The Letters of
ERNEST DOWSON

Title: # The Letters of
ERNEST
DOWSON

Collected & Edited by
DESMOND FLOWER
and
HENRY MAAS

Cassell & Company Ltd.

CASSELL & COMPANY LTD
35 Red Lion Square, London WC1
Melbourne, Sydney, Toronto
Johannesburg, Cape Town, Auckland

Printed in Great Britain
by W. & J. Mackay & Co Ltd, Chatham, Kent

F.567

Contents

Illustrations

Preface

ERNEST DOWSON became famous after his death, but his life was short and for the most part poor and solitary. He kept few papers and wrote no memoirs, and few of his friends left more than random recollections of him. Luckily, however, several of them kept his letters, and these, providing a wealth of biographical information, add enough to our knowledge of the literary history of his time to justify publication.

The largest collection of them is his correspondence with Arthur Moore, his lifelong friend and collaborator in two novels. These letters, with a few exceptions, are now in the Pierpont Morgan Library, New York. Dowson's letters to William Theodore Peters are in the Berg Collection, New York Public Library. There are important groups of letters at the Museo Horne in Florence, in Manchester University Library, in Princeton University Library and in the Library of Dartmouth College, New Hampshire. Numerous other libraries and private owners hold smaller sets of letters which they have generously placed at our disposal. We are particularly indebted to the University of British Columbia, who, after discovering Dowson's letters to Conal O'Riordan and planning to publish them in a limited edition, sacrificed their project in the interests of this book. We are grateful to Mr. Robin Skelton for his sympathetic help in this matter. We have noted the present location of each letter wherever this is known to us, but many of the originals have changed hands several times since they were made available to us, and in such cases, if we have not traced the present ownership of the letters, we have given the source from which we obtained the text.

Five previous authors have published collections of Dowson's letters. The first was Victor Plarr, whose *Ernest Dowson 1888–1897* (1914) contains thirty-three letters, many in fragmentary form. A few more appeared in *Cynara*, a novel by his daughter, Miss Marion Plarr (1933). Mr. John Gawsworth's lecture *The Dowson Legend*, delivered to the Royal Society of Literature in 1938, quotes at length from an incomparable group of letters to Samuel Smith, of which only fragments now survive and are in the collection of the British Museum. Dowson's letters to Herbert Horne were edited by Mr. Ian Fletcher for *Notes and Queries* (March 1962). Finally Dr. Mark Longaker's *Ernest Dowson* (1944, second edition 1945) quotes, often in full, fifty-two letters, many of them previously unpublished.

Dowson usually wrote his letters in haste and his spelling and punctuation are erratic. We have none the less decided to print them as they stand. The addresses are abbreviated after the first appearance of each, with no distinction made between written and printed headings, and the dates as a rule are put into standard form. We have sometimes used our discretion in paragraphing and replacing underlinings by the use of italics. Where a reading is doubtful we have generally chosen the normal spelling. Dowson's cancellations are indicated except for a number that we judged too unimportant to be worth noting. All editorial interpolations are in square brackets. Otherwise, except where we have indicated that the only source is a printed one, the texts are taken directly from the originals or photostats.

Many friends and correspondents have helped us. Anyone working on Dowson must be indebted to Dr. Longaker, who was the first to produce a comprehensive life of the poet. Desmond Flower, the elder of the two present editors, had the great advantage of discussing Dowson with some of those, now dead, who knew him: Arthur Moore, Father John Gray, W. H. Woodward, Sir William Rothenstein, Horace Annesley Vachell among them; and he is grateful for the help and vivid impressions which they gave him. Mr. John Gawsworth and the late A. J. A. Symons were most generous in placing their material at our disposal. Mr. Ian Fletcher has helped us by his discovery of the letters to Herbert Horne and Don Patricio Gannon has undertaken some difficult researches for us in Paris. We are very grateful to Mr. Dominick Spencer for his devoted help in checking the text and to Mr Ernest Mehew for his careful scrutiny of the proofs. We owe a special debt to Sir Rupert Hart-Davis. His superb edition of *The Letters of Oscar Wilde* (1962) contains a large body of information on the period without which our task would have been much harder. He has discovered letters for this book, given constant encouragement and made countless improvements.

To the many others who have helped us we would here offer our apologies for not naming them individually and our gratitude for all they have done.

We are grateful to all the owners of Dowson's letters who have allowed us to use manuscripts in their possession, and who are mentioned in the list of attributions, and also to The World's Work Ltd., for permission to reprint R. Thurston Hopkins's 'A London Phantom'.

Introduction

THERE were many distinguished poets in England in the last years of the nineteenth century. Bridges and Hardy were in their prime. Meredith, Morris and Swinburne were still active, and Binyon, Davidson, Housman, Kipling, Alice Meynell, Francis Thompson and William Watson all made their reputations between 1890 and 1900. But most of these seem hardly to belong to the eighteen-nineties at all. The poetry that best represents the decade is the work of the younger poets who thought of themselves as 'the movement', 'the *fin de siècle*' or the Decadents. Among the best of them was Ernest Dowson.

The popular impression of these writers is all too familiar. It is a likeness that the succeeding generation accepted from a few survivors of the period, like Arthur Symons and Frank Harris, who seem to have wanted above all to convince their later audience of their own wicked youth. The group which shuffled back and forth between Fitzroy Street and the Café Royal was, we are to believe, idle, penurious, drunken, promiscuous, living with its head in a cloud of artistic ambition but doing little towards its achievement, tempted towards drugs and perversion, often addicted to them, producing exquisitely fashioned small works, but doomed, after material failure, to an early death.

Ever since Symons edited the first collected edition of Dowson's poems in 1902[1] and prefaced it with an introduction which is more fiction than fact, the poet has seemed the archetype of this allegedly feckless generation.

Literary historians have generally accepted Symons's account without question and despite the corrections made by Dowson's friends[2] even authoritative reference books combine an uncritical adoption of his exaggerations with an amazing inaccuracy in simple questions of facts and dates. It is hardly too much to say that in books of literary history and gossip Dowson generally appears as an alcoholic, drug-addicted tramp, earning a pittance by translating French pornography.

In fact he was nothing of the kind. As a young man he worked

---

[1] In the United States. The British edition did not appear till 1905.

[2] e.g. Edgar Jepson, 'The Real Ernest Dowson' (*The Academy*, 1907); Victor Plarr, *Ernest Dowson* (1914); W. R. Thomas, 'Ernest Dowson at Oxford' (*The Nineteenth Century*, April 1928).

for six years in an office and left it only when through no fault of his the job ceased to exist. His free time was spent dining with friends, at parties, theatres and exhibitions. For holidays he liked walking tours in France or he went sailing. He was carefully, even smartly dressed, and as welcome in fashionable drawing-rooms as in bohemian pubs and cafés. In his later twenties, when he was dependent on his writing and often in wretched health, he worked with surprising diligence. In the four and a half years before his death he translated six books, four of them of considerable length. His publisher only once proposed a really pornographic book, the *Lysistrata* of Aristophanes, and then Dowson avoided the commission. The authors he translated were of a different order— Zola, Voltaire, Laclos, Balzac and the Goncourts. At this time, weakened by tuberculosis, he began to neglect himself. He drank too much and was often short of money. But he was certainly not a drunkard or a drug-addict and was not destroyed, as one encyclopaedia has said, by 'evil living'. He did not die in squalor, but decently cared for in a friend's house.

Had he wished, he could easily have chosen a more conventional life, but he avoided it because he was a poet. As W. B. Yeats later wrote of Dowson and his friends:[1] 'unlike the Victorian poets, almost all were poor men, and had made it a matter of conscience to turn from every kind of money-making that prevented good writing, and that poverty meant strain, and for the most part, a refusal of domestic life.'

Yeats himself is the only one of Dowson's contemporaries who now receives widespread critical attention, but it may be of interest to note here the comments of three recent critics on Dowson. Professor Tillotson has emphasized the precision of Dowson's writing:[2] 'He does not snatch at the first things that come to a poet's eyes for the sake of saying them divinely, does not transform a modicum of complex but limited impressions into a thousand lines of lyric. He may be dreadfully intent on writing poetry that shall be flawless as verbal music, and that music may be of an exacting and subtle kind, but all this is only half his activity. Dowson does give minute attention to working over and over his lines, to punctuation, to placing capital letters as a refinement for indicating accent: and yet beside all this, he is putting in an equal amount of work on improving his meaning. He succeeds in the use of forms like the villanelle because he can write lines which are substantial enough to bear repetition, or to make minute variation worth while.' T. S. Eliot, acknowledging that his re-

---

[1] *The Trembling of the Veil* (1922), p. 177.
[2] G. Tillotson, *Essays in Criticism and Research* (1942), pp. 153 ff.

peated 'falls the shadow' in *The Hollow Men* derives from Dowson's *Non sum qualis eram bonae sub regno Cynarae*, says: 'The derivation had not occurred to my mind, but I believe it to be correct, because the lines have always run in my head, and because I regard Dowson as a poet whose technical innovations have been underestimated.'[1] Easily the most important critical study of Dowson is that of an Italian scholar, Signor Agostino Lombardo, in his meticulously detailed *La Poesia Inglese dall' Estetismo al Simbolismo*.[2] He speaks there of Dowson's 'spontaneous capacity for song, a quality of music inherent in the feeling itself, the extraordinary purity of the effect attained'.

Ernest Christopher Dowson was born on 2 August 1867, at The Grove, Belmont Hill, in Lee—now part of the sprawling suburb of Lewisham, to the south-east of London. He came of a well-to-do middle-class family. His father, Alfred Dowson, was an intelligent, highly literate man, who owned a dry dock in Limehouse; his mother was a very beautiful woman who had within her a neurotic streak which eventually led her to disaster; her inner sadness showed in her features and years later Conal O'Riordan wrote:[3] 'I recall Ernest showing a photograph of his mother to me and I was moved to tears (being barely twenty-one at the time) by something extraordinarily pathetic in her charming face.'

The Dowsons had one other child, another boy, christened Rowland Corbett, born in 1877. He emigrated to the United States about 1895 and died in San Diego, California, in 1913. He seems, for part of his life in the United States at any rate, to have been a farmer.

There had been Dowsons on the Thames for many generations. They were originally in business at Richmond, but eventually moved down the river. In 1788 they were established at Chamberlain's Wharf, off Tooley Street to the east of London Bridge, where they had a 142-foot frontage with a crane for landing goods. By 1804 Messrs. Christopher Dowson and Son (the great-grandfather and grandfather of the poet) were proprietors of Bridge Dock, Limehouse, which in the Land Tax Books is called a 'Ship Yard, Dock and Blacksmiths Shop. Counting House and Wharfs on the opposite side of the street'.[4] Christopher's sister Sarah and his brother Joseph also owned property in the district. In 1817

---

[1] *The Times Literary Supplement*, 10 January 1935, quoted in Tillotson, op. cit., p. 156.

[2] Rome, 1950, p. 236.

[3] Letter to D.F.

[4] Archives of the Port of London Authority and the Guildhall Library (in Thames Conservancy papers).

Messrs. Dowson and Olds successfully submitted a petition requesting permission to extend the entrance wings of the dock out into the river bed. It was this property, Bridge Dock, which Alfred Dowson inherited and of which Ernest himself was one day to be the manager.

The Dowsons were a family of intelligence as well as initiative. Years later the poet still owned a picture of one of his forebears in the reign of George IV acting on a stage with Corinthian columns.[1] This may well have been his grandfather Christopher, who had become a man of substance in Limehouse and was a member of every committee governing the Thames River, its docks and its wharves.

A close friend of the Dowson family was an eccentric character called Captain Pritchard, one of whose whims was never to let anyone know where he lived. He it was who introduced Christopher Dowson junior, Ernest's grandfather, to Robert Browning, whose earliest known letter is written to Christopher Dowson, beginning, 'You are probably by this time aware of the unfortunate state of our friend P[ritchard].' When the old eccentric died in 1860 he left £1000 to Browning and £500 to Emily Dowson.

Browning in turn introduced Christopher Dowson to Alfred Domett, a man of letters, sometime Prime Minister of New Zealand, and remembered as the model for 'Waring'. A close friendship resulted and in 1836 Dowson married Domett's sister Mary. We catch a glimpse of them in a letter from Browning to Domett dated 22 May 1842 in which he writes: 'The 7th of May last week was my birthday and on that day I dined with dear Chris Dowson and your sister. We were alone and talked of you and little else.'

It was in this kind of atmosphere that Alfred Dowson, the poet's father, inherited Bridge Dock, which was at that time let to and worked by another company, the Dry Dock Corporation of London Ltd. He was therefore a man of adequate substance and considerable leisure, friendly with his uncle, Alfred Domett, and with Robert Browning. He was a foundation member of the Arts Club, as was his uncle, and one of his son's close friends later described him as 'a remarkable man, a wit, the friend of half the interesting artists and men of letters of his generation'.[2] A typical glimpse comes from Domett, who records in his diary that in September 1872 he went to dinner with his nephew at the Arundel; the other guests were W. G. Wills, in whose drama *Charles the First* Irving was playing at the time, and 'a square-headed man with bright

[1] Plarr, p. 18.
[2] Plarr, p. 18.

reddish hair who turned out to be **W. S. Gilbert**'. Plarr also records that on one occasion he fitted out a barge like a prehistoric house-boat and cruised about in the vicinity of the dock, putting in from time to time for supplies; the celebrities on board as guests included Burnand, the editor of *Punch*, and Swinburne.

The house in which Alfred Dowson lived when he married, and in which Ernest was born, was a large residence in a pleasantly laid-out garden suburb. Alfred Dowson spent a good deal of time travelling abroad, often in the south of France, and as the years passed he used frequently to take his elder son with him. The charming photograph of the boy in Highland dress, after p. 48, was taken by Schemboche, a photographer with studios in Turin and Florence.

In the winter of 1873 he met Robert Louis Stevenson when both were staying in the Hôtel du Pavillon at Menton, and the two struck up a friendship. Stevenson had been ordered south by his doctor in early November and, travelling by easy stages, arrived at Menton on his twenty-third birthday, the 12th. He was lonely and in looking round for someone with whom to spend his time found Alfred Dowson. He wrote home: 'There's a very nice man here called Dowson, with a pretty wife and son; he talks literature heavily with me. . . . Dowson and I expressed mutual incredulity in each other's bad health. . . . I have made myself indispensable to the Dowsons' little boy (aet. 6), a popularity that brings with it its own fatigues as you may fancy; and I have been fooling about with him all afternoon, playing dominoes, and learning geography with him, and carrying him on my back a little.'[1]

W. H. Woodward, sometime editor of *The Times*, has recorded that, after coming down from Christ Church in 1877 and spending a year abroad, he took up residence at 396 Commercial Road, on which centred a group of people who were teaching voluntarily in the East End. One of the group was Alfred Dowson, who, Woodward said, at that time showed no particular signs of ill health. Dowson was about 5 ft. 10 in. tall, with brown curly hair, ruddy cheeks and a fine voice. At that period in 1878 he seemed to spend a great deal of his time teaching, and his pupils were largely the children of thieves and prostitutes, who often at the age of fourteen could not read. Woodward clearly remembered Dowson making these children sing together, while he stood before them beating time. The whole group used to meet at the house every Friday night, and on these occasions Dowson would often read poetry. He

[1] No. 3339, *The Stevenson Library of Edwin J. Beinecke*, vol. iii, Yale University Press, New Haven, 1956.

was particularly conversant with a great deal of Shelley; but above all Browning was an open book—even the wilder tracts of *Sordello* were clear to him. His reading aloud was extraordinarily good. He was also extremely fond of music. These regular meetings continued for two years, and thereafter Woodward kept in touch with him for a few more years, which, we may assume, takes us to 1883 or 1884, at which time Alfred Dowson, despite his earlier tubercular trouble, still seemed to be in good health.[1]

There is no evidence that Ernest ever went to school, and the presumption is that his father taught him, which, W. H. Woodward insisted, he was quite capable of doing. Certainly Ernest Dowson seems to have taken his entrance examinations to Oxford in his stride, although once he got there he did not stay the course. If he was brought up at home and on his father's travels (there is a suggestion that a priest in the Italian village of Senta had a hand in the affair at one time), the state of his father's mind, health and purse are of obvious importance. We believe that Ernest's adolescence and early manhood, whether happy or unhappy, were certainly not adversely affected by his father's affairs, nor by his mother's mental health. He once said to his friend Plarr that his upbringing had been pagan; that would seem to indicate an education without bias, and following the welcome dictates of personal taste.

It was this young man, brought up in an unorthodox but intelligent way, who entered Queen's College, Oxford, for the Michaelmas term, 1886.

[1] W. H. Woodward, personal statement to D.F.

Part I
1888-1889

IN spite of the irregularities of his education, Ernest Dowson seems to have been accepted by Queen's without any difficulty. To begin with, he had rooms in college, at the top of Staircase 5. Among the first undergraduates to make his acquaintance was Arthur Moore. Moore introduced him to W. R. Thomas, whose reminiscences form an invaluable record of Dowson's life at the University.[1] Moore was Captain of Soccer in the college and designed the cap, which remains unchanged today. Thomas lived on a staircase known as the 'rabbit warren' and hence is often referred to in Dowson's letters as 'le lapin'.

Friends remembered Dowson as round-shouldered, with irrepressibly curly hair and blue-grey eyes. His teeth were bad and were to be a marked feature later in life when he had neglected them. He had a vague voice, a vague indistinct manner, was barely audible in conversation and completely inaudible when reading aloud. 'His manners', says Thomas, 'were charming. Of pose he had, at that time and throughout his life, no trace whatever. He came up, of course, with a dislike for convention, and for what he held to be English insular hypocrisy. His roamings on the Continent had given him a somewhat wider knowledge of such places as the Paris music halls than most undergraduates possess. But his frail body was almost free from the power of the flesh, though its psychological study interested him . . . The Dowson who came up to Queen's had certainly done some hard thinking, and the pessimism to which he always remained faithful had been based, in the main, on the writings of Schopenhauer . . . But his intellectual creed did not affect his personal happiness.' Thomas records that the authors in whom Dowson was most interested at this time were Baudelaire, Poe and Swinburne. His copy of *Les Fleurs du Mal* was annotated from cover to cover, and it was at his prompting that Thomas put down a request for Swinburne's works in the suggestion book of the College Library. Another great interest of Dowson's at this time was the Jacobean dramatists. They also shared an enthusiasm for the novels of Zola. They

[1] W. R. Thomas, 'Ernest Dowson at Oxford', in *The Nineteenth Century*, April 1928.

LED—B

planned to send an anonymous letter from two Oxford under-graduates to the great French novelist, but in the end did not do so. Thomas read a paper on Zola before the Addison Society. On the day it was to be delivered, they sat down to a rubber of whist after lunch. About 4 p.m. Thomas realized that he had not yet even considered what he was going to say; so while he wrote his paper Dowson translated selected passages from the novels for incorporation therein. It was a great success.

Dowson either liked an author enormously or not at all. He had no time for Corneille, Racine or Molière; he liked Diderot a lot, Voltaire less, but had no interest in Rousseau. He had an un-bounded admiration for Maupassant, whom he had met at a country house in France. His earliest statement concerning the novelists whom he admired is contained in an annotation in his copy of the second edition of *The Story of an African Farm* which he bought at Oxford in 1887. The last sentence of Olive Schreiner's preface reads: 'Sadly he must squeeze the colour from his brush, and dip it into the *grey pigments* [ECD's underlining] around him. He must paint what lies before him.' Beneath this Dowson wrote: 'This is the greater method—the method of the novelists who are not popular, but great and the method of Tourguénef—of Gustave Flaubert, of George Meredith & of Henry James. The time for romance, for novels written in the stage method is gone. In a worldly decaying civilization, in an age of nostalgia like the pre-sent—what is the meaning of Mr. Rider Haggard? He is an anach-ronism. It is to books like *Madame Bovary* & de Maupassant's *Une Vie* to books like these one must go to find the true signifi-cance of the XIXth Century.'

Nor was Dowson uninterested in sport, although there is no record of his playing any games himself. Thomas says that he ran along the tow-path supporting the college boat, and an interest in sport appears in his letters long after he had gone down.

Dowson was already writing seriously and had begun the note-books in which he kept fair copies of his verses with notes as to their fate.[1] Some thirty poems had been completed by the time he went down from the University. The first to be published was *Sonnet of a Little Girl*, one of a cycle, which appeared in *London Society* in November 1886; *To Nature—Morituri Te Salutant* was written in August 1887 and printed in the same periodical in the following March.

---

[1] The one plain black-covered notebook which has survived was succes-sively in the possession of A. J. A. Symons, Sir Newman Flower and D.F. It is now in the Morgan Library, New York. It contains some loose sheets from another notebook, the rest of which is apparently lost.

Thomas, however, points out that at this time Dowson was not thought of by his friends as a poet but as a prose writer, and indeed throughout his life Dowson took prose more seriously than verse. His first short story, *Souvenirs of an Egoist*, appeared in the January 1888 number of *Temple Bar*, and he had already begun to write a novel, *The Passion of Dr. Ludovicus*, in collaboration with Arthur Moore, with whom he had made the first of many trips to the Continent together in the summer of 1887.

During that same summer he spent some time visiting his cousin Spencer Secretan in Reigate—together they decorated the lawn with Japanese lanterns for Queen Victoria's jubilee, and went with the family to watch the procession in London. Miss Dulcie Secretan recalls his visits to the family with great affection, and says that he never failed to bring her and her sister a box of chocolates.[1]

During his first year Dowson had impressed the college authorities sufficiently for them to agree that he should read for an honours degree, and this was a suggestion which he accepted.

It is customary for undergraduates at Oxford to spend their first year in college and the following two in lodgings, and in consequence at the beginning of the Michaelmas term, 1887, Dowson moved to 5 Grove Street. Thomas records that 'with the removal to Grove Street his life assumed a darker shade. Early in the term I noticed his marked depression. We both took it seriously.' From this statement it has been concluded that some change had occurred in Dowson himself, but we think that this is too narrow a view, which does not take into account the known pattern of his family's life. Certain statements made by Thomas have been taken out of their context. For example, 'It was at this time that he went in search of fresh sensations. His first remedy was alcohol, but the experiment was a brief one.' Thomas goes on to say that Dowson, whose normal drink at that time was Chablis and soda, decided with his friend to experiment with whisky; their first evening led to their becoming agreeably merry with good conversation, their second was a failure, and that ended the matter. This episode has been seized upon as the first step to depravity, in complete disregard of Thomas's final statement on this subject—that 'in the use of alcohol his [Dowson's] habits were simply those of many undergraduates at that time'—or, one may add, any time. Another myth is contained in Arthur Symons's one damning sentence 'At Oxford I believe his favourite form of intoxication had been haschisch'. The basis for this fabrication subsequently appeared in Thomas's reminiscences. In the autumn of 1887 an Indian student

[1] Statement to D.F.

came up to Queen's and, as a result of what he had to say on the subject of bhang, a party was arranged one evening after hall to consume pills of the drug. The effect, says Thomas, was 'slight, but on the whole satisfactory'. A second experiment produced no results at all, and a third—more intensified—necessitated a visit to a chemist in the High for an emetic; after which unfortunate experience the delights of bhang were forsworn. Nobody, one notices, has as a result of this referred to Thomas, in later life a respectable citizen of Liverpool, as a 'haschisch' addict.

The change in Dowson's outlook on life may more probably, although there is no definite evidence, be attributed to the decline in the affairs of his family. The company which had leased Bridge Dock, on which the Dowsons' income mainly depended, was running into such trouble that before the end of 1888 Alfred Dowson was to be forced to take over the management, for which he was neither mentally nor physically equipped. His wife may have been already showing signs of the mental aberrations which were soon to destroy her. The family had moved from their home in Lee to a house at Woodford, Essex. For a young man, sensitive and pessimistic by nature, these changes must have been unsettling. Small wonder that he was not the same in the autumn of 1887 as he had seemed three months earlier.

At 5 Grove Street there were many evenings spent in whist, poker and conversation—all three pastimes in which Dowson delighted. It is apparent that he was highly regarded by the circle of undergraduates in which he moved. Despite his pessimistic philosophy, life was not intolerable. Yet when the spring came he brought the whole thing to an abrupt close. In March 1888 he sat for Honour Moderations and completed the first few papers; then suddenly one evening he told Thomas that he would have no more of it, and refused to sit for the remainder. Thomas said there was no evidence of any trouble with his tutor. He went down at the end of term. It is perfectly possible that this sudden decision was brought about by melancholia and pessimism. But it is equally possible that the decision was based purely on finance. Thomas records that Dowson was regarded almost with awe by some undergraduates because a myth had grown up that he was the wealthy son of a docks magnate. In fact Bridge Dock had ceased to produce any substantial revenues and it is not improbable that Alfred Dowson may have told his elder son that the cost of keeping him at Oxford had become a strain, but a strain which would willingly be borne if it were serving a constructive purpose. And Ernest, who throughout his short and troubled life never lacked a broad streak of common sense (as we hope his letters will show), would have replied that a university degree would add nothing material to his welfare and would have suggested that he should come down. Perhaps—and this is the remotest speculation, but not out of keeping with what we know of father and son—they may have agreed that Dowson should sit his examinations and review the situation thereafter. Since, as Thomas records, Dowson did not think he had done well in his first papers, he may have decided then and there to throw in his hand. Thomas's memory of him, as he departed, was of his 'thinking power, his sincerity, and his entire freedom from any form of affectation'. He always possessed great pride, and the son of the reputed magnate was not the man to explain that his family no longer had the money to keep him in residence; he preferred just to go down and leave his many friends to think what they might.

It was at this time that Dowson met Victor Plarr, who was to become for some years one of his closest friends. Later, as we shall see, they drifted apart because the poet still wished to pursue the uncertain career of a man of letters, whereas his friend graduated into respectability. That they saw so much less of one another was regretted by both, and Plarr certainly remembered their friendship with the deepest warmth, as his memoir of Dowson shows.

They met, Plarr records, early in 1888 and were introduced by Charles Sayle. 'There is a man whom you ought to know,' Sayle said, 'a young poet just down from college, a man exactly like Jepson only, if possible, more so.'[1] There must have been something in common between Dowson and Jepson, because Plarr constantly confused them in his mind and frequently called one by the other's name; indeed, this confusion persisted so that he admits that he had addressed the survivor (Jepson) by the name of the dead poet even on the day before he began to write his memoir published in 1914.

The first conversation between Dowson and Plarr, the latter records, opened with a few phrases which are most pertinent to the mental attitude which they and their friends shared at this time:

'Shall you ever feel old?'

'No; I am static—about four years of age.'

'Like Victor Hugo at the age of eighty.'

When Dowson left Oxford he went home to live with his parents in Woodford. There is some evidence that he began to read for the Bar. If he did, his heart was not in the work and it is certain that he was more interested in writing. In the autumn a most important event took place in the Dowson family's affairs. Alfred Dowson

---

[1] Plarr mentions the parallel solely as 'J', but it was undoubtedly Edgar Jepson to whom Sayle referred.

instituted proceedings to recover possession of Bridge Dock. He succeeded; and henceforward he was himself saddled with the management of a decaying property and his son was committed to helping him. Ernest had his own office in the dock buildings in Narrow Street. Although his home remained his parents' house at Woodford, he would from time to time after a late night in the West End take the early workmen's train back to Limehouse and sleep for a few hours on the couch in his office. In the first novel which he and Arthur Moore published, *A Comedy of Masks*, Dowson described the dock, and since it was for a time his home—the last home he was ever to have—his description may be quoted here:

> In that intricate and obscure locality, which stretches between the Tower and Poplar, a tarry region, scarcely suspected by the majority of Londoners, to whom the 'Port of London' is an expression purely geographical, there is, or was not many years ago, to be found a certain dry dock called Blackpool, but better known from time immemorial to skippers and long-shoremen, and all who go down to the sea in ships, as 'Rainham's Dock'.
>
> Many years ago, in the days of the first Rainham and of wooden ships, it had been no doubt a flourishing shipyard; and, indeed, models of wooden Leviathans of the period, which had been turned out, not a few, in those palmy days, were still dusty ornaments of its somewhat antique office. But as time went on and the age of iron intervened, and the advance on the Clyde and the Tyne had made Thames shipbuilding a thing of the past, Blackpool Dock had ceased to be of commercial importance. No more ships were built there, and fewer ships put in to be overhauled and painted; while even these were for the most part of a class viewed at Lloyd's with scant favour, which seemed, like the yard itself, to have fallen somewhat behind the day. The original Rainham had not bequeathed his energy along with his hoards to his descendants; and, indeed, the last of these, Philip Rainham, a man of weak health, whose tastes, although these were veiled in obscurity, were supposed to trench little upon shipping, let the business jog along so much after its own fashion that the popular view hinted at its imminent dissolution. A dignified, scarcely prosperous quiet seemed the normal air of Blackpool Dock, so that even when it was busiest, and work still came in, almost by tradition, with a certain steadiness—when the hammers of the riveters and the shipwrights awoke the echoes from sunrise to sunset, with a ferocious regularity which the present proprietor could almost deplore, there was still a suggestion of mildewed antiquity about it all that

was, at least to the nostrils of the outsider, not unpleasing. And when the ships were painted, and had departed, it resumed very easily its more regular aspect of picturesque dilapidation. For in spite of its sordid surroundings and its occasional lapses into bustle, Blackpool Dock, as Rainham would sometimes remind himself, when its commercial motive was pressed upon him too forcibly, was deeply permeated by the spirit of the picturesque. . . .

Rainham had a set of rooms in the house of his foreman—an eighteenth century house, full of carved oak mantles and curious alcoves, a ramshackle structure within the dock gates, with a quaint balcony staircase, like the approach to a Swiss chalet, leading down into the yard. In London these apartments were his sole domicile; though, to his friends, none of whom lived nearer to him than Bloomsbury, this seemed a piece of conduct too flagrantly eccentric—on a parity with his explanation of it, alleging necessity of living on the spot: an explanation somewhat droll, in the face of his constant lengthy absences, during the whole of the winter, when he handed the reins of government to his manager, and took care of a diseased lung in a warmer climate.

Dowson's life through the latter half of 1888 and the whole of 1889 was the healthy and normal one of any young man—the solemn Plarr indeed describes it as 'a strange period of undergraduate rowdiness'. But in another context he added that Dowson 'wasn't lurid, though he tried to be'. He saw a number of his Oxford friends; he met a group of medical students, mainly from Bart's. He came up by train to the West End more evenings than not, and enjoyed himself. He was interested in sport, the theatre and girls. He met many girls, with varying results, but by November 1889 he had met the child—for then she was no more—whose name is most closely associated with his: Adelaide Foltinowicz, the daughter of the Polish proprietor of a rather indifferent restaurant in Sherwood Street, where the Regent Palace Hotel now stands.

This same period was also one of great literary activity. Besides several poems, Dowson wrote what he called 'a shocker', which was offered round but not accepted, and is now lost. At the same time he wrote a novel called *Madame de Viole* which likewise did not find a publisher. Then he and Arthur Moore resumed work on *Dr. Ludovicus*, their first novel together which they had started writing at Oxford. Their method was to write alternate chapters in notebooks which they passed one to another. Occasional coordinating conferences were held. By April 1889 *Dr. Ludovicus* was finished and was on its way to a publisher. In mid-May it was rejected by Frederick White; in August it returned from Arrowsmith; in November Chatto & Windus turned it down. In the end it came to nothing, but while it was going the rounds Dowson and Moore were at work on their next book, *Felix Martyr*. This, too, was destined not to find a publisher, and it is improbable that it was ever completed. Nevertheless it was another step forward at a time of hard work and great pleasure. During 1889 Dowson also had another job. In April, Victor Plarr was offered the unpaid sub-editorship of a not very successful weekly called *The Critic*. He did not want the post, but passed it to Dowson, who took it. The main attraction was that it carried with it the office of dramatic critic, which meant free seats for any theatre. As the letters for the remainder of this year show, Dowson took full advantage of this amenity. But *The Critic* remained unsuccessful, although, like Charles II, it was an unconscionable time a-dying; towards the close of the year Dowson spent less and less time at the sub-editorial desk, but he wrote a number of essays which appeared in the magazine, and he remained a constant and devoted theatre critic.

1. *To Arthur Moore*[1]
   13 November [*1888*]

Church End, Woodford, Essex

My dear Moore,
   I am beginning to be seriously alarmed—d'abord, news that your liver has broken down—ensuite—silence—what meaneth this thing? I hope however that it only means that you are now reposing from the fatigues of law, cares of office etc & laying in a stock of hygiene many

---

1. Arthur Collin Moore (1866–1952) was the son of J. C. Moore, a well-known portrait painter, and the nephew of two equally distinguished painters, Henry Moore, R.A., and Albert Moore. He was a year senior to Dowson at Queen's, and on coming down in 1888 joined a firm of solicitors, Longbourne, Stevens and Powell, of Lincoln's Inn Fields. He was admitted a solicitor in 1891 and remained with the firm until his retirement in 1937. He collaborated with Dowson on *Dr. Ludovicus*, which was begun at Oxford, *Felix Martyr* (see above p. 16), *A Comedy of Masks* (1893) and *Adrian Rome* (1899). He also published stories in *Macmillan's Magazine* and *The Yellow Book* and a number of novels.

kilos from this foggy, pestilent metrop. Not that I mind it much—when one gets a glimpse of daylight—i'faith I have had a right merry time in it lately—a time quite unprecedented indeed in the annals of my London life. Dost know the "Bedford",[2] mon vieux? As fate would have it last Wednesday, Bouthors,[3] Lefroy[4] & self took a box there—& "thats how my story begins" The box opposite us—there are only two in that noble house was occupied by four medicals one of whom Lefroy thought he knew—although he had not seen him for years. He sent his card round & we joined company, became most intimate in no time. As the programme proceeds we have the chairman in to binge with us & he asks us to stay on after the affair is over, to a smoker—& be introduced to the singing tarts. A medical offers me a sofa which I accept—& eventually the whole lot of us adjourn to the side & make the acquaintance of many aimiable "pros"—the sisters Graham, Miss Agnes Hazel[5]—the Jappa troupe[6] etc. It was most awful sport—& I consummated it by sitting up all night drinking unlimited coffee with a man named Anty[7] of Barts—whom, mind you, I had never seen before in my life. You must go to that café-concert, mon gros Arthur, it is worth it I assure you. We had a box there again on Friday—i.e. my host of Wed, anothers Barts man & Lefroy—your humble servant having previously dined Miss Hazel of music-hall fame at the Cavour[8] & driven her up. There's a beautiful inconsistency for you! And I regret to say that I purpose doing exactly the same to morrow—only as my star sings in two places a night this week, 1st at the "Star"[9] Bermond-sey—2nd at the "Bedford"—there will be probably rather more agre-able tête-à-tête drives.

These Barts men are really capital fellows. You must know them, & my chanteuse (am I at all épris?—I really don't know—but I am afraid unless I take care I shall be) my chanteuse is charming. She has a good deal of chic on the stage—sings fairly & has a pleasant north country or possibly Irish accent.

Friday night I also spent in town even more festively—after the Bedford at the same man's rooms—with the other Barts man Morris

---

2. A small music-hall in Camden Town, painted often by Sickert.
3. Louis Bouthers, a Frenchman living in London and at this time a close friend of Dowson's.
4. Walter John Magrath Lefroy (1870–1955), who had gone up to Queen's in 1887. He was now studying medicine at the Middlesex Hospital but in 1891, after a stay in France, he went to Canada, where he remained as a journalist and editor until shortly before his death.
5. A serio-comic with whom Dowson was briefly acquainted.
6. Actually the Zaro Troupe of acrobats.
7. Probably John Sylvester Anty (born in Manchester, 1864). He did not qualify in medicine.
8. A restaurant well known at the time, in Leicester Square.
9. A second-rate music-hall in Necking Road, south of the Thames.

—,[10] an acrobat French & his "wife" (?)—an immensely vivacious girl who sat up with us imbibing copious café au cognac & smoking cigarettes until 6 A.M., when we adjourned to the St Pancras buffet for breakfast—I without showing the smallest fatigue. I never saw a girl who could make a night of it like that before—& I did not believe she existed. The evening reminded me of la "Vie de Bohême"[11] more than any other episode I have been through—& the beauty of it was that it was all perfectly proper. The girl was very pretty—fire enough to be jolly but nothing more—altogether, mon vieux, a consummate sportsman. We should not have broken up when we did only our host was in a mortal terror of his landlady. O it was the merriest jest. I wish you had been there. I shall never go any more to the "Empire"[12] if I want a merry evening—it is not in it at all.

We ~~always~~ had some one of the company in our box the whole evening—sometimes one or two.

Once even (to my great delight) an awfully clever little American child who dances and sings exquisitely was brought in & had a lemonade. I dare say you have seen her at the "Pav"[13]—"Little Flossie"[14]—she figures in the bills. She was a most amusing little lady —aet 9—chattered like a jay—& I have promised to throw her chocolates at the "Star" to-morrow. I suppose you are out of town or I would ask you to join us to-morrow. If you are not however & get this letter in time, you will know where to find us.—All this gaiety is deucedly bad for literature, & you can imagine how it interferes with "Madame de Viole"[15]—but the oof will be out soon & then I shall take up my pen perforce, if it is only pour tuer le temps.

Gad! what a long epistle—I shall expect a reply in kind.

I wish you could join us at the Cav. to morrow.

I have been analysing my emotions & after all I am not much épris. One only believes once in one's life in la dame aux camélias—happily. But I shall let the liaison run its course—it will be very amusing & not as costly as an affair with a regular horizontale ("mélinite"[16] by the bye is the latest word vid Gil Blas[17]).

I wish women had never been invented—or men if you like—but

---

10. C. E. M. Morris, who died in a canoeing accident six months later, see Letter 31.
11. Henri Murger's novel *Scènes de la Vie de Bohème* was published in 1851.
12. The music-hall, with its famous 'promenade', in Leicester Square, where the cinema now stands.
13. The London Pavilion in Piccadilly Circus, opened in 1884.
14. Billed as 'The American marvel'.
15. The novel on which he worked intermittently for the next year. It was not published.
16. Originally the name of a high-explosive invented in 1886 and later used of the French music-hall singer Jane Avril.
17. French literary and political paper which began publication in 1882.

since they exist, it is profitable to study them. After all too it is not les filles de l'opéra or horizontales that I protest against—it is les jeunes filles de société—& I keep deucedly well away from them. Au revoir, vieux frère—Write speedily

Yrs ever   E. C. DOWSON

2. To Arthur Moore
[*late November 1888*]

Bridge Dock, Limehouse, E.

Dear Moore,

I will await you at Café Monico[1] at or from 6 P.M. onwards to-morrow evening—Friday. Otherwise wire to me here some time to-morrow morning. You will be much amazed at the heading. I will explain it to you hereafter—briefly now.

I have expected to date from this salubrious spot for some time but was surprised myself when I found it settled a few days ago. I believe my governor is about as surprised as I am myself. !!!!!! It is really rather a jest.

The place has been in the family for many generations but has been let to a Company for the last ten years or so. The company was not very litigious satisfactory, my governor is very litigious—after a good deal of ragging with Chitty J.[2] two days ago, the affair was settled & the governor took possession again. Hence me voilà—bien entendu. We are going to work the affair until it can be let again. We neither of us know anything about dry-docking but we have an excellent foreman. "Dowson" has one office—"Son" the other & there is another one for the Clerks who have not yet arrived. At present the only occupation of the firm has been to smoke a good many cigarettes & write a few letters. The place is very open with a ripping view of the River

---

1. In Piccadilly Circus.
2. Sir Joseph William Chitty (1828–1899), Judge of the High Court since 1881. These proceedings formed part of the protracted Chancery Court action Brodie v. the Earl of Kilmorey. By an order of 29 October 1888 the lease of Bridge Dock was surrendered by the bankrupt Dry Dock Corporation of London to its liquidator, Alexander Young, from whom Alfred Dowson now recovered it.

It is nearly 3. o'clock—the Senior partner has already retired & I am thinking of following his example. We will go whither you will tomorrow. My own preference is "Le Monde où l'on S'Ennuie".[3]

I am just going to write to my "petite Californienne".[4]

I hear nothing of my shocker wh. is at "All the Year Round"[5] & has been there for a month & more.

> Yrs
>
> in the utmost amazement   E. C. DOWSON

À demain.

3. By Pailleron, played at the Royalty from 21 November to 1 December 1888. Jane May was in the cast.
4. Little Flossie (see Letter 1).
5. A weekly periodical started by Charles Dickens which ran from 1859 to 1895.

3. *Postcard to Arthur Moore*
13 December 1888

Bridge Dock

Votre lettre reçue. Je crains que je ne pourrai pas te chaperoner au Royauté[1] samedi parceque le soir je suis engagé—et l'après midi je ne puis pas laisser le quai avant 3h. Donc j'espère vous voir ici—après demain—je vous ferai voir tout ce qu'il y a de voir dans ce triste quartier. On five-à-o'clocque vers 4h. où whiskey si vous le preferiez.

Esperant d'entendre tout de suite de vos nouvelles. Toujours à vous.

ADOLF[2] DU QUAI-SEC DE LA RIVIÈRE

P.S. Niniche sera encore sur les scènes cette semaine prochaine—donc nous y irons si vous voulez.

1. To see *Niniche*, a farce by Hennequin and Milland, performed by the French Repertory Company, which remained at the Royalty until 1890.
2. A reference to the introspective hero of Constant's novel *Adolphe* (1816).

4. *To Arthur Moore*
   Thursday night [? *3 January 1889*]

re le Rêve

Woodford

Dear Moore,
   The adage of the whist player—"When in doubt play trumps"—is of course fatuous. I amend it, it seems, into "When in doubt write to A. C. Moore". I have been reading "Le Rêve",[1] & I must tell you my impressions before I forget them. It is worth reading, you know, if you take Zola as seriously as I do—(I take him of course more seriously than anything else)—otherwise possibly not. I started with immense prejudices against it. I end by accepting it—or at any rate being grateful for it. You have seen the reviews—they have not understated its extreme innocence. It is idyllic & pure & graceful to the last degree—& there is a sort of pleasant unreality about it an ambiguous glamour which can hardly be without intention from a man who has such a unique power of vivid evocation. It strikes me chiefly as a sovereign piece of irony—hinted at in the title & corroborated in the last sentence. "*Ce n'etait qu'une apparence qui s'effacait, après avoir créé une illusion. Tout n'est que rêve. Et au sommet du bonheur, Angélique avait disparu dans le petit souffle d'un baiser*" From the literary point of view it is certainly a pretty idyll—artistically written—of a kind that it is quite excusable for a man to write when he has give one "L'Assommoir"[2] & "Pot Bouille"[3]—even if there was not the undercurrent of irony which anyone who really knows his Zola will discern. And the touch of the master is visible everywhere. An' you read it which I advise, I would call your attention to a score of pages that no one but our Emile could devise. I will mention only now the chapter in which Monsignore brings the extreme unction to the girl who is supposed to be dying. It is Zola at his best—& I hope you will admit that Zola at his best stands above all other novelists living or dead. He reminds me—or rather this episode reminds me—(excuse this desultory criticism) of Pater—a strange conjunction but it is so. I suppose it is the superficial resemblance of incident to the last few pages of "Marius".[4] It is a pity by the bye that Pater can not write a *real* novel. If he had the force of concentration necessary it would be a book unsurpassed & not surpassable. I am thankful for the two of them—but should like them hugely rolled into one. You must read the 'extreme unction' pages even if you can't stomach the whole. The purifying of the separate orifices of sensation

1. By Zola, published in 1888.
2. 1877.
3. 1882.
4. *Marius the Epicurean* (1885).

with the consecrated oils strikes me as an excessively fine notion.[5] I think if I have a death-bed (wh. I don't desire) I must be reconciled to Rome for the sake of that piece of ritual. It seems to me the most fitting exit for the epicurean—after all one *is* chiefly that—& one would procure it—(it seems essentially pagan) without undue compromise or affectation of a belief in "a sort of a something somewhere", simply as an exquisite sensation, & for the sensation's sake. . . . . .

A quotation flashes across me. "Les femmes sont faites pour commercer avec nos faiblesses, avec notre folie, mais non avec notre raison"[6]—I don't quite see the connection of thought—but it is there. I was thinking partly of the article you mentioned by Lucas Malet[7]— partly on what a double life—(triple possibly?)—one leads. I don't mean anything so obvious as the Jekyll & Hyde[8] business, but something more subtle—too subtle for me to express—although no doubt you see my point. Depend upon it there is something radically weak in a woman's brain. One *should* only know them carnally—I doubt if one *can* know them otherwise—& that is why the hot blooded, entirely sensual men are not puzzled by them as we others whom the devil of analysis has entered into. The biblical use of the word "know"—in reference to a woman is full of suggestion. I won't ask you to explain the insane attraction they possess because of course you can't. The sensual hypothesis does not quite fit—it is certainly not sentimental— vanity no doubt enters in—but will hardly account for all these phenomena. What the devil else remains? Is it curiosity? Case for Mr. A. C. Moore 1 gua. Thank the gods my particular puzzles are retiring but I can not hope they will be the last. What a charming world it would be if they did not exist—or rather if they never grew into their teens. And yet it is folly to try & escape from them. One might succeed if one became an inmate of La Trappe—a conversational monastery would be quite useless as one would certainly talk of them. Or one might adopt a child & cease to trouble about them—only then she would grow up—(for of course it would be she—was there ever an un- objectionable small boy?—) & so one's last state would be a million times worse than one's first. I wish I could believe, as I imagine you do—in a "sort of a something somewhere" in the way of womankind, but I don't, won't & can't. I am not in the least bitter against them. I am simply bewildered. They are fascinating, foolish, irrational, pretty, sensuous, omnibibulous creatures & if their society brought us in £5 a minute instead of being, as it is, ruinously expensive, it would be devilish dear at the price. Excuse this chaotic tissue of truisms & come

5. Dowson clearly had this passage in mind when he wrote his poem *Extreme Unction*, reproduced in Letter 275.
6. Chamfort, *Maximes et Pensées*, 'Sur les Sentiments' xi.
7. Pseudonym of Mary St. Leger Harrison (1852–1931). She was a daughter of Charles Kingsley.
8. R. L. Stevenson's novel was published in 1886.

and see me on Saturday when, if you like, we will ignore the existence of the sex altogether & talk of kings, cabbages & what you will—

Yrs ever—at present—sleepily ECD

Gad! when I think of the stupendous fatness of my corr. with you & the slackness of a certain Welsh friend of mine[9]—I feel our letters ought to be printed & presented to him as a wholesome moral lesson in energy.

9. William Rowland Thomas (1867–1936) was a close friend of Dowson's at Queen's and continued to see him from time to time in the early 'nineties. He spent most of his life in Liverpool.

5. *To Arthur Moore*
   [*c. 11 January 1889*]

Woodford

Cher et gai Lothario.[1]

Sorry Editha[2] is to be deferred & hope next week we shall have plus de chance. Your letters positively make my head go round; they breathe the vertigo of the rollicking polka & the languishing valse. Enfin, amusez-vous bien, mon cher! I am serenely self satisfied just at present because so far I have declined three—six in effect, for does not one danse accepted infallibly let one in for another? I mean to accomplish a record in that respect this year; next year I will free myself from the intolerable *corvée* of the *mondain* dinner—& après?—well, who knows but that the demi-mondain may follow?

You really must however work an evening next week or I shall retire in disgust to the North & canvass my clientèle. I knew you would appreciate the Daudet.[3] When you have done it I shall be awfully obliged if you will do it up & direct it—or somehow convey it—to

Victor Plarr Esq.[4]
40 Gt Russel St.

1. An allusion to the character in Nicholas Rowe's *The Fair Penitent*, first produced in 1703.
2. *Editha's Burglar*, a one-act play by Mrs. Hodgson Burnett, given as a curtain-raiser at the Globe; it was taken off on 11 January.
3. Probably *L'Immortel*, 1888.
4. Victor Gustavus Plarr (1863–1929) was born at Strasbourg of an Alsatian father and an English mother. He lived in England from the age of seven.

I dined with the above named yesterday at the Holborn.[5] The dinner
was excellent & the band sufferable—we must vary our salle-à-manger
I think & give it a try. We spent some hours afterwards in the familiar
smoking-room which was beautifully desolate. My beverage I admit
with shame was café au rhum. We are busy very in the East now—
three heavy collisions—one in our own dock, one in the Regent's Canal
& 1 at Tilbury & a barque to be painted coming in alongside of the
"Krystal"[6] to-morrow. I enclose a second letter from ma petite Californienne. Is it not touching? Is not the spelling divine? Some of it
however seems to me a trifle obscure. I am going to send you a Pall
Mall[7] in which is an interview with a lady of palmistic (! ?) fame whom
I imagine to be your "Vicious Camel"—of the BMR.[8] Will you come
with me & be showed up by her? I will cheerfully offer her my 5/- if
you will join me in the excursion. But oh—an' it were the Camel. I
would not give up hope of LS.[9] I have had similar experiences & the
MSS has returned. Why not call on the editor in person & awe him with
your eagle eyes.

I have not read the new Howells[10]—nor the newest but one. He's
a lesser light than James, n'est ce pas?—though "Indian Summer" is
delightful simply because of Effie.

How about Bruges? Will you come? If you think the two days or
so are not worth it I have no doubt I could arrange to be away for about
a week. Let me hear of this. I am taking up my classics again so great
is the dearth of novels here. Pliny is charming so is Ovid:—of Horace
I find, a little goes a long way. But ah—Sir Thomas Browne. I have had
a nodding acquaintance with him for a year or so but have lately
become intimate. Read him, read him—or better still get somebody else
who can read to read him to you. He's the only man anterior to Flaubert

He came down from Worcester College, Oxford, in 1886 and met Dowson
through Charles Sayle two years later. He became librarian of King's
College, London, in 1890 and of the Royal College of Surgeons in 1897.
In the early 'nineties he contributed articles and poems to several periodicals and published a book of verse, *In the Dorian Mood*, in 1896. In the
years around 1910 he was associated with Ezra Pound, who later satirized
him cruelly as 'Monsieur Verog'. His memoir *Ernest Dowson 1888–1897*,
published in 1914, gives a sympathetic account of the friendship.

5. A restaurant on the corner of High Holborn and Kingsway, pulled down
   in 1956; it was famous for its cellar.
6. The *Krystal*, bound up-river with a cargo of ice, was in collision with the
   Umzito in the afternoon of 2 January. She had to be beached at Limehouse with her after-hold flooded.
7. *Pall Mall Gazette*, 10 January.
8. i.e. British Museum Reading Room.
9. *London Society*, in which Dowson's first published verse had appeared in
   1886.
10. William Dean Howells (1837–1920), American novelist; his new novel was
    A Hazard of New Fortune. Indian Summer had appeared in 1885.

who had the "passion for the right word. I could die happy if Sarah
Bernhardt would declaim "Hydriotaphia" to me for an hour or too
first. No news of Thomas? Here, none! Au revoir.
Write speedily & name the day.

Yrs.   ECD.

I must add a note entreating name of some readable novels. I am
désésperé. I am looking for the Lucas Malet[11] you mention. The tribal
work I doubt if I could digest. I hate the Jews & all their works—&
can't even stand Daniel Deronda.[12] I am reading my Balzac now—
Have you written any more?—Write, write, write, it is the only endurable employment except when one is fortified with a glass of absinthe.

I have discovered an adorable child here, hailing from one of the
three publics that surround us on either side—"which pleases me
mightily" as Pepys would say. It is astonishing how pretty & delicate
the children of the proletariate are—when you consider their atrocious
after-growth. Of course it is the same in all classes but the contrast is
more glaring in Limehouse. This child hath 6 years & is my frequent
visitor, especially since she has realised that my desk contains chocolates.

I wish we could do something about "Ludovicus".[13] I was looking
over an odd chapter the other day & it seemed to me that we might
have done something.

I have got the idea of at least three novels germinating in my head—
& shall start off on one of them immediately M de V is finished.

But basta! basta! I am giving you too large a dose of this illegible
scrawl. ECD.

Know you of any shop where one can buy a hat (silken) of Parisien
shape?

11. Probably *A Counsel of Perfection* (1888).
12. By George Eliot (1876).
13. *Dr. Ludovicus,* the first novel on which Dowson and Moore collaborated.
    It was completed in 1889 but all attempts to publish it failed and the
    manuscript is lost.

6. *To Arthur Moore*
18 January 1889

Bridge Dock

Cher Confrère.
I have been meditating an epistle to thee for many days & I embrace
a slack moment of the morning to reply at once. I am glad rather that

our merrie meeting is deferred until next week—(but next week il faut absolument, mon cher),—as I too have been, although not in social bondage—yet somewhat a victim of the 'varsity invasion of this period. I met a potent socker man of C. CC[1] & Empired & Holborned with him; & the wily Swanton[2] was up until last night & absorbed a good deal of my time. He was down here with Lefroy yesterday & I finally saw him off with Sayer[3] by the 9.15 to Alma Mater last night—feeling greatly blood-stained & depressed as the train bore them away out of my sight. I should have rather liked a Royalty matinée with you to-morrow but I am destined to take my brother & 2 desmoiselles of tender years to the Surrey pantomime[4]—so we must positively fix an early meeting in the ensuing week. I shall be very oofless tho' & ~~we~~ must I fear be a Pinolitic pittite[5] on the occasion

I am condemned to bite my—lip in society on Tuesday—not praise Jah in a ball room but at a musical evening which is almost as bad:—for the rest, any day you fancy afterwards will seem to me "supremely fitting".

I have received no news from Clement Scott[6]—who has been honoured for the last month with the custody of my "Between the Acts"[7]. I have just sent back the proof of a Sonnet which is to appear in the April number of Temple Bar.[8] I enclose it to you though of course I don't pretend to write verse seriously. I believe however that T.B. gives me a gũa. for that sort of balderdash.

My p.b.[9] hangs on hand: when completed it goes to "Atalanta".

"Madame de Viole"—progresses—slowly but withal steadily. I will send you the next vol. as soon as it is therein copied. I tremble at the final revision:—oofless or otherwise I shall hire an amanuensis. I am sketching out a little tract—burlesque, blasphemous & satirical which with Swanton's connivance will probably be produced in a few weeks at Oxford. Ça s'appelle: "Heaven & Hell. or "The Lost Undergraduate".[10] It is very poor—but I flatter myself contains a *little* more humour than J.A.F.[11]'s "Visit".

1. Corpus Christi College, Oxford.
2. Calvert Hutchinson Swanton (1867–1914). Went up to Queen's College, Oxford, read law and was called to the Bar in 1894.
3. J. B. Sayer (b. 1866) was at Queen's from 1885 to 1889, when he became curate of Birkenhead St. Anne.
4. *The Forty Thieves*, at the Surrey Music-hall.
5. Dining at Pinoli's, a famous inexpensive restaurant in the Strand, which continued until the Second World War, and sitting in the pit.
6. 1841–1904, Dramatic Critic of the *Daily Telegraph* and Editor of *The Theatre*.
7. This short piece eventually appeared in *The Critic* during Dowson's connection with that ill-fated periodical.
8. *April*, subsequently included in *Verses* as *My Lady April*.
9. Pot boiler.
10. This appears never to have been published.
11. John Arthur Fallows (1864–1935) was at Queen's 1883–1888. He was

I need not say that it will be anonymous & will not bear the printer's name.

I also send by this post a rejected pot-boiler, (Argosy & All the Y.R.)[12] to London Society.

Write soon & settle a meeting place time & day:—where we go to, I leave to you—for it seems inevitable that any piece which I particularly wish to see runs precisely one week—: to wit "The Dean's Daughter"[13]—"Brantingham Hall"[14]—"Editha's Burglar! There's always the Royalty tho' the incomparable[15] has departed & "Paul Jones"[16] & ? Captain Swift[17]

By the bye I very much wish to go & see the Old Master Exhib.[18] Could you work it with me one Sat. afternoon. I particularly want to study the Watteaux.

I have got another charming photo of Bootle's Baby.[19] I hope she will be done in the fancy dress in which she was to appear last night at Menpe's[20] children's ball. Write soon.

Tout à vous.   ECD

ordained in 1891 but renounced his Orders three years later. He published a number of books, including *Introduction to the Study of the French Revolution* (1914). Towards the end of his life he told Plarr that he had a batch of 'early irreverent' letters of Dowson's, but these have not come to light.

12. *All the Year Round.*
13. By Sydney Grundy and F. C. Philips, from the latter's novel of the same name, opened at St. James's Theatre on 13 October 1888.
14. As W. S. Gilbert's first serious drama, this play excited considerable interest. But it was a disappointment and ran only from 29 November to 30 December 1888 at the St. James's.
15. Jane May, who was in *Le Monde où l'on s'ennuie* and *Le Voyage de M. Perrichon*, but did not play in *La Cagnotte*, which opened at the Royalty on 16 January.
16. Adaptation of the French comic opera *Surcouf* by Planquette, produced by the Carl Rosa Company at the Prince of Wales on 12 January 1889.
17. One of the current successes, written by C. Haddon Chambers; it opened at the Haymarket on 20 June 1888 with Beerbohm Tree in the cast.
18. Loan Exhibition at Burlington House. The Watteaus were lent by Sir Richard Wallace and Alfred de Rothschild, so that the paintings which Dowson was anxious to see were substantially those now in the Wallace Collection.
19. Minnie Terry (b. 1882), Dowson's favourite child actress, then on tour in *Bootle's Baby* by Hugh Moss (from the story by John Strange Winter), in which she scored her first great success in London in 1888. Dowson had a collection of photographs and souvenirs of her.
20. Mortimer Menpes (1860–1928) was an Australian who described himself as a 'painter, etcher, raconteur and rifle-shot'. He was a well-known figure in London's art circles and a friend of Whistler.

7. *To Arthur Moore*
[*c. 23 January 1889*]

Bridge Dock

Mon chéri Alphonse.[1] I recvd. your letter with much pleasure & look forward to to-morrow with much hope. I presume we meet at the one & only Monico in vestibulo. But of that you must let me know. If you have no special inclination for the evening what do you say to dining at the Holborn & dropping in vers 9h½ at the Princesses for which I have tickets. I am aware that Princess "vieux melo",[2] is not all that can be desired but we have had to invest in these tickets for some seafaring benefit business & they may as well be used. We shall probably find "Paul Jones"—more agreable when the first rushes are over. I trust you will get this to-night if so send me a line as to your plans. If I don't receive either a response or an independent epistle I shall take it for granted that the Monico rendezvous will suit you. I have a corvée on to-night in the shape of a [dinn]er[3] at at Blackheath—of a shipping & parliamentary ἦθος[4]—[so] I shall simply live in thought of our diner à deux to-morrow. [If] you write ∴. Address me here for I shall sleep with the Blackheathens & come straight here to-morrow. I heard from J.A.F. yesterday: he is still Germanizing & does not contemplate return for another year.

What do you think of the startling innovation at the B.M.R?—It will arouse discontent.[5]

I hope to talk over Ludovicus with you. I agree with you that the diary form is a very inadequate method. I sent a story to T.B. yesterday but without much expectation as it has already been rejected by Blackwood & othrs.

The Surrey pantomime is rather excellent: we laughed much over it. I hope you will come with me to the Watteaus on Sat afternoon—but of that we will converse anon. No more now.

Tout à vous.　　　GUSTAVE[6] DE LA RIVIÈRE

P.S. I enclose the tickets—on second thoughts—as if you will come with me—you might get the seats booked as it will be nearer for you than me—on your way down to-morrow.

---

1. i.e. Daudet.
2. *Hands across the Sea*, a melodrama by Henry Pettitt, opened 10 November 1888.
3. This letter is torn, damaging part of the text.
4. Probably a mistake for ἔθνος, tribe.
5. The Trustees of the British Museum on 12 January 1889 adopted a regulation by which novels published in the last five years could not be consulted in the Reading Room.
6. i.e. Flaubert.

Don't trouble however to go out of your way, for even if we don't go somewhere else after all, I daresay we should get good enough places by presenting our tickets at the door. ECD

Letter no. 2

Your small epistle to hand.

I don't mind what we do but as we have the tickets I suggest we look in at the Princesses, about (damn the hair)[7] ten—but let us act as the spirit moves us. I will not meet you outside the Empire an' you don't mind as I prefer a sheltered rendezvous in these parlous times. You will however find me taking an absinthe in Monici vestibulo at or about 6 p.m.—when we will proceed to Pinoli or where you will.
T.O.[8]
Act à votre discretion in the matter of booking seats—if you think that we shall be very much bored don't fix them.

Just off to Blackheath—οἴμοι ταχος τῶν κακῶν ὀτότοτοι[9]

Ton ADOLFINE

7. A hair got into his pen and smudged his writing.
8. Turn Over.
9. A tragic exclamation of despair, a parody of several phrases found in Aeschylus.

8. *To Arthur Moore*
   [*30 January 1889*]

Bridge Dock

Dear Moore.
By this post or the next "please receive" vol 2 of "Madame de Viole". I apologise for the bad writing but hope you will be able to fathom it & report at your leisure. Please be free with your criticisms & don't hesitate to comment on any places that may meet with your disapproval or "si forsan" their should be such—particularly—with your approval on the opposite blank leaf. I *particularly* want you to do this if you don't mind for I look on your criticism in fiction as final and shall be able to revise or at least try to do so according to it. Let

me know also of the style—how it strikes you in the *ensemble* & where it falls & when into the Burlesque. I have in some sort you know, the modern "passion for the right word" & I should like to know if the booklet ever strikes you as reaching a certain fitness of phrase which is what on the whole I care most about. Criticisms on the ἦθος[1] also will be welcome, though of course I don't expect you, or indeed anybody, quite to endorse it. However take your leisure.

Re Saturday—I forgot the old Masters for the moment in conversing with you on Sunday—but of course I would prefer them an' it suit you to accompany me. Otherwise I shall go to a Royalty matinée: but I shall hope to hear from you on the matter. I see the "Théatre Libre" is shortly to appear in Dean St. We must certainly go to that, if not to Coquelin.[2] Is he *the* Coquelin, par exemple or is he another? I am not quite clear on that point. What do you think of the Boulanger Victory?[3] Stupendous, n'est ce pas? I don't quite know whether to be elate or indifferent. One can't regret the Republic—the beau idéal of rampant mediocrity but there seems nothing to follow. The Comte de Paris[4] whom I should prefer is impossible—Plon-plon[5] no less so & the Géneral is too fatuous a bonhomme not to make some irretrievable blunder directly he comes to the top. I suppose that it simply means that France will be managed for some time to come by the extreme left —& so long as they respect the liberty of the naturalistic novelists, & do their best to squash the insufferable little squirt who calls himself William II of Germany[6], Je m'en fiche diablement. It will be interesting to watch however. Re Ludovicus—I have given much thought to it— & the result is simply that we had better continue it on the original lines & chuck the diary & the Princess & restrain our analytic instinct to the best of our power. Give your mind to this however & I will do the same.

I went last night to rather a decent musical "crush" where I had the pleasure of meeting Mrs Grossmith. There was some excellent music &

---

1. Moral tone.
2. There was a resident French company at the Royalty Theatre in Dean Street. Their manager, M. L. Mayer, invited the Théâtre Libre, a semi-amateur company from Paris, to occupy the theatre for a season and they opened on 4 February. The eminent French actor Coquelin Cadet appeared at the Royalty for one week in April.
3. In the elections held on 27 January, General Georges Boulanger was returned to the Chamber as member for Paris. At the time his victory seemed to mark the imminent collapse of the Third Republic, but at the last moment he flinched from using force against the State. Subsequently he ended his life by shooting himself on the grave of his mistress.
4. The Orléanist pretender.
5. The Prince Napoléon (1821–1891), the Bonapartist pretender.
6. William II became German Emperor in 1888 at the age of twenty-nine.

towards midnight several theatrical celebrities turned up, including Geo Grossmith[7], Jessie Bond[8] & Miss Philippi (?)[9] of the Court. I put up at the First Avenue[10] & reached Woodford at about 9.00 this morning, a most incongruous looking creature, in full dress, just as people were beginning to start townwards—

My recent social experiences of the last two Tuesdays have not given me much reason to change my view of the entire fatuity of these sorts of gathering. The young girl seems to me if possible rather more inane than when I last spoke to her a twelvemonth or so ago. And nine out of ten of the married women are just as bad—only happily, occasionally one can esconce oneself into a sheltered corner with the tenth—as I did last night—when the evening becomes endurable. Still I would sooner sit through the stiffest of melodramas than face the ordeal again for a month or so.

I regret that owing to my having lunched not wisely but too well I forget what has preceded this sheet. At the risk of being tautological I beg to hope that you will write & fix a rendezvous soon—a Pinoli & a smoke—or "what you will". I am exceeding oofless—so I can't rise above the modest Pit at the most. Ancient masters I presume on Sat? Write write soon. I heard from Swanton this morning. He says S. Smith[11] has gone down. I fancy that at least half of my noble year have been prematurely cut off. Eheu fugaces!

Do you know the Noons?[12] I met them with Lefroy on Monday (Edith & Evelyn): he wanted me to join him in theatrizing them—but I refused. Theoretically I don't mind those Mesdemoiselles "Tout-ce-vous-voudrez-mais-pas *ca*" to whom you can say everything & do nothing—but practically they are not attractive. I feel infinitely bored—ennuyé to the last degree: that is my only excuse for boring you with this aimless epistle. I want to reduce you to the same condition as myself. Good-bye. Write soon. I feel rather drunk. I am very much bored. Au revoir.   E C D

7. George Grossmith (1847–1912) created the main comic roles in the Gilbert and Sullivan operas. Author with Weedon Grossmith of *The Diary of a Nobody* (1894).
8. One of the Savoyards, who created the parts of Iolanthe and Pitti Sing.
9. Rosina Filippi (1866–1930), an actress then appearing in *Mamma* at the Court Theatre. She had achieved a marked success that winter by writing a pantomime, *Little Goody Two Shoes*.
10. The First Avenue Hotel in High Holborn.
11. Samuel Smith (1867–1938) was at Queen's from 1886 to 1890. He then taught for ten years in preparatory schools before going to Enfield Grammar School, where he remained until his retirement in 1931. In 1896 he made the translation of *Lysistrata* which was issued anonymously with Beardsley's illustrations. Though not a close friend of Dowson's, he was the recipient of his most intimate letters.
12. Untraced.

9. *To Arthur Moore*

Dimanche [*3 February 1889*]

Woodford

My dear Moore.

Here goes for my accustomed Sunday yawn to you! Thanks for your note. I meant to have called for Bouthors this afternoon & then have tried to get hold of you: but the weather appalled me & I stayed & looked at it ~~from~~ at a respectful distance instead. I shall hope to meet you one evening soon:—to-morrow, Tuesday, or Wednesday will see me equally & discuss "Ludovicus" & other matters with you over a 2/- *diner* at the Café Gall (opposite the Princess's) wh. I think you will admit to throw Pinoli entirely in the shade. We must come to some settlement about the order & distribution of the chapters. Then my idea is that we start a small manuscript book in which we *both* write—& wh. shall fly backwards & forwards between us viâ the penny post. e.g. You write chap I & send it me. I then return you the booklet with chap II & so on. Each writing on one side of the page only—& each having liberty to add & interpolate on the fly leaf of the other's portion. How do you think that will work?[1] Of course we must get at least 1 chapter done a week.

I went to "Hamlet"[2] on Friday night. I am able to say that the scenery is everything that could be desired & the dresses excellent. *Du reste*, I am still suffering from it—Wilson (—the great & good) made about three points in the play—Miss Eastlake struck me as being about as inconceivably bad an Ophelia as it is possible to see. I go to the "Princess's" no more. I have, by the bye, just conceived of what strikes me as rather a good—or at least, original idea on which to found a novel. Perhaps I shall work on it when "Madame" is done. Imagine a man of low origin, extremely strong, cynical & determined to "arrive" —& not caring particularly by what *means* he obtains the desired result. Next, a girl, young, & of excellent family, & rich—but who has *fauté* & has to be married off hand to save an *esclandre*. Of course here is the chance for my protagonist—he makes his own terms—high ones of course—marries the girl at once & retires with her until he can reappear with his wife & child without the risk of awkward questions being asked as to dates & birthdays. Then I should trace the gradual process by which the pair, whose marriage rests on such a cynical basis, come in time to tolerate each other—& finally to set on their union the

---

1. This, in fact, was the method by which *A Comedy of Masks* and *Adrian Rome* were written.
2. *Hamlet*, with Wilson Barrett in the title role, opened at the Princess's Theatre on 28 January 1889.

sanction of affection. That would be one dénouement—or it might be better to work it out more tragically. In any case it seems to me there would be ample material for a study of morbid anatomy in the vein of Paul Bourget—only, do you think a story starting from such a motive, would ever go down? Of course it would require delicate treatment? Perhaps we might collaborate?—[3]

I shall let it simmer in my brain however until 'Madame' & Ludovicus are in the hands of the pilfering brotherhood.[4]

Louis Bouthor's brother "Jean Thorel"—has just sent me his book "La Complainte Humaine".[5] I will bring it to you—though it is not much either in your line or mine. It is worth reading however if only for its charming style. He purposes sending copies to English gens de lettres & has asked me for names & addresses. I have suggested Swinburne & Pater, Lang, Oscar Wilde & Lady Dilke as the most feasible— also Austin Dobson. Can you add any others? I must stop this now as I have various other letters to write, which have already been due for some months. I get up on Sundays at 12.0 but only begin to wake up after "five o'cloque" & as I am a chrysalis again after supper I have to make the most of my few hours of energy. I wish my other correspondence would run off my pen with as little effort as this of yours entails to yrs—ever-à-bientôt—n'est ce pas?—   E C D

"Between the Acts" has come back from Clement Scott at last— endorsed "Very pretty but will hardly suit. Declined with thanks."

3. This project came to nothing.
4. i.e. publishers.
5. Pseudonym of Jean Raymond Virgile Bouthors (1859–1916). This was his first book.

10. *To Arthur Moore*
    6 February 1889

                                                          Bridge Dock

Dear Alphonse:
    Yrs to hand. I have not yet looked at your scheme as my own is not yet devized & if I did so I should not be able to resist unconscious cribbing. Here is my order. We will compare & draw up a "revised version"—when we meet—say Saturday?—though an earlier day will suit me best—

Chap I[1] Introduces Dorothy (also Daisy)—Blake (?)—Ludovicus etc at Duneton. Meeting between Blake & Ludovicus.
Chap II—Lud. calls at the Manor. Proposes to Dorothy. Refusal. D. explains that she has been engaged to Blake for some time. Anger——mutual recriminations.

Chap III Picnic—Dinner etc Lud. leaves the Manor—he meets Blake who offers to drive him home. He accepts & decoys Blake to supper with him.

Interval of 2 or 3 weeks

Chap IV "What has become of ~~Edward~~ Richard?—He calls at the Manor—Dorothy reproaches him for his long absence. His curious manner. Entry of Ludovicus—much agitated. Curious scene—highly incomprehensible manner of Lud. & Blake. Dorothy puzzled—Mr Lemaitre irritated.

Chap V Arrangements for the marriage. Ludov. appeals to Lemaitre to stop it. He declares that Blake is really a most ineligible parti. Lemaitre much agitated but declines to interfere. Ludov. makes 1 final appeal in the presence of Dorothy & her lover.
    Dorothy very wroth. Ludov. threatens he will prevent it: he "has a trump card in his hand." Dorothy defies him: Blake obviously uneasy.

VI Ludovicus at bay. He disappears to Paris. The marriage day. ~~No bridegroom. The body in the Morgue.~~ Bridegroom uncomfortable. "How Mr Richard has changed! Can this be Dick!" The death of the bridegroom. Annoyance & surprise of the bride. Something odd about the corpse. The Doctors speak not.

VII The body at the Morgue! Suicide in the Cathedral of Notre Dame! At what hour? At the same hour at wh Blake died.

VIII The Princess Czatoriska visits Duneton. I am his aunt! Whose? Blakes? No. Ludovicus'? No. Whose then? Prince Ludvig Casimir Soboievsky, Phil. Doc. Leip! "I can a tale unfold"—She unfolds it. Hair of the reader & of Dorothy rapidly acquires a perpendicular permanent stiffness. Dorothy understands. Finis.

This is very crude & much cannot stand but at present it is the best I can do. I am now going to read yrs.
    I have done so & should think we can make a fairly good revise. I see you have 1 chapter more than I, but I expect my programme could not easily be compressed into less than 9 chaps. 10 would be the right number. I am anxious to see you this week—as well to discuss this matter as to hear your detailed criticisms on "Madame". Is Iseult a

1. Dowson's original chapter numbering is given. He altered it after reading Moore's suggestions.

little too "stiff"? Will the British public swallow her? I was obliged to put the colour on her rather thickly—otherwise the readers sympathies would have gone entirely with her & not with Lucien—who indeed even as it is will not I fear be a very sympathic person to the B.P.

Write again soon & state plans for Saturday. Let me know if poss. by Friday as my theatric plans on that day will depend greatly on whether you are not good for a Pinoli on Sat. night.

11. *To Arthur Moore*
[*c. 15 February 1889*]

Woodford

In the High Court of Justice
Intoxicating Liquors Division

Whiskey
v   Lay in a packet
Absinthe

Dowson J ruled that the defendant be non-suited. Leave to appeal refused.

Dear Hayfield,

How went it with you? I had a jovial journey home as I had the fortune to stumble into a carriage of which the only other occupant was a genial old gent retiring from a Holborn banquet who was exactly $3°. 55'. 14''$. more intoxicate than myself.

On the whole it is a mistake to get binged on the verdant fluid. As a steady drink it is inferior to the homely Scotch. I sobered sufficiently to read your criticisms through before I went to bed (many thanks for them, en passant—all your emendations seem to me most happy & I shall expect you to treat the first vol. similarly)—but awoke this morning with jingling nerves & a pestilential mouth on. I shall anxiously await Ludovicus & have already jotted down a few alterations of my old 2nd Chap. I understand that absinthe makes the tart grow fonder. It is also extremely detrimental to the complexion. I believe that even in the full swing of the campaign of my last term I never presented a more deboshed appearance than I do this morning.

Believe me, my dear Heathcote,
Yrs very affectionately   DAISY MALONEY[1]

---

1. Mayfield (not Hayfield) and Daisy Maloney were characters in the revised synopsis of *Dr. Ludovicus* (see Letter 12); Heathcote was probably Mayfield's first name.

A p.c. addressed to W.R.T. &
inscribed with a simple "Scribe"
(not Pharisee)—will be dispatched
from here to-morrow, the first of a
series of 8 to follow daily.

12. *To Arthur Moore*
18 February 1889

Woodford

My dear ~~Sayle~~[1] Moore,
    Excuse this palpable economy but paper seems to be scarce! Here-
with—rather before, "please receive" chap ii Doctor Ludovicus". I was
disgusted with my old chap. ii & so wrote it afresh with small draught
on the old one—but am painfully conscious that my chapter is still
eminently unsatisfactory & probably worse than the other. Ma chè
vuole? I have not felt myself since my generous allowance of the potent
green on Thursday & was right 'orf' the fascinating fluid yesterday
which I spent in large part with Bouthors. To day for the first time I
awoke without a head but am still très las.
    ˙ I am delighted with your chapter which defies *improvement* though
as you see I have taken the liberty of making 1 slight *addition* which
seemed admissible.
    I must apologize for having failed to come to the scratch—I mean
for having meandered along without bringing Ludwig to a proposal.
Mais en effet—that seemed to me a little abrupt. I hope however it wont
inconvenience you in your chapter. I think you had better bring the
proposal off in your next chapter—whether at the dinner—or the picnic where he would no doubt have ample opportunity. Erase without
hesitation any passages in my portion which strike you as ὀλίγιστα πρός
τι.[2] I check my rambling style as well as I can but am conscious
that I wander off a great deal too often into the dominion of the
roman des moeurs. Let me have a fresh instalment as soon as possible

1. Charles Edward Sayle (1864–1924) met Dowson at Oxford (he was at New
   College). During 1888 he had rooms at Gray's Inn and it was here that he
   introduced Dowson to Plarr. In 1889 he went to Cambridge as assistant
   librarian at St. John's College and in 1893 moved to the University
   Library, where he remained for the rest of his life. He published several
   volumes of verse, including *Erotidia*, 1889, and *Musa Consolatrix*, 1893,
   which contains a sonnet addressed to Dowson.
2. In no way to the point.

& by the bye tell me at the same time or by return of post if possible what will have happened when I am next to resume the story. For I am afraid my incurable propensity to let the action halt, may have thrown our written programme out of gear. Excuse the drunken metaphors. I think bien entendu, we had better let the chapters grow as the spirit moves us a good deal—although of course sticking to the skeleton of the revised programme. Did we revise it though? I am hazy! Or how soon did the nectar take effect? We must meet again soon more soberly. My beverage shall be milk & soda. Bouthors by the by will be dining with me at Gall on Sunday. Can you not be of the party? If so write & I will arrange details of rendezvous. It will presumably be his last Sunday in Albion. I now return to Madame de Viole as I can not resume the other until I know the substance of your next instalment. Wherefore acquaint me speedily thereof. For at present I am a little bit in the spirit of it—& living more or less with the people. I want to strike while the iron is hot. Daisy you have made very visible to me. Quelle dommage qu'elle n'existe pas! Work at it, mon vieux, with a vengeance & shortly we will see it on every bookstall. I wrote most of my portion at the office to-day. No more now. Keep yourself up & abstain from alcohol & amourettes. So shall we inherit the Kingdom of—Mudie![3] Let me recommend "Bovril" as a cheap & efficient lunch. I partake of it daily—thereby scoring 7d of the firm. Au revoir à bientôt n'est ce pas?

Toujours le votre, cher collaborateur,   ERNEST DOWSON

P.S. I enclose a second scheme—How will it do? & is it different from our former one? I feel terribly sure that the difficult chapters are those yet to come.

$$\sigma\chi\hat{\eta}\mu\alpha^4$$

Chap I   The garden party. Introduction of $\tau\grave{\alpha}$ $\pi\rho\sigma\hat{\omega}\pi\alpha^5$ Ludovicus appears.   A C M

Chap II   Ludovicus calls us at the Grange. Daisy makes an impression. Lemaitre introduced.   E C D

Chap III The picnic at Allerton Mere. The belle Americaine & also Aunt Charlotte. Dinner (past) alluded to. Ludovicus & Daisy. Proposal. Refusal. Tableau.   A C M

Chap IV   ? Ludovicus chez soi, alone. He meditates flight. Evening. Ball. Unexpected entrance of Mayfield. Thought he would just look in. On his way home. Ludovicus has a thought. They retire to the labratory.   E C D

3. The largest and most influential circulating library.
4. Scheme.
5. The characters.

Chap V   Daisy at Mayfields. Timid unaccount nervousness of Aunt
Charlotte. Ominous suggestions! Daisy & Mayfield. Curious
interview. Daisy puzzled by the new method of his wooing.
He presses her for an earlier day. She consents. Annoyance
of Adrien.   ACM

Chap VI   Ludovicus calls at the Grange. Presses Daisy with an air of
assured triumph. The arrival of Mayfield creates a curious
consternation in both men. Daisy frightened. Finally they
both depart together. Fragment of their conversation to titil-
late the reader's curiosity in approved Braddonian style[6]
without satisfying it. They defy each other.   ECD

Chap VII Ludovicus announces that he is going to Paris. Shortly
afterwards to Adrien's somewhat annoyance Mayfield implies
that the marriage will take place in Paris. Dorothy secretly
alarmed consents rather than appear to mistrust Mayfield.
Enter L. Sensational interview between the three persons in
which Daisy finally declares that she is of Mayfield's side. ACM

8.—In Paris Ludovicus at bay. He threatens Mayfield to do his worst.
"You will shoot me?"—"No, myself: Mayfield pales! The catastrophe on the marriage morning.   ECD

9.?

10.?

6. Miss Braddon (1837–1915), whose great success, *Lady Audley's Secret*,
appeared in 1862.

13. *To Arthur Moore*
21 February 1889

Bridge Dock

Dear Moore.
Le Lapin[1]—
Yrs to hand: with much joy recvd. Write at once & fix a meeting as you
suggest—Monico—at 5.30 or 6. We will take him to Gall—or elsewhere.
I absolutely decline to see socca' matches but will matinize with
you whither you list.

1. W. R. Thomas, also referred to in this letter as the Man of Wales.

In writing to The Man of Wales prithee make the foll: points—
1stly. How far nobler it would be to come with us to a matinée of
(say)—"Yeomen of the Guards"[2]—than to be spectator of the rival
teams at—where? (Queen's Ground I suppose).[3]
2nd. How essential to the harmony of the evening it will be that
neither Mamma nor any other man of bad character do accompany us.

———

The first point you will miss: the second *must* be made: Men *must* be
squatched.

———

Ludovicus

I await Chap iii eagerly. It seems to me the best chap possible
though at present I can't quite grasp how Daisy is inveigled into the
House on the D's. However no doubt you will arrange it with admirable
tact.

We must talk of these things on Saturday. Unless I hear from you
to the contrary I shall look for you outside the Anglo-Austrian[4] as soon
after 2.30 as possible—I shall be there probably some time before.

Yrs in profound excitement   ECD.

P.S. I don't feel much like matinizing at the moment mais *nous verrons*

P.S. I enclose a P.C. wh. I had just written—it is no longer necessary
—but you may as well post it.

2. *The Yeoman of the Guard* by Gilbert and Sullivan opened at the Savoy on
   3 October 1888.
3. The University Soccer Match was played on 23 February and resulted in
   a draw, 1–1.
4. The Anglo-Austrian Club was at 7 Mill Street, Hanover Square.

14. *To Arthur Moore*
    [*22 February 1889*]

Bridge Dock

Dear Moore.
     Thanks for your epistle. I am impatient to return chez moi to dis-
cover the new installment.

Unless I receive a wire from you re Lapin, Matinée & othrs. I shall probably be a little later than 2.10. Ergo I suggest give me until 2.15 outside the A. Austrian & then adjourn to the portico of the B.M. I express myself badly—I mean the platform with the doors & the drinking fountain, where are seats & elderly gentlemen thereon munching sandwiches.

I take it therefore that in the absence of electric communication to me here before 12. (in which case I will turn up anywhere at any hour) —an' I do not find you by the A.Au. I may look for you on one of those same seats—or at the furthest in the R.R. near the door.

I am bound to say that at the present moment I feel right on for a matinée either with you alone, or in conjunction with the decoyed one. However not I think *La Doctoresse*[1].

Suggested Programme

2.10 Meeting of the 2 inferior persons.
3.0   Matins.
5.30 The one & only Trinity in conjunction at the Café Monico.
5.35 Pernod à trois
6.0   Charter-party executed of a two-wheeled hutch to convey the prize rodent to Gall.
6.15 Arrival at Gall. Arrangement with the proprietor that no dogs shall be admitted
6.30 The ménu.   Potage Rolandaise

                Homard à la Kismetics

                Queue blanche

                Pâté Zola   Vins divers

                Choux-fleurs à la Reine

                Lapin Rôti.

                Pudding au lait.

                Glaces des Nuits Arabiens

                Dessert à la Burton[2]

7.30 Dissolution of several buttons on the beatific waistcoat.

---

1. A comedy by Ferrier and Bocage which opened at the Royalty Theatre on 18 February.
2. Sir Richard Burton's translation of *The Thousand and One Nights* was published in sixteen volumes, 1885–1888. The 'menu' also alludes to two plays, *Kismet* by J. Wilton Jones, which was on tour in 1888, and *The Arabian Nights* by Sydney Grundy, which ran at the Comedy during most of that year.

7.35   do.   do.—the beatific bags.
8.0   Emotion. Tears. Hysteria. Profanity.
8.15 Removal of the prize rodent. Paddington. Blue fire.
10.0 Pernod à deux.

Good old Pigott![3] Cat out of the bag at last. Poor Dicky Webster, what a notch! Vive la Bagatelle.

3. Richard Pigott, who had supplied a spurious Parnell letter to *The Times*, appeared before the Special Commission on Ireland on 21 February. In cross-examination it became clear that he was himself the forger. Sir Richard Webster Q.C., the Attorney-General, was counsel for *The Times*.

15. *To Arthur Moore*

Sunday [*24 February 1889*] 9.25 p.m.

Woodford

Dear Moore—

The worst I hope is now over. it has been bad though not I am deeply thankful as bad as I feared. I awoke early & immediately swallowed the contents of my water-bottle. I then waited in much distress fearing the worst. But the worst did not arrive. I resolutely refused to eat—although at one moment I almost *desired* that relief or the more thorough one of immediate dissolution. A cup of very strong tea began the cure & at 11.30 I rose & plunged into a tepid bath. I was rather off dinner but later on at tea time was able to eat largely & comprehensively. For the rest except that I have a beautiful pea-green complexion & am still suffering from an absolute impotence to do anything except sit in an armchair with lowered lights, the cure is complete. How are you? Have your sufferings been of like nature with mine?

To-morrow I begin a severe course of caring for my liver & the remaining coat of l'estomac. In two or three months I may possibly venture on a glass of claret & water. We must dine soberly however one day this week—any day except Wednesday will see me.

I need not say I have not written a line of Ludovicus. I will try however & commence Chap IV to-morrow. Great Scott! I am so exhausted. The effort of this epistle has entirely dissipated my last remaining shred of energy. I would give much to see the Rabbit at this moment. Thanks to a merciful something or other I only had 1 whiskey

& that early in the day: otherwise I should be, I feel convinced, already being measured for my little blue coffin.

Write soon & assure me that you are still in the land of the living. This must be positively my last "binge". By a miracle I have survived it but a repetition would infallibly take me down to Hades.

Au revoir.

Ton	ADRIEN

Monday A.M. Yrs to hand.
Am now pretty fit

16. *To Arthur Moore*
Friday [*1 March 1889*]

Bridge Dock

Dear Moore.

I regret to say that partly owing to the deplorable state of my health Tues & Wed, partly to the extraordinary difficulties in the conception Chap iv has proved a stumbling block to me & I shall be surprised if I am able to let you have it by to-morrow. I will try to do this however & in any case if you can *possibly* work it meet me somewhere to-morrow afternoon or evening.

Let me have a line by to-morrow morning to say whether or no I may find you 2.30 at the BMR or where?

Otherwise I am due at Orchard St[1] by 5.0 on Sunday & can devote the interim from 2.30 thereto with you if you could manage to meet me smwhre. I should however vastly prefer Satdy: (to-morrow). Mind & write or wire.

Yrs in gt haste	E.D.

PS. Rcvd a letter this mrng from Mabel.[2]

1. Miss Margaret Roberts, a 'witty old lady' acquaintance of Dowson's, lived at No. 8. See Letter 199.
2. Probably Mabel Vance (see Letter 153); untraced, but likely to have been a child actress.

17. *To Arthur Moore*
    Saturday [*2 March 1889*]

Bridge Dock

Dear Moore.

I am painfully conscious of the miserable failure which I have made of chap iv—wh will I hope reach you to-night. I worked at it from 9 PM to 3 AM last night without a break & after about 900 abortive chapters now in Gehenna set down the version which you have as better than coming to you to-day or to-morrow with empty hands. In daylight it seems to me worse than ever altho' the Doctor's soliloquy is really an admirable burlesque of the G. Meredith love scenes. I refer you to the "Tragic Comedians"[1]. Alter it & emend it as much as you can: the less like itself it returns to me the better I shall be pleased.

I am sorry you could not manage to meet me to-day. However I shall be at Baker St. as you prefer—w.p. shortly after before 3.0, to-morrow—I shall probably compass a matinée or a soirée to-night.

Suggestions for Chap **V**.

———

Arrival of the groom at the house. 11 p.m. Sonia. Ludovicus comes out of the labratory—looking very much exhausted. "The fumes of some chemical he was brewing had overpowered them". Mayfield follows him —curious impression of the groom: bring in some chance remark of Ludov. to M. overheard by the groom: such as. "Bear in mind what I have told you."—or of a more puzzling nature. The drive home: Aunt Charlotte anxious sitting up. *Her* strange impressions.

Previously I should recommend a *strong* scene in the kitchen—the groom & the old woman sitting, waiting: intently: harrow up the reader's nerves to the best of your power. They might grow so nervous, or rather *he* for Sonia is imperturbable as to make a rush for the labratory. No sound. They thunder at it. Presently the door slowly opens. "Your master & I have had a narrow escape. Open the window: brandy—Mayfield you are all right now take care of yourself. Wrap up well: have a cigar.

———

I believe this is rather different to the proposed Chap V: but I think it will be as well to prolong the real sensational business this way especially as hitherto we have shown a tendency to slur it over. Use your own judgement however. Au reservoir? Turn up to-morrow if you possibly can.

1. Published in 1880.

I apologize for my slackness but I have been really so awfully seedy this week—spending my time on a sofa & Tuesday & Wed partaking of nought save beef tea au cognac.

By the bye so far I haven't the very faintest, remotest conception of what my next chapitre is to be about.

Yrs   E D LUDWIG VON SOBOIEVSKI

I heard from my petite Californienne yesterday.

18. *To Arthur Moore*
   Tuesday [*5 March 1889*] 11 p.m.

Woodford

Dear Moore.

Here goes for a ream or so! I have got your card & regret that Lud:s delays, shall hope to see him to-morrow, & will do my best to complete my portion by Saturday. Par exemple! we *must* meet this week & talk over the subsequent line to be pursued. I wrote a long epistle to you yesterday but subsequently destroyed it. I thought on the whole that a bulletin of me might be with advantage deferred especially as I am decidedly of weather-cock constitution. Let me recommend by-the-bye, that if any of my voluminous correspondence with you survives, you endorse the relics with a scathing allusion to consistent inconsistency.

I quite agree with your advice on Sunday & shall abstain from the Pot de Feu[1], except as far as a casual cup of coffee is concerned when *we* pass in the neighbourhood.

I had a very charming epistle of 5 pages from "Lena". It confirmed my opinion that if the experiment is to be made, this girl is the right one. But I am not sure whether it is altogether advisable—and I am even a little sorry that I am unable to rush into the thing in Bartholomean[2] fashion without thinking or reasoning about it at all. I doubt mon vieux after all if our analytic habit is altogether a happy one. I know of course that in sober moments this critical fastidious attitude is what chiefly makes life tolerable. But *après*—?—doesn't one risk missing some fine sensations by being too critically curious about the why & the wherefore of them? If the substance of the gods' gifts smells suspiciously of the dung-heap is that any reason for losing faith in the

1. The Horseshoe, in Charlotte Street, where he first met the barmaid whom he called Lena.
2. He refers to his medical-student friends at St. Bartholomew's Hospital.

shadow which I am convinced, the fabulous dog[3], in spite of Aesop, preferred *wisely*. Moore, mon vieux, this is a hyper-critical age & we who are so intensely modern are not of it with impunity. We are "Sebastian van Storck"[4]. I must look out the quotation—"And at length this dark fanaticism losing the support of his pride in the mere novelty of a reasoning so hard & dry, turned round on him *as our fanaticism will*, in black melancholy". That is perhaps not so true of you as of me, for although I gather, your views practically coincide with mine you are not fanatic: & I am afraid I have been, possibly still am. I have been worrying part of this evening with the aid of Bohn,[5] through parts of the "Symposium" & the "Phaedrus". But I am sorry to say that Plato on "Love" still seems to me less convincing than Schopenhauer.

All this in view of a—no, don't say "barmaid"—*grisette* is better— may strike you as highly ludicrous, I dare say it is: but my practice never gives me any tangible satisfaction unless it fits in a little with my theory. And this don't & won't. And yet what the devil is the good of a philosophy which doesn't save you from ennui? I suppose I shall continue to plague myself with these questions until I am drunk or dead. The girl wrote a nice letter. I have written her one: it is a perfect letter in its' way; I should like to have shown it to you; I recognize in it, thou' I say it as shouldn't what Pater calls "a delicate tact of omission"; and the only defect in it was, the vital defect, that it was perfectly factitious, & that unless the girl is exceptionally naïve she *must* see that I didn't believe in it myself. She is a literary girl by the way with a certain amount of *esprit*: e.g. she reads Dickens etc, quotes Tennyson, says that when you have read one of R. Haggard's novels you have read them all, & acquiesced in my announcement that I shd. call her 'Lena' au lieu de C——e, with the remark that you couldn't make a silk purse out of a sow's ear. She is very young & I suppose innocent— as innocence goes after the earliest teens—& therefore if the experiment is to be made, isn't she about as good a specimen as I could find? I suppose the experiment will have to be made—n'est ce pas? I contemplate nothing gross, mind you—which is perhaps only another objection to the experiment—or at any rate to it's success.—But then I have no real expectation that it will succeed. Have you? I wish you would start an "experiment" of your own, though?—i.e. a spiritual mistress taken from one of the classes outside Society: we might compare notes with mutual advantage & work our result when the disillusionment comes, into an agreeable étude—in collaboration.

I am sorry for boring you in this way, but you know my habit of

3. Aesop, Fable 233 in Halm's edition.
4. The third of Pater's *Imaginary Portraits*, first published in 1887. The passage Dowson quotes appears towards the end.
5. The translations in Bohn's Classical Library.

seeking your spiritual counsel in these matters. I hope this will be at any rate the last.

Plarr & Image[6] & those people are "no good of" at all. They are "naturalists" who quite fail to grasp the position, & contemplate a colony à la Thoreau, of "Hobby Horse" people & a few elect outsiders each with a "belovèd"—(please mind the accent) where there will be leisure only for art & unrestrained sexual intercourse.[7] The only point on which we are quite at one is that no "belovèd" is admissible who has breathed the poisonous atmosphere of a drawing-room. Write soon & express your views with freedom, & be not chary of your advice.

I shall have leisure to consider it during the interim which must elapse before Lena gets a free afternoon or evening,—when that happens,—unless I decide in the meanwhile that the experiment be abandoned—

We propose theatrizing together or some similar amusement—if it be Sunday, with your connivance? possibly the Zoo. Next Sunday being the first since her arrival she has to spend in the bosom of her family. I am not yet in love with the girl though I foresee that with a very slight effort I shall become so. Her greatest charm is her youth: also (a little) her blue apron.

In any case I will not allow this affair to distract me from Ludovicus, although I fear Mme de Viole must lie fallow until the dénouement comes. What dénouement is possible? It must inevitably be more or less melancholy, unless one can keep the thing the whole time in the tone of persiflage. And that I fear is impossible?—

How long do you prophecy that it will last? A month from to-day at the longest! Eheu fugaces amores! And yet it makes me extremely tired to think of it lasting longer. Great Scott! What a fantastic paradox is life! I feel so exhausted that I think this must be at least my 90th. incarnation. And I fear I am not yet on the way to Nirvana. Adios: write soon:—with all my inconsistencies

Always yrs   ERNEST DOWSON

6. The Rev. Selwyn Image (1849–1930), Vicar of St. Mary's, Soho, poet and artist, later Slade Professor of Fine Art at Oxford. At this time he was an associate of A. H. Mackmurdo and Herbert Horne in the production of *The Century Guild Hobby Horse* (see Letter 69).

7. The simile is not exact. Thoreau was a bachelor, of whom Stevenson said, 'He was no ascetic, rather an Epicurean of the nobler sort . . . He left all for the sake of certain virtuous self-indulgences.' The *Hobby Horse* group set up their establishment in Fitzroy Street, off Tottenham Court Road, but it was probably more respectable than Dowson suggests. Victor Plarr, a highly respectable man, lived there for some time before his marriage, and so did Lionel Johnson.

19. *To Arthur Moore*
   [*c. 6 March 1889*]

Bridge Dock

Dear Moore.

I must really send a line since your letter has come to protest against your valuation of Chap V. I consider it *distinctly the best* chap of the whole bundle & there is nothing except (perhaps) the two last pages which I can criticize. And they only want a little expansion not alteration: the rest is entirely admirable & I would not wish to change a word.

I have already begun Chap vi, but it is amazingly difficult & I fear may not be ready after all by Sat. I promise it however by Monday morning. I think—rather I am sure I can dine with you teetotally on that night. Let us fix it therefore. Let me know where to send Lud to:—I mean to say will you go to the office at all on Monday or shall I bring it with me? (If ready on Sat. to 19 PPV.[1]?)

Your letter gave me great & immeasurable joy & I shall reply to it at leisure. As you say, fiat experimentum—in corpore tenerrimo (?). I have not been to Charlotte St since Sunday & shall not look in for a café noir till Saturday—if then. My idea is that if my hare is trappable by any Pot au Feu competitor—then she is not worth the trapping as far as I am concerned. But I think I have her. You say Mimi[2] does'nt exist. I am afraid you are right—but it is a great pity.

What a joy to think Ludovicus progresses so hopefully. When he is in the hands of a friendly firm we must seek a fresh field for our inexhaustible genious! ? a novel à la Phillips[3]—or an étude Jamesiensis. Joy of your Hants expedn. I go Brightonwards[4] shortly. Au revoir. Écrivez

Tout à toi   ECD.

I enclose rather a waggish article
by Andrew Lang.

1. Moore lived at 19 Park Place Villas, Maida Vale.
2. The heroine of *Scènes de la Vie de Bohème*.
3. F. C. Philips (1849–1921), a popular novelist and playwright.
4. Where his uncle, J. R. Dowson, lived.

20. *To Arthur Moore*
      Sunday [*10 March 1889*]

Woodford

My dear Moore.
      Here is your extra special Sunday edition!—
                  L'Art.
      Ludovicus is a great difficulty at the present moment & the harder I
cogitate over Chap vi the less I make of it. I hope however that between
now & the small hours I shall manage to knock together something to
show you to-morrow.

      Thanks for your letter which I have perused more than once. I am
not quite sure whether I can or can not detect a vein of Olympian irony
running through it, which mitigates from the completeness of your
agreement. If that is so however you are probably right.—As you
remark it is the "après" wh. spoofs us. I foresee it in this case & although
I cease to consider it, can well imagine that the aftermath will be of a
kind which will make all my former pessimism seem by comparison a
rosy cheerfulness. N'importe. La jeunesse n'a qu'un temps. And at the
present moment I am surpassingly buoyant. The pity that it can't last!
I also feel surprisingly *fit*, more fit than I have for years, in spite of the
fact that yesterday owing to Swanton arriving & my dining with him
& seeing him off by the good old 9.15. I was joyously drunken—but on
Koch fils. And to-day I am still buoyant. The girl is an admirable
creature. I grovel for having so blasphemed her & her adorable age in
the past—this, mind you without prejudice, & reserving my full right
to assume the old attitude when the glamour is gone. You are wrong
by the way—we are no longer capable of the "Bartholomean rush": we
make love with infinite reservations & are always conscious that there is
something factitious about it. As for *esprit*—je m'en fiche—there never
was a woman spirituelle before she was thirty. She writes a delightful
letter though & is certainly the right type. I saw her Friday & also for
about five minutes yesterday—but there is no doubt that this is a
liaison of the spirit which will have to be conducted chiefly on paper.
      I am impatient to see your fair—find her out & that with speed—
your liver & the state of your purse will cease to annoy you. I am merely
conscious that I am alive & almost for the first time find the sensation
a pleasant one. It would certainly be more enjoyable to isolate the girl,
after your notion, but she would hardly find it amusing & as one is
prepared to offer her the devotion—not of a life-time but of a calender
month at the longest—perhaps the "consideration" of the compact is
not a valid one. I suppose you are now in the solitudes of Hants. Lucky
man. Shall I see you this week? I hope so. I hear that Bourget has just
published a certain volume of "Pastels"—10 études on "les femmes" wh.
by & by will be savagely enjoyed by me. In the meantime I resume my

acquaintance with Tennyson, so that I shall not be at a disadvantage in conversing with "Lena"—who, as I probably told you, is delightfully literary. Shall I, do you think, ever succeed in educating her to the point of view of James? I fear not: still I will take what I can find & drop the critical attitude.

I shall ask you shortly to procure me Zoologicatickets for Sunday— but at present no such prospect is possible. Only a theatre this week is on the cards. I suppose it will have to be a sentimental melodrama— e.g. "Tares"[1]—: or perhaps "Sweet Lavender"[2]. I shall not be satisfied until you are in the same condition as myself. But you may go further than the "Pot au Feu", (insufferable as the place is) & fare worse. I consider that I was simply miraculously fortunate in getting a look in the first day. That doesn't happen twice I fear. It was I think the blue pinafore which subdued me—also not a little, a certain youthful timidity which at first repelled advances & then gave way to an exemplary graciousness. And I notice the same trait in the letters. But enough of this amazing balderdash.

Poignée de main   ERNEST DOWSON

1. Written and produced by Mrs. Oscar Beringer at the Opera Comique on 21 January. The cast included Forbes Robertson and Kate Rorke.
2. By Arthur Pinero; opened at Terry's Theatre on 21 March 1888.

21. *To Arthur Moore*
[*15 March 1889*]

Bridge Dock

Dear Moore.

At last I am able to send you Chap vi. I finished it at 2.0 AM precisely. It is very bad, very long, & distinctly "penny awful" not "shilling shocking"—: curtail it at your pleasure.

I hope you have not been cursing me very bitterly for my delay. My only excuse is that I invested in "Robert Elsmere"[1] on Wed. & have been unable to tear myself away from it. However I will reserve my criticism for the present on that criticism-suffering book. I can't give you any ideas for Chap vii except that it ought to contain love-making between Daisy & It—between Daisy & Ludovicus—some gentle cynicism by Adrien as a sort of ironic background to the tragedy and *possibly*

1. Mrs. Humphry Ward's great success appeared in 1888. It was reviewed by Gladstone and became the subject of fierce controversy in the pulpit.

a second more violent interview between the 2 Ludovici. I feel too drained & exhausted by chap vi. to write more at present. Nevertheless I feel fairly hopeful about the opus—although for some obscure reason, presumably excessive tea drinking during this week of temperance— my nerves this morning are annoying me somewhat. I had a letterette— assez gentille from Lena yesterday, but have not been to Charlotte St since I was there with you last.

Write a line or so by return if you can—I am feeling rather aghast at the thought of the inroad of the barbarians to-morrow—but I am not sure that I shall not run down to Brighton from to-morrow till Tuesday. I hope we may meet some part next week.

Ever yours   ERNEST DOWSON.

P.S. How cursedly we are at the mercy of the changes of the weather.

22. *To Arthur Moore*
Dimanche [*17 March 1889*]

Woodford

Cher Confrère.

I *did* go down to the ABC[1] after leaving my atrocity with you on Friday—hunted upstairs & downstairs—had my boots cleaned outside & then searched through the Law Court refreshment bars—but in vain; finally I took a hansom in disgust at your inaccessibility & partook of an omelette in Charlotte St.—Did you aerate after all O Moore?

I am anxious to hear what your next chap. will be & will then try & get on with mine. I muchly fear that I shall not be able to do an evening with you this week. If any it must be Saturday or perchance Friday. But I foresee great—great—ooflessness—as the result of this week— much dissipation—& one evening will have to be devoted to Lena. However we will compare notes & arrange, if possible, later. This is only the good old ordinary Sunday afternooner. Did Tweedy[2] arrive? If so kiss him for me with a holy kiss. Were you at the Empire last night? If not you were well off: it was the most infernally hot, stifling, crowded place conceivable. We were only there from 9.30 to 11, but my head still throbs from it. By we of course I mean et ego et Swanton et Lefroy. Afterwards supping at the St James,[3] we beheld a striking

---

1. Short for Aerated Bread Company, a well-known chain of tea-shops.
2. Charles Winstanley Tweedy (1867–1909), Dowson's contemporary at Queen's. In 1890 he went to Chile, where he spent the rest of his life.
3. The fashionable restaurant of the day in Piccadilly, often called Jimmy's.

instance of the ups & downs of fortune. A "lady" brushed past our table
& bowed graciously—for the moment I could not conceive in what
place or how the gorgeous vision had known me. Then we grasped the
situation—it was Minnie Turner. Great Scott! How dress changes a
woman. She was positively radiant—a creamy creature, with splendid
arms & delicious flesh tints—& a toilette that was really admirable &
for a wonder not too much décolletée. Great Scott. She seems veritably
to have arrived. And there surged up another vision—of a private room
at the "Rising Sun"[4]—a creaking sofa—& "little Hewett"[5]—I was
obliged to chortle.

I just caught my train by a fraction of a minute: I shall probably do
an "all night" though one of these next few days. Perhaps we may run
across each other with our respective parties, at the Empire or
Alhambra?[6]

My liaison progresses—no new developments except that at the girl's
request I go no more to the "Pot au Feu": although my intercourse with
the "patron" is again quite amicable. Is the request favourable or the
reverse? The most obvious inference is that as she means to get some
outside recreation with me she does not wish me to see her coquetting
with the somewhat mixed clientèle who are no doubt amusing. It is
just possible I suppose that she is sincere in the reasons she gives—
which are of course of a little more flattering nature. I simply put
myself these questions out of curiosity: personally I am quite content
to let the affair develop itself in the way—I prefer—on paper. She seems
an exceptional sort of girl however—& is both quick & receptive: e.g. I
write her an alliterative sentence—& allude to Swinburne:—In her
answers she also "alliterates" not without effect & remarks "Swinburne is catching". That is fairly good for a *grisette*, though you may
say that my judgement is already warped & I lay too much stress on
detail. It can't last however, & I am not sure that I should like it too.

"Robert Elsmere" I have finished. You should have made me read
it before. It is a great book though it has enormous faults & might be
compressed with advantage. Catherine repels me almost more than
Dinah in "Adam Bede"—& Robert is an eminent prig. The terrible
man Green—I find it horribly hard to be tolerant of people like that—
also vitiates the $\mathring{\eta}\theta o\varsigma$ of the book & Robert's final position is a great
deal more ridiculous even than Xianity. But Langham is a stupendous
creation & I am jealous of Mrs. W. for having forestalled me in discovering him. The love passages between him & the violin girl are the
most ghastly & fascinating things I have ever read. And it is, in my
mind to Mrs HW's artistic honour that she saw & set down the close
of them—inevitable to a man with critical passion. Can you tell me by
the way where the quotation comes from—"The small things of life

4. A pub at Long Crendon, near Oxford.
5. Henry Victor Hewett (b. 1868). Went up to Queen's in 1885.
6. The famous music-hall and theatre in Leicester Square.

are odious to me & the habit of them enslaves me: the great things of life are eternally attractive to me & indolence & fear puts them by."[7] It is very well put—very. The Madame de Netteville episodes are also clever—but how passionately serious all these Arnolds[8] are even to the third & forth generation. Write soon.

Tout à toi   ERNEST DOWSON

7. This quotation made a great impression on Dowson. Some years later he gave it to Jepson to write against his name in a birthday book.
8. Mrs. Ward was the granddaughter of Dr. Thomas Arnold and the niece of Matthew Arnold.

23. *To Arthur Moore*
Saturday [*23 March 1889*]

Woodford

Dear Moore.

Thanks for yr. notes & vol iii: vol ii will doubtless arrive later. I don't like Chap vii as well as some of them but there are excellent things in it. I have already made some progress with my next chap: but it promises to be degrees worse than yours.

Am just off to dress for Faustus.[1] I don't expect to enjoy it much, but n'importe. Can you spin out your Park promenade to-morrow until 4.0? My plans hinge on those of a certain fair damoiselle whose plans in their turn depend on the whim of a blasted old fool. From 3.20–30 I await her outside the Horseshoe. If she turns up wh. is problematical, we go down to Buckhurst Hill together. If she doesn't I will proceed post-haste to the Marble Arch on the chance of finding you there at 4.0 Then we might have an hours stroll—& then I should go t' Orchard St.

I am anxious to have a chat with you but don't inconvenience yourself for it is quite on the cards that I mayn't turn up & even if I do, & you are not there I can go to O. St an hour earlier.

We must meet however early next week. Adios.

Yrs. in haste   ED. STULTISSIMUS.

Did my letter depress you? My dear fellow depression is not the word. Que diable allons *nous* faire dans cette galère.

1. *Faust-up-to-date* by G. R. Sims and H. Pettitt, which opened at the Gaiety on 30 October 1888.

24. *To Arthur Moore*
    Sunday [*24 March 1889*]

                                              Woodford

SPECIAL SUNDAY EDITION

Mon cher Ami.

    I wont apologise for having *manqué* the rendezvous this afternoon—partly because I don't suppose you were there—partly because I am sure you will be glad to hear that I carried out my other programme successfully, & feel a good deal the better thereby. In fact my mental & moral balance is now in large measure restored. I was the least little bit nervous, my faith in Mdlle Lena's taste, in spite of the blue pinafore not being very large & expected to be disillusioned when I met her endimanchée. Imagine my joy therefore when she turned up, a little late, attired most daintily in the most perfect taste: there wasn't a single bit from hat to shoes which I could have wished away. Mon vieux, I really think I am rather fortunate in this instance. I believe she is fairly unique. *Du reste* I could only complain of the small time she was able to give me for I had arranged to take her down to Buckhurst Hill (on my line) where she was going to spend the evening with her aunts & unfortunately I have to be at home this evening so she must go back alone. However I made the most of the occasion—we had an agreeable drive to Livpl St. & thence secured "the privacy of a first class compartment" Buckhurst Hillwards. It was very pleasant & (as I said) it has restored my mental balance. I expect there will be strange complications though for Mddle Lena is evidently a young lady of great independence & as self-willed as one of Rhoda B's[1] heroines. It appears that there was some difficulty about her getting furlough to-day. The patron consented yesterday: she sent me a wire. To-day the patron repents, he says he can't spare her. Mddle Lena says nothing: the patron goes out: Mddle retires, puts on her most charming hat & levants. It seems to me that the very obvious result will be that my charmeuse will be chucked! She doesn't seem to care however—& now that I have got a little headway on—I don't care how soon she leaves the most noble "Pot au Feu". I hope to goodness she has the sense to stay at B.H. to-night with her people & doesn't return to face the infuriated patron. But she is capable of anything—is impulse & imprudence personified, & would be to anyone so inclined, the easiest prey imaginable. Have you found *her* yet or looked for her? I should say "seek" or "refrain"—as it might be the first or the second experience. It doesn't do to ignore it—for the artist—but it is bathos to go through it twice. It isn't essentially ridiculous, you know, (in spite of what I

---

1. Rhoda Broughton (1840–1920), author of *Belinda, Dr. Cupid* and other popular novels.

may have said through ignorance) the first time—but repeated it becomes absurd & what is worse still reflects a sort of retrospective absurdness over the previous experience. I don't know how soon this will finish or in what way—there doesn't seem any dénouement possible to a Platonic attachment & yet few things are more finite—but I am very sure it shall be the last. I will let the subject drop however for the present: excuse my boring you with the lady in this reprehensible way. I want to talk of Ludovicus, also of the Gaiety. I am glad I went, I must confess. Mookerjee,[2] Swanton, Lefroy & myself made up the party. We had excellent seats in the second row of the stalls—Lonnen[3] is delightful & Florence St John[4] had exactly the kind of naughty impudence which a burlesque Marguerite requires. Yes, she is very nice: but après—fifteen times! mon ami I could no more go *twice* than I could to an Adelphi *melo*. No, after full & due consideration I am inclined to believe that English burlesque is a mistake. It's all puns & propriety:—the former element is unpardonable anywhere & what *is* the good of a burlesque unless it is risqué? I expect your attraction to the "Gaiety" is entirely one of association.

The only form of drama I really appreciate is the comédie de moeurs —the more cynical the better. Dumas fils easily first—après the playwright who most approaches him.

We *must* dine together next week & if you can let us go & see "The Weaker Sex":[5] any day in the earlier part of the week will suit me. I am sick of 'varsity men & shall leave on Friday for Brighton & so escape whiskey & whores on boat race night.[6] If you meet anybody of my acquaintance please anticipate my departure & remember that I am already there.

This appears to be an *extra* special: it is overunning all limits. Excuse my diffuseness. With regard to Ludovicus—I hope to be able to send you chap viii to-morrow & with it vol ii. My last chapter *was* too long, but if it requires mersion it must be with your chap vii—not chap v which must certainly stand. Chap vii has very good things in it but I think it doesn't carry on the action enough. In conjunction with chap vi it seems to drag rather. All the same I don't think there is any real need for compression—eleven or even twelve chapters would not be too much. People *will* have their shillingsworth. Before anything can be done however we really *must* have a meeting. How about Tuesday?

---

2. Satis Chandra Mookerjee, b. 1868. Went up to Queen's College, Oxford, 1887. He was called to the Bar in 1891, and entered the Indian Civil Service. He was the Indian undergraduate who had introduced Dowson and Thomas to bhang (see pp. 11–12).
3. E. J. Lonnen played Mephistopheles.
4. The outstanding *opéra bouffe* singer of the period.
5. By Arthur Pinero, produced at the Court Theatre on 16 March with Violet Vanbrugh and the Kendals in the cast.
6. 30 March.

Even as it is I am not at all sure that my working out of the chapter in hand is not all wrong & contrary to the σχῆμα. It is very gruesome & ghastly you know: it's a horrid idea. I really am beginning to feel frightfully sorry for the girl. By the way, I'm afraid I must after all object to the name "Jim". Can't it be "Frank" or "Hugh". I have an unreasoning objection to "Jim". We will settle that however in revision——

I am not going to roost yet & I am not quite ready to write my promised letter to Lena; wherefore I had better fill this page with bagatelles. What a hole I should be in if I ~~hadn't~~ wasn't able to confide all my fantasies to your aimiable patience. It is really excellent of you to wade through my correspondence . . . . There is no doubt in my mind that given the desirability of an amourette, this *is* the right type of girl. A girl in society is too much fettered & cramped—another sort of girl is always bringing you down suddenly to the most base material standpoint—but here you have the refinement of the mondaine with the independence of the cocotte—& conjoined the special, enchanting quality of the grisette. It is quite new to me too, to meet with a girl who takes one's love-making shyly—with whom it's not merely an exchange of persiflage. For in spite of her audacity in public, when one has her to oneself, Mddle Lena is really shy—blushful—full of charming reticences. She must be extremely young & presumably innocent. You will gather from this that your unworthy collaborateur is pretty far gone. Oh I don't deny it, I'm even glad of it: c'est le printemps. Write to me soon & fix a day & don't deny yourself the satisfaction of writing me down an ass. Dear old ass—so are we all asses—all—though I admit my asinine quality is now colossal. To think that —Great Scott! truly this is drôle. Oh, breathe it not in Gath.

yrs merrily   ERNEST DOWSON

2 AM. Bon soir. Have just finished my poulet. Vive la jeunesse: it has actually lasted 3 weeks. Unprecedented!

Those eyes the greenest of things blue
The bluest of things grey"—[7]
Did you note them? How I *loathe* swarthy black eyed women. Ah that horrible Tuesday. But *She* is all that is most fair & blonde Excuse me. I am sleepy & incoherent but really now—black women are the devil.

---

7. Swinburne, *Félise*, in *Poems and Ballads*, 1866.

25. *To Arthur Moore*
25 March 1889

Bridge Dock

Cher Confrère.

I hope my Sunday edition hasn't driven you to a self inflicted grave. I have written Chap viii & if (as is highly probable) I have leisure to copy it to-day) you will please receive it this evening at 19. PPV. It is on the whole, I think, not quite so bad as some of my chapters—but one can never tell of one's comps. & ∴ I shall believe you if you prove me wrong & tell me it is the worst.

For the rest I think I can see the remaining *two* chaps. pretty well & I give you my notes for what they are worth.

Somehow or other you must kill Lud & It. in the next chapter, wh. will have to be rather a long one— & will I suppose plunge or at all events *glide* after very small preface to the wedding morning—or ? the day before the wedding. Details I leave to you. I will then take up the thread with Chap X & last. The Princess alas! must be sacrificed. Lud: (according to my view) after his death leaves a written explanatory confession to Dr. Mugford—which of course Doctor Mugford treats with bland scepticism & burns. The confession is put before the reader however—during Mugford's dubitations whether Daisy is to be told: of course Daisy is *not* told & never knows—& does not I think lose her reason. Of course I will finish up with some characteristic paragraphlet concerning Adrien. . . . How does this strike you? feasible? impossible? It is the best dénouement I can suggest but I am, I need not say, open to emendations. I am deeply thankful that in the natural sequence of things Chap ix falls to you. You have my sincere sympathy in your arduous task but I am *absolutely* barren of *any* ideas as to ways & means of that chapter. Only *remember* the little phial—also Sonia—also Aunt Charlotte: one or more of these may help you.

But ἅλις σπουδῆς.[1] I am smoking "Cubeb" cigarettes & have a profound catarrh. I am not going down to Brighthelmstone till Sat. so any day before that shall be delighted to go round with you. I am happier in my mind, as my health appears once more to have escaped. But Gt. Scott! what a frightful risk—in retrospect! Write—write

Yrs ever   LUDWIG VON SOBOIEVSKI

P.S. Excuse a certain suggestion of Family Herald in my new chapter. Love-making is certainly not my speciality. I believe by the bye—that in the bond you took all that on your shoulders. N'importe—revise—

---

1. Enough about serious things.

where you can. You don't revise my chaps. half enough. I will send vol ii when I have done a little in that way. L VON S

P.S. Couldn't get it off yestday—so send it herewith. If you can dine with me to-night somewhere drop me a wire to Bridge Dock before 5.

26. *To Arthur Moore*
[*30 March 1889*]

c/o J. R. Dowson Esq, St Aubyns, West Brighton

Mon cher.

I just send you a line to explain that I came here yesterday morning after all & so could not send you word of my port of embarkation. I have absolutely no ideas as Chap ix—& very few as to Chap x. I feel jubilant though to think how skilfully we have guided the ship-let into port: & am already meditating on the new novel of more sustained interest.

Brighton is not so full as usual, I suppose owing to the boat-race it will no doubt fill up later on in the day. I don't think we are going to win myself.[1] Were you at the sports—enthusiastic worthy patriot that you are?[2] I perceive from the morning journals that we were not in it there—as usual. "The service is going to the Devil"—

Praise the gods that in their great & unspeakable goodness they have brought "Pepa" over to the Royalty.[3] We must go next week: there is no piece I have more wanted to see. I read a few isolated scenes of it that appeared in "Gil Blas". You ask me about the "Episode". Floret floreatque. The Patron has condoned the effrontery of Sunday. At least so I gather from a meagre note I received in the middle of the week. When my *charmeuse* will get out again however—lies very much on the knees of the gods—& I am strenuously forbidden the "Pot au Feu".

The last *epistlette* however—I suppose it was the result of my Sunday exertions—for the first time dispensed with the formal Mr. I shall return on Monday & shall hope to see you as soon after as possible. "My Lady April"—is out[4] & I have pocketed the guinea. No more now.

Yrs ozonely   ERNEST DOWSON

1. He was right; Cambridge won by 2¾ lengths.
2. They took place at Queen's Club the previous day, the 29th.
3. Coquelin Cadet, Mlle Reichenberg and others from the Comédie Française joined the French Repertory Company at the Royalty Theatre for the last three weeks of their long season. These gala performances opened on 1 April with *Pépa*, a comedy by Meilhac and Ganderax.
4. *Temple Bar*, April number.

27. *To Charles Sayle*
    [*1 April 1889*]

Woodford

My dear Sayle.
    Such a charming letter as yours ought to have been answered before
this: many, very many thanks for it. I am free from the Law, to begin
with myself—and am occupied in Dry Docking!!—it is hardly the lot
I should have chosen had choice been vouchsafed me. But I—or I
should say, my father—has suddenly become burdened with an ancestral Dock in Limehouse owing to the collapse of a Company to which
it had been let and for the present, to prevent absolute ruin are carrying
it on, until the white elephant can be re-let or, which we should prefer,
sold. We know nothing at all about it, but have implicit belief in our
Foreman and so far jog along fairly well. On the whole it is less disagreeable than the law would be an' I took the latter seriously, and it gives
me ample leisure. I exist, you perceive, and much more than that I
have never done. *Du reste* I do not suppose "la joie de vivre" will be
revealed to me any more at Limehouse than in the Temple. Enough of
a disagreeable subject! So you are a Catholic! I envy you hugely:
Catholicism is about the only beautiful "ism" left nowadays and I feel
many degrees nearer you than when you dubbed yourself Anglican:
none the less, mine own habit of mind becomes more stable daily.
Thank you for writing to me,—honestly; thank you: write to me when
you can and dont quite give me up though I am very indefensible.
    Tell me the title of your book, of course I will get it.[1] But a farewell
—I wont and can't believe it! I should like much to come and see you
and will still hope that it may become possible. But a sort of apathy
has come over me of late and anything involving an effort, no matter
how great a pleasure it promises, has become impossible to me.
    Society, in the technical sense, I was abandoning even in your Gray's
Inn days: now I have quite retired from it. And of late, as I have
hinted, it has become difficult to me even to see my friends. I suppose
in time my faculty of correspondence will be affected and I shall drop
away altogether from everybody. My novel wants and has wanted this
long time a chapter to completion. I hope to finish it shortly but do not
expect and to tell you the truth have ceased very much to care that it
finds a publisher. If it goes anywhere it shall go to Bentley. I have a
Sonnet in this month's "Temple Bar": that is all and that is nothing
for I have never done any more than play with verse.
    Are you still busied with Wicliff and his writings?[2] The "Complainte"

1. *Erotidia*, published by G. E. Over, Rugby.
2. Sayle had produced two works in 1887: *Johannis Wyclif de Officio Regis*,
    edited in collaboration with A. W. Pollard, and *Wyclif*, an historical
    drama.

is not by me, nor is the spirit of it greatly revealed to me. Do you like it? I think there are fine pages in it, here and there. Bourget sent its author "Jean Thorel" a most pretty letter, in return for a copy. I hope, if you can say any good of it, you will do the same. I envy you your library[3] and your pure country. One should be able to isolate oneself well in a library, and when all is said and done, that is the great thing, to isolate oneself, from men & women—chiefly from women but also perhaps from men. But beyond everything I envy you your Catholicism. I have seen, I think, no one of our mutual cognizance save Plarr, and him recently only once. You know doubtless "Seafaring"[4] is afloat again?

I heard also not very long ago from Arthur Fallows—from Germany. I still scribble occasionally—pour passer le temps, and devote most of my leisure to the French Renaissance—chiefly to the Pleiad.

But one is not with impunity of this damned, fastidious, fascinating century. And sooner or later to everything in life or art, the cursed critical devil pops up with his eternal "Cui bono?"—And I, for one, can not answer him. But I must really wind off this unconscionable scrawl. Forgive my prolixity and rate me when you write for a morbid fool, scarcely sane.

None the less

Yrs ever   ERNEST DOWSON

3. The library of St. John's College, Cambridge.
4. A periodical published 1888–1892 to which Plarr contributed a number of poems.

28. *To Arthur Moore*

Monday night [*1–2 April 1889*]

Woodford

Mon chéri.

Thanks for yours recvd this morning. I am once more as you see, near to the "hub of all things"—& was greatly cheered on my journey by your note as well as by an emotional one from Charles Sayle which I found awaiting me. It seems that Catholicism "pleases him mightily" as my friend Pepys would say. Lucky man! If I could see things—or hoodwink myself—? as he does I would take a first class single for La Trappe to-morrow. He has just published another Vol: I am anxiously awaiting chap ix: but with very mixed feelings—as I tremble at the thought of the task which Chap x will entail. With all my heart I agree with you that a passionate finale would be disgusting.

But before I set a word on paper I must see you at leisure & discuss with you. Make it Wed: if possible: we *must* see "Pépa". Were you at Lonnen's benefit this *après*:?[1] I didn't arrive till about 5.

Ah, how I look forward to our next collaboration. Have you any ideas? I haven't seen the new edition of the Master[2]—unless it is like the 2/ ed: of "Princess Casamassima"—which is of some eld.

It is excellent of you to endure my minute episodiography. I myself somehow take rather the third person's point of view, most frequently. After all—only a corroboration of my theory that one consists of manifold selves which can be generally separated. Women however are simplex creatures—therefore (this is not a paradox)—more complicated. With weaker animal passions & weaker intellectual capacities, it is impossible to them to draw a hard line between the senses & the spirit. They are "naturalist"—par excellence: & just as they are, *for the most part*, incapable of the defensible sensuality, wh. is utterly without a ray of sentiment—so their *sentiment* is always a little bit fleshly. This is a pity—but one must take them as they are—or not at all I suppose —Whitely not providing[3] the ideal woman or girl,—I think you are wise however if you refrain—although I find the attraction pleasant enough when one doesn't analyze it or look forward. Nine tenths of one's time however the cursed critical devil pops up with his eternal "Cui bono?"—And one can only lay him—not answer him. (This letter is taking the proportions of the Sunday ed: which the Brighton ozone —or rather the coziness of my cousin's club delayed—) I didn't *mean*, when I began, to send you an essay on the affections—so pardon my ill-tamed pen. I seem to have the spleen to-night, though I don't quite know why I should—having no special grievance that I can precisely fix. Try & arrange for Wed: a dinner with you (? Gall)—will do more than anything else to cheer me: & I have hopes of "Pepa". Hercle! though, how I detest this cursed London: it gives me a sort of mental asthma whenever I return to it after an absence—however short. No it is not London—it is Great Britain. It was a very cynical star which dropped me in these islands. Adios: forgive my drivelling in this way & write soon.

Yrs ever   ERNEST DOWSON

1. A gala matinée given at the Gaiety on 1 April.
2. Probably the two-shilling 'yellowback' reprint of *Washington Square* issued in March 1889.
3. Messrs. William Whiteley of Bayswater, London's first department store, advertised as 'the universal provider'.

LATEST EDITION

Tuesday Morning

Bridge Dock

Just an addendum to tell you the latest development, which, after all, has greatly cheered me. It is a wire (opened of course by the foreman) to this effect, recvd: on my arrival here this morning. "Can you manage Percy Street seven tonight. Lena."

That I imagine implies a theatros: you can guess my response. My spleen is temporarily dissolved: nevertheless I still send you the letter of last night. Néanmoins I would I were more equable.

always yrs ED.

P.S. Grieved to hear of your health. I am taking care of myself: follow my example: no spirits—half a pint of beer & a little burgundy. I have a most rampant catarrh: & have almost coughed away my lungs. These are parlous times.

29. *To Arthur Moore*
Friday [*5 April 1889*]

Bridge Dock

Dear Moore.

Just a line to tell you that I have begun Chap x on somewhat diff. lines to those originally proposed. i.e. I only give selections from the Confession: & bring out the more striking incidents in a conversation between Adrien & Mugford before they commit the MSS to the flames. Will this do?

To-morrow? "Pepa". May I leave it open until 2.0 o'clock to-morrow. You will find me at that hour at the corner of Percy St. where it comes into the Tottenham Court Rd: and then I shall be able to decide. The episode has taken complicated form: whence this vagueness. Some last straw the nature of which I have not yet discovered provoked Mdlle Lena into a summary departure "I couldn't stand it any more" she writes—(I haven't seen her since the rupture). In the meantime she is going to share lodgings with the other waitress, the tall, gaunt woman whom you may remember & wait there until *something turns up.* That seems to me the beginning of the end & I am more sorry than you will believe. I implore her to go back to her people but unsuccessfully. There is really nothing that I can do: I haven't time or inclination to set up as a sheep dog, & she is such an absolute child that there can be only one *dénouement.* But I admit I am savagely annoyed about it.

If 2.0 PM. Percy Street will be too late for you—go straight to the Royalty Pit. The chances are that I join you there about 3.0. You shall have Lud: on Monday: & perhaps Tuesday or Wednesday we might meet here & revise. There will be no interruptions—& we will get as drunk as lords. Adios　　　　　　　　　　　　　　　　　　　E.D.

P.S. I hope you have lost your bruises & feel no ill effects.[1]
　　　Bah! Do you see *any* cheering possibilities? If so—

1. Moore had had an accident in a hansom cab.

30. *To Arthur Moore*
　　[*6–7 April 1889*]

Woodford

Cher Ami.

I hope, mon vieux, that the office engagement was bona-fide this afternoon? Or at least that no consideration for me prevented you joining us? You know I consider the number three essentially the enjoyable number, when you & I are two & a Mdlle Lena the third. And I had contemplated inducing you to be of us to-day, supposing she turned up which I hardly anticipated. I particularly wanted it in fact —desiring more & ever at this critical juncture your valuable & unbiassed opinion. Anyhow I am awfully glad you saw her & hope you were pleased. After we left you we passed some hours together in the Zoo, tea'ed together modestly at an A.B.C & finally parted at Liv'pool St at 8.15. You were right by the bye as to age. She will not be seventeen until the 30th May next! I am a little more easy in my mind than when I wrote last—but still uncomfortable. But I must get you to study her yourself. She is quite presentable, n'est ce pas? I assume as much, in that we were accosted in the Reptile House by an old lady of friendly demeanour who required information as to an animal—and I suppose that would have hardly have been the case unless we had appeared conventionally allied. But what the deuce will be the issue of it, is the question which unceasingly poses me? I am in the condition of the perplexed lover in "Daisy Miller".[1] Is she amazingly innocent or impudence personified? There is however a certain contagion in the delight which she takes in her liberty, and at times I am inclined to believe that she is, as she declares, quite able to take care of herself.

1. Henry James's first great success, published in 1878 in the United States, in 1879 in England.

But you must be with us for a longer period soon & give me your theories. We shall do a theatre on Tuesday night. Couldn't you work it somehow also? It will probably be the Court or else the 'Vaudeville'. I hope also that you were not annoyed that I didn't come to "Pépa". I really had so little hope that she would turn up after the sermons I have preached her in the week that I thought I could safely undertake to go with you. However I shall await your report—if you went—& if it is favourable perhaps we can do it next week. I am going to send her a James—the "Madonna of the Future"[2] vol. to-morrow. *Will* she appreciate it? ? ? . . . ... Do you think she gains or loses in attraction clothed & removed from the "Pot au Feu" environment? I apologize for boring you in this primitive way, *ma chè vuole*? I ought to write re Ludovicus which is almost complete: but I can't at the present moment. The episode still flourishes—and yesterday I told myself that it was done! It is not philosophical—nevertheless I can not help being glad. This is the Sunday edition, though I have not yet been to bed—(it is the fault of our Dorothy with whom I will be as gentle as I can)— therefore it is lawful for me to be discursive & violate a second sheet. To morrow I spend in bed. Lena is going to pass it with her people, who, as you probably gathered, are still in the dark as to her departure. She seems to devote most of her leisure to looking at the shops & walking about. I suppose it is just possible that she do not join the majority. It is a pity that I have so vivid an imagination & so very little faith. I am surprised that I should care so much. I think it is chiefly because she is such an absolute child. Besides there are times when she becomes very soft & charming indeed. And in spite of obvious faults, she is on the whole pleasant to look at.

The most objectionable & laughable result of this curious *liaison*— is the utter havoc it plays with my digestion. Absolutely except on the evening of your hansom accident I haven't dined since I was at Brighton! Entirely owing to interviews, or abortive interviews, or theatre going with Mdlle Lena! And my people are simply rampant—and suspecting the worst. It is immensely droll if you come to think of it & how entirely Arcadian it is. 'Tis a censorious world—*sans* charity. Write & answer any of these inconsequences that you can. You will probably gather how desirous I am of your opinion—also not a little of your advice. I will send you the Chapter completed no doubt on Monday. re Tuesday I will communicate with you. Wednesday, unless the episode calls me away—perhaps you would devote to revision at Bridge Dock? I hope we may get this opus off & have another on the stocks into which I can throw myself when or I will say "if"—for the omen's sake—the catastrophe comes. With regret I write myself—a damned fool—though

always yrs   E D

Sunday proper. I haven't somehow managed to get this off so may as well scribble down to the bottom. I have had an intensely lazy day;

2. Published in 1879.

have smoked many pipes, laid on sofas, written to my Deliciae, analyzed myself copiously, and other people including yourself, not less, and— I regret to say, *meditated* only—on Ludovicus. You *shall* have it however by Tuesday morning. Forgive me, your most unworthy collaborator. I am in such a puzzle. I wish to goodness I could take the humourous view of it, which must be so distressingly obvious to the impartial spectator—personified in you. Here I am, having hated nothing so much in all my time as responsibility—and look at it how I may, I am becoming more & more impelled to believe that I *am* responsible in this matter. I hope you credit the purity of my intentions because I am quite sure nobody else would. And the worst of it is that I have lost my faith in the inherent viciousness of the feminine nature. And I ask myself whether after all what I am doing may not be almost as unaesthetic as a vulgar seduction? Horrid thought: even if she doesn't come to grief, I must give her her first disillusionment. Absolutely I don't know whether the episode hasn't been the most essentially immoral thing I have ever done—& worse still the most vulgar. Write to me, mon cher, you are the only person whose criticism one way or the other would affect me.

Yrs　　　ED.

Excuse the incorrigible length. The gist of the letter lies in the postscript as usual.

31. *To Arthur Moore*
　　　Tuesday [*9 April 1889*]

Bridge Dock

Dear Moore.

"To-morrow & to-morrow & to-morrow etc" I really am profoundly sorry: but the Chapter *will not* be finished, and parts of it I re-write and re-write. I will try & let you have it to-morrow though, & we must revise here, I think at the end of the week.

I was decoyed into the social act yesterday evening or it would have been doubtless done. To-night I have to meet Lena: but I am working on it at the Dock this morning & expect a slack day. Did I ever mention to you a man named Morris? I expect I did, as my chief pal of the Bartholomeans & by far the most excellent. I said adieu to him a week or 10 days ago—when he was off to Ely—and last night receive a nasty jar by coming suddenly in the Echo on a report of the inquest on him— drowned canoeing in the Ouse.[1]

1. C. E. M. Morris was drowned canoeing late at night near Cambridge. The inquest was held at Littleport on 6 April.

I don't pretend to be hugely cut up, but it has somewhat depressed me. However—we have had glorious nights together in our time.

Adios: write soon & if possible forgive my slackness—and name your own night for these wilds.

Tout à toi   ED

P.T.O

2 P.M. Your epistle has just arrived & has slightly cheered me. Bank Holiday although of course we *must* meet thereon, is too remote.[2] Will Friday or Saturday do for you either here or elsewhere. Or could you come down to Woodford from Satdy next to Monday. There will be less whiskey than at Stepney but we shall possibly do more work. And you needn't fear Sunday! I believe my mater occasionally goes to church but she doesn't proselytize. And family prayers, nine o'clock breakfasts & such abominations are quite unknown. Anyhow however we will meet, n'est ce pas, on Saturday aft'noon, & arrange. I told you, I believe, that I am to meet Lena to-night. I have not however received confirmation of the rendezvous and if she doesn't turn up I go to "*Pépa*". Perusing your letter again I see that on the whole you corroborate my feeling. Be it so. I can do no more than I have done. I can't understand about the supplies. I gather she is *staying* with the gaunt woman. N'importe Τὸ μέλλον ἥξει.[3] When one is constitutionally slack and a confirmed fatalist these things don't annoy one very long. However a conjunction of causes—the failure of the experiment, the d——d weather, the social ordeal last night, the difficulties of chap x—and Morris's death have made me feel, what the English people in Hy James call "blue". I have also a "graveyard cough" tho' my catarrh has yielded to Cubeb. It must be d——d unpleasant to be drowned. I hope all this drivel will not reduce you to the same state of languid depression in which I pen it. * * * * * * * If anything could possibly have made me more dejected than before!! Those stars have been filled by an interval of some three quarters of an hour in which our worthy foreman has been declaiming to me on the errors of Home Rule & the superiority of the present administration to all others. Damn all administrations. "A plague on both your houses"—is my most hearty sentiment. Write "at your earliest convenience."

ED.

4.30. The familiar wire "Percy Street 7 to-night. Lena" has just arrived. So I suppose *Pépa* must be deferred.

---

2. Easter Monday was 22 April.
3. 'What is to come will come', an allusion to Xenophon, *Anabasis* VI. i. 21.

32. *Postcard to Arthur Moore*
   Friday [*Postmark 12 April 1889*]

                                        Bridge Dock

Yours to hand, Shall expect you here to-night as soon as you can get
away & will have chap x for you. Bring the other vol. if possible. I am
afraid Limehouse won't produce a dinner but if you can stand it
"possibly my old Sonia's larder may rise"[1]—not "to the occasion" but
to a scratch tea à la Grove St.[2]
   Turn up to Stepney Station from Fench. St: & ask for Bridge Dock.
Narrow St. I shall wait here for you.

                              Yrs   ED.

1. An allusion to *Dr. Ludovicus.*
2. Where Dowson lodged in his second year at Oxford.

33. *To Arthur Moore*
   14 April 1889

              ⅅ   Woodford

   The only original Sunday edition. None other is genuine.

Cher Moore. Excuse pencil: am in more than my usual Sunday slackness, quite incapable of writing any Ludovicus or indeed of anything
at all which cannot be worked in an easy chair halfway up the chimney.
Tea will arrive shortly however & then invigorated & braced by the
admirable fluid I will try & describe the manipulations in the labratory.
So far they have not been revealed to me.
   Yesterday, mon vieux, was the 6th. hebdomiversary of the episodion!
It was a beastly day—nevertheless we boated to Greenwich & pro-
menaded in the exceedingly desolate park. You, I presume, are in
Reading. I am told you were seen in Regent Street about or rather
shortly before 2.0. Is that so? Shall I tell you our programme: at least
I will give you a list of the trains we travelled in. Ridebis et licet rideas!
(Plin. Ep.)[1]

              Lewisham to Cannon St.   20 min.
              Cannon St (M.R.) to Charing X 15 ,,   ,,

                    *   *   *

1. Pliny, *Letters* I. 6. 'You will laugh, and you may well do so.'

Charing X to Bishopsgate	20 min.
Liverpool St to Stratford.	15 min.
Stratford to Liverpool St	15 min
Bishopsgate to Aldersgate St.	10 min

Society must be in a parlous state when one can only secure privacy for one's Platonics in the Underground Railway. The utterly purposeless journey to Stratford & back was a sublimely facetious proceeding.—On the whole however I enjoyed myself assez bien. We spent 8 hours together from 2–10 not unpleasantly & the Episodion still flourishes most healthily. We are contemplating a new frock for the summer. It is to be of white, made plainly & without further ornamentation than a sash from Liberty's round our adorable waist: the colour & shade thereof left to me. Shall we say amber—or maize—or a shade of blue? If we shall not compromise you too much, we shall hope to walk with you in this toilette in the Park, at some future day. Personally my only objection to meeting any—almost any—of my relations is the fear that they wouldn't be scandalized enough. They wouldn't at all appreciate the position. I will give them plenty of chances however, as we contemplate another journey to Buckhurst Hill to-morrow: it would be supremely funny if the governor got into our carriage. Ye gods how sleepy I am. I have fallen asleep about six times in the course of these absolute bagatelles. Lena goes back to her people to-day (only for the day of course): they are still in the dark, and to remain so. I have given up all attempts at conjectures as to results. I shall hope to see you some evening next week after you have recvd. Chap x but shall probably have neither oof nor leisure for a theatre. "Pépa" will come again & Mdlle Reichenberg presumably—mais la jeunesse n'a qu'un temps. Have you shown vol I to your Mater yet? I feel very nervous & wish much that there was no distinction of hands. Write & report

Yrs   ERNEST DOWSON

34. *To Arthur Moore*
   [*16 April 1889*]

Bridge Dock

Cher Ami.
   Your letter to hand. Copying is as you remark a notable trial; in fact, a "demnition horrid grind".[1] The 2nd. vol. shall be forwarded to

---

1. *Nicholas Nickleby*, Chapter 64.

you as soon as I have completed copy of Chap vi, which will be done in the course of to-day. We must get it before (?) F. V. White & Co next week.

Your remarks re Chap x are appreciated, but my patience failed me and I trust to you to make it sufficiently explicit. For the love of all the Gods send it not back before it is licked into shape.

Re Easter

I feel rather slack and have refused an invite to eat the Pascal lamb at Reigate:[2] neither can I quite bring myself to face the enthusiastic Sayle.[3] Do you feel inclined for two or three days tramp—say into Surrey? Otherwise—i.e. unless I can face the *campagne* with the support of your society, I shall remain in London. Write and tell me your plans. I think we ought to work one meeting at least during these holidays. I am glad the maternal criticism was on the whole satisfactory. What about Satdy night? If you are in town could we not meet? I don't feel equal to a theatre at this season. Everywhere will be so deucedly crammed. However a *Gall* might be managed.

This copying is exhausting *à mourir*. I wish Sarah[4] would come to England—as the Despard.[5]

O Hercules! to think of Italy at this season! When shall we be there when, when? . Firenze? . . Baveno . . Cadenabbia . and Switzerland . . Oh this cursed island.

Yrs dismally   ERNEST DOWSON

P.S. We MUST make some oof by our fluent pens. If Ludovicus gives us a ten pound note apiece . . . this collaborator for one is in Champagne—at Auxerre within a week. Adios. I can bear up in the winter, I can bear up in the summer—more or less—but at Easter I think of the lakes—I think of the opening of the passes—of the banquette in the diligence & I weep.

---

2. Where his cousins, the Secretans, lived.
3. Sayle had invited him to Cambridge.
4. Sarah Bernhardt usually gave a short summer season in London, but she did not come in 1889.
5. Léna Despard in *Léna*, an adaptation by Pierre Berton of F. C. Philips's novel *As in a Looking Glass.*

35. *To Arthur Moore*
Tuesday 23 April 1889

Bridge Dock

Dear Moore.
I am sorry I have not yet copied out my portion. But I have played the part of the 5 Virgins of historic folly. Wh: being interpreted means to say that I ran out of Chncy fcp on Sunday and so as far as th' Opus was concerned yesterday was non-existent. To-day I have laid in a new stock. Thanks for your letter. I am sorry we missed one another Satdy. I was at the National Gallery: also at Gatti's:[1] we should have met. Let us pour a libation to the gods some time to-morrow evening for that at length this tyranny of Sir J. Lubbock's is overpast.[2] I shall await a note or wire from you to that effect. If we dine however mon cher, it must be most modestly. I am sorry you have emended Chap X so scantily. However I will insert your emendations and do my best. By the by there was *no knife used*: it was poisonous gas. This is important. I hope it does not come to you too late. I thought of wiring but refrained as I knew not where you were. I hope to have finished my copying to-morrow. I shall bring you the result to get "green sewed" as I have not the wherewithal.
With regard to publishers I am of opinion that we had better try "Geo. Routledge & Sons", Broadway, Ludgate Hill. I have just read a curious "s. shocker" published by them (one of the "Ludgate Novels") by one Edgar Saltus[3] an American,—entituled "Eden". It is interesting though grotesque: you must read it. It chiefly edifies me in that it strikes me as a *flamboyant* example of the "p for the r.w."[4] ~~school~~ carried to a ridiculous excess. "Eden listened as were she assisting at the soliloquy of an engastritruth".—"If you haven't had the forethought to cuirass yourself with indifference, truth can cause a hydrophobia for wh. the only Pasteur is time." . . "In the back ground the moon glinted in derision, and directly overhead was a splatter of callous stars" . . . I select at random. And mind you it is not by any means intended as burlesque: it's serious. Nevertheless Routledge is, I think, as good a man as anyone to begin on. We must meet however *to-morrow* evening as a cousin of mine, confound him, a midshipmite elect comes to us from Thursday to Monday, before joining his ship and I must devote myself to him. If it would the better meet you for Wednesday night to tea with me here, let me know: wire or write to that effect. Otherwise

1. A restaurant in Queen Adelaide Street, near Charing Cross.
2. Sir John Lubbock, M.P., had been responsible for the Bank Holidays Act in 1871. Dowson regularly refers to the incidence of a bank holiday by some allusion to Lubbock.
3. Edgar Everton Saltus (1855–1921) wrote studies of Balzac and Schopenhauer, historical chronicles and 'spicy novels of murder and adultery'.
4. Passion for the right word.

say—outside the Holborn 6.15. I am looking for mottos also for a title. How does—"The Deathly Dilemma of Dr Ludovicus". suit you or "The Crime and Dilemma of Dr L.". When the last word of your portion is copied begin, I beg, to excogitate the *opus* to succeed. Enough for the present.

Yrs ever   ERNEST DOWSON

36. *To Arthur Moore*
26 April 1889

Bridge Dock

Arturo carissimo.

Th' òpus neatly ordered & complete is done up ready to go to Routledge, the letter is written. By this afternoon they will have arrived. And now to watch & pray! . . . . . Oh!

I am going down to Cambridge to morrow till Monday to stay with Sayle. At least that was my intention but as Swanton arrives for three days this afternoon & I meet him at the Empire to-night—it is possible I may be seduced into staying up & put off the Cambridgeshire till next week. No more Brompton oratories though!

By the by—a most amusing incident which may lead to a strike of "ile". Plarr has been offered—but stay. I enclose his letter & you can read the story for yourself. Here followeth the enclosure.

Mr Herbert Williams has given me an appointment to-day at 5 in order to "talk things over". If I can work it without too much loss of time to the Dock I shall take the unremunerative subeditorship of his most comprehensive journal for as long as he will have me.[1]

The experience in journalism won't be a bad thing & it will be an immense jest. But perhaps I count *sans* my host. If you get this epistle before leaving— ~~you might meet me say outside the Hol~~ but no—I will call on you if possible before 6 and we may converse a moment before I run off to meet Swanton. Watch & pray and write

adios   THY COLLABORATOR

1. This refers to the sub-editorship of a modest, indeed failing, weekly, *The Critic*; although it had not long to live, it was proud of its title, 'the oldest established weekly newspaper in the world' (it dated from 1719). The offer was made to Victor Plarr, who declined it and passed the suggestion to Dowson, who accepted. Herbert Williams was the proprietor and editor.

37. *To Arthur Moore*
    Monday [*29 April 1889*]

Bridge Dock

Chéri.

A lengthy letter to compensate for the omission of yestday: also to console me for my return here. I have just come back from Cambridge & found your letter. Yes—"Ludovicus" is at Routledges. My pápa took it himself with his own right hand & left it. One Mr Moon,—he was referred to—the reader of Routledges. Mr Moon however was out of town but would be back to-day. The MSS is at his office awaiting his pleasure. ἅλις σπουδῆς. I went to Cambridge with Plarr on Satdy morning &—yes, it was pleasant though we all of us found the rival Alma M. sadly wanting. Would you had been with us! We talked much —& of most things in heaven & earth—in the old Oxford fashion and the Cantabs, who came in at intervals were silent & comprehended us not. Our final impression was that they are not subtle, that there is an indefinable something which they can not assimilate—that they are horridly earnest—sane & detestable & that above all the Renaissance has not yet reached them. Sayle adds the damning word that in the library of Johns there is no copy of Johannes Secundus. I can't go so far as that: because until Sayle introduced me to him I (and Plarr was with me) had not heard of Johannes Secundus. Henceforth he becomes an article of our faith and I intend to devote all my spare time to searching the London bookstalls for a copy of him. How shall I describe him? He is Alfred de Musset in Latin—no: he is Catullus and more than Catullus rendered into Renaissance Latin. Simply he is divine: look for him on the bookstalls & buy him if you see him.

Ah, but this Saturday to Monday has been very estimable: it was with grief & pain that I tore myself away. The thought that you were in London was the one thought that consoled me. When am I to see you? When are we to see "The Profligate"?[1] Soon—soon!

I saw Herbert Williams on Friday. He was very bad: not quite so bad though as Plarr's caricature. He was a greater snob but not quite such a cad. He wanted me to give him "all of myself"—in other words to spend the day in Took's Court. I declined. I have written from Cambridge offering my services after 5. Thus the matter stands. I am not particularly keen though on his accepting my offer as Sayle has almost converted me to his faith that journalism is the second death. His new book is charming. The Amaryllis poem, which probably you know, is in it. Will he ever do it again? Does one do these things twice? . . . . . .

Oh when am I to see you again! Write to me & that soon. The

---

1. By Arthur Pinero; opened at the Garrick on 24 April, with John Hare, Forbes Robertson and Lewis Waller in the cast.

Episode, alas, alas, perishes for lack of sustenance. It is not yet dead but it dies—and it shall be the last. The theory of episodes in the abstract we discussed exhaustively last night. Plarr posed as the absolute sentimentalist! "l'amour" he maintained was the supreme $\tau\epsilon\lambda o s$[2]—Sayle was neutral but inclined that way—, I at the risk of appearing a humbug (to Plarr at least)—maintained that sentiment was the very devil & l'amour an impossibility.

Is it not so? But what a pity! . . . .

I will confess therefore once for all that the experiment with me as with our friend Ludwig has signally failed. I was perfectly right when I deprecated the critical spirit. It makes life tolerable—it gives one immense compensations of an intellectual sensuous character—but the price one pays for them is the withering away of one's emotional capabilities. Fiat! henceforth the episode will cease to all practical extent. It has become a corvée & I will break it off as quickly as I can without disillusioning the girl too much. I fear that disillusioned a little, she must be! N'importe—let us talk of pleasanter things. Like Ludwig's cigars—it—(the Episode) was good, while it lasted: let it be the last. I will now return to "Madame de Viole".—until you are ready to collaborate with me once more.

I want you by the by to meet Plarr. Could you manage Friday here, Evening. I think he would be able to come that evening. Write soon.

always yrs   ERNEST DOWSON
P.T.O.

PS. After all, I doubt if it is the girl's fault: not often! I think it is very largely our own—& society's. I very rarely find myself in agreement with V.P. but I entirely see the force of his theory that in any decent future life there should be a special, deepest circle of Hades reserved for the British Matron & her embryo the British young lady. It is they after all, far more than Sappho, who are responsible for our scepticism in the matter of woman.

Forgive this drivel & its predecessors. Henceforth I will try & write less trivially. But alas for the Episode—alas!   ED

I wish you joy of your letter to Thomas: I love the man still: but I can write no more. Tell him so: nevertheless commend me to him & entice him here if you can. By the by—I walked all the way home on Friday night, & arrove at 4.15 AM. It rained the whole time!

2. Purpose or end.

38. *To Arthur Moore*
2 May 1889

Bridge Dock

Chéri.

I owe you a letter, I believe. Anyhow I will write one & first thank you for the "Stolen Hand".[1] It is an admirable idea—my criticisms in detail I will reserve until I see you—(tis a consummation devoutly to be wished)—& only say here that I think it would be better if there were more of it. What did the "Argosy" suggest? You will have got Routledges acknowledgement by this time. I apologize for not having sent it you before: but the thing 'scaped my memory. I feel hopeful: th' opus only needs reading, & will, I gather now, at least be read. I don't know when we can meet: Satdy is my only suggestion: but even for Gall the oof is not with me. Ah, when only our merits are recognized & rewarded—substantially—*forsan et haec olim meminisse juvabit*.[2] At present, mon vieux, they are very damnable indeed! I—i.e. we—was at the Royal[3] on Tuesday evening for some time & half hoped you would be there. When are we to do the "New Gallery"?[4] Th' Academy can, I think be postponed though *on dit* great things of it.[5] Alas, why is "Albert"[6] so slack? And why doesn't Henry[7] cease pot-boiling and Bourget[8] from idleness?

This is real April weather. In this accursed country the months are always in arrears. As long as March however is accomplished! I—(i.e. we) shall probably be at the Royal again to-morrow night. Can we not hope to see you? I haven't yet gone to the "Profligate".—nor to "Doris"[9]—nor in fact to anything.

1. A story by Moore, possibly an early version of *Second Thoughts* which appeared in the *Yellow Book*, October 1894.
2. Virgil, *Aeneid* I. 203.
3. i.e. the Café Royal.
4. An exhibition of modern painting which opened on 1 May; it included Watts's *Fata Morgana* and Sargent's *Ellen Terry as Lady Macbeth*.
5. The Summer Exhibition opened on 2 May.
6. 'Albert', who is referred to again in Letter 144, is most probably Arthur Moore's uncle, Albert Moore, who after a brilliantly successful start as a painter of, *inter alia*, scenes of Roman life executed with great verisimilitude, went to pieces and repeated himself *ad nauseam*. He became an impossible figure and was never elected to the Royal Academy, as one would have expected from his early work.
7. Since *The Princess Casamassima* (1886) James had published three collections of stories and one volume of essays, but no novel.
8. Bourget was silent between *Mensonges* (1887) and *Le Disciple* (1889); in between he began a novel called *Cosmopolis*, but abandoned it when he found that in subject it clashed with his friend Maupassant's *Fort Comme la Mort*.
9. A comic opera by B. C. Stephenson and Alfred Cellier, produced at the

? Motto for Ludovicus. "My life is not life". Calderon.
"Woman thou hast subdued me". Calderon or "Let it be—pass on—
                    No good can come of it—it is not well
                    To meet it—it is an enchanted phantom—
                    A lifeless idol—" Goethe
That is all I can suggest at present. For the novel to be I have no idea
at present but doubtless the idea will leap into being suddenly when it
is least expected.—A note from Plarr has just come announcing his
approaching arrival to "5 oclocque" and enclosing this translation of
"Epitaphium Citharistriae"—
                    "Oh, for it would be a pity
                    To o'er praise her or to flout her,
Chaste is it not?   She was wild & sweet & witty—
                    Let's not say dull things about her."[10]
May I ask you, an' you pass some of the more *solid* old bookshops (not
Holywell St[11] but à la Quaritch[12]) to enquire the price of (if procurable)
Johannes II—his opera. The *Basia* alone I can get for 7/6 but I would
prefer to give a little more & get the whole lot. No more now. Write soon.
                    Yrs.   ERNEST DOWSON

In case we don't meet before can you fix the B.M. Reading Room about
2.0 on Satdy. I want to be there for an hour or so

    Lyric Theatre on 20 April, with Ben Davies and Hayden Coffin in the
    cast.
10. The third and last stanza of the poem by Plarr, collected into *In the
    Dorian Mood*, 1896.
11. Off the Strand, the centre of the less reputable second-hand book trade.
12. The well-known dealer in antiquarian books and manuscripts.

39. *To Arthur Moore*
    Sunday [*5 May 1889*]

                                           Woodford
Chéri.
                 Re Syndicate[1]

    Your scheme meets my considered approval. Nevertheless I have
decided not to come in till Monday week as my capital will not be
sufficiently assured. After that however I am with you. Perhaps in the

1. Moore backed horses and had proposed a syndicate.

meantime I may rise to a little guerilla practice if you will put on a bob or so occasionally as I may send it to you. But of that anon. Success go with you.

Re Tuesday

As I anticipated my Mater is not particularly keen on my dining out while the Governor is away ∴ *mon cher* let me entreat you to accept my amendment—come down & dine here with us, & sleep here. We will go to town together as early as you like the next morning & may possibly during our ante-somnal smoke evolve a brilliant *roman*. If it is absolutely necessary I could send you back the same night at 10: but it would surely be better to stay, especially as your Mámma will have to sit up. I needn't say that my Mamma joins with me in hoping you will be able to turn up & sleep. We shall not dress: come in a blazer if you like.

re Varia

It appears fated that you & I are to go to the "Garrick".[2] We[3] made an attempt last night—a gallant attempt—got wedged in at the Pit entrance until about ten minutes before the doors opened—then alas! we fainted—& I tottered out with the swaying, senseless burden in my arms. Per Baccho—we are heavy I can assure you. I feel strained & weak from the ordeal now. Finally when we had recovered & had partaken of cognac—we insisted on a theatre (against my advice) & so adjourned to the "Court".[4] We got there at 8.30, had a good seat in a thin house, and saw one of the most clever, witty & original comedies I have ever seen on the English stage, without further disaster. I may as well mention, for Tuesday's sake that you came with me to the "Weaker Sex" last night. I hope you enjoyed it. You must really see it (again): Mrs Kendall is at her best & Annie Hughes as you say *une parfaite ingénue*. Is it genuine? Kendall by the by was indisposed & had a substitute.

~~Have just been reading my "Star" etc. If you can work it could you put 2/6 for me on "Millstream" for the Chester Cup.~~
Second thoughts. no: I will wait till the 13th. & stick to the system. Probably you will be on Millstream anyhow?[5]
Write & let me know of Tuesday etc.

Yrs   ED.

2. To *The Profligate*.
3. He went with Lena.
4. Where *The Weaker Sex* was playing.
5. Fatal second thoughts! The Chester Cup, run on 8 May, was won by Millstream at 13 to 2.

40. *Postcard to Arthur Moore*
   Monday [*Postmark 6 May 1889*] 8.30 PM.

Liverpool Street Station

Chéri. You will probably have seen our current number[1] by this time &
have seen also that you were right & I rong in the question of space.
Proofs are deceptive creatures. Tell me (write)—when to see you &
prithee prepare a New Gallery critique as good as t' other. We will go
there together an' you will.   E D

1. Of *The Critic*, No. III, Vol. I (New Series). Arthur Moore wrote critiques
of art exhibitions under the pseudonym 'Arthur Charters'.

41. *To Victor Plarr*
   [*c. 7 May 1889*]

Bridge Dock

Dear Plarr.
   I ought to have answered your delightful letter before but what with
Dry Docking & "The Critic"—I am simply "decayed" with work. I
was sorry you could not come down here on Thursday but hope your
visit is merely postponed. You will be sure of finding me this week—
(save Saturday) any day you care to turn up, before 4. as my parent
is in Scotland & the cares of office confine me here constantly.

   I have not I find despatched this epistle but will endeavour now.
Come to-morrow if you can to lunch, or (preferably) to afternoon tea
at say 3.30—or when you like, next week. I must try & look you up
but feel it is difficult unless I can catch you at "Seafaring" as the
"Critic" claims my evenings & I am—for the present—its special
correspondent for all Music Halls. It is rather a jest, I find, visiting
these familiar places in the character of a pressman. If we survive our
third number—it seems problematical even that it appears—I shall be
greatly amazed. Mais—quoi donc—enfin—craque!—vive la bagatelle!
I can't secure a Johannes II. Have been to several places. Have you
been successful? I must write to Sayle: haven't done so as yet. Have
just finished another *nouvelle*,[1] very short which I want to show you.

1. Probably *The Diary of a Successful Man*, which *Macmillan's Magazine*
accepted in June 1889 and published in the following February.

Adios—for the present. I am celebrating this delicious weather by the finest & largest catarrh which I have had this year! I was immensely pleased with the epigram. One has such a large feminine acquaintance of whom one can say that much—& nothing more—"wild & sweet & witty"—Eheu! respectability is a blighting influence. Once more au revoir—à bientot n'est ce pas?

Tout à vous   ERNEST DOWSON

42. *To Arthur Moore*

[*c. 10 May 1889*]

Bridge Dock

Dear Moore.

As if my precarious state of health (including choice complications of catarrh, bronchitis, asthma & pleurisy) was not bad enough—this morning the last cup of bitterness is added to my drop by the enclosed letter ! ! ![1]

Pilules! What in Heaven's name do they mean! I have examined scores of shilling shockers & they don't make 120 pp. It's a blasted pretext Sir—it's fudge Sir & that's what it is Sir and be damned to them, Sir.

We must hold a conference on Satdy afternoon. Where?—I await your ukase impatiently. I feel like a protoplasm in the embryo of a troglydyte. If you see a second hand, roomy coffin, fairly cheap will you please purchase same & have it sent down here. Bill to be sent to my exectrs.

Write to-night fixing rendez-vous.

Yrs   ED

PS. Thanks for the Grosvenor critique.[2] I am quite sure it was very admirable but have not seen it, as it was in the printers hands before I turned up at the Office. Adios.

1. The rejection of *Dr. Ludovicus* by Routledge.
2. Review of an exhibition of contemporary paintings at the Grosvenor Galleries by Moore in *The Critic* of 11 May.

43. *To Arthur Moore*
    15 May 1889

                                                    Bridge Dock

Cher Collaborateur.

Sickness of mind, body & estate, (the latter twain still very present)
prevented the accustomed Sunday special. I now write to say that
"Doctor Lud:" is once more away to F. V. White.[1] Good fortune attend
it. You will have seen presumably the Critic (current)[2] & observed
yourself—& myself with many obvious errors such as Bousquet for
Bourget—"thunder & cannon" for thunder of cannon"—in print.

We await a critique of the New Gallery.[3] Swanton promises an
Oxford letter.[4]—If the journal lives they will be inserted—it is gasping
however & threatens mortality. Good old Field Club: quelle spoofe-
mente.[5] By the by I have discovered that the Opus was read—at least
the first vol as someone Moon methinks, has made feeble verbal alterations passim with a pencil! I have no great opinion of Messrs Routledge
—nor of their readers literary taste. I have not written to ask for a
criticism. Won't you do it or better still go to see them?

I can meet you any day & any time almost after six for the New
Gallery or a lager. I can't work a dinner—at least before Satdy. Next
week possibly I may be ready for the system. How goes it? Write to me
soon I beseech thee. To-night we go—the Editor & myself—to the
Princesses.[6] We have had stalls sent us without asking for several
matinées this week but only one for each. I may have to go to one—
the Comedy on Thursday.—[7]

Is there anything you are particularly keen on as I think I shall
write for a couple of seats *somewhere* this week while the paper lives.

---

1. It was rejected by him a month later.
2. The 11 May number to which Dowson contributed a notice of *Oh! These
   Widows* at Terry's Theatre, the variety shows at the Empire and the
   London Pavilion, and also the Paris letter in which, under the name of
   Pierre de Lombard, he dealt most graphically with the opening of the
   Exhibition. Moore reviewed the paintings at the Grosvenor Gallery.
3. An exhibition of modern paintings which was reviewed by Moore in the
   following week.
4. This appeared the following week, 18 May.
5. A gambling club in St. James's which was raided on 12 May; seventy
   arrests were made.
6. A revival on 15 April of *The Silver King* by H. A. Jones and Henry
   Herman. Wilson Barrett and Miss Eastlake were in the cast. The
   production was favourably reviewed by Dowson in the following
   number.
7. *The Inheritance* by Cecil Raleigh, which was given a trial matinée on
   16 May. It was given a good review by Dowson on 25 May.

It was the great Williams whom you saw at the Gaiety.[8] No more—
adios.

always yrs (although afflicted at present with croup, bronchitis,
pleurisy, consumption and melancholia.

ERNEST DOWSON, PIERRE DE LOMBARD etc. etc—

8. *Dick Turpin the Second* by W. F. Goldberg, first produced 6 May.

44. *To Arthur Moore*
    [*19 May 1889*]

[*Woodford*]

DEATHS

On Saturday 18th. inst at 16 Took's Court Cursitor St, Chancery
Lane—the "Critic" Weekly Review, very suddenly in its fourth number.
Deeply regretted.[1]

The above is my excuse for putting you off yesterday. The *Garrick*[2]
had only one seat to give away but promised something for next week.
I could no doubt have got something for somewhere else—but with
affairs in so precarious a state I thought you wouldn't mind letting me
put it off. Sudden is not the word for the death: it was instantaneous.
The cursed printers! Everything was ready—when they somehow got
wind that we were perfectly broke & struck for £11—or so before they
would move. £11 could not—nor can—be procured—& in spite of our
impressing on them that their only chance of getting a cent was by
publishing & not losing us our advts they refused to do so &——the
Critic is a deader !!! Hélas . . . . hélas! The Editor is almost off his head;
& although we went to see Mrs B.B.[3] in the afternoon I think he had
hardly realized then that it was all up with the affair. Then he went &
saw the Ed. of "Pump Court"[4]—who talked of taking up the paper &
had actually at one time gone so far as to tell us to mention him to the
printers as guaranteeing this number. It was his backing out of this

1. Dowson's obituary was premature; the fourth number did, in fact, appear,
   and the periodical continued for some time thereafter.
2. *The Profligate.*
3. Mrs. Bernard Beere in *Still Waters run Deep*, a comedy from the French
   by Tom Taylor, first given in 1855 and revived at the Comedy on 19
   January 1889.
4. Subtitled *The Temple Newspaper and Review*, published 1883–1891.

engagement I think which more than anything put the printers back up & finished the business. In the evening we sat dejectedly in the office but were obliged to admit finally that it was a case of "spoof".

Enough of this most melancholy affair. I am sorry your article is wasted but I am in the same boat with a critique, a review & the P.L.[5]

I have simply worked like a nigger this week & its annoying to feel my labour vain. Write soon.

I am now going to bed for a week.

Let me have your views re: Ludovicus.

And now chéri confrère, trusting that you will join me in a hearty malediction on everything which is in Heaven & Earth & the waters etc and especially on the race of publishers & printers, believe me

Yrs   E D

D'you want a colley dog? One 2 years old, "handsome & gentle & clean", etc. is at your service—My great aunt wants to find a home for him as apparently he can't get on with 6 or 7 of her other dogs. *Early reply requested.*

5. The Paris Letter.

45. *To Victor Plarr*
    [*20 May 1889*]

Bridge Dock

Cher Confrère.

I must apologize deeply & profusely for not turning up on Sunday morning as per arrangement & hope that I didn't muchly inconvenience you. But the exertions of the week & notably of Satdy—were so stupendous that I calmly slept on & on, missing the 9 oclock train—after which there was a blank (Sunday) in our railway arrangements until lunch time when of course it was no good. I regret to have to tell you that The Critic—*died* very suddenly on Saturday afternoon in its 4th number. I am afraid it is now past recovery. No iv was all ready—the whole thing set up, advts & all—proofs corrected etc—& it only remained to machine it—when somehow the printers got wind of the financial state of the affair & refused to budge a step until their little bill was settled. There is weeping & gnashing of teeth in Took's Court in consequence & we expect a bailiff in hourly. This is very melancholy —my journalistic career is evidently going to be severely chequered. I shall hope to look in on you shortly & bring my apologies in person. Meanwhile adios

Tout à vous   ERNEST DOWSON

46. *To Arthur Moore*[1]
[*26 May 1889*]

[*Woodford*]

Agnosticism—not of course à la Mrs H. Ward—but a reasonable Huxleian agnosticism is logical & consistent—but when you come to forms of belief—there is only Pessimism & Catholicism. They are the only respectable "isms". Theism strikes me as about the worst kind of balderdash that I have yet come across except perhaps Positivism. I apologize for this unnecessary & fatuous digression. But—I have been reading "John Ward—Preacher"[2]—& you know my little weakness for speculative correspondence.

By the by the "Episodion" is not yet dead. I received a letter yesterday—when I had hoped it had passed finally into the limbo of forgotten follies, crapulous yesterdays etc—& yes, it liveth. And I fear I cannot give the death stroke to it at present without being rather brutally plain spoken. As an experiment though it is finished & the result is as I expected—i.e. I am more than ever convinced of the futility of bringing any kind of sentiment into one's relations with Woman. The whole idea is essentially false & impossible: the evil that is done in perverting & warping one's intellectual vision by vicious & trashy novels, such as "Dr Ludovicus" is simply incalculable. For Heaven's sake let us assert our reason & soothe our consciences by writing an antidote—a novel without any love-making in at all—or with only love making à la Zola.

Seriously though be quick in fashioning a plot at which we can begin to work—and work this time with no prostitution of our most chaste pens. I say "our" because you *must* surely see that my view is correct—that—oh damn it all—I am muddled but never mind—ἅλις σπουδῆς—Write to me soon & forgive my remissness. Call on me to-morrow at Tooks Court if you like—vers 6.h. & I may be able to walk with you for un petit quart d'heure. And in any case let us meet soon. I have embarked in a sweepstake (Derby)[3] which hails from the Stock Exchange but the drawing is not yet. Of course I shall draw blank.—I am doing this week the Opera—the "White Lie", a novel & the Parisian letter—& Heaven knows what besides.[4] I think that the paper's life

---

1. The first sheet of this letter is missing.
2. By Margaret Doland, 1888; the story of a rigid Calvinist's struggle with an agnostic wife.
3. The Derby was run on 5 June and won by the Duke of Portland's Donovan.
4. It was, in fact, an extremely hard week's work. In the number of 1 June Dowson reviewed *Aida*, *Les Pêcheurs de Perles*, *Faust* and *Lohengrin* at Covent Garden, *A White Lie* by Sydney Grundy with Minnie Terry in it at the Court, *Now-a-Days* at the Princess's, *The Scarecrow* by Charles

may be short but it will certainly survive its staff. I have had a dinner to-day & so feel temporarily invigorated but I shall be hungry ~~again~~ & at deaths door again by Tuesday at least. Journalism Sir, is by no means all beer & skittles. N'importe—it's a good joke for a short time. Don't forget No 2 Academy notice[5]—you had better read up the first notice so as not to be tautological. Now—adios. I go to my balmy couch to dream no doubt of theatrical criticisms.

Yrs   CLEMENT SCOTT JNR

Thomas for a matinée at the Strand, *Frou-Frou* by the French Company at the Gaiety, and a novel by Mrs. J. K. Spender called *Kept Secret*.
5. This appeared in the following number, 1 June.

47. *Letter-card to Arthur Moore*

Friday night [*7 June, postmark 8 June 1889*]

The Critic, Tooks Court, Strand, W.C.

Dear Moore

Shall not be up here probably to-morrow as th' Editor will be away. ~~Will however look in or endeavour to do so at Café Royal between 2 & 3.~~

If we fail to meet write me your plans for Sunday & Monday remembering that at Woodford English postal arrangements are in vogue—i.e.—write me by Saturday night

ever thine   CRISTOPHE LE CRITIQUE

P.S. On second thoughts meet me if you are free at Rathbone Place[1] 2.30. I have a project.

1. Selwyn Image lived at No. 51.

48. *To Arthur Moore*

14 June 1889

Bridge Dock

Cher Ami,

Your letter of yesterday plunged me into a profound depression which has prevented me from replying to it before. I rather hoped moreover that you would turn up last evening at Took's Court?—I can suggest scarce anything. Use your own judgement—but I should say it rests now between using the introduction of your aunt, the publisher killer or trying a magazine.[1]

What do you say to seeking an interview, (armed with Sampson Lows etc's letter) with the editor of Cassel's Satdy Journal—something might come of it & he is a 'Varsity man himself—the "Q" of the Oxford Mag & of "The Tale of Troy Town".[2] Perhaps we could work an introduction to him. I forget his real name but probably you will know it.

I am not sailing till Wednesday, I believe, now:[3] so we should meet —if not to-day to-morrow. Look me up about 6: at T.C. if you can— this evening.

Read my Ibsen critique in the forthcoming "Critic".[4] It is the only serious criticism, save that of "A White Lie" which I have attempted. You *must* go & see it. I fear I can't get anything more in the seat way out of Harrington Baily[5] but if you don't mind pitting it or amphitheatring at 1/6 with me we will go together to-morrow night.[6] I must go again—that is clear & you, *at least*, once. I hope this will catch you & that you will turn up. If you can't come round to-morrow afternoon. I shall be at the office by 2.30 at the latest probably before. But write to make sure.

No more now

Yrs ever   ERNEST DOWSON

I went as a Pigottist to '*Which Wins*'[7] on Wed: afternoon. I promised to bless—(as one of my old ladies is going to put the notice before the elder P. the Censor)[8] but I felt sadly inclined to curse. I think *bien entendu* that "Which Wins" is the *very* worst play I have ever seen. Alas for Conscientious Criticism!—But buy the P.M.G. of yesterday: the ruffian Buchanan is attacked in a most withering & delicious letter by one Shaw.[9] Buy it!

1. *Dr. Ludovicus* had once again been rejected, this time by Sampson Low, Marston & Co.
2. Arthur Quiller-Couch (1863–1944), later Professor of English at Cambridge and editor of *The Oxford Book of English Verse*.
3. To the Broads. In fact, he left on 29 June.
4. His enthusiastic critique of *A Doll's House* appeared in the issue for 15 June. It is reprinted in Appendix A.
5. Actor and theatrical agent, d. 1908.
6. *A Doll's House* with Herbert Waring and Janet Achurch opened at the Novelty Theatre on 7 June.
7. A comedy drama by J. W. Pigott at Terry's Theatre.
8. E. F. S. Pigott, licenser of the plays in the Lord Chamberlain's office, died 1895 aged seventy-one. He had the distinction of having refused to license Wilde's *Salomé*.
9. *Pall Mall Gazette*, 13 June. Bernard Shaw contributed a short but ferocious article on Robert Buchanan's review of *A Doll's House*.

49. *To Arthur Moore*
  [*c. 19 June 1889*]

Bridge Dock

Cher Thorvald[1]—
  Actually for once pas spoofé. The Diary has commended itself to
Messrs Macmillan's editor & he will send me "the proofs in due course".[2]
This is extremely pink.

Ranke[3]—M.D.

I trust I shall see you in the course of a day or two. I am doing a
matinée with Mdlle on Sat. but shall hope to see you at the Royal—say
5.30 after. I will *not* bring my editor this time although I may have
Mdlle with me. However—Come & bring much copy round to T.C.
about 6 to-night.—

1 and 3. References to Thorvald Helmer and Dr. Rank in *A Doll's House*.
2. *The Diary of a Successful Man* appeared in *Macmillan's Magazine*,
    February 1890.

50. *To Victor Plarr*
  [*c. 19 June 1889*]

Woodford

Cher Ami.
  Thanks immensely for the most piquant invite.[1] I hope that I may
be able to go—but can only hope—as I wait hourly the order to sail—
and fear that I shall be on the high seas by Sunday.
  Have you seen your article in this week's *Critic*:[2] it makes a most
imposing front to an unusually meagre inside. I hope you will give
us some more copy "at your earliest convenience"—I have, by the way,
actually scored another point at last in my battle with the obdurate
editorial mind—i e. I have just received acceptance of a story from
"Macmillans". When it will appear I know not—but at any rate it *is*
accepted.
  Du reste—I am more or less of a corpse, what with the intolerable

1. To the Rev. Stewart Headlam's party (see Letter 51).
2. *Anecdotage as an Art*, which occupied the whole front page of *The Critic*,
    15 June 1889.

ennui of this office & my laborious efforts for the unhappy "Critic. but doubtless the society of my respectable old buccaneer & the ocean breezes—not too much of 'em, I hope,—will revive me temporarily. Go & see *A Doll's House*—I have been twice & go again. It's the very finest play that has been seen for years.

I hope we may meet on Sunday 'twixt 8–4.

Poignée de main   ERNEST DOWSON

51. *To Arthur Moore*

[*23 June 1889*]

Woodford

Cher collaborateur.

It is some time since the Sunday ed: has gone to you. Let it be resumed. I trust you arrived chez toi—in all sobriety last night & accomplished the de[s]census Av—I should say omnibi with discretion. I feel to-day that I possess a liver—doubtless the result of that little green absinthe. I know not whether I sail to-morrow. If I do not let us dine together Tuesday. Let it be arranged. In any case come round tomorrow Monday night to Took's Court on your way home. The Editor will be away at Cromer, but I shall be there.

I have nought else of especial to say to you. I can not conceive another story. I feel barren, sterile—what you will. O, prithee, bethink thee of a good plot & let us start on it. I have purchased & am reading "Germinal".[1] According to L.B.[2] it is the most powerful of the Rougon-Ms.[3] I like it myself less than several. I should by now be dancing neath S. Headlam's[4] Chinese lanthorns with fair sylphs of Th' Empire & Alhambra. But somehow I couldn't come up to the scratch. The liver & the spleen, chiefly the latter have stood in my way. I am rather sorry because it would have been novel & unconventional to say

1. Published in 1885. Referred to by Zola himself as 'a leap into the stars from the springboard of exact observation'.
2. Louis Bouthors.
3. *Les Rougon-Macquart*, the cycle of novels published by Zola between 1871 and 1893.
4. The Rev. Stewart Duckworth Headlam (1847–1924), founder of the Church and Stage Guild, editor of *The Church Reformer* and for many years a member of the L.C.C. The Guild, whose purpose was to break down prejudice against actors and dancers, held a ball twice yearly. Its monthly meetings were attended by many men of letters. Shaw was a regular speaker and in 1890 gave a lecture on Ibsen.

the least of it. But my dancing days are over & even the disrespect-
ability of my partner wouldn't be sufficient temptation now. If Macmillan forks out before Sept. which is improbable, I shall go *at last* to
Auxerre. Would that I could tempt you away with me. But I suppose
that is impossible. What a bore Sunday is to be sure, & what a d——d
nuisance that Monday comes with its intolerable *corvées* of The Dry
Dock & the Critic. Are you on the river now? What a man you are! I
assure you I am aghast when I think of your unconquerable energy! I
could no more go down to Richmond & row now than I could—go to
church—or to S.H.'s ball. Indeed it is as much as I can do at the
present moment to hold a pen. Hélas—hélas! Would the Gods I had an
idea! Would the Gods you would invent a plot. Would that you were
not such a beastly slacker—or rather would transfuse some of your
enormous energy into less unprofitable channels than *la danse* & la
rivière! Oh this cacoethes scribendi.[5] The ideal world—as I have no
doubt remarked before to you—would be one in which one can see clean
paper without wishing to spoil it & woman without wanting to kiss
her! I wish Stevenson would come back.[6] I have been reading some of
his old letters to my governor and would send him *Ludovicus* like a
shot if he were only accessible—I can't get on with Madame de V. Have
you forgotten that I had a novel on the stocks so entituled? I almost
have myself. The Episode has postponed it—but by all the Gods it
shall be finished. And no more episodes for me—none none—none. J'en
ai assez. Shall hope to see you to-morrow 5.30–6.30.

                 Thine   APEMANTUS.[7]

5. Juvenal VII. 52; an incurable itch to write.
6. Stevenson was far away in the Pacific and never returned.
7. The cynical philosopher in *Timon of Athens*.

52. *To Arthur Moore*
     29 June 1889

                                     Bridge Dock

My dear Moore.
     I am off to Lowestoft—or rather Olton Broad directly: my people
are already there. I shall be back here on Monday & shall hope to see
you in the course of the week down here. I am down in the mouth. The
Episode has been practically over this fortnight or so but I only found
out decisively last night that the girl had bolted. It has finished after
the fashion which I foresaw. Truly women are strange beings. She must
be a most accomplished little liar—after all it's one of the qualities of

her sex—to have hoodwinked me so long. I grasp her attitude now which hitherto I confess puzzled me. There are depths of cynicism which one doesn't easily realize. Do you remember the episode of Mdlle Niniche in "The American?"—[1]

It's sublimely fatuous that I should mind—but entre nous it has quite spoofed me quite. I have no heart left for anything not even for a debauch.

Bah—it doesn't bear thinking of or writing of. Let us drop the subject. Write to me & tell me if you have yet discovered an idea. Oh ye Gods I wish this intolerable Norfolk business was over. I never thought I could be notched so severely by anything as I have by this cursed, ridiculous affair. And I wonder if—and where & when I shall see her again? It would be rather ghastly.

No more now. Excuse this maudlin scrawl.

always yrs   ERNEST DOWSON

You *must* come & see me or dine with me early next week—I am just going to have a holocaust of letters & reliques. I am triste à mourir. Oh Heavens what a fool I have been.

1. By Henry James, 1877. 'Niniche' is a slip for Mlle Noémie Nioche, the accomplished but elusive French girl who finally gives Newman, the hero, the slip.

53. *To Arthur Moore*

Sunday [*30 June 1889*]. about 2 o'clock

Yacht "Rover"—river Waveney—between Oulton & Beckles

Cher Ami. This is the Sunday edition. I write at a disadvantage on the flyleaf of "Diana of the Crossways".[1] It's a perfect day. At the present moment I have dropped a little astern bathed & dried myself & now lie in the dingy sunning myself, my painter (?)—tied to a bank. This method of ruralizing has distinctly its points. We have a most swift & commodious little craft a 12 tonner—I go back to-morrow morning from Beckles but return on Saturday & pick up the ship at Yarmouth. By the end of my time I expect I shall believe in the Broads as devoutly as you do. We reach Beckles where we lay to for the night about 6. At the present moment we lie at anchor—& I believe the whole family

1. By George Meredith, 1885.

sleeps. You will have got my Saturday outburst. To-day everything is so green & sunny & still that the mere physical sensation of living & slacking is quite enough for me. Would that you were here. (I perceive that my brother[2] who is on shore is endeavouring to cast me adrift. Excuse me while I go & demolish him)—I am now safely tied astern & prepared for any issue. But oh—it is difficult to write in a dingey. I have been reading Meredith—with satisfaction. I think the best thing a man can do who has made a great & blatant fool of himself is to take a course of Meredith. He is freer from the slightest taint of sentiment than anybody I know brilliantly clever—& hard & cold as a piece of crystal.

I mean presently—when I feel a little less slack—to give my whole mind to our future opus.[3] Do thou likewise. I feel ready to write now: there is nothing at all to distract me—nothing. And you must come & give me your ideas on Tuesday. It is astonishing how change of scene clears a fellow's brain. Mine will get muddy again no doubt in London —but that's only to be expected . . . . . . Yes there is certainly a charm about English river scenery—even English. It gives one a sensation analogous to that which one gets from a supper off sponge rusks & milk. I am tranquil—may it last.—The yacht moveth & it bears me in my light craft gibbing behind. This is charming. I feel like a champagne cork. Excuse this egoistical small talk. But after being the victim of a tragicomedy for a fortnight it is dulce dissipere in cymba.[4] The pace is increasing. I fear this scrawl must terminate—We are passing a hillock grass green which runs down to the river's edge dotted with elms—rather a pretty spot. I didn't know Duneshire was so attractive. However as yet I see not the Dunes—& the Daisy alas neither here nor anywhere. Du reste I return comme on revient toujours, à mes anciens amours. I think it is possible for the feminine nature to be reasonably candid & simplex, up to the age of 8 or 9. Afterwards—phugh! Be of my advice, profit by my experience, & I hope in the future by my example   Yrs   E.D.

2. Rowland Corbett Dowson, ten years younger than Ernest and the only other child of his parents.
3. *Felix Martyr*, a novel which they did not complete. See Letter 54.
4. Cf. Horace, *Odes* IV. 12: *dulce est desipere in loco.*

54. *To Arthur Moore*
    Sunday [*7 July 1889*] 3 p.m.

Yacht "Rover"—off Wroxham

Cher Théophile.[1]

It being wet & Sunday & as we do not purpose moving on to Horning until to-morrow morning what better object have I than the epistolary one of 7 Lincoln's Inn Field?[2] Excuse me for straining after the Meredithian but I have been reading "Diana" until I am pink and my brain quavers. To return to *our* Diana. She has been developping steadily ever since I left you on Friday night! She improves on acquaintance. I propose in Chap I—shortly to be submitted to you to introduce Felix Martyr fellow & tutor of—— Coll: Oxon: aet 40 spending a week or so in Paris after the May term & anterior to the Grand Prix. With him one Lord Hildreth his chief pal. Their characters are still rather sketchy to me at present but light & shadow will come in composition. (Hildreth perhaps the cynical chorus?)—To them appears Comtesse Diane de Lussac—who has pretty well spoofed our unromantic Felix ten years before when she was a bright meteor of Commem—the beautiful Miss Lucerne. A chapter of retrospect—the original jilting of Felix by Diana & her entrapment of de Lussac. The meeting: subtle—suggestive conversation. Invitation to Madame's place in (?) Britainy—Provence (latter I think), (call it— / . . . . ? Interspersed chapter—by you?—at Oxford or London. They go to *Lussac*. Madame very obviously but not too obviously after F.M.: F.M. right off but wavers until the sister turns up (?) from her convent (Elsie Lucerne) when (?) he falls in love with the sister. Hildreth & others staying in the house. Diana jealous. Other characters the village curé, charming, refined, sceptical, conforming—living with his child (niece) aet 7. (You must not blackball this character—I give you carte blanche to introduce corresponding specialities of your own). The curé & Hildreth "pal up" & discuss things in general & the Lussac ménage in particular.

*   *   *   *   *   *   *   *   *   *   *   *   *   *   *   *   *   *   *

The part of the novel denoted by those stars is to me a void: I look to you to supply it with incident, characters & analysis. The dénouement I think is this—Madame sees that she has hopelessly lost F.M. & being enragée decides that at any rate he shall not marry her sister. She intrigues to that τέλος & finally plays her most successful coup: she tells Elsie that the marriage is an impossible one & delicately suggests that Felix has originally been her own lover. The girl is horrified retires

1. i.e. Gautier.
2. Where Moore was working in the solicitors' firm of Longbourne, Stevens and Powell.

LED–G

into her convent & refuses to see or enter into any explanation with Felix. The end comes when Felix discovers through Hildreth or the Curé the mendacious ruse of Diana & taxes her with it & the curtain falls (?) upon his precipitate return to London very much dégouté but not a little relieved that after all he has not taken any positive act. Elsie I conceive as a very ingenuous & childish & charming young person but perfectly helpless in the hands of a woman of genius like her sister. She is a sort of Ophelia sweet but savourless—without character, whose condition of life is absolute sunshine & who at the least breath of misfortune withers away with the hopes of those who have leant on her. It might possibly be more subtle to make her simply give up FM. & accept a lover of her sister's choosing without any revelation of the kind suggested above but simply through her sister's opposition. That is for you to decide—Felix of course, in contrast is *très fort*, solid & determined but with less true perceptions & less savoir vivre than either Hildreth or the curé. Voilà, mon vieux. There is my (purely provisional) outline. Fill it up & emend it & write upon it at your will. Write to me to-morrow posting your letter before 5 to Horning Ferry— as after that our movements are vague: but there we shall be until Tuesday morning. (A large jack has just been landed—I renew after the excitement which it has caused is allayed). Mind & write as I want to get on with the work & shall wait for your suggestions. The weather is rather dull to-day & it has been raining: I prefer the Broads at temperature of 70 upwards. We have been here since last night at anchor. I went for a sail in our dinghey this morning over Wroxham Broad. It liked me much—there were many boats & yachts about. Tyro & Nellie with full companies aboard lying opposite: the Kate of Worsterd (wherry) has passed down. The Clive & Volunteer also the little Buttercup anchored a little above us. No more now: the skipper & my brother are just going off with letters—Write: write. My governor tells me to tell you re Horning Ferry that "Annie is gone & Emily has come". *I* don't know what he means. Perhaps you may

Yrs ever   ED.

55. *To Arthur Moore*
[*13 and 14 July 1889*]

Yacht "Rover"—Oulton Broad, Suffolk (?)

Mon cher Algernon.[1]
No sailing to-day owing to the rain—so I will take the opportunity

1. i.e. Swinburne.

of addressing you once more & thanking you muchly for your most acceptable note to Horning. I regret to say that the novel develops so far chiefly in my fertile brain: a little of it however is on paper. But sailing is an exhausting process & en effet my hands have so suffered from the perpetual straining upon recalcitrant jib sheets that when the day's run is over & we moor at some Acle or St Benets—the most I can do is to lie prone on the cabin sofa quaff shandygaff,[2] smoke & give to the novel—my most earnest consideration. The governor arrives this evening however & we wait for him here—so I may have a turn at scribbling & chuck the halyards to day. We have had some excellent days—but the winds have not favoured us. Our cruise has been one prolonged beat. I am amoureux fou of Horning (tho' not of Em'ly)—ditto of St Olaves—Yarmouth has the very vilest stink of any city or sewer which I have yet met with—and I have been to Marseille: also the approach to it from Acle—with tide & wind against you conduces to profane imaginings—Breydon Water is glorious: we beat across it at 7. AM on Thursday morning in a gale & although my hands were skinned thereby I maintain it is glorious. The Ant is a fraud: I skulled my people up to Barton & cursed the tide. These tidal rivers occasionally exhaust one's vocabulary. But enough—enough—what of Ludovicus?—what of The Critic? What of things in general? I am anxious to hear your developments & characters in Felix Martyr? If you can write to morrow, *do*: as we shall be here till Monday morning when we start probably for Norwich. There is some doubt how much longer we can have this yacht for: we may possibly be turned out on Monday over to the *Cynthia*, but we shall stick to this ship if we can. I will keep you informed however of our shiftings. I think I saw the Anonyma:[3] obviously a ship's life boat—small—lug-sailed—tiller handle fantastically shaped & having a yellow paint line. Recognize you her? Have just read Bernard Shaw's novel—"Cashel Byron's Profession"[4]—wh. I recommend as one of the most strikingly clever books I have read for some time—& certainly not the least original. Get it—& let me have your opinion. I will refrain for the present however: we have swopped our dinghey for a centerboard & so tempting a breeze has sprung up that I must e'en go & test its sailing quality. Write—write—write

always yrs   THE REEFER.[5]

I shall be back next Saturday I expect. Will you be in town then? ED

2. Beer and ginger beer or lemonade.
3. Dowson and Moore used this name for the yacht mentioned in *Adrian Rome*, 1899. It was also used for a yacht in a story by F. N. Paton in *Temple Bar*, March 1890.
4. Published in 1886.
5. Slang for a midshipman.

Sunday

en route to St Olaves

I continue to-day as I discovered the erraticism of the Sunday posts & Saturdays & refrained from sending the foregoing. Also as you see from above our plans change. Address me (to-morrow Monday if you can—Post Office Norwich.): we stay in the "Rover" until Monday—possibly longer. If we shift it is into the "Arrow"—we may be at Norwich two or three days—excursing in the centerboard. It is a glorious day again: the governor sails the ship so I rest me thus below & write you inanities after my fashion. I have also written about ½ Chap I & hope to send you the whole in a day or two. I have also been frivolling with subsequent chaps: sketching out my curé at Ost. 0lb. & his ménage. Madame & her sister ? Elsie—Effie. Gladys—Beryl—Olive . . . what you will? are still rather blank to me. For the love of Bacchus meditate & report on them. I leave blank face sheets of Cap I for your alterations, *interpolations* curtailments & comments: especially I want the underlined. I think such a method will make the chapters more complete. We are just reaching St Olaves: oh for some 'baccy other than shag! I shall send this via: my governor who returns to town to-morrow morning. Try & write—& write to-morrow.

thine   ALPHONSE DE NORFOLK.

St Olaves, Sunday night
Write to Norwich before Tuesday night

56. *To Arthur Moore*
17 July 1889

Yacht "Rover", Thorpe, Norwich.

Dear Moore,
Your scintillating letter has been a perpetual source of joy ever since I reaped it this morning—as the reward of a 4 mile pull to the Norwich post office. I have read it many times: & time at present being heavy on my hands, can not resist replying to it. Knowest thou this place? If not you must certainly visit it in your "Anonyma". The last two or three reaches before you sight Norwich are to my mind the prettiest part of Norfolk which I have yet seen—& I have seen most of it now. I envy you much your glimpse of Mignon[1] undivided by the footlights—& under

1. Minnie Terry, referred to as Mignon because of her part in *Bootle's Baby*.

such favourable circumstances. It was a privilege that befell me often when I oscillated round the B.M.—but since an unkind fate has distracted me from the Bloomsbury paradise—(after all its the one place in the metrop that one would weep to see conflagrated) to the purlieus of Limehouse & Fleet St—I haven't seen "la petite"—save in the White Lie—which I regret to see has given place to one more of these unspeakable, brazen faced, confessed farces.[2] Is she not—("la petite"—I mean) verily a sight for sair eyes? I look forward to possessing the new photo . . . . I refer again to your letter. Like you I do little except curse my fate & everything connected with shipping—only on Bass not Lager. The Broads are certainly pretty but after a fortnight of them I shall come back to London with a certain thrill. I give what energy is left me from much sculling & infinite tacking to the new . . . .? what d'ye call it? The first chapter progresses—I may send it but I shall more likely bring it. I'm not at all satisfied with what I've written: it's jerky, affected, indelicate & all that is unjamesy. Oh what would I not give to discover his secret—inimitable—inimitable method! Talk of Meredith talk of Thackeray—talk of Zola (yes, Zola)—they are powerful, brilliant, ingenious—what you will— but when you come to delicacy—subtlety—there is only H. James & his master Tourguénef of novelists—& of—? semigods the one Pater. I had thought of Lucerne Snr. but venture to suggest that he is only *alluded* to (in your chap. of retrospect) as the dead & insignificant husband of the faded, flimsy, fashionable, medicine-chesty Mrs L. ((matre pulchra)[3]—at Oxford with her daughters, one marriageable, Diana,—the other in the shadow— Elsie (?) not yet grown up)—to suggest the adventuress as though he were perhaps rather mythical. This sentence defies analysis: don't attempt to scrutinize it. Lord Sheldrake is good: but you must explain me his part. You will see my view of F.M. in Chap I—in Hildreth you will recognize my old inevitable friend of half a dozen rejected MSS & two accepted: who is right off action of any kind, but can be drawn on ad lib. for moralizing more or less inanely to any extent. So far no new characters dawn upon me—I look to you for the necessary half dozen or so still required.

Fancy P.L.A.[4] incredible! You shall have "Cashel Byron" & various other more or less inane works for your cruise. You will note if you see current "Critic"—(one has been sent me) that we are both wildly

2. *Aunt Jack* by Ralph R. Lumley succeeded Sydney Grundy's *White Lie* at the Court Theatre on 13 July.
3. *O matre pulchra filia pulchrior*, first line of Horace, *Odes* I. 16. O lovely mother's lovelier daughter.
4. Percy Lancelot Andrews (b. 1866) went up to Queen's in 1885. He got a first in Mathematical Moderations in 1887, but followed it with a third in 1889.

appealed to in the Answers to Correspondents.[5] You should study Lee Crighton,[6] an you meet him. He is a silent man, by no means the bounder that, I admit, he looks—and as deep as our worthy chief is shallow. I have found points in him . . . . . . Yes, the roman will be developped most surely over absinthe. Dine with me—Cavour—Solferino[7]—Previtali[8]—or somewhere on Tuesday—or on Wednesday —or on Monday—next. Fix your day, but dine with me. I shall be alone again all next week at Bridge Dk: so perhaps you will also be able to work an evening there with me. We leave here to-morrow for Cantley & thence to Oulton where for the rest of the week a letter will find me an' you have time to pen one. I received at the same time as yours, an epistle, incoherently joyous, from V. Plarr, written at the Café de la Frégate—in the only city. I wish we were all there—with pockets—but enough, enough of these *souhaits*.—Par exemple—title for a novel—our next—à la Bourget—or Bosquet as The Critic prints it—"Wishes"? I really hardly dare to ask your pardon for penning you this absolute bagatelles. Drivel describes it mildly. But I write as the spirit moves me—& have to fill up the time between "fife o'clocque" & supper. It has just struck me that by this time Cassells have written. Well, I anticipate it. Break it to me at your leisure . . . . . I suppose you have read "Diana"? I'm not sure that it isn't the best. Would the gods I had some absinthe on board! Good old Café Royal. P's letter—envelope rather, lies before me on the table & the post mark on it depresses me.[9] It begins to rain. I look forward to basking beneath your eagle glance on Tuesday. I suppose you will be off to these quarters before we have time to turn round. May you be more prolific of pen then ~~is the parting prayer~~ than your unworthy collabr has been under similar circumstances. Adieu   Poignée de main   ERNEST DOWSON

I go back to *the* roman.

5. The 'appeals' read as follows:
    A. C. Moore. We are not aware of your address or would write. Have no means of knowing it either. Pumpkins (i.e. E.C.D.) has departed for foreign climes, or Hades, we are uncertain which. Do you know? The Editor is consequently alone. Note change of address. Thanks for MS which is used.
    E.C.D. If this should meet your eye at any spot on mortal or material earth please remember that the sunshine of the office is now but a thing to be remembered—a fact existing in name only. *When* shall we see your luminous countenance? The Sub, who is famous for alleged letters and post knocks, is absolutely becoming a mere skeleton. Hurry up, thou sluggish traveller, to the new address and crack a bumper of the vin ordinaire with thy pals of the pen!
6. A contributor to *The Critic*.
7. A restaurant in Rupert Street, Leicester Square.
8. An hotel in Arundel Street, off the Strand.
9. After the words 'the post mark on it' Dowson inserts a rough sketch of the postmark, bearing the inscription 'Paris 12. 89'.

57. *Postcard to Arthur Moore*

Friday night [*19 July, postmark 20 July 1889*]

Yacht "Rover"—Oulton

Dear Moore: Just a line to tell you that I have decided on coming back to-morrow—so perhaps I may see you on Sunday. Am going to Orchard St at 5—& will wait at Baker St Station for you (on the chance) for 10 minutes 3–3.10.

Yrs ᴇᴅ

58. *To Arthur Moore*

26 July 1889

Bridge Dock

Dear Moore.

I greatly fear that Saturday will not see us united. My mater is *de retour* on that day & I am pretty well bound to put in an appearance at dinner as she will probably be alone. Let me hear your plans for Sunday: we might compass a walk in the afternoon. I am sorry to say that the work does not proceed. I cannot get into the vein: I am going to send you a revised Chap I with blank interludes for you to fill up with brilliant & pointed dialogue.

I have been busily engaged on what I believe will be positively the last number of The Critic.[1] Come & look us up: the new office[2] (it was the *Gentleman's*,[3] of libellous fame; & we have entered into its inheritance, chiefly a set of very waggish office rules on the wall) is a most palatial one. At least we die decently. Come & look us up: this evening. I shall be there at six.—Anyhow write. I found it difficult to choose between the half-dozen new & equally charming photos of Mignon. On the whole however the "doggy" ones liked me least. I think I have the prettiest now. This weather I find depressing: also most other things. I have a liver. I have spheroids which I gnaw. I have the reliques of a catarrh. Barabbas as you know was a publisher. Tartarus is the metropolis of England[4]—one of its most hideous circles being Limehouse. O why am I not now in the British Museum! There are many things I

1. He was again unduly pessimistic.
2. 9 Cursitor Street, Chancery Lane.
3. *The Gentleman* appeared from October 1888 to February 1889, and was notoriously scurrilous.
4. Cf. Shelley, *Peter Bell*, Part III . 'Hell is a city much like London.'

want to do there: here there are none—none that I want to do—& none
that I could do an' I wanted to, which I shouldn't an' I did. I fear that
I can't possibly spin this letter out for more than another ten minutes.
It is now 11.30 AM. I am morally bound to stay here till 5!!!! 5 hours ½
—without a novel—& without ideas. I recommend you to read my review in the next Critic on "Toilers in London". It's a most successful
essay in fictitious enthusiasm I've done! οἴμοι: Come in & see me ce
soir if you can. We will walk to the Royal & absinthe: that may restore
me: besides I want to buy the new Bourget.[5] Come—come—come.
Mais—enfin—que diable—bah—

Tout à toi   ERNEST DOWSON

5. *Le Disciple.*

59. *To Arthur Moore*

31 July 1889

Bridge Dock

Mon chéri.

Thanks for your note & copy which is all that could be desired. I
am as yet ignorant whether or no the special no. has reappeared. As
probably however you care about that—for yes or no as little as I do
myself let us pass on. I write to tell you—I may though see you before
this arrives—that I have written for Gaiety[1] tickets & am prepared to
go with you if they come which is probable. In any case perhaps we
may work a modest repast & confer on the important subject of *the*
roman. If I can get away from the corvée to-night I will give myself to
it. It—(the corvée) seems painfully tenacious of life. I wish it no harm
—notwithstanding that if it had its deserts— — ! ! — but I am very
weary of it—& above all of it's editor. If it is really going to live permanently I will send in my resignation at once. If on the contrary it
seems likely to die in a fortnight I will stay to the end. I presume you
are with me.

Du reste I am very very low. I have knocked off whiskey, allow
myself tea only at breakfast and curtail my smoke: it makes no difference; I still continue to plumn the depths of depression. I hope you will
find the Broads more productive of tissue, liver and equanimity than

1. *Circumstances Alter Cases* by I. A. Ascher opened on 27 June 1889.

I have done. Aesculapius attend you! If I can only shake off Cursitor St I will go to the oeuvre like one oclock. Prithee do so likewise. For the night cometh etc.

Yrs de profundis   ED.

60. *To Arthur Moore*
Sunday [*4 August 1889*]

Woodford

My dear Moore.

You should receive by this post Chap I of "Felix Martyr" whereof I have just completed the fair!!! copying. I hope you didn't inconvenience yourself to meet me at the B M on Satdy. I felt so decidedly below the mark that I didn't even get as far as Limehouse. My rest however has been so far beneficial that I feel now considerably fit—and have as you will see, at last finished off a first chaper of sorts. Emend the same as much as you can: it wants it greatly. I hope we may be able to work an evening at Bridge Dk before your departure, some time this week to discuss further developments. I needn't tell you that I dislike Felix extremely—almost as much as Paul Muniment (I have just been reading the "Princess Casamassima")—but I have purposely made him rather a bounder. The Princess (not Casamassima) but what you will— I conceive as an old pal of Lord H's mother—but more interested in Martyr than the other & as you will gather matrimonially disposed. I think she may be useful chiefly of course as the possessor of rather a brilliant *salon* at which Diana etc may be produced—& also later as a confidante of various of our personages. The development, I confess, is still very vague to me—only I think it is essential that Felix should generally score off everybody else, while at the same time the sympathies of the reader are to be enlisted for the people who are spoofed. But enough—give these things your consideration.

I have been investing lately in some Brownings. Do you know the "Blot on the Escutcheon".[1] It amuses me to think of the excellent, bourgeois Browning writing a prurient poem, with its false morality & its fulsome, sickly sentimentalism worthy of "Aurora Leigh"[2]—and then of his fanatic following reading papers on it & flinging mud at the French psychologists. I hope I'm pretty Catholic—one should certainly read Browning & I intend to do so at my leisure. But what can you expect of a nation which reads the "Blot on the Escutcheon" and

1. Published in 1843.
2. By Mrs. Browning, 1857.

boycots Bourget. It makes me despair of England. After all these years —the most important contribution to the sexual question by the man who, we are told, is the "subtlest-souled psychologist" of them all—is simply another "Daphnis & Chloe"[3]—with all the pruriency and only the poetry of the original left out! It's very depressing. And when the literature is so fatuous it's not surprising that the people make one vomit. An infamous ass who is simply rolling in oof and has something to do with ships told me on Friday with the most disgusting complacency that he had just produced twins! He seemed to expect me to congratulate him—or at least to enquire after his beastly wife. It's astonishing how proud your average Englishman is if he's only prolific. If he only had one spark of imagination he ought to deify the Rabbit. I think I never fully realized untill within the last year of what depths of imbecillity the human animal is capable. Des bêtises—des bêtises des bêtises! Upon my soul in another year I shall hate my brother man as much as I do woman.

And the best—or the worst of it is that these fulsome idiots with whom one has to brush shoulders don't understand one's language. They can stamp on your toes with their great ~~infamous~~ hoofs but you can't retaliate because their density is so great that they can't conceive such a possibility as your disagreeing with them—in toto—I can't say as I should like to—"My dear Jones, with your twins, and your smug complacency, & your beastly respectability, and your narrow vile mediocrity, you can cease talking to me, and worse still taking it for granted that I agree with you—because I *don't*. Roundly speaking I loathe you: personally I detest you, but infinitely more I detest what you represent. Your atmosphere affects me like a drain: your conversation rasps upon my ear like a file. Your ideals—such as they are are abhorrent to me,—if I were to tell you mine you would think me a maniac—and your holiest of holies I look upon as a pigstye. If I thought I had any one of your virtues or had ever committed one of the things upon which you pride yourself—I would never hold my head up again. I would go and shoot myself. MR JONES 'GIT' "—I can't say this in the first place because it would not lead to business and secondly because the animal would not understand. He would simply put me down in his gross apology for a mind as a lunatic. I apologize for this outburst but *enfin* I am sick of these people. I can't stand very much more of them. And really your cultured Hegelian optimists are not much better. They disgust me less but they irritate me more. All their superficial refinement is simply a gigantic fraud. They simply try with more or less success to gloss over repulsive facts—they don't dispute them or fight against them. I think the time is coming when I shall not be able to compromise any longer. I have had to give up society almost entirely because it became so painful to me but it can't end there. So long as I live at home I have to wage a sort of perpetual war for my isolation.

3. The Greek pastoral novel, attributed to Longus. *c.* A.D. 300.

And it's wearing me out—and to no purpose for I shall never come to terms with τὰ ὄντα.⁴ The nuisance is that I doubt if anyone understands. Unless one has established, orthodox convictions properly registered & classified in the book of convention one is assumed to have none & however carefully argued out a course of conduct one may follow it is put down to eccentricity.

This is a long yarn—I commend your patience if you get through it. I shall hope to see you next week some evening when we can devote our whole time to the novel. My health is entirely recovered—I trust you will be able to give me a good account of yours and of your liver which, if I remember rightly, you told me, is of a delicate purple colour, relieved with crushed strawberry spots & old gold stripes.

Yrs ever   ED

P.S. Yr: epistle to hand—vid arsenical enclosure.

4. Things as they are.

61. *To Arthur Moore*
    [*c. 5 August 1889*]

Bridge Dock

Mon cher.

The work has arrived:[1] by this time you should have received the fragment of its successor. Arrowsmith's letter is certainly riling—& obscure. And if Joseph Hatton[2] has been cribbing our motif—then all I can say is more shame to Joseph Hatton. Blast the whole race of publishers. Curse—damn—damn—curse—curse curse—damn—damn —*crescendo*

damn curse blast . . . .! the whole race of publishers. DAMN. I am going to send it to Scott of Newcastle: also I intend writing to the Editor of the Pall Mall Budget and asking him if he wants another serial shocker! But first there is a weird thing in it which I must show you—on Wednesday night. Do you know the handwriting of the rejecting?

Try & fix Wednesday. I have a corvée on to-morrow which I vow by all my gods shall be the last. I look forward also to the death of the

1. *Dr. Ludovicus* once again rejected.
2. Journalist and popular novelist (1841–1907).

Critic this week. Have you seen No the last It's very bad. I will look
out the novels for you. Write   ED

PS. Have written to the Editor of the P.M.B.

62. *To Arthur Moore*
    Sunday [*18 August 1889*]

                                           Woodford

My dear Moore.
    Enviable man—so you are actually in the regions of "John Barley-
corn". I hope your thermometer announces a less icy temperature at
Potter Heigham than it does here. But I am very unhappy—I have no
tobacco . . none . . none & see no prospect of obtaining any till to-
morrow morning. I will write with great pleasure for Aunt Jacklets[1]—
& if they arrive, despatch them "as per" your letter. The P.M.B. main-
tains a stony silence. I shall send the opus to-morrow to W. Scott. But
things are bloodsomely pink. My liver is stupendous—chiefly I think
owing to Friday night which I passed at the Royal & at Marshalls[2] with
Plarr, who is in town for two or three days. We both got assez gris—&
finally toddled back together to Gt Russell St[3] where we slept on floors
& sofas till the morning. The issue a liver! I shall simply be comatose
now until my release at the beginning of Sept! I prithee keep me more
or less informed of your movements & I will throw you out a word &
a "Star" in my waking moments. I don't think "The Critic" has come
out this week. If it has, unless there happen a miracle it is positively the
last number. I will send it you if it should appear—it contains an article
by me on stage children.[4] I heard from J. A. Fallows yesterday—from
Hannover—8 pages, chiefly abuse of the German character. He is sending over an American pal, of rather a Jamesy type, I gather, who is to
seek me out at Limehouse when he comes to London.
    Du reste—absolute deadness—à Londres, personne—partout la
bêtise, triomphante, insolente—. The novel progresses, I am well on
with Chap III. Elsie by the by can't be the sister—she might be Diana's
daughter—cousin—(the last perhaps best)—but she *can't* be the sister.

---

1. *Aunt Jack* at the Court.
2. Probably Archibald Marshall (1866–1934), novelist and journalist.
3. Plarr's lodgings.
4. *The Cult of the Child*, 17 August, occasioned by the agitation against
   children under ten years of age appearing on the stage. It is reprinted in
   Appendix A.

The difference in the age would be too ridiculous. I apologise for the absolute banalité of this letter. But I positively faint with ennui. Happily afternoon tea can not long be delayed. Allons donc! Look out for the "Rover".[5]

5. Instead of a signature Dowson adds a rough sketch of a yacht. Moore's cruise took him over the same waters which Dowson had so recently traversed in the *Rover*.

63. *To Arthur Moore*
Thursday night [*22 August 1889*] 11.30

Woodford

Mon cher vieux. Excellent man indeed—to write. I can't resist replying —of a sort—though I know not when or whither I shall send the Effusion. Methinks I will try Acle! So you woo slumber at this hour in a dank deep well on the misty Bure—while I sit smokingly by a roaring fire. It is even so—alas that this should be August. I deeply sympathize with your inability to transfer the *roman* to paper. Myself, in conditions more favourable, I suffer from the same difficulty. I was weak enough this evening to purchase "Far From the Madding Crowd"[1]— & consequently did nothing at all after dinner but skim its facile pages. Hardy is an admirable man; his rustics are not so veracious as Meredith's & his style is not so uniformly good—neither, I think does he ever have those flashes of insight, of veritable genious, of which each book of Meredith's contains half a score perhaps of examples: but his characters are far more human. What impresses me most of all in everyone of his books is the extraordinary insight he has into the feminine character. There is only Bourget to match him. Excuse this drivel. Your letter cheered me some: otherwise I have been fairly maudlin since you left. Swanton writes to me to-day from Co Cork that he will be in town next week. That will mean I fear, an alcoholic debauch—but no more Brompton Oratori-os!!! Once bit twice shy—& the wily crustacean of Yarmouth is now my nightmare. Chap III of the novel advances very—very—slowly. I tried to take up Mme de Viole—for a change but found that I was not yet sufficiently cured. So I betook me, weakly enough to the writing of rondeaux. I send a specimen thereof.[2]

1. By Thomas Hardy, published 1874.
2. Rondel *To Hélène*, eventually printed in *Temple Bar*, September 1893. as *A Roundel* and subsequently in *Decorations* as *Beyond*.

Despise me. Certainly emotion is the devil & one pays for it a great deal too dearly. These are listless days—I look forward only to your return when I trust that the action of the English Channel & the Bure on our respective miserable livers will enable us to appreciate the exceptionally attractive programmes with which several West End houses will inaugurate the autumn season! (This sentence—N B—is modelled on the "leader" à la very-bad-man-Williams)

(i) the only original Nelly Farren,[3] whose points you shall point out to me

(ii) The Middleman[4] at the Shaftesbury with Maude Millet & Annie Hughes therein

(iii) Roger le Honte[5]—containing in the caste la chère petite—now, I am glad to say, recruiting herself after her exertions on the Brighton Sands.

I will send you some more journals. You will have seen Damala's death.[6] Fouquier's mot is good—the divine Sarah a *widow*! "Il était dans sa destinée à tout connaître". The strike of all these stevedores & people is annoying us pretty considerably.[7] We have had two steamers & a ship fixed for dry docking all this week—& lo they can not be discharged & lie idly in the West India Dock while B.D. is empty & yearneth for them. The Critic if it is published at all will simply be a réplica of last week. But I think it is dead. I went with the editor to the Shaughraun[8] the other night. I was astonished to find what an excellent play it is—quite a hundred degrees above the Sims—Pettitt atrocities[9] & in my own opinion—breathe it not in Gath a better, in that it is a less pretentious piece than The Profligate.[10] There is genuine comedy in it

3. *Ruy Blas or the Blasé Roué* by A. C. Torr (i.e. Fred Leslie) and H. F. Clarke, with Fred Leslie and Nellie Farren, opened with great éclat on 21 September.

4. *The Middleman* by Henry Arthur Jones opened at the Shaftesbury Theatre on 27 August, with E. S. Willard and Annie Hughes.

5. *A Man's Shadow*, adapted by Robert Buchanan from the French *Roger le Honte*, opened at the Haymarket Theatre on 12 September. The Trees, Julia Neilson and Minnie Terry, were in the cast.

6. Jacques Damala, the husband of Sarah Bernhardt, died on 18 August, aged forty.

7. The strike began in the East and West India Docks on 15 August. It spread throughout the London docks and continued with considerable disorder and rioting until 19 September.

8. An Irish drama by Dion Boucicault, revived at the Adelphi Theatre on 2 June.

9. George R. Sims and Henry Pettitt wrote several Adelphi melodramas, including *The Silver Falls*, in which William Terriss had been playing.

10. By Arthur Pinero.

also. I congratulate your brotherlet.[11] Does he make the shores of Bure re-echo to sweet melodies of Burmah? I suppose I had better cease this idle strain & go to my little pink couchlet. Keep me informed of your whereabouts. I foresee that the spirit will frequently move me to communicate with you tho' also I can say nothing to the purpose. Adieu. Au revoir

Ton Dévoué   ED

11. E. A. Moore (b. 1869) went up to Queen's in 1887 and was selected for the Indian Civil Service in the same year.

64. *To Arthur Moore*

Dimanche, 1 Septembre 1889

[*Woodford*]

Mon cher ami.

Merci—(no it's too much grind)—thanks for the letter. I respond at once & shall send this to Yarmouth tho' I gather that you may not be there till the week's end. I expect you have got all my effusions by this time with the exception of a couple of postcards which matter not. I hope to be off soon & await a wire telling me in what spot of England, Ireland or France I am to join my ship. I live otherwise only in the expectation of your return. Sam Smith & Swanton have turned up & have taken a flat together which they are now furnishing. I have knocked about with them *some* during the last week. Smith is exactly the same. Entre nous I am not altogether delighted with the prospect of their—or rather of Samuel's—becoming a permanent feature of the metrop. I dined with them & Martin[1] the other night at Previtalis. Martin is an awful wreck—we two, mon cher, are visions of radiant health in comparison. I haven't done much more to Chap III & think I must chuck it now until I have read your chapter. In the meantime I have been working away at "Mme de V." & hope to have it completed for your criticism by your return. I had a letter from Dornford[2] yesterday after more than a year's silence—so perhaps there is hope of Thomas.

The last three "Critics" have been simply triplicates to save expense until the Company is floated—Critic Press Lmtd of which prospectuses are out. This by the way in confidence. I like it not myself—& have

1. Probably J. P. Martin (b. 1864), who went up to Queen's in 1884.
2. Unidentified.

practically withdrawn from the concern—& look to my absence from London to complete the rupture without offence. They sent us tickets for the 2nd night of The Middleman to which I went with Williams. It's a fairly good play of the class romantic. Willard is a man of genius Maud[3] is too heavily weighted as the inevitable seduced maiden but Annie Hughes is delicious & I shall make a point of watching her career with interest. The weather here is exquisite & makes my mouth water for the Broadlets. I suppose I shall be just in time for a good old gale in the Irish Channel. I am sorry to see the Septr Macmillan doesn't include me. "Ludovicus" is off to Scott. I regret to say that owing to great slackness on the part of your unworthy collr it has not been gone very long. I enclose rather a quaint little leaflet wh. may amuse you. Chap ix is delightfully cynical. There are floods of letters which I meant to write to-day but I suppose that as usual they will not be written. This strike which is possibly over to-day has been something extraordinary. It has almost paralysed the river & if it goes on two or three days more there will be such a shindy as we have never had in London yet. I am going now to smoke a pipe, read a novel & lie in a large chair for several hours, when I shall go to bed. Adios. Write soon

Yrs ever   ERNEST DOWSON

Have been trying to indite you a "Ballade of the Norfolk Broads"— but the 3rd verse won't come[4] Shade of François Villon come to my aid.

3. Maud Millett.
4. This Ballade has not survived.

65. *To Arthur Moore*

8 [*actually 13*] September 1889

Bridge Dock

Chéri.

How art thou? Why was't thou not with us on Wed: night at Gall & afterwards at the Royal.—where we consumed many Lagers & disputed concerning many things. What of tomorrow? I shall endeavour to pass the après midi at the British Museum—at Desk I as I contemplate *faisant des économies* to pay my Doctor's bill. May I look for you there? Or if not where, when and to what end? If it is possible to let me know of these things: do so. If not try & turn in to the R.R of the B.M—some time after 2.0.

I intended going to Victoria this ~~afternoon~~ evening to see the last of

Ernest Dowson. From a drawing by William Rothenstein

Ernest Dowson, aged three,
photographed in Turin

▷
Ernest Dowson
and his group at
Queen's College, Oxford.
He is second from the
right, standing

Ernest Dowson
as an undergraduate.
The photograph is
inscribed to
William Theodore Peters
▷

Ernest Dowson in 1868,
aged nine months,
on his mother's lap

Ernest Dowson, and three friends at Queen's: from left to right,
Arthur Moore, W. R. Thomas, Dowson, P. L. Andrews

the noble Louis.[1] But Destiny in the shape of a furious & raging "head" has prevented me & purpose retiring immediately to a sofa at Wood-ford.

My editor is becoming too much for me: after the brief holiday which I had from him during his sojourn at Margate this week—he returns overwhelmingly. And I suffer—suffer—& foresee that either the Critic's death or my own must shortly ensue. Therefore "O subtle & sanguine Arturos"[2]—meet me to-morrow if you can & over the modest Lager & the pastoral pipe we will bewail the general grossness of vision especially of all editors & publishers and cry with one accord, pouring a libation of Bock—From Dry Docks and all that is connected with shipping, from all journalism, & from the fetters & service of the Law and from bloody London

Good Diabolus defend us.

Thine   E D .

1. Louis Bouthors, returning to France.
2. cf. Swinburne's *Dolores*.

66. *To Arthur Moore*

Sunday night [*22 September 1889*]

Yacht "Varani", Waterford, Ireland

Dear Moore.

I have meant to write to you frequently during the last week but—! It has been immensely jolly & I have been immensely slack & so I can only write now to announce my return which begins to-morrow. We have been cruising about the S of Ireland for the last week & I am entirely delighted with the counthry & the ghurls who are the most beautiful taking them all round of any that I have seen. Certainly I saw more pretty girls in Cork & Queenstown in one day than I have in England in the last year. Also are their curling eyelashes indescribable—& the brogue merely gives to most sweet voices the last piquant touch. We arrived here this evening after having been at sea 26 hours & as I cannot wait for the yacht which does not start for Falmouth till Tuesday I propose leaving here to-morrow at noon by the good s-s —— due to arrive at Fresh Wharf, London Bridge some time on Thursday.[1]

1. For his return journey see Letter 69. It seems that he did, after all, return via Falmouth.

May I hope to find a note from you arranging a rendez vous for Saturday afternoon at the Royal or the B.M? It is long since our horny hands grasped. Adios! I am going to have one more pipe on deck, do a pie in the "whiskers" & then turn in. Till Satdy.

Yrs ever ERNEST DOWSON

P S. Bethink thee of me the next two days on the wild ocean wave. I really don't care though if it is rough. I have so enjoyed the tossings about we have had on and off this week that I think even in a steamer now a calm would quite disgust me.

67. *To Arthur Moore*

Wednesday, 9 September [*actually October*] 1889

Bridge Dock

Cher Vieux.

Thy letter filled me with mingled joy & consternation. Forgive my slackness due to the unprecedented purpleness of my liver & nerves. Yes—I suppose I am now convalescent. Allons donc—ces barbares! Between the devil & the deep sea—the Tweedy & the hospitable flat Hildreth, Diane et Cie seem likely to languish.[1] N'importe—a time will come. In the mean time how about a junction of forces on Satdy?— always supposing—in my case at least—"que l'estomac soit en état". Perhaps—or rather—certainly I shall see you before that—at 6.0— tomorrow? However everything lies on the knees of the gods! Sufficient for the day is the whiskey thereof. Good old Bedford! Good old Supper Club! Good old Exposition des Vices![2] As you remark with such truth & fervour the only end *is* death"! All the same, though its a fearful drain on the constitution "Our Flat"[3] is an amazing funny institution: you must really give it a look in.

I foresee that we shall have to meet at B.D after all—but when? Name your own day next week & if I am alive—! Don't go to "A Man's Shadow"[4] without me—that's all. Damn! I think I must be getting softening of the brain. These are parlous days. By the by that

---

1. Tweedy was now in London, taking up Moore's time, while Dowson spent his mostly with Smith and Swanton at their flat at 4 Museum Mansions, Bloomsbury.
2. See note 2 to following letter, No. 68.
3. An allusion to the farce by Mrs. Musgrave, which opened at the Prince of Wales on 13 June 1889.
4. Opened at the Haymarket Theatre, 12 September.

Roundel I sent you has been taken by Temple Bar.[5] Acceptable guinea!—when it comes. I am many months ahead of my income. Allons—allons—we must really meet once more before our last lucid interval is over. I date mine—at this rate—in about one week's time. Give my love to Tweedledum—or Tweedledee—wh: is it? but not to both—& tell him that it will give me delight to press his honest hand. For the present adios—au revoir. Keep me informed of your movements—as I will do thee of mine—even if we can't rencontrer & let us pray that this tyranny may eventually be overpast. Thine, in luctu et squalore

AN F... O.. BINGER.

5. See Letter 63 and note.

68. *To Arthur Moore*

Wednesday morning [*16 October 1889*]

Bridge Dock

Lugete

Cher Vieux. Woe! Woe! Woe! Alas! Eheu! Sacré nom de Dieu d'une bordel!—Your letter is the one & only consolation which has come to me for many returning days. What I wish to remark is—when will this tyranny be overpast? Tweedy told me last night that his stay in town was "indefinite"—O Lord! Samuel is apparently a permanency. O Lord! O my liver! O my nerves! O my poor blasted constitution! I am getting to such a state of chronic insobriety that even the morning after my legs—as now—are tottering. The only thing that preserves my reason is this futile attempt at an epistle. I am *so* largely with you re. Music Halls. They are unutterable.—Algernon, Algernon, wherefore are we thus? Confirmed sleepiness has fastened its fangs on me. I drivel but I am awake. Yes—I will one day soon stay my tremulous course outside No 7[1]—& we will absinthe—be it never so deleterious. What is one more drink among so many?

1. i.e. Lincoln's Inn Fields.

D——. it is an awfully weird feeling to feel as drunk as I do now at 11.30 AM. who have been binging cold water all the morning. Finish the chapter & write to me. *Above all write to me.* To find an epistle awaiting me when as this morning I have dragged my weary & jaded way from Gt Russell St about 10. AM. having been to bed at 6. is the first gleam of the sun.—Good old duel à la whiskè. But I should have put my money on Thomas. In lager I can understand their spoofment but—whiskè!!!!!!!!!!!!!!!! I fear to-night will again see me on the war path. Mercifully my little sample with Swanton of an exhibition in a purlieu of Leicester Square so absolutely sickened me with the feminine nudity that my debauchery hasn't since extended beyond the bottle.[2] But this cannot possibly go on for ever! Come & stay with me soon—else shalt thou follow me to Woking[3] only—a callid porpse. I'm becoming more mixed every moment.

I've been kissing my hand aimlessly from the window to une petite demoiselle of my acquaintance—also par exemple a Minnie & presque aussi gentille as her prototype. This has temporarily revived me. I will shortly have breakfast. Whiskey is unsatisfying to me—phiz is the most god-forsaken beverage that was ever created.—bah.—there is nothing in the universe supportable save the novels of Hy. James, & the society of little girls. Music halls are all that you say of them—the woman of Leicester Square is a beast—the Woman of Society is unmentionable—the Grisette is a fraud.—whiskey is also a fraud & phiz a poison in addition. Nay—as I have remarked before—the idea of the little girl is the only one which doesn't make for bloodiness.

Excuse this awful drivel I must be drunk still I think. O God—I dine with Lefroy to-night. Perhaps we meet at the Cri[4]—before you get this—O God—Prince of P.mp Sh.p! Ugh!—

Good-bye—au revoir. Bethink thee of coming to stay with me. If you don't come this next Sunday I shall be in Gt Russell St & perhaps you will call in in the afternoon Sunday & breakfast with us? However we shall doubtless meet at Philippi. Au revoir

Thine in consumption, general debility, delirium, enlargement of the liver, & tears

THE MOST WRETCHED BINGER
WHO EVER GAVE THE SHIFTER POINTS
Write.

P.S. Get me that plaque of Minnie if you see it.

2. Baedeker's *Guide to London* at this time warned visitors of dubious establishments in this area.
3. The Crematorium.
4. The Criterion, Piccadilly Circus.

69. *To Arthur Moore*
18 October 1889

Woodford

Cher Algernon.

I didn't mean to inflict on you a reply to your last most acceptable effusion at once but I perceive you mention "Looking Backwards"[1] I write to save your life. *Don't* DON'T, DON'T read that most . . . . of shockers. I bought it at Truro coming up the G. WR lately & before I got to Plymouth it had retired out of the window. It isn't a shocker—its a dreary fraud—it's J. A Fallows at 5st 7lb. Verb. sap. To continue—you really *must* come down on Sat. next. I insist—in fact I can't admit an excuse. To begin with—I haven't seen you for a blue moon & I want a large dose of your society to take the taste of the infinite bloodiness of the last fortnight out of my mouth—2nd My worthy sire retiring on that day (the 25th) also till Monday, I under solemn bond & vow to remain at Woodford with my mama. 3rd but after all 2 good reasons are good enough. Woodford on Sunday is only endurable when it is fortified by congenial society. Ergo come—come! Come.

Thanks for the plaque[2]—I will fetch it as soon as I am next in town —at present I feel as if that would be never. Let me know the wash however whether I turn up or not. I was beginning to pine for another picture & this will content me till the new Haymarket photos[3] are out.—Yes we will go to the Gaiety[4]—but not yet. By the by I hope I was not grossly rude to the Tweedle who looked me up at BD ~~the other day~~ yesterday—I did my best to enthuse over him but my health had suffered from three Bloomsbury nights running & there must have been intervals of very depressing silence. I suppose you have seen him since? One would that all these aliens would take to themselves wings of the doves—but Smith is a fixture at any rate for all this term, & Tweedy from what he tells me, is a six monther. With regard to movements—I feel inclined (for the moment) to lie very low. But life is strange—& I may still muster heart to turn up in Bloomsbury to-morrow night. But oh me! oh me! I tremble at the thought of my liver & the period of frightful & unprecedented ooflessness which cometh. By the by it was Leeson[5] who asked me to tell you about the Grosvenor.[6] I am ashamed to say that I haven't seen Williams or produced a

1. By Edward Bellamy (1850–1898), American novelist, 1887.
2. See PS. to Letter 68.
3. Of Minnie Terry in *A Man's Shadow*.
4. *Ruy Blas or the Blasé Roué.*
5. Probably M. R. Leeson-Marshall (1859–1939), at this time in chambers in the Inner Temple.
6. The Grosvenor Club, which Dowson joined in 1891.

line of copy for the bally rag for 3 weeks! When we meet I have many adventures to tell you of—some assez saugrenues. But enough—enough—perhaps we had better draw a veil over τα ἀπόντα[7] (?)—I enclose you the latest Minnie Terrianum in my collection—which kindly return. Send the novel—write—come to B D—*above all* come here next Satdy & smoke a sad smoke & binge a lemonade & water with all that is left of your devoted

ALPHONSE-ADOLFE

P.S. I go to read "Le Lys dans la Vallée" (Balzac) & a very bad shocker "The Boy Princes".[8] Adieu. I think I must have a shot at the enclosed genre of versifying. I know Macmurdo. Horne[9] I have not yet met but have heard a lot of. He edits the Hobby now. I don't know Randall Davies[10] but seem to know the name well though I can't connote it. Have you seen "The Germ"?[11]

How about the new "Arts & Letters Club"?[12]

---

7. What is absent.
8. *The Boy-Princes, or Scions of Royalty cut off in Youth*, by J. G. Edgar, 1857.
9. Arthur Heygate Mackmurdo (1851–1942), was an eminent architect who in 1882 gathered round him a group of craftsmen, called the Century Guild, so that together they could undertake the whole construction and decoration of a building. In this group Selwyn Image was responsible for stained glass. Mackmurdo founded a periodical, *The Century Guild Hobby Horse*, in 1884 to express the ideas of this group. Herbert Horne (1864–1916) in 1881 asked Mackmurdo to give him instruction in ornamental design and in 1885 they became partners. In 1890 the partnership was dissolved. *The Century Guild Hobby Horse* continued until 1892; then Horne and Image took it over and produced three issues, as *The Hobby Horse*, to which Dowson made a number of important contributions. Horne was by inclination a writer and art critic; Professor Saxl has described him as 'perhaps the most accomplished historian of art this country [Britain] has produced'.
10. Art critic (1866–1946).
11. A short-lived periodical published by Rossetti in 1850.
12. Dowson joined this club in 1890.

70. *To Arthur Moore*
  [*c. 21 October 1889*]

Woodford

Cher Vieux
  Eheu! Eheu! Let me send you a line before I fall into a little pink slumber. Actually I am going very shortly (about 9.30 I guess) to sleep in my own bed. O God—but Tweedy of Barts[1] is an aI almond poor sight, I don't think . . . . Enough. We really must meet soon. Our meeting on Satdy night was very sad. It seemeth to me on the whole that our glass is well nigh run. Will you come down here from Satdy to Monday—next or the next after as may suit you best? It will delight me—need I say—& possibly prolong my life—as otherwise I shall be reduced to Gt Russell St with its many exhausting—tho' I admit agreeable accompaniments. Come, if you can. We have arrears of conversation & literary projection to make up. Then there's the Haymarket.[2] By the bye—I had a delightful glimpse of Mignon this afternoon from Plarrs window. She was disporting herself in a superb way in Gt Russell St—hatless & in a "pinny" with a diminutive sister (?) in her arms, sporting with the bambina of an Italian organ woman. We threw pennies & chocolate down to the bambina & to our great delight Minnie Terry collected them & handed them on. It was a delightful picture & restored my equilibrium vastly. Allons donc—I wish these TweedlecumSamuelses[3] would aroint them & allow us to possess our souls in peace. Write to me O Alphonse the Great & Good: tell me of the state of thy liver & thy soul. Also—where—oh where is Ludovicus to go to? Tomorrow I go with one Walton[4] to "Caste".[5] We dine at Pinolis:—if you feel inclined to join us———? I am reading Le Rouge et Le Noir—(Stendhall)—several Balzacs & a Turgénev,— writing nothing—not even roundels. I am very slack, very sleepy— (last night to bed 5. AM up 8.30 AM—Satdy 6 AM, up 11 AM—Thurs 4.30 up 8.30) but tolerably fit otherwise. Good night—good night— good night. *Write.*
  Tout à vous   EDOUARD ARMAND GUSTAVE DE POLISSON—
                                        DEMI MORT-IVRE

1. C. W. Tweedy's younger brother Reginald (1868–1917). He became a doctor and practised in Kenilworth.
2. *A Man's Shadow.*
3. Tweedy and Sam Smith.
4. F. W. Walton, later librarian of King's College, London. He and Plarr were joined by Dowson in the task of annotating Olive Schreiner's *The Story of an African Farm,* see Plarr's *Ernest Dowson,* p. 42.
5. *Caste* by T. W. Robertson, revived at the Criterion Theatre on 5 October.

71. *To Arthur Moore*
[*27 October 1889*]

Woodford

No 999   Special Sunday Edition   1ᴰ
                   The Desultory Driveller

Cher Vieux.

Delighted to hear of your recovery wh. is, I hope, decisive. also to receive Chap II which has one fault only its length—& that I hope to see rectified in an early installment. It is really though extremely good & plunges me into despair when I compare my own abortive IIIrd which is really deucedly difficult & wh. I have already begun 3 times on totally different lines.

Thanks for your notes. I am obliged for you suggestion—but fear that I have still a soul above tractlets or else—am too far gone. I did not know you were *en evidence* last week or would have made a pilgrimage to your bedside. Please accept the will for the deed. When shall we meet again . .? Are you equal to Bridge Dk.? Any evening this week is for your choice—given 24 hours notice. Beverages—weak whiskey & water or milk & soda. Also the Haymarket? . . These things I leave to you: all volition has absolutely departed from me . . . So there is a choice of plaques? Methinks I cannot run to 2! Ergo, if you will guide me one evening to the window in which they are displayed —perhaps I shall be able to summon up energy for the selection. Yes— that will be best—for we positively *must* meet one evening this week— neither as mules nor muleteers. There are 3 *romans* I want you to read & shall make you cart away with you on an early occasion. (i) Le Rouge et Le Noir—Stendhal (ii) Premier Amour. Turgénef. iii—Le Lys dans La Vallée. Balzac.—The last author I am reading systematically & I have discovered that he is really very great. Methinks also that the three above-named masters are responsible for the evolution of Hy James. The poem from The Globe is, I agree with you "drivel".[1] If the execution however is inferior the impulse is praiseworthy. When are you going to call upon The FLAT? On the whole I have been agreeably surprised as regards Samuel. Whether he has acquired more tolerance, or that I with increase of slackness have gained in amiability, I know not, but undoubtedly, intercourse with him is cosier. You must certainly come to Gt Russell St—it is an institution worth of study. But let us meet first in some less fervid atmosphere—for I have much to say concerning Hildreth et Cie, I apologize for the absolute triviality of this letter. In effect I hardly know what I write. I can only imagine from the chaotic state of my brain that paralysis has actually com-

1. Anonymous political doggerel by members of *The Globe* editorial staff.

menced. Come to the Dock if you can, or Pinolis—or here?—the first or last in preference. But n'more! ἅλις, Adieu.

always yours   ERNEST DOWSON.

Fancy the Cambridgeshire!!!!!![2] Write!

2. Run at Newmarket on 24 October and won by Laureate, an outsider.

72. *To Arthur Moore*
    31 October 1889

Bridge Dock

Chéri.

Thanks for yours. Also for Chap IIB. You will by this time have recvd Chap III B. Don't let it startle *you* into a premature grave. Emend it all you can—a lot more than Chap I at any rate. Your letter depressed me—but I will try & live till next week. Satdy I go to a matinée of Minnie T. with Williams so may not see you—but also may. Go to the Leicester Sq. place on the chance. Afterwards I am due at the Flat. To-night I also purpose spending at the Flat.

I saw Williams this afternoon at the Kettledrum.[1] He told me of your praiseworthy industry & incited by it I have weakly promised to "do" Emile Augier's funeral for to-morrow.[2] As you remark this *is* a purple world. Yes—your letter depressed me! Don't let it occur again. The chapter though worked the other way. Parts of it are brilliant—& the Princess is really an admirable study. I know her so well. Keep up to it & I will do my best also. Slack & I shall get slack. But we mustn't get slack. Won't you join the "Arts & Letters"? I have sent in my application, the prospectus was attractive. There are to be 500 original members at £6.6. Arthur Severn the artist is my sponsor.[3] You ought to join. Forms (to be had of A. E. Bright Secty. 37 Albermarle St. Picadilly) must be sent in by Nov. 4th.

No more now. I am just getting rather drunk—or sober—I'm not sure which. Write soon

Yrs always   ADOLF, GUSTAVE DE L'ASSOMMOIR.

1. Probably the Kettledrum Tearooms in New Bond Street.
2. *The Nobility of Art in Death* appeared in *The Critic* for 2 November. It is reprinted in Appendix A.
3. Arthur Severn (1842–1931), the son of Keats's friend Joseph Severn. He exhibited regularly at the Academy and in Paris.

PS. Read "Pastels" 10 Portraits de Femmes par P. Bourget. C'est de l'oeuvre!

PS 2 I will treat your complaint as in the strictest confidence & the more easily as I have not yet grasped its precise nature—but gather that it is venereal? Or is it—no—is it—no—not Crustacean!!![4]

P.S. 4. Was it the issue of the railway carriage p—ke? Fi donc! Shocquing!

4. Presumably 'crabs'.

73. *To Arthur Moore*

     7 [*actually 9*] November 1889, 3 p.m.

                          Middlesex Hospital College

Cher Alphonse.

Lefroy is dressing. Methinks I will wile away the hour of his toilette by a fragment of the Special Sunday. Your letter cheered me greatly. It dissipated the aftermath—more or less—of last night au Bedford. To come to your epistle

(i) Bernard Shaw *is* on the "Star".[1] i.e. I only accept your statement with explanations.
(ii) I am going to send you another cartload
(iii) Mind you do send it
(iv) Hear hear (v) Good—There is a biography of Minnie Terry in this month's "Theatre", containing also a photo which I had before. It bears out my repeated assertion to sceptics concerning la chère petites age. She was born in the Gironde Jan 1. 1882.

     I am dining to-night with Samuel at a Polish Pot au Feu in Sherwood St, Glasshouse St. Soho.[2] I discovered it. It is cheap; the cuisine is fair; I am the whole clientele, and there is a little Polish demoiselle[3] therein (Minnie at 5st 7—no not quite that—whom it is a pleasure to sit & look at. Excuse hopeless grammar. I know not of the rag, altho'

1. Shaw was music critic of *The Star* 1888–1890 under the pseudonym of Corno di Bassetto.
2. The first reference to the restaurant run by Joseph Foltinowicz in Sherwood Street which in subsequent letters he generally calls 'Poland'.
3. Adelaide Foltinowicz ('Missie') (1878–1903), the proprietor's daughter.

there was some thing which I wrote for it—at the Governor's request—
which I wanted to appear—a fulsome panegyric of "Wanted a Wife"
writ by a pal of his & produced on Monday at Edinburgh.⁴ I think
however it is dead. I am glad at the 11th hour I did *not* put any money
on the L'pool C—as I should have done but for an accident. I was
going on Quartus.⁵ By the by—mark that horse & when he runs next
plump on him with all your available capital. Verb Sap. This tip I may
add doesn't come from Museum Mansions but from a man who spotted
Primrose Day for the C'wtch. I am taking my mater one day next week
to see Minnie—but any night bar Wednesday I will dine & theatrize
with you. I went to the Savoy⁶ on the night I saw you—I believe I
and not mine astral came but it was a spectral interview as you say.
I meditate on *the* opus & will continue when—thou slacker—Chap III
returns. In the meantime I work on a little study of the over critical
man and an amourette.⁷ Write to me soon, & remember that tho' the
heavens fall etc we *must must, must* meet next week.

   Goodbye. I go to enter into temptation. Eheu. Adieu

thine ED.

I have just upset the ink. Lefroy curseth.

4. By J. H. Darnley, produced at the Theatre Royal, Edinburgh, on 4
   November.
5. Quartus was struck out of the Liverpool Cup at 12.15 on the day of the
   race.
6. *The Yeoman of the Guard.*
7. *The Story of a Violin*, printed in *Macmillan's Magazine*, August 1891.

74. *To Arthur Moore*
    [*11 November 1889*]

Bridge Dock

Cher Algernon,
   So sorry to hear of your new complications of complaints. The world
is decidedly pea green. I write with this promptitude because in your
eagerly received instalment of this morning you enclose a blank sheet—
& methinks you may have made a mistake. Explain! . . . Yes the Lord
Mayorlet's Tom Foolery was a nuisance.¹ I spoofed it successfully by

1. The Lord Mayor's Show that year celebrated the seven-hundredth anniversary of the Mayoralty of London and there was a procession from the
   City to Charing Cross on 9 November.

going from Limehouse to Bloomsbury by tram. My Satdy night was like yours a wet 'un—but praise the gods my virtue didn't suffer as much as my liver. I will come & see you any evening next week you name—social functions barred—an' you care to see me, & can not come here or elsewhere. This long abstinence from you is preying on my constitution, & is distinctly bad for Diana. I have however rather a large faith in time. You must certainly come to Folitsocxs² with me. The place is unpretending but less grimy than the "Pot au Feu" & perfectly deserted. One dines there well for about 1/5 inclusive. By the by I have une *petite affaire* on hand which promises some amusement at any rate. The tart is aged 15¾ & belongeth to a tobacconist of Picadilly who apparently views his paternal responsibilities lightly. The circumstances *attending* the origin of our acquaintance I will tell you some other time.—She hath the *torso* of seventeen, at least, and wonderfully fine eyes—she has vouchsafed me a rendezvous for Sunday, when I tea with her at the Abode of Prophecy (No 4. M M)³ and for Satdy when I take her to a theatre. I have also made lavish vows of correspondence & am now contemplating an effusion,—a task of some difficulty. I confess I have not quite grasped the situation. How does it strike you? The name, I may mention is Bertha Van Raalte!!!!! May I hope to see you at the Mansions on Sunday afternoon & submit the demoiselle to your psychologia? Enough however of this paradox. I was very much annoyed about *Quartus* but—"I'll have him by & bye".⁴—also Goldseeker. What is your tip for the M'ter November H.? Well, we are all mules or muleteers. Good old Tweedy—give him my blessing. I wasn't in bed all last night but started from Bloomsbury at about 8.30 A M—after rather a moist night. We all—Smith especially— got sublimely drunk & then divinely sober without sleeping at all—a phenomenon which has only occurred once before with me. Write.

                                        Yrs ever   E D

2. The Foltinowicz restaurant.
3. Sam Smith's flat at 4 Museum Mansions.
4. An allusion to one of Lonnen's most successful songs in *Faust Up-to-date*.

75. *To Arthur Moore*
   16 [*and 18*] November 1889

                                        Bridge Dock

Mon cher Vieux.
   Your letter greatly cheered me—especially by the hope it held out of a meeting at Philippi. Soit! Next Wednesday let it be. I answer

now ∴ I shall be spending the next 40 hours or so in Flatland & I may be prevented of the S'nday edtn. What, I wonder dost thou to-day? I shall probably, as I did last Satdy, play about 600 of Bigliardo with Lefroy.

There is no doubt that the Van Raalte in question is a scion of *the* V.R. Perhaps I gave you a wrong impression of the worthy man. He may be a doting parent for all I know, he is at least an inefficient duenna. I had an epistle from Fraulein Van Raalte yesterday which was most quaint & touching & in such a superior school-girl-hand.

You are perhaps right in being "off" Gortsachoff's[1] though the cooking is less deleterious than Pinolis. But the environment—with the exception of Minnie Terry—would depress you. Let it be for a later day. What shall we do afterwards par exemple? A theatre? I think the Critic is dead—but haven't seen the Bad Man for a fortnight or more. I blush at the thought of Ludovicus. There has been no morning for the last two months on which I have not risen vowing to dispatch Him. Simple slackness alone has prevented me. It shall I swear go to somebody on Monday. I will refrain from speaking of the Opus novissimum until I see you. Ye gods what of the Manchester Nov.[2] I have been tipped (i) Lady Roseberry (ii) Goldseeker (iii) Phil—(by you). (iv) Mercy (v) Rêve d'Or.

At present I contemplate 5/- apiece on Goldseeker & Mercy for a win & 5/- on each for a place. But then, Phil? And I should dearly like to be on Vasistas. Why shouldn't that superior filly redeem herself at the last? Fletcher[3] of Queens is staying at the Flat to eat his dinners . . . . .

MONDAY

Just back from Bloomsbury—in a more or less dilapidated condi-tion—varying this time from forlorn liver to a dog bite on my lip & a Jemsmithian ear[4] from a drunken brawl! on Satdy night. I look for-ward to Wednesday however.—Last night we had rather a quaint hour or so: I had an appointment with Miss Cigarettovitch at 6.0 & as she turned up with a girl of Swanton's acquaintance, we repaired after an interval at the Anglo-Austrian to number 4—which had been previously cleared of the profane. Then the 4 of us, Swanton, Bertha, the 2nd damigellina & myself spent a most profitable & platonic evening on the sofa, "each with each", until 10 o'clock & the entrance of Smith & Co routed us. I must certainly show you my latest Amaryllis. I am going

---

1. i.e. Foltinowicz's.
2. The Manchester November Handicap was run on 23 November. The only successful horse fancied by Dowson was Phil, which came in third; the rest were nowhere.
3. E. E. Fletcher, b. 1869. Went up to Queen's College, Oxford, in 1887. Called to the Bar (Lincoln's Inn) in 1892.
4. Jem Smith, the famous prize-fighter; hence, a cauliflower ear.

to take her to the "Savoy" on Thursday or Friday. Good old Van Raalte. But enough of this perfunctation for which I apologize. Write & let me know where to meet you & what you propose doing.

Yrs ever   ERNEST DOWSON

76. *To Arthur Moore*
26 November 1889

Bridge Dock

WRITE SOON

Mon cher.

Many thanks for yours & apologies for the non-arrival of my own special Sunday. The spirit truly was willing but the hand was shaky. I saw you & Tweedy by the by on Sat'dy aftn'n when I was having tea with my mater in Gattis—even as in a procession you passed through the good old Adelaide[1] until the throng received you out of our sight. How did *you* like the Haymarket? *We* were badly spoofé as for Miss Minnie Terry the play bill contained the name of Miss Dorothy Harwood. The latter is a very clever little girl but she is not pretty & she is not *mignonne* & my mater & I were both extremely bored by the play in consequence. I am glad you were not too depressed by the flat. Perchance we shall meet there again? re Van Raalte—I fancy that it has begun to pall. We spent a somewhat monotonous evening on Thursday & after I had sat for some two hours & a half on the sofa with my arm round the waist of the demoiselle & Lefroy ditto with his—we agreed that in view of the new act[2] le jeu ne valait etc. And as we neither of us kept an appointment which we had made on Sunday evening with them & haven't written to explain since I guess the thing is off.

Have you read La Bête Humaine[3] yet? I am anxiously looking forward to it.

re. R.O.[4]

I believe we agreed (i) that I was to go on writing retrospect, bringing in Oxbridge (ii) that you were to go on writing Chapters like Chapter 2 (iii) that Elsie (cf Pansy "Portrait of a Lady"[5]) is stepdaughter of Diana (iv) that you were to invent a plot. (v) both parties

---

1. Gatti's restaurant was in the Adelaide Galleries.
2. The Criminal Law Amendment Act of 1885 raised the age of consent from thirteen to sixteen. Until 1875 it had been twelve.
3. By Zola. The first edition is dated 1890, but the book must have been announced and expected in the latter part of 1889.
4. The abbreviation is mysterious, though here and in the next letters it clearly stands for *Felix Martyr*.
5. By Henry James, 1881.

to hurry up I am really going to stay at home this week & nurse myself & go on with the Opus—& shun the "bitter delights of the" flat, & try & reduce my tongue to a decent size & a colour a few shades less lurid than it is at present. I will send you the result some time soon or better still if you can meet me Saturday aftn'n will bring it with you & matinize. As the Critic I hear is not dead but has "turned the corner"— I am expecting seats. It will outlive us, *mon cher* that evil sheet, depend upon it. Eh bien—for the present adieu. The governor is away— things are slack—I propose to sit in front of the fire for the rest of the day, slack, sleep & read Stendhal. Write.

always thine   E D

PS. When will you dine at Kossuth's with me?

"Ludovicus" has gone to Chatto & Windus. How will enclosed advt do for next time?

77. *To Arthur Moore*
29 November 1889

Bassin du Pont

Cher Alphonse.

A line to acknowledge yours. I shall probably be out of town to-morrow & (certainly) Sunday otherwise I would try & meet you after your theatre which is I presume la Gaité.[1] If I am still in Babylon I shall go to see the last of the "Yeomen of the G"[2] I shall be delighted to squat beneath your mahogany *any* day next week so far as I know at present—unless the beastly catarrh which shivers my handkfs at present seriously increases. However advise me of this at your leisure. I have been thinking of the R.O. but have done nought further yet— chiefly ∵ I have been busily engaged on the "Study" whereof I told you & which should-be finished to-night. I will send it to you as soon as it is f. c'd for your criticism & suggestion for title & destination. At present I contemplate "Murrays", "English Illtd" or "Blackwoods". Hoping to see you soon. I will write shortly.

always yrs   E D.

PS. I have been such a good boy all this week—off alcohol & beer—off pastry (fig) not up in Flatland since Sunday & writing hard all the week. "So there"! Love to Tweedie.

1. *Ruy Blas or the Blasé Roué.*
2. 30 November.

78. *To Arthur Moore*
    24 December [*1889*], 12.30

                                                     Woodford

From Ernest Christopherovitch the slack man to Arthur Moorevitch the Parkplace vilain with all good wishes for this most melancholy season—Greeting!
Mon cher vieux: I am sorry for the unprecedented length of my silence. Ma chè vuole? I have been a prey to my d——d, vacillating inability to come to a decision since we had that charming—always-to-be-delightfully-recollected evening. And finally I have decided—& wrote yestereen to CHS. to cry off.[1] Eheu inertiam! I have racked my brains in vain to work the scheme with my people's connivance & I fear that my present relations are too strained to permit me to carry it out without—i.e. without risking the total cutting off of supplies. And now I have neither the energy nor the courage to contemplate the winning of "the wages of going on & not to die" by any other process than that of sitting, sitting, sitting. I fear it must be Bridge Dock ad infinitum. Well so much the more time for Hildreth, Martyr et Cie. I can, now the roulette idea is settled, give all the more time to those eminent people & I hope within a day or two to send you the result of my cogitations. Come back though soon to your old habitations even to the ~~square~~ fields of Mesech, & let us Haymarket & Gaietieize & and Polandize to the end of our days. It is written so! I have been to the Gondoliers[2] to-night with Smith & Lefroy. It is clever—witty—musical—the scenery is charming—the dresses are all that could be desired—& the general impression, at least on me, was unsatisfactory in the extreme. It is certainly inferior to the Mikado—Patience—& Ruddigore—to say nothing of the Yeomen. And bien sur in the whole score there is nothing so deliciously brimming over with melody as the "Sing me your song oh!" Last night—lo what a theatrist I am becoming—I went to Benson's "Midsummer Night's Dream".[3] Very little Shakespere—very much Mendelsohn is my criticism—with a rider however to the effect that if one must have Shakespeare diluted I prefer Benson's dilution to that fool Irving's.—However the theatre is a great resource, Nothing has been more cheering to me than the sudden resurrection of my delight in the play, which I feared a month or so back had become finally a weariness to the flesh of me. I am becoming once more a whale at it & intend to continue so to do. See the advisability of going through

1. C. H. Swanton had apparently suggested that Dowson should join in some kind of gambling venture which would have involved his absence from Bridge Dock.
2. *The Gondoliers* opened at the Savoy Theatre on 7 December.
3. Opened at the Globe Theatre on 19 December.

a course of London Music Halls! Bar burlesque & Penleyan[4] comedy I am becoming tolerant of this insipid British drama. Even bad melo doesn't cause me to vomit as it did of old.

To return to our muttons—come back to Babylon & we will

(i)   dine in Poland.—?—

N.B. I dine there every night now & little Mdlle de Poland is beginning to greet me with a smile.

(ii) go to Ruy Blas—

(iii) go to A Man's Shadow

(iv) dine at the Arts & Letters.

N.B. This is contingent on the arrival of sundry Xmas pourboires from sundry Aunts which will probably not come. Parenthetically let me also remark that the said A & L is the dreariest, most sombre, respectable, Philistine, solemn & depressing institution in London. Still we will haply sample it—moral—A bohemian should no more think of belonging to a club than of taking to himself a wife!

(v) Do some Pantomimes via. Herbert Williams.

(vi) Swear solemnly by the bones of Aeneas NEVER to go to that bad show of Barnum's.[5]

N.B. Ugh!

(vii) develop *Felix Martyr* (This is also a no I—feature of the programme).

(viii) Do a Bridge Dk. Slack.

ix—? La Tosca.[6]

x. The Middleman.

Of good truth thse Xmas mock-merry makings about take the cake for pure a I almond spirit-shakers! Would they & the d——d indigestions they ensure were over. I fly away from them immediately after early dinner to-morrow & remain with Smith, "Blafonski"[7] & Co. until Thursday. But I fear I shall not even so escape the general depression. I hope you are sharing it. Why—oh why—haven't we done away with anniversaries—Why do we have watches or clocks or hours at all—at all?—I believe—en passant—that I have trapped the influenza! Well—well pardon this fooling & write soon & copiously. Methinks I will swear off wine & women & weeds & late hours & confine myself to the writing of the r.o, & the cult of Minnie Terry. Otherwise there is no balsam in Gilead![8] Quels miserable fools of fortune we are! Why can't

4. W. S. Penley was an actor appearing at that time in *Penelope*, a musical comedy at the Comedy Theatre. Later he scored a great success in *Charley's Aunt*.
5. At Olympia.
6. Adapted from Sardou by F. C. Grove and Henry Hamilton, produced at the Garrick Theatre on 28 November with Mrs. Bernard Beere, Lewis Waller and Forbes Robertson in the cast.
7. Probably a nickname for Swanton.
8. Cf. Jeremiah viii. 22.

we accept the beastly limitations of our cursed existence—or if not, score off nature in the only way that is final—by the happy despatch. Shall we write a novel—the study of a man *two-sided,* i.e. by temperament etc, humanus, pleasure loving, keenly sensible to artistic impressions, & to the outward & visible beauty of life—& ~~equally by temperament etc~~ at the same time morbidly conscious of the inherent grossness & futility of it all—& so trace the struggle between his sensibility & his fanaticism—until the latter has spoilt the whole of art & nine tenths of life for him, & made him either a suicide, a madman or simply a will-less, disgustful, drunken debauchee. I don't see any other possible dénouement for our novel. Well—write soon.

always yours   ERNEST DOWSON.

79. *To Arthur Moore*
Dimanche [*29 December 1889*]

Woodford

Mon cher Vieux

What news of thee, thou unconscionable? I alas—am in the same case with the King of Portugal, the Czar, Randy & other crowned heads—though by a singular oversight the daily press does not publish bulletins of me.[1] Since Xmas day I have been prostrate with Russian influenza alias grippe & know not yet whether I am out of the wood. I trust that you are not in like case? Write speedily to inform me thereof or give an account of your silence. Yes: la grippe has gripped me & I stay here wrapped in tarpaulin jackets, consuming handkerchiefs by the score & reading all the trash the Woodford Cirng Library contains. I prithee write. Quelle sacrée climate. Are you back in the triste metrop yet? I can't compose my mind to the manufacture of fiction but can only peruse it. Goodbye Sweetheart[2]—that silly, sentimental, unwholesome, readable book I have just read again—also Dust by J. Hawthorne[3] which is Besant-ly—a Gaboriau[4] or 2—and now I am tackling Dr Paulus.[5] How my soul abhors the blatant good-humoured, self-

1. An influenza epidemic raged throughout late December and early January. *The Times* on 26 December reported that the King of Portugal and the Tsar were ill, but 'Randy' is mysterious. There is no record of Lord Randolph Churchill being ill at this time.
2. By Rhoda Broughton, 1872.
3. Published 1883.
4. Emile Gaboriau (1835–1873), the originator of the modern detective novel.
5. *Herr Paulus* by Walter Besant, 1888.

satisfaction of Besant & his school. I think I must read L'Immortel[6]—over again for a change. I know not when I shall be let out again. When I am we must meet. *Write soon*

Yrs   E D.

6. By Daudet, 1888.

Part II
1890-1892

THE early years of the eighteen-nineties were the best of Dowson's life. Eighteen-eighty-nine had seen him settling into the rather dismal routine of Bridge Dock and escaping from it into dissipations that were harmless but wasted his time, while his efforts in literature brought him little success; talented though he was, by the end of that year he had written only one poem that he thought good enough to include when he collected his work in *Verses* in 1896.

His life in the next few years showed no great outward change, but he was settling down, seeing less of his wilder friends among the medical students, making new ones among his intellectual equals, and writing with a far surer touch. Perhaps the most important development was his growing friendship with the young poets who formed the Rhymers' Club. The Club owed its existence largely to the enthusiasm of Lionel Johnson and W. B. Yeats. Johnson, whom Dowson had known slightly at Oxford, came down from the university in June 1890 with a great reputation as scholar and critic and took up residence with Horne, Mackmurdo and the other disciples of the *Hobby Horse* in Fitzroy Street. He and Dowson soon became close friends. Both were passionately interested in literature and shared similar tastes, including one for conversation late at night. Like Yeats, Dowson held Johnson in some awe and paid great regard to his opinions.

The Rhymers' Club began meeting regularly, about once a month, early in 1891, usually at the Cheshire Cheese in Fleet Street, and offered its members a sympathetic and discerning audience for their work. Dowson was a frequent contributor and his work became well known among his friends for some time before it was published. He disliked reading aloud, and whenever he could he would persuade someone else to read his verses for him. Other members whose work survives include Arthur Symons, John Gray and John Davidson. Wilde was an occasional visitor, and the American W. T. Peters, for whom Dowson wrote *The Pierrot of the Minute*, was among the small group of 'permanent guests'. In the summer of 1891 plans were made for the publication of a joint volume of verse, in which each member was entitled to be represented by a maximum of six poems. G. A. Greene was the secretary of the club and the organizers were Yeats and Lionel Johnson, with a good deal of help from Dowson. There was an editorial committee on which Greene, Lionel Johnson, Le Gallienne, Todhunter and Dowson were included. By the autumn most of the material for the book was collected and Yeats wrote to Elkin Mathews on 12 November:

> Dear Mr. Mathews,
> Lionel Johnson, George Greene and myself, three members of the Rhymers' Club, wish to see you about the publishing of "The Book of the Rhymers' Club" (a volume of poems by the members) and propose to call on you next Monday about 3 o'clock . . .[1]

The discussion went well and in due course Mathews made a proposition; on 23 November Greene wrote: 'Yours of today received. I have communicated with Mr. Yeats, and he will at once do so with Mr. Lionel Johnson: the rest will be informed promptly so that the matter may be settled without delay. I may say that, for myself, your proposal appears to me to be a fair one.'[2] The rest did indeed agree and the volume appeared early in 1892. Dowson was represented by the maximum permitted number of six poems. Norman Gale promised to send his quota, and as an earnest of his serious interest sent in four light-hearted pastiche verses beginning:

> One more unfortunate
> Volume ungodly
> Rashly importunate
> Gone to the Bodley.

In addition to securing his place in the Rhymers' Club, Herbert Horne gave Dowson practical (though unpaid) encouragement by printing his work in *The Century Guild Hobby Horse*, and there can be little doubt that the sudden flowering of Dowson's talent at this time is at least partly due to his knowledge that anything he offered would readily be published. The magazine had only a small circulation, but the approval of its readers was valuable, and Dowson's work began to be known largely on the strength of the story (*A Case of Conscience*) and the four poems, including *Non sum qualis eram bonae sub regno Cynarae*, which appeared in *The Century Guild Hobby Horse* in 1891. The poems that Dowson copied out in

---

[1] Michael Holland Collection.   [2] ibid.

letters to his friends at this time show him at the height of his powers. There is no way of knowing his methods of writing verse, but it seems probable that poetry came quite naturally, if infrequently, and that he wrote with ease, though he was punctilious in revision.

Beside *A Case of Conscience*, Dowson published two other stories in 1890–1891, *The Diary of a Successful Man* and *The Story of a Violin*, both in *Macmillan's Magazine*. In June 1890 he began with Arthur Moore the novel that was eventually published as *A Comedy of Masks*. *Ludovicus*, which, it must be admitted, seems to have been a really inferior production, had failed to find a publisher, and its successor, *Felix Martyr*, was apparently abandoned after a few chapters. *A Comedy of Masks*, on the other hand, went ahead smoothly, was finished within two years, and accepted by Heinemann soon afterwards. By the summer of 1892 Dowson and Moore were at work on its successor, *Adrian Rome*.

The task which demanded Dowson's most concentrated effort was the composition of his play in verse, *The Pierrot of the Minute*, which Peters commissioned in October 1892. Dowson had barely three weeks for it, and his brief notes to Peters at the time show him in the throes. The play was put on at the Chelsea Town Hall as part of an evening organized by the Primrose League on 22 November. Dowson had eight tickets, and his guests were satisfied that the play had gone well. It was to be published five years later by Leonard Smithers in an extremely handsome edition with designs by Aubrey Beardsley, who referred to it somewhat unkindly as 'that foolish book'.

Dowson had had no holiday abroad in 1889, but in these years he was in France every summer and it was in 1890 that he first visited Brittany. On this occasion he travelled with A. C. Hillier and in July 1891 he had a few days by himself in the Landes. But a few weeks later, and again in 1892, he returned to Brittany with Arthur Moore. The Breton countryside made a deep impression on him which is reflected in many of his stories and poems; and when he found himself able to live wherever he wished a few years later, it was in Brittany that he chose to settle.

At the end of August 1891 Dowson's parents moved from Woodford to a house in Maida Hill. Here he was living close to Moore and in consequence correspondence between the two was seldom necessary; this unfortunately deprives us of the almost daily record of his doings which he had previously written to his friend and collaborator, but it enabled him to see much more of his other friends. During the day duty kept him at Bridge Dock, but at about 6 p.m. he arrived in the West End. London at that time, like Paris, was still a cluster of villages and any circle of friends habitually frequented the same small area. The usual rendezvous was The Cock in Shaftesbury Avenue, and those arriving much after six would generally find Dowson already there with a glass of absinthe in front of him writing verses on a scrap of paper or the back of an envelope. At seven he would go, either alone or with friends, to dine in 'Poland'. If he had no theatre engagement, dinner lasted a long time. If there were others dining with him they would adjourn to the Café Royal or a public house when they had eaten, while Dowson would stay on. As soon as all the other diners, mostly Frenchmen and Poles, had been served, he would coax Adelaide to come and sit at his table. She would come and talk, and sometimes they played cards until about ten o'clock, when her mother called her to go to bed. She was intelligent and vivacious, with dark hair and blue eyes; her face was oval, and her nose a little crooked; she spoke with a slight foreign accent. She had warm colouring and the freshness of youth. During 1890 and 1891 the relations between her and Dowson widened and deepened; his letters to his friends became more and more serious; he was falling in love.

Adelaide at thirteen was still more child than woman, and it must have been some time before she understood the strength of Dowson's feeling for her. She was wayward and could tease him into paroxysms of jealousy, but nothing seemed to shake his devotion. Being in love with a girl of such an age caused numerous difficulties. The chief of these was the fear of being misunderstood, and in 1891 there occurred an incident which threw Dowson into a prolonged depression. During August 1891 the papers were filled with reports of a case of abduction. A sixteen-year-old girl named Lucy Pearson had given reporters a gruesome account of the treatment she had received at the hands of her captor, a man named Newton. Dowson first read of the affair at the beginning of September and was filled with horror; immediately he felt that the innocence of his relations with Adelaide had been shattered—'this beastly thing has left a sort of slimy trail over my holy places', he wrote to Moore[1]—and he imagined that her family and his own friends looked askance at him, questioning his motives. This was all the more bitter since his behaviour towards her had always been scrupulous and the thought of acting otherwise would never have entered his head. On 3 September he wrote to John Gray, 'the gods have been torturing me with a grievous neuralgia in France; and since I came back they have devised a peculiarly refined and indefinible form of moral torture, which on the whole

[1] Letter 162.

is worse than the neuralgia.'[1] And on the 22nd he wrote to Arthur Moore: 'This thing is killing me. Since I came back, nothing has been the same: I've tried to persuade myself that I'm wrong, but I give it up. Her people are as kind and cordial as ever, there are no obvious differences made: only I can feel that there is a difference and that it will become more apparent daily. C'est fini.'[2] It was in this mood of depression and disillusion that he had written on 13 September *Ah, dans ces mornes séjours*, the saddest and most exquisite of all his poems:

> You would have understood me had you waited;
> I could have loved you, dear, as well as he.

After a time he appeared to recover, but the blow had been a heavy one. It was almost certainly under its impact that he finally made the decision to follow his friends Charles Sayle and Lionel Johnson into the Roman Catholic church. He was received on 25 September 1891. For a time he took his religion with great seriousness, but he did not find consolation in it for long, and from this time forward we hear more often of the depression which gradually deprived him of his natural gaiety.

In February 1892 Plarr became engaged and Dowson sometimes wrote ruefully of the contrast between their situations. He longed to declare himself to Adelaide and her parents, but could not bring himself to do so, partly for fear of shocking them, partly through an unwillingness to face the inevitable sharp disapproval of his family and friends, who were already gossiping about his affairs and missed no opportunity of telling him what they thought. Lost in indecision, Dowson did nothing, but the experience was the most intense of his life. 'Though I have done, nor said, nor suffered anything tangible since I last saw or wrote to you,' he confided to Plarr, 'I write as an *illuminato*: I seem to have seen mysteries, & if I fail to be explicit, it is because my eyes are dazzled.'[3]

Though she probably never knew it, Adelaide was the inspiration of almost all Dowson's best work. During these years the clouds were already beginning to hang upon their relationship, but she remained none the less his chief source of happiness—perhaps the only one.

[1] Letter 163.   [2] Letter 168.   [3] Letter 184.

80. *To Arthur Moore*
    Sunday [*5 January 1890*]

           The Arts and Letters Club, 27 Albemarle Street, W.

Mon cher.
    Voyez-vous donc! I am cured—(although I have started a bad cold since la grippe left me). I will Haymarket any day this week you like. Only if possible give me a choice of days as I have several noxious engagements this week & must fix them up early in it. This is rather a dull place *bien entendu*, but one can slack here with some comfort. You must come & find me here one day. I hope the plague hasn't seized you. By the bye where is Ludovicus? I can't write now somehow—not "Felix Martyr" nor nothing. I am usé. Meet me as soon as you can & we will Poland & converse. The 2nd instalment of Hy James[1] is almost as bad as the first—but Hardy on Candour in Fiction is worth the 6d.[2] No more now. Write to-morrow if possible.
                    Yrs ever   ERNEST DOWSON

1. *The Solution*, serialized in *The New Review* from December 1889 to February 1890.
2. Hardy's article in *The New Review*, January 1890, was entitled 'Candour in English Fiction'.

81. *To Arthur Moore*
    Wednesday [*8 January 1890*]

                        Arts and Letters Club

Chéri.
    I have mislaid the effusion which I wrote to you from Limehouse & so send a brief note to express the extreme satisfaction with which I will call for you to morrow evening (Thursday) at the hour of six or thereabouts & introduce you & be introduced by you respectively to Poland & "Good for Nothing". Thursday is the best day for me also
    Au revoir à demain
                      in haste   ED

82. *To Arthur Moore*

Dimanche early morning i.e. 1.30 Saturday night, 11–12 January
1890

Woodford

Observe this *is* dated.

Caro mio.

I have nothing on earth to tell you ∴ I may as well set to & write
you a lengthy epistle. Merci for a most acceptable night on Thursday.
It was certainly most annoying about Mignon:[1] also the "Arts &
Letters" quart d'heure was cheerless but otherwise I enjoyed myself &
"Good for Nothing" was quite good enough. I went last night with
Williams (two more stalls out of that wretched sheet!) to "Tra La La."[2]
Will you esteem me more or less if I tell you that I enjoyed it,—more
than "Faust Up to Date". I will go with you to it when you have seen
at least 1 act of La Tosca. Otherwise you will not appreciate it as the
entire point of it lies in the marvellous caricature which Miss Ayrtoun
presents of the Bernard Beere. I positively chortled aloud at times.
Arthur Roberts is Percy at 5st 7. The Queen is an excellent caricte of
Miss Leclercq, music pretty, libretto often waggish,—chorus, dancing,
supers & stage management unutterably bad.—We must do the Middleman[3] next however—n'est ce pas?—I feel my courage rapidly waning
for to-morrow & fear that after all my horror of dances will outweigh
my curiosity to sample Stuart Headlam's ballet girls.[4] I have changed
my mind as to the immediate submittal to you of "Ysabeau".[5] I am
in train for another chapter which I have just laid down & shall resume
when this letter is finished. And you may as well be bored by 4 as 3
chaps of that unfortunate work while you are at it. I think they are
beginning to bore me horribly those estimable personae of mine. I am
very much annoyed in fact—because they have all got (those few who
are left) into such a distressfully lofty atmosphere that it is quite too
much of a strain on my harassed mind to make them converse. And the
petite damoiselle whom I meant to make much of doesn't seem to fit in
quite, so I can't let myself out on reporting her—which is also annoying.
Talking of petite d's by the bye I am afraid you were not favourably
impressed by Poland. Or rather you were less disgusted with the Pot
au Feu character of the cooking than I feared—& didn't enthuse as

---

1. Minnie Terry appears to have missed the performance on 9 January.
2. *Tra la la Tosca, or the High-toned Soprano and the Villain Base* by F. C.
   Burnand opened at the Royalty on 9 January. See also Letter 78 note 6.
3. At the Shaftesbury Theatre. Dowson had already seen the play in August
   1889.
4. See Letter 51.
5. i.e. *Mme de Viole.*

much as I expected over *la petite personne* who gives it so much local colouring. This is not as it should be. Half the charm of dining there lies in the fact that you are honoured with the conversation—if you are an habitué—of that little lady. I would dine off fish snacks in Whitechapel for a similar privilege—which is certainly more than I would do for the society of any "jeune fille" in existence. I shall take you there again however—but you shall have (i) mock tartel (ii) salzgherken (iii) veal cotlets—instead of "hearts" which I confess gave me a mighty indigestion on Thursday. Excuse these pilules—but I warned you that I had absolutely nothing to say. I am meditating still on "Felix Martyr"—so far with no brilliant result. I will let you have a sample soon though & shall expect you to send me the nucleus of a plot in your Sunday edtn. I am sitting in my great-aunts dressing gown & demolishing 1 oz of honey dew[6] & 1 bottle of Burgundy. I wish you were here. Perhaps when the influenza retires you will do a Satdy to Monday. By exemplary behaviour during the last week—for me—I am once more on terms of amenity with my people & my governor is going to retire to Hastings shortly. By the bye—I was at the Museum this afternoon working away like a nigger at my Chamfort[7] when lo—ye Gods imagine what strange sight I saw! Sitting negligently graceful *on the table* of the Vicious Camel[8] & talking to her with great & intimate urbanity was the celebrated Herbert Williams—proprietor, editor, staff & office boy of *The Critic*. He tells me that she is a niece of Tay Pay[9] of The Star—a Miss O'Connor & he belongs to the same secret society with her—where they cast horoscopes & produce astrals etc. I chortled! All the rest of the menagerie were there as usual at the same old desks. Do B.M. readers ever die? I shall have to give up going there if it tends to immortality in this way. Did you see Tweedy to-day? I am quite delighted with the burst of energy—(plumistic)—which has come over me since I saw you. I was afraid that after the effort of refusing the attractive offer of Swanton—blackest ennui would seize me. On the contrary it has rather produced the opposite effect. I suppose that the overdue depression will come on to-morrow. I am wise therefore to ensure the Sunday edition. Lefroy writes me dismally that his people are sending him to a French school to teach English & be instructed in that subtle tongue—a ruse to obstruct him from the alleged immoral woman who is supposed to have hold of him, which he resents. I shall miss the dear obstinate fool immensely but if he comes back an accomplished French linguist!!! Could you support him on the Broads?—But now in the name etc etc

always yours   ERNEST DOWSON

6. A brand of pipe tobacco.
7. Dowson was working on an article on Chamfort, the French eighteenth-century moralist, which appears never to have been published.
8. The palmist; see Letter 5.
9. T. P. O'Connor (1848–1929), Irish journalist and Member of Parliament.

83. *To Arthur Moore*
   27 January 1890

Bridge Dock

Mon Vieux.

Thanks for yours. I was afflicted with an abnormal lethargy yestdy which must excuse my silence. I am sorry you didn't look in at the B.M. on Saturday. I fell a victim to that godless journalist Williams— & was reduced by three hours of his society to the verge of suicide & murder. He is certainly the meanest thing alive, & the most illiterate. In the evening I slacked & eventually met Image & Horne at midnight outside the "back door" of the Alhambra! & was introduced to various trivial coryphées. There was something eminently grotesque in the juxtaposition. Horne very erect & slim & aesthetic—& Image the most dignified man in London, a sort of cross in appearance between a secular abbé & Baudelaire, with a manner du 18me siècle—waiting in a back passage to be escort to ballet girls ~~whom they don't even~~ ——— !!! I confess this danseuse-worship escapes me!! Horne seems a man of merit however. I am going to tea with him this afternoon. By the bye— I see that my "Diary of a Successful Man" is advertized for appearance in Feb.[1] Good old chequelet. How I shall curse if it's less than a tenner.

On the strength of it I am going to invest in a plaque which I have found in Wardour St—(supposing I can get it for a reasonable amount). I should like you to view it. It is coloured & is possibly meant for Mignon but if so—the likeness is marvellously idealized. It is possibly from a picture: in any case it's ideal loveliness & the first time I remember to have come across it.

I am glad you are not reduced à vomir over Ysabeau etc. I am afraid it's awfully high-falutin. I meant to write one chapter more—but whereof I know not. If you think it should end there it shall. That must be considered when we meet & I prithee, mon respectable ami, let the meeting be soon. Any day you like—Thursday or another—save Saturday when I may very likely be at Cambridge. Yes, make it Thursday. Excuse my babbling on. It is but 3.0 & I can't leave till 4. & there is nought else to do. My correspondence has assumed enormous dimensions of late & is one of the most consoling parts of my existence. En passant if you want a perfectly charming half hour—buy, borrow or steal Hy. Jame's "Partial Portraits".[2] They are a lot of criticisms— probably you know them—including G. Eliot, Emerson, Daudet, De Maupassant, & Stevenson. Some I have not read: those I have, fill me with wonder & amazement. None of his novels contain happier sentences. e.g. he says that women in R.L.S' are so many "superfluous

1. In *Macmillan's Magazine.*
2. Published in 1888.

girls in a boy's play". But he touches the bull's eye as easily in every page. I am also reading Stendhal's "De l'Amour": with mixed feelings. But like James, his worthy disciple, Stendhal is always piquant, although unlike James one often disagrees with him. He says "l'ennui ôte tout, jusqu'au courage de se tuer."—elsewhere: "On convient qu'une petite fille de dix ans a vingt fois plus de finesse qu'un petit polisson du même âge. Pourquoi à vingt ans est-elle une grande idiote, gauche, timide et ayant peur d'une araignée, et le polisson un homme d'esprit?" . . . The typical English woman he guages thoroughly "la véritable Anglaise *accomplie,* déstinée à satisfaire pleinement à toutes les convenances et à donner à un mari toutes les jouissances de l'orgueil aristocratique le plus maladif, et *un bonheur à mourir d'ennui*"—

Again—"Rien n'ennuie l'*amour-gout* comme l'*amour-passion* dans son *partner*" Pardon these extracts.

I am glad you have done the "Middleman". On the whole I agree with your remarks thereon. I have a great & unreasonable aversion to Garden[3] though—in whatever he plays.

Smith & Swanton are both at Oxford now. They want me to come up & I have half promised—but I think my courage will fail me. I am afraid it would be too depressing.

I am beginning to feel hopeful about Ludovicus. It's a good work. At any rate I have no doubt that publishers will leap for it when "Hildreth" has appeared. I am going to let myself out on that now. Keep it rolling round in your luminous mind even if you haven't time to write much of it at present.

Let me wind up this effusion before I drift on to another sheet. Write soon & do your level best to keep Thursday or any other day you prefer this week, open for us.

thine ever   ERNEST DOWSON

---

3. E. W. Garden (1845–1939), a popular actor at the time. Dowson had previously seen him in *Hands Across the Sea.*

84. *To Arthur Moore*

4 March 1889 [*actually c. 4 February 1890*]

Bassin du Pont

Mon gros Prosper.[1]

This is to inform you that the poor fool who sub-edits "The Argosy" has returned "The Passion" to *me* with the usual banalités. Whither

---

1. i.e. Mérimée.

shall I next dispatch it? Trischlers?[2] or Chambers? or where? . . . .

Yours gratefully to hand. Next week or this (—*almost* any night—) I shall be delighted to see you here. Jambon au Skrish—n'est ce pas? Some time soon I must go & see the curtain-raiser at the Avenue[3]—& sample the quality of a new infant phenomenon whom I am told I shall like.

This week I must economise!! I was weak enough to pay a book seller's bill of about £4.10. I dined with a naval cousin of mine at the Cri. rather recklessly yesterday—& now after purchasing *Marius*—I am rather more oofless than usual in spite of Macmillans (Or is it because?) modest cheque. Praise the gods at least that none of it has passed into feminine hands. Write re: Lud. at your earliest.   ED

I am sorry to hear of the death of Mrs H. Moore.[4] A funeral is more detestable than anything I know of except a wedding. I heard by the way from Lefroy yesterday. He sends me a most rueful account of his ménage—sleeping as he does in a "*dortoir* containing 16 French beds" (? what is the peculiarity of a French bed?) & without proper washing accomodation. I have also writ to Thomas—Please assure Tweedy that I shall be delighted i̶f̶ to see him down here any afternoon. Or send him to Poland vers 7h. He will find me there bar accidents to-morrow, Friday & Sat. Perhaps on the latter day I shall see you. No more now.
                                                                    Hastily   ED

2. i.e. *Atalanta*, which was published by Trischler & Co. of New Bridge Street, Blackfriars.
3. *Fool's Mate* by F. W. Broughton, which opened on 1 February; the phenomenon was Gracie Murielle.
4. Elizabeth Moore, the wife of Henry Moore, R.A. (A.C.M.'s uncle), died on 2 February 1890.

84A. *see page 422*

85. *To Arthur Moore*
    7 February 1890

                                                                    Bridge Dock

Caro Mio.
    If you are not going to do anything particular to-morrow (Sat. afternoon) will you lunch with me at the "*Arts & Letters*" (27 Albemarle St) at about 2.15 oclock. Drop me a card there at once if so. I want to converse with you re Ludovicus etc. I shall not be able to get there before 2.15 I fear.
                                                                    In haste   ECD

P.S. If you get this letter to-night post your answerlet to this basin. Then I shall probably go straight to the Museum if you are not able to turn up.

86. *To Arthur Moore*
    Friday [*7 February 1890*]

Arts and Letters Club

Dear Moore.
    Just a line to say that I am sorry I shall not be here to-morrow, after all—as I am going to take Missy to the Egyptian Hall[1] & afterwards have to meet Hillier[2] to take him down with me to Woodford. Write
Yrs   ERNEST DOWSON

1. Maskelyne's entertainment of magic.
2. Arthur Cecil Hillier (b. 1858) had been at Worcester College, Oxford 1882–1886, and was now London correspondent of the *New York Herald*. In the summer of 1890 he went with Dowson to Brittany. He contributed poems to the two books published by the Rhymers' Club and collaborated with Dowson and G. A. Greene on the translation of Muther's *History of Modern Painting* (1895–1896).

87. *To Arthur Moore*
    Monday [*?10 February 1890*]

Bridge Dock

Caro Mio.
    Je suis désolé. Have only found your card this morning. But although I hardly expected you I *was* at the A & L from 2–3.30 lunching there in solitary boredom. Pourquoi oh pourquoi did you not enquire of me from the Cerberus?
in haste   E D

P.S. I live in anticipation of Thursday. Mind & come. Sunday edn is at Woodford, left there inadvertently. Will be posted to-night—

88. *To Arthur Moore*
     Tuesday [*11 February 1890*]

[Bridge Dock]

Mon Vieux.

My *edition de luxe* is so out of date that I will refrain from inflicting it on you & merely write a line to thank you for yours received this morning & once more express my regret for our avortement on Satdy. It was lucky that you met Money.[1] But wherefore did you not rout me out? However better luck another time. I went last night in solitary state to the Avenue.[2] Little Miss Gracie Murielle, in a curtain raiser which has more merit than most I have seen, is worth seeing—but don't, oh don't—if you go for that be deluded into sitting through the insufferably dreary farce which follows. I perceive "Mignon's" matinée is to be at the *Globe* on the 25th in a sketch by C. Scott.[3] I am going to book a seat—is there any hope of your being there? I wish the show did not include a play for which I have such an extreme aversion as "Adrienne Lecouvreur".[4] Still one must be thankful for small mercies—

I have been reading "The Passion of Dr Ludovicus". It is an *extremely* good work: I can't believe that publishers will persist in their evil ways. I will positively send it off to-night quelque part! I have however the most unaccountable aversion to doing up parcels. I have also been writing a new 2n Chap for "Mme de V" to fit in *between* the original chaps I & II. I hope to have it complete for your criticism when you come here on Thursday. For you will—must come. I will kill the fatted porker & deprive the oranger of its choicest fruit for you. Let me have a card to-morrow to acquaint me if it is a fixture. Eh bien—no more now. I have a bad cold, leaden spirits, and in fine feel all round a pretty fair "pourriture". Au revoir.
     Thine

                              in senitio omnium   E D

1. Walter McLachlan Money (b. 1866), Moore's contemporary at Bradfield and Oxford. He was called to the Bar in 1891.
2. A farce, *Dr. Bill*, by Hamilton Aidé, with Fred Terry and Albert Chevalier in the cast. The curtain-raiser was *Fool's Mate* (see Letter 84).
3. F. R. Benson lent the Globe Theatre for a charity matinée on 25 February. Minnie Terry's sketch was called *On a Doorstep*.
4. By Scribe and Legouvé, first performed in London by Sarah Bernhardt in 1880.

89. *To Arthur Moore*

Dimanche [*16 February 1890*]

Woodford

Caro Mio.

I was very glad to get your letter, wh. partly dissipated the depressing results of your mother's alarming p.c.—I was coming up—had not that letter arrived—to the Vale of Maida to make my enquiries in person—Lud: is at Chambers now. May it find a haven there—& at any rate not return too soon. The effort of doing it up & dispatching, is to me something stupendous. I stayed last night with Smith in the Wood.[1] He keeps his term there from Sat. to Monday as a rule. He tells me that (i) we have bumped Exeter in the torpid,[2] chiefly owing to Swanton's excellent rowing (2) that Thomas is not up this term owing to the death of his father. He has rooms with S in St Ald's. & they want me to go up before the term is out. But I doubt if I shall be able to. With regard to a meeting—let it be soon! any day you like this week will be equal for me. At Bridge Dk. or in Poland—whichever you will, but oh—let it be *somewhere & soon. I* too am exquisitely bad—& I have a graveyard cough of the most alarming dimensions. We will compare our symptoms when we meet. My people all go away shortly to Southampton & Hastings severally. I know not whether I shall go to the Dock or stay here. It will depend on whether our cook who is pretty & young or our housemaid who is old & ugly as sin goes for a holiday—If the former I shall be permitted to rest here. In any case I hope to see something of you. I dine almost invariably in Poland now. The atmosphere of the place has the most cheering effect on me. The dear child becomes daily more kind & gracious. The other day she came & sat by me & conversed with great affability all the time I was there. She is really the most quaint & engaging little lady—& she can play the fiddle very prettily. Do you remember, par exemple, Pater's note in "Marius"[3]—to the effect that when one's pain in life seems just a stupid, brutal outrage on us & one can seek refuge from it, at best, only in a mere "general sense of goodwill, somewhere, perhaps"—sometimes the discovery of that goodwill if it is only "in a not unfriendly animal has may seem to have explained & actually justified the existence of our pain at all". That is really almost true. Certainly the mere friendliness of a child has some such effect on me—seems to me at times to be not merely a set-off against one's innumerable unliquidated claims against life but a quite final satisfaction of them—an absolute end in itself— Corollorary (& my apology for dilating to you so much on quite trivial incidents)—that

1. St. John's Wood.
2. The Torpids were rowed 13–19 February; Brasenose remained Head of the River for the fifth year in succession.
3. Chapter XXV.

there is really after all nothing so important as that one should be constantly trying to multiply these moments & to make them last. Well—
no more now. Write at your earliest etc,—take care of yourself, don't
get la grippe & come speedily to

Votre devoué   E D

90. *To Arthur Moore*
Wednesday, 19 February 1890

Arts and Letters Club

Caro Mio.

Just received your undated note. The Cerberus tells me it was left
on *Monday*—But am I dreaming or did we not meet on Monday? Or
was it yesterday or perchance to-night?—A question I cannot answer
until I see you.

Let that be to-morrow n'est ce pas?—as soon after six as you like I
~~was down~~ shall be living at the Bridge from to-morrow.

in haste

yrs   E D

91. *To Arthur Moore*
[*23 February 1890*]

Bridge Dock

—The Back Office—in an easy chair before a colossal fire—time about
9.P.M.—Sunday.—Would you were here. Still if a pencil is permitted
au lieu of the less facile pen I will endeavour to send you the accustomed
chronique—I did a weird thing yesterday. I heard that there was a
special 10.15 "Socker"[1] train from Paddington & I repaired there—
(why did not you?) & found a great Pandemonium, many men I knew
—amongst them Evans[2] of Merton, Swanton, De Castro[3]—etc. In the

---

1. The University Soccer match was played at Queen's Club, London, on
   22 February, when Cambridge won 3–1.
2. Rev. A. C. Evans, b. 1868. Went up to Merton College, Oxford, in 1887.
   He became curate of Abergavenny in 1891, Vicar of Welton, Yorkshire,
   1919–1935.
3. Rev. E. H. G. de Castro, b. 1868. Went up to Keble College, Oxford, in
   1886 and graduated in 1890. He became curate of Beaminster, Dorset, in
   1891, Vicar of Halford, Craven Arms, Shropshire 1902–1919.

issue I found myself at Oxford (naturalich) at about 11.40 PM. &
stayed with Swanton. I came back to-day—finding it supremely triste:
did not go near Queen's at all—nowhere in fact. A place which is born
again every 3 years has its drawbacks. Never again, mon vieux. Cambridge as often, as you like, but not Oxford. Mon Dieu comme j'étais
content de revoir ce fichu Paddington. Don't forget that we must try
& work a theatrum this week. Il le faut absolument. Otherwise—
This fire is certainly an excellent business. I expand under its cheerful
influence. I positively beam. Would I could muster the energy to open
a bottle of Burgundy. I assume you had no plans yesterday as you
wrote not: I dined en Pologne as usual yesterday, & wished you had
been there. I went later than usual & it was agreeably quiet & private.
—(I am getting too slack to write—the above three sentences have
taken me over an hour to indite—

Would I could light a pipe—but the tabac (caporal—by the bye in
blue packets) is on the table.

No news fr. Chambers. I still remain perfectly sterile—can neither
complete what is begun, devise new stories or think of our Felix. The bad
taste of "Yeast"[4] is still in my mouth. I try & rectify it with "Marius".
To read Chamfort—as it implies cutting the leaves—I am far too slack.

Enfin—enfin—write & tell me how you are finding yourself. Perhaps
though I shall call for you to-morrow on my westward way. But write—
write. Certainly my ideas flow not at all to-night. I apologize for this
perfectly inane scribble. It is the expression of a long & fairly comfortable yawn. If only Thursday did not loom over me with its vista of
drawing room inanities! I wish you could come to Mignon's matinée on
Tuesday. I guess I shall skip Adrienne Lecouvreur. We must go to the
Garrick,[5] n'est ce pas? I am beginning to feel exquisitely sleepy. Yes—
il faut le dire—bon soir—bon soir thou dreamer of commentaries.

Tout à vous   E D[6]

4. A novel by Charles Kingsley, published in 1850.
5. *A Pair of Spectacles* by Sydney Grundy (adapted from the French) opened
   on 22 February.
6. A rough sketch of a yacht is added after the signature.

92. *To Arthur Moore*

Tuesday morning [*4 March 1890*]

Woodford

Caro Mio.

May I look upon Thursday as fixed? Or—how would Wed: suit you
as I rather want (excuse my banal taste) to do a St Jame's Ballad

Concert.[1] Whichever day you like however. And I am really quite anxious to see Fred Leslie.[2] I have just completed fair copying Chap II (new) of Mme de V. I will bring it when we meet next & get you to read it. It's all analysis. I had a very pleasant evening on Satdy. after all, my flight was precipitate—I had to wait 40 min: at L'pl St for my train. Hope your constitution (& reading) proceeds well. Mine is AA1.— special survey. I thought of looking you up to-night but I arrived rather too early & so went & played bigliardo with Walton. Dined as usual in Poland. La pétite would not allow me to sit in my usual place but led me up above the salt to the fireside table You can imagine how "gratted & flattified"[3] I was. I hope she will be expansive when you come there with me next—it will amuse you to study her I think. She is the most charming little chatterbox & we are quite on a footing of *vieils amis* by this time. The Roumanians have retired to Roumania—viâ Paris this morning—so unless the Bohees are equally vociferous we may be able to dine there at an earlier hour than 7.30 with comparative quiet.

I am still—alas—perfectly unproductive—can't write a line or get a solitary idea. I skimmed through "Bel Ami" on Sunday. I think I must have confused it with Maizeroy's novel—for it was new to me. It's clever, n'est ce pas?—cleverer I think than "Une Vie"[4]—but without the pathos of that. I prefer "Marius". By the bye have you noted— but my pipe expires—the small hours are getting perceptibly longer. Je vais me coucher. "Dormez bien et moi aussi"—as Adélaide says. W^RITE

Yrs   ED

Where oh where is that unhappy "P of L"[5] to seek a home now? *Do* suggest somewhere.
>?All the Year Round?
>Family Herald?

---

1. The Ballad Concert in the St. James's Hall, Piccadilly, on 5 March had Sims Reeves and Edward Lloyd among the soloists.
2. In *Ruy Blas or the Blasé Roué*.
3. A spoonerism attributed to the Duke of Cambridge (1819–1904), Commander-in-Chief of the Army 1856–1895.
4. Maupassant published *Une Vie* in 1883 and *Bel Ami* in 1885. Dowson seems to be referring to Maizeroy's novel *P'tit Mi*.
5. *The Passion of Dr. Ludovicus* again.

93. *To Arthur Moore*
    9 March 1890

Bridge Dock

Caro Arturo mio.

Excuse pencil. I went to the St. James[1] last night with Plarr & Walton. The house was crammed: the play very disappointing. Bourchier indeed as Jacques (pronounced there Jaykez!) although far too genial acted extremely well. The Jersey Lilium is a fine animal—I had never seen her before—but a most unideal Rosalind. Cautley's Orlando is a most offensive performance & Sugden's refined Touchstone an absurdity. Celia—a Miss Amy McNeil—was too bad & inartistic to talk about. The show, in short, is a bad show & Mrs Langtry is an éspèce de type that I should detest even if she could act wh. she can't. Tace! I hope to see you shortly Mon. or Tues. even if, as I half fear from your vague remarks on Friday that we dine not this week. By the way in my Chap II anent my 18th cent cultured roué you pencil "cf New Republic"[2] Does this mean that I have plagiarized? I have a sort of vague fear that I may have reproduced a passage from that excellent work but have not the book to refer to. Tell me I prithee if this is so that I may amend accordingly.

Par exemple—read *last* week's "Speaker" Grant Allen of all people therein takes up the cudgels for American fiction,[3] Howells & James—chiefly Howells & speaks of Silas Lapham as a Great Work of art to rank with Vanity Fair & Richard Feverel! I am going to make an effort when I have finished this scrawl to begin my Chamfort article. Where you at the Museum yesterday? I was there at two thirty—got out half a dozen books—met Plarr & went & lunched with him in that dismal bun room—strolled round the Elgin marbles for about half an hour & came back again. We then read for some 5 minutes—recognized the lanky figure of Williams & beat a hasty retreat to Image's. So as usual my afternoon's severe reading at the Museum did not come off. Are you going to see Benson's Hamlet?[4] I may go. Oh me—I wish I could get into the vein for producing some more copy & oof. Send me the right idea for a short story & we will share the problematical proceeds. I read Bellamy's "Dr Heidenhoff's Process"[5] the other afternoon. It is better than "Looking Backwards"—though that does not say much. What an exhausting day Sunday is! It is impossible to have any ideas on Sunday.

---

1. *As You Like It* with Mrs. Langtry and Laurence Cautley opened at the St. James's Theatre on 24 February.
2. *The New Republic* by W. H. Mallock, 1877.
3. 'The Novel of Character' in *The Speaker*, 1 March 1890.
4. F. R. Benson's *Hamlet* opened at the Globe Theatre on 6 March 1890.
5. Published in 1880.

It is a mistake to get up on Sunday. I put off that operation as usual until 1.0 oclock but I feel as if I had got up several hours too soon. Let me conclude these bagatelles. Write soon.

Yrs ever   E D

94. *To Arthur Moore*
14 March 1890

Bridge Dock

Caro Mio

I am sorry that I have not been able to look you up thus far. Perhaps to-morrow? Could you—supposing you matinize & I don't see you previously at the B.M)—could you then five-o'clocquer with me at the Arts & Letters at 5.30. To-night as the governor is away I dine at Woodford: to-morrow I shall probably Polandize. Send me a card to notify your movements *as early as possible,* to *the Club.* I was in St John's Wood on Wed. night with the Prophet[1] who went back to Oxford yesterday but returns to-day (if he can spoof collections)[2] for good.

I purchased another photo of Mignon yesterday—a Man's Shadow one (Act iv costume) a very pretty one but singularly like Mdlle Adélaide. My collection now comprises 3 cabinets 2 cartes de v. & 1 plaque. I heard from Bouthors yesterday. He comes to England about the 1st prox—for how long or with what intent he does not state. I really must try this time & work a réunion between you. This is real May. The river looks charming & I have been sitting with open windows.

Are you reading Lucas Malet's "Wages of Sin" now appearing in the *Universal Review*[3]—It strikes me as rather excellent. I believe I told you I purposed going to Hastings next week. It will be a corvée but I suppose it must be endured. Would the gods it were over. I have just consented to be *entremetteur* of a critique Plarr has written of his pal Boas' play[4] to the Critic. I hope it doesn't bring the great Williams down on me again. Excuse this unnecessary flow of ink *de nihilo.* I believe my brain must be softening.—The effect on the river now is most charming

---

1. i.e. Sam Smith.
2. 'Collections' are College examinations. Smith appears to have had leave of absence from Queen's in order to read for Final Schools.
3. It appeared in book form in the following year.
4. *The Favourite of a King* by F. S. Boas and Jocelyn Brandon opened at the Comedy Theatre on 11 March.

—the sun very much chastened by the clouds just lightens it up without colouring it at all. Dominant tones grey & gold—effect very cold—like a French landscape with a coldness which doesn't reach one's temperature.

However the tempus appears to be 4.45 & I will even take my homeward way. Adios.

Thine   E D

95. *To Arthur Moore*
   [*28 March 1890*]

Woodford

Mon Vieux.

Quelle dommage that I have not seen you this week—more especially as I am rather spoofed to-morrow & shall be at Bridge Dock till about 4.0. I took an afternoon off to-day instead but thought it would be no good looking after you. Well—we must meet & *dine* next week without fail. Swanton took me—sane invitum—to the Empire on Tuesday. It was in usual state of pommade. I met a good many men I knew however—& slept afterwards with Smith at the Wood—after many b & s's: the reason I suppose that my liver & nerves have been in such a rasped condition ever since that I have not mustered energy to look you up. Thanks for the Purloined Relique.[1] I will do my best but it seems to me really extremely good & I am not at all confident that any emendments I may make won't spoil it. I wanted to go to the French Artists[2] this afternoon & study the Corots of which I hear there is a good assortment—but the gods would not give me the energy. I suppose you have been—n'est ce pas? My health annoys me very much just at present. I should like a new liver & kidneys to match. I have barely anything for breakfast, no lunch,—latterly not even afternoon tea—& then after forcing myself with some nausea to swallow a cutlet in Poland suffer from indigestion half the night. This is not as it should be. I literally live on tobacco nowadays. We must really effect a speedy juncture & compare our symptoms. Read the summary of Tolstoi's latest (unpublished) novel "The Kreutzer Sonata" in the current Universal[3]—I did not know that Great man had such excellent views on sexual questions. He talks of marriage as a heinous crime against morality &

1. Apparently a story sent by Moore for Dowson's criticism: it may have been a revised version of *The Stolen Hand* (see Letter 38).
2. Romanticists' Exhibition at Dowdeswell's, New Bond Street.
3. *The Universal Review*, 15 March.

humanity—vituperates as strongly as I could wish against the monstrous division drawn between licensed & unlicensed lust—by the conventionalist & the pedantic, banal Hegelian—& in fine ~~proposes~~ preaches Laurence Oliphant's "sympneumatic" affection purged of animalism.[4] All this from a Xtian of the deepest dye is eminently surprising and admirable. Another article in the same review (in French) on the décadent poet Paul Verlaine is also stimulating—chiefly for the digression on Rimbauld (Verlaine's friend & master) "le grand déclassé"—who was so consistent in his social hatred that he threw away his identity & dropped finally into the crowd just when he was at the zenith of his success.[5] Verlaine parted from him in Metz in 1876—& since then no one has heard of or seen him. That was a worshipful man, my masters. Please contrast our worthy Hegelian laureate, Browning William Morris et Cie! I think if I can work that incident up a little it will form a very fitting dénoument to my unhappy "Mme de V." wh: (en passant) I may mention is likely to be fair copied about the A.D. 1900. This must stand, mon cher, for the Sunday edition & entreats an answer. Excuse my beastly prolixity but I am deucedly disinclined for slumber & have no literature to peruse. I am going to the Garrick with my mater very shortly.[6] I suppose I shall have to dine at Prévitali's or Gatti's. I should like to take her to Poland but I suppose at a reasonable hour for theatre going it would hardly do? Ces sacrés Bohées! I am sure she would be charmed with my little lady. My dinners there now remind me more than anything else of certain hospitable "nursery teas" at which some years ago I was a frequent visitor before my cousins who partook of them had grown up into formidable young ladies.[7] La petite comes & sits by me & paints or talks as a matter of course whenever I have not "company"—and her adoring mama from time to time favours me with anecdotes in most unintelligible English of her amazing qualities & her extreme gentilesse. Children certainly reconcile one—(at least in my case) more than anything else to one's life but on the whole I am more & more convinced each day that there is nothing really worth doing or having or saying. At least I can't fix on any tangible object or aim in life which seems so desirable as the having got it finally over—& the remaining *in perpetuo* without desire or aim or consciousness whatsoever. "Tout casse—tout passe—tout lasse".—"Enfin on se lasse de soi"—

M. Aurelius' optimism—wh. certainly had no "secret of cheerful-

---

4. War correspondent, novelist and mystic (1829–1888); author (with his wife) of *Sympneumata* (1885) in which he advocated spiritual enlightenment through physical love.
5. By Edouard Dujardin. Arthur Rimbaud (1854–1891) disappeared for fifteen years, during which he lived chiefly in Aden and Abyssinia. He returned to France shortly before his death.
6. *A Pair of Spectacles.*
7. Miss Dulcie Secretan and her sisters.

ness" in it reduces itself to that at last—to the very blankest Pessimism—the impression which Pater's epicureanism leaves on you is very much the same.

~~In the meantime~~ "For there is a certain grief in things as they are, "in man as he has come to be, as he certainly is, over & above those "griefs of circumstance which are in a measure removable—an in-"explicable shortcoming or misadventure on the part of nature itself—"death and old age as it must needs be, and that watching of their "approach, which makes every stage of life like a dying over & over "again"—8

No there is no "secret of cheerfulness" in Pater.

Excuse my boring you in this perfectly unnecessary way with these most trite & obvious reflections; I suppose certain lucky people ~~don't~~ aren't so constantly conscious of the general futility of things.

And indeed I am not remarkably depressed to-night, but I never really escape from a depressing theory. The value of contact with children is chiefly I think that it enables you at least for a time to consider with a sort of mellow melancholy what you would otherwise do with extreme bitterness & acrimony. But I am really exceeding even my own usual long winded-ness. Forgive me & write soon.

always yours   ED.

8. *Marius the Epicurean*, Chapter XXV.

96. *To Arthur Moore*
Monday [?*31 March 1890*[1]]

Woodford

Mon bien Cher

My rheum, possibly through the cadaverous atmosphere of that "billard", assumed such proportions—but proportions! on Saturday night, that ever since I have been captive to it here. It is slightly better to-night; or, at least, I shall consider it so; and return to my Docks to-morrow; and to Poland. I fear however, that I shall hardly face the Aeolian Corner.[2] So you must write, mon Vieux, and explain your intentions. I may go to Brighton, from Good Friday to the Monday: The

1. The date of this letter is uncertain. It could also be 23 March 1891. Cp. Letters 132 and 140.
2. The corner of Lincoln's Inn Fields, near Moore's office.

Octave of Blessed John Lubbock is rather a depressing season, in London; but nothing is fixed as yet. I have been reading Virgil and Browning, to-day, I have found some superb mottoes in the 6th Aeneis to hang some melancholy modern sonnets on: when I can write them! As for Browning! Mon cher—if our Henry, if Turguénef, if Bourget had written their masterpieces in verse they would have been like that. The subtility, the tact of omission, the Morbidezza! "My Last Duchess", par exemple, is pure Henry James. I must have read it a dozen times before to-day: but I have only just appreciated the full subtilty of it. It is wonderful. Talking of morbidezza by the way—and Browning reeks of it—, what a stupid cant this is, of the Philistines, & Saintsburys:[3] the sanity of genius! and the joyousness of the great literature! Fudge! Virgil is easily the master of melancholy sound. Shakespere and his Sonnets! Montaigne & Molière! The XVIIIth Cent has a complacency of demeanour which is merely good breeding: Johnson & Swift & Sterne let the cat out of the bag. And as for now, the two people considered, I suppose, sanest, Browning and Meredith,—!—What an absurdity! As for Pater & Newman—the two greatest men of the century, surely? I doubt if even British suburban criticism could discover much health or sanity in them! . . . .

Yes: I shall probably go to Brighton: cura ut scribas, anyhow. Friday, Sunday, Monday, the doors of Poland will be shut & you will be on the river—or playing poker, and I shall have no resources. I am grievously indisposed: mind & body. When will this long, long winter end? I want the summer & "Ploumariel",[4] with the advantage of your society. In the meantime, let me subscribe myself

Yours   ERNEST DOWSON

3. George Saintsbury, literary critic (1845–1933), known for his disapproval of the French naturalist novelists. His *Essays in English Literature* appeared in 1890.
4. Imaginary French village name used by Dowson in two of his short stories, *A Case of Conscience* and *Apple Blossom in Brittany*.

97. *To Arthur Moore*
    [*8 April 1890*]

[Bridge Dock]

Caro Mio

When come you back? I wanted to write & try & persuade you to escape the clutches of Thomas on Wed. & come with me to the prémière of "April Showers"[1] for wh: H Williams (now at Bournemouth) has sent tickets. But your whereabouts was doubtful & so I arranged to go with the 1st man I met (Hillier of Worcester & the New York Herald). I suppose application to you would however have been futile.

Can you dine with me somewhere on Thursday? Afterwards we might slack or break up early as I shall have had rather a plethora of Theatre—I do definitely at last do the Garrick show with my mama on Wed evening. So *Thursday* or *Friday* at your pleasure, but one of them I prithee.

La chère petite has been shut up with a cold lately—but yesterday I was taken up to see her & sat with her for some time in an upper chamber while she had her dinner. The patron came & "drank wine" with me (a quaint brand of Port)—& portraits of Adélaide in various periods of infancy were exhibited. It was quite a charming episode & cheered me mightily. Du reste everything is extremely pink altho' the domestic atmosphere is I am glad to say clear again.

Hoping to see you soon

yrs FLEUR D'ENNUI.[2]

P.S.
I see Miss Annie Hughes was married yesterday to one Devereaux.[3] "Mon Dieu", as Bouthors is fond of exclaiming "comme les hommes et les femmes sont bêtes."

1. *April Showers* by Bellamy and Romer opened at the Comedy on 9 April. Annie Hughes was in the cast.
2. An allusion to *Les Fleurs d'Ennui* by Pierre Loti, 1882.
3. On 7 April at St. Mary's, Cadogan Street.

98. *To Arthur Moore*
Friday [*16 May 1890*]

Bridge Dock

Cher Notaire.
As you say it is a sanguinary world. If it had not been so I would have written to tell you. I have been dining with Bouthors also with a French journalist & his maitresse taking a week's congé in this land of eternal night. Otherwise nothing—save a glimpse every now & then of Smith or Berridge.[1] I regret the aratrum[2] but do not much

1. Richard Berridge (b. 1870) went up to Queen's in 1888.
2. The Law Society's examinations for solicitors were held 15–22 May. Moore evidently expected to be 'ploughed'.

believe in it. I will perhaps call in on you to-night "alle sei" (*6*)

In any case let us meet somewhere to-morrow. Send me a card to the "Arts & Letters" with a rendez-vous. My governor is in bed with gout & rheumatism & I am consequently very much tied to this very pink basin. I have done nothing to the "Stolen Hand" & have written nothing else not even a letter for an aeon. Because like the respectable Queen of Sheba there is no longer any spirit left in me[3]—

Let us meet soon & do some good round cursing together.

Yours   E D

3. See 2 Kings x and 2 Chronicles ix.

99. *To Arthur Moore*
   Monday [*19 May 1890*]

Bridge Dock

Mon bon.

Grammercy le votre. I purposed a letter last night but exceeding great slumber intervened. So I will even answer yours now—an empty Dock, the closeness of the atmosphere & the absence of the paternal relative per gout—all conduce to it. I supposed you were bathing on Saturday afternoon. I had several "fortunate hours". W Herbert (not the critical Ischariot but the actor)[1] sent me 2 stallocks for what transpires to be the last matinée of *Nixie*[2] and I duly repaired there in company with notre petite Polonaise. She seemed to like the play which bien entendu is a werry poor one. "Nixie" is a clever child enough but not as pretty either as Mignon or my little Missy herself. *She* looked very sweet & charming, though I confess the superior smartness in which she appeared for the occasion did not commend itself to me so much as the familiar black pinafore. We intend to have some similar excursions on future occasions.

Let us say Thursday for dinner. Very likely though I shall see you to-night at the Corner. Digby & Long[3] are perusing as you say. Du moins je l'espère. I did not go to Macmurdo's Swarry on Saturday. Plarr meant to be there though. I wonder if he met your sister. We go

1. William Herbert (1844–1896). The 'critical Ischariot' was no doubt Herbert Williams.
2. By Mrs. Hodgson Burnett at the Globe Theatre. It closed on 17 May.
3. A firm of publishers to whom *Ludovicus* had been sent.

to Cambridge on Saturday next. I was staying in the Wood till yesterday afternoon. You should turn up at No 9 some Sunday. There was quite a formidable tea party there yesterday—Mayhew the brother in law of Berridge who digs with Samuel now is an excellent man. He has the Thomastic way of sitting perpetually on the music stool & playing snatches of opérette—Gilbert & Sullivan, Sultan of Mocha[4] etc. He also sings extremely well, and—praise the gods—has no *"comic"* songs. Congratulations on your wins. But systems, mon cher, are precarious things. *"J'ai vu ça, moi!"* Au revoir—till this evening.

Yours in sec. seclm[5]   E.D.

4. *The Sultan of Mocha*, a comic opera by Alfred Cellier, first produced in 1876 and revived at the Strand Theatre in 1887.
5. i.e. *in saecula saeculorum*, for ever and ever.

100. *To Arthur Moore*

Sunday [*1 June 1890*]

Woodford

Mon cher.

Has this weary old world been too much for you? Was it a razor, or the braces & door peg or how? Or is it the social function which conceals you from our view—and how long shall these things be. In the meantime I break to you gently etc, etc . . . . .[1]

It is back again with the usual formula of regrets & thanks. It has the appearance of being read—the dirty editorial thumb mark—Now *you* shall have it & cart it round for a while. Write to me soon I prithee. I am wasting away slowly with a cold & a graveyard cough—superadded to the profoundest ennui. Plarr was down with me on Thursday & after dinner we sat & smoked for some hours hatlessly on the balcony. Hinc illae lacrimae.[2] This damp June Sunday is also extremely disspiriting. I wish I was not so sensitive to the influence of the weather. My ooflessness is such that I can't buy books even now & my shelves make me weep spleen when I consider how long it will be before they contain (i) Appreciations[3] (ii) the complete works of Newman (iii) Gibbon—his Histories (iv) Morley's 18th Century Studies.[4] Eheu! I

1. *Dr. Ludovicus* rejected once again.
2. Terence, *Andria* 126.
3. By Pater, 1889.
4. *Diderot and the Encyclopaedists*, 1878.

have been lolling over Poe's "Valueless Verse" this afternoon. My latest
Valueless Villanelle[5] I enclose you. It has been sent to "Atalanta" & I
await its return with a philosophic resignation which I would I could
muster equally where my prose is in question. Plarr has some pretty
versicles coming out there, of a little girl playing a violin[6]—a Polonaise!
(My mother is exasperating me at the present moment ~~by~~ with reminiscences of Dijon—Macon—Amiens & other unattainable places
which oughtn't to be mentioned in Woodford. Tace!) I went with
Victor P the other night to the United Democratic in Chancery Lane.[7]
The room (done by William Morris) was excellent—the people very bad
& blatant—Morrison Davison[8] all that but amusing because he was
drunk. On the whole I don't know that democratic rant doesn't irritate
almost as much as the conservative bigotry of the city ship-owner.
What is the reason of the intolerable vulgarity of the present day—at
least in England? I am beginning to think it must be chiefly the effect
of Protestantism. Let's blow up the City and the City Tabernacle.
Even when people make an effort to make the hoardings a little less
hideous—as in this matter of the Zaeo[9] atrocity—they do it from such
ridiculous motives that reasonable persons can't sympathize with them
—I have just had supper & am a trifle less spleenful in consequence.
Nevertheless things are generally pink. Will you be able to come here
next week or will you prefer a dinner and Adélaide? I don't mean of
course that you couldn't have a dinner here—but here there is no
Adelaide. Write & inform me of these things for I feel as if I should
never again be robust enough to beard the piercing draughts of L.I.F.
I am now going to hunt for something to read. Here are olives and
Burgundy. Let me get down "Marius"

always yours   ERNEST DOWSON

5. Probably *Villanelle of Acheron*, which was completed on 25 March. The
    editor of *Atalanta* accepted it in October, but the poem did not appear in
    that magazine. Dowson entered *Villanelle of Sunset* in his notebook on the
    day following this letter, but there is no note of its being submitted to any
    paper.
6. 'The Violin Player', *Atalanta*, November 1892.
7. The United Democratic Club was one of the occupiers of Victoria Cham-
    bers, 55–56 Chancery Lane.
8. Morrison Davidson [*sic*], a barrister of the Inner Temple and author of a
    number of books on socialism.
9. Zaeo was an acrobat performing at the Royal Aquarium, Westminster,
    which advertised her show with a huge poster showing her clad in scanty
    gymnast's costume. As a result of the proceedings brought by the National
    Vigilance Association on 22 May 1890, the Bow Street magistrate ordered
    that the poster 'ought not to be allowed in any public place in London'.

101. *To Arthur Moore*

Sunday [*8 June 1890*]

Woodford

Carissimo.

You missed a Symposium last night after all—Bouthors, Smith, & another man named Smith all turning up. Du reste the evening passed without incident worth noting & I left Tweedy for the wood of the Evangelist soon after midnight. I told you methinks in our too, too brief interview that an idea had come to me for our new Besant & Rice[1] pudding. It is not particularly good or particularly original but it may do. It will be pommade I am afraid, this novel—but it is that is it not which the many headed Beast demands? I propose to take our old friend the self-sacrificing lover of romantic fiction, ditto the weak good looking, backboneless, egotistical, shallow successful lover of— ditto the charming girl & work out their history with a sort of mélange of romantic realism in the way of Norris.[2] Nothing much of an idea there you will remark. Let me proceed—& for the sake of explicity call our personages for the time being—Andrew—Alphonse & Dorothy. Andrew aet 38, both lungs gone, in love with Dorothy but lets conceal- ment prey on his damask cheek etc; of Alphonse his friend he has not a very high opinion but as Dorothy is in love with him & he knows noth- ing very damaging about him he doesn't actively oppose their marriage. When they marry which happens in 1st Vol. his entire object in life is to promote her happiness which is of course variously threatened. In several minor ways he is successful when behold a crisis occurs. An old flame of Alphonse's, a girl of the people whom he has seduced turns up ? with a child & threatens exposure. Tremendous ructions occur which culminate in a strong scene between Alphonse, Andrew, Dorothy & the Frail one (or better perhaps the Frail one's revengeful lover—she her- self being dead) in which as a last chance of ~~keep~~ propping up Mrs Alphonse's happiness & her faith in her husband Andrew takes the affair on his own shoulders and declares that it was he & not the actual guilty party who ruined the girl. The result of which is of course that Mrs Alphonse in her revulsion from suspecting her husband altogether repudiates Andrew & shuts her door on him. The estrangement might be final, Andrew of course dying soon after or be cleared up at his death—as we should decide in discussion. Crudely stated the above is my idea: melo of course & rather violent but the sort of stuff which takes in this country & might be shaded in a good deal beside. I have a good many minor people & episodes in my head as well which I will

1. Sir Walter Besant and James Rice collaborated in fourteen novels between 1872 and 1881.
2. W. E. Norris (1847–1925), author of *Matrimony, The Countess Radna* and several other novels.

give you shortly & no doubt you will add some more. The chief point
of course & the idea which I started from is this voluntary blackening
of his own reputation by Andrew. It is for you to decide if we can start
upon it & if it is practicable & not too risqué a situation. My conception
of Andrew is a rather ironical person whose devotion to the girl is not
suspected by any other of the dramatis personae & only revealed
allusively to the reader—who is considered generally too cold blooded
an individual & too much a persifleur to be capable of a grande passion.
Alphonse is of course a plausible blackguard who arrives—(cf Bel Ami)
& Dorothy our old friend the jeune fille of a million vaudevilles, loved
of the British public—but not very dear to me. The seduced maiden
Nancy might be a model, Alphonse being an artist—or possibly Andrew
might be in some commercial occupation, be manager of works, or a
dry docker & Nancy his foreman's daughter? I should also like to weigh
in rather strongly with her child (Minnie Terry x Nixie x xyz^2) and an
old confidante of Andrews Lady Lowndes who knows him better than
other people. If we placed as I suggested Andrew in a Dry Dock &
Alphonse in a Studio it would have the further advantage that we
could divide the work easily & both weigh in somewhat heavily with
our personal impressions & our actual acquaintance. Give this your
careful consideration & report on it at your early conve.[3] I will try &
look in on you to-morrow. If I don't see you then—write at once as I
am engaged on Tuesd. & Wed. evenings. Perhaps you could dine &
spend Sat to Monday next here & talk it over? Do if you can. However
ἅλις σπουδῆς I am delighted with the sudden lifting of the spell of
sterility which occurred on Friday but fear it will not last. Anyhow I
hope to have my story, now in hand, finished early this week—I am
going to call it, I think, "Fin de Siècle".[4] Parts of it satisfy me more
than most things I have done; parts I am afraid are exuberantly bad.
It is simply a study of the incomplete amourette of a modern whose
critical sense has rather outworn his powers of action—told in the
autobiographical manner of both my printed stories. There is more
psychological motive in it and less of "ficelle" which Bouthors objected
to so in the "Diary". I am half afraid however that the average editor
is less tolerant of morbid psychology than of artistically indefensible
misdirected letters. Well I will even wind up this protracted scrawl
now I go to make a rough synopsis of our new "substitute for Thackeray". Let us call it, par exemple—what? "For Dorothy"? (Pommadish)
  Device
—"A Covenant of Service"?—Wages. ? (be content with your wages),
"The Uttermost Farthing". But no matter. The people are already
beginning to become real to me; may the become so to you to. Au
revoir

           Thine E D

3. This is the first tentative synopsis of *A Comedy of Masks* published in 1893.
 Dowson generally refers to it as *Masquerade*.
4. *The Story of a Violin*, begun in 1889, but not completed until June 1891.

102. *To Arthur Moore*
  [*10 or 11 June 1890*]

Bridge Dock

Mon cher Collaborateur,

"*The World's Wages*". (?).[1] I just send you a LINE! to inform you of a new minor personage whom you might work into your synopsis— Conceiving of our hero as an artistic "stung for lifeur"—with a good deal of *talent*, of an arrivable quality, who arrives at academic renown by backstair influence—let us bring in as a foil—an irreconcileable— entirely disreputable artistic *genius*, refusing to adapt himself in any way either in art or life to convention: He might eventually die of excessive absinthe drinking & general disgust at the bêtise of a public which boycotts his oeuvre & buys Chomondley's pretty little ineptiae. & his friend the hero should previously have calmly appropriated some idea or picture of his & have toned it down into a flamboyant success.

Rainham knows of this but for Dorothy's sake hushes it up—& ?— persuades the injured artist to allow What-is His-Name to take the picture. (They *must* be artists I think).

The *révolté*—call him Oswin for the moment—I conceive as a violent & rather venomous person with however de bons mouvements— & I should suggest that he foregoes his purpose of exposing Chomondley (he must have a better name than that by the bye)—from a semi- cynical aesthetic appreciation of Rainham's devotion to Dorothy—who however had better not be Dorothy. Or Oswin himself might have a sort of uncouth affection for Dorothy too?—On the whole I think the first notion the best. This is one development since I saw you last. 2nd The two artists—with some other artistic & Bohemian types might meet in the early part of the book in a Soho restaurant based on Poland— Chomondley however introduced by Rainham to his old friend Lady Lowndes is taken up by Society & turns a cold shoulder on Bohemia & especially on Oswin to whom of course he is under large obligations.

3rd ~~in vol III~~ previous to the marriage Rainham having a vague suspicion that Chomondley is mixed up with the disappearance of Olga Nethersole remonstrates with him & is assured that it was merely a slight flirtation which has been finished a long time since.

and 4thly he might in the 3rd vol. discover the whole thing & be brought face to face with the Nethersole by picking up her child lost or strayed & restoring her to her mother.

5th I should say that the best dénouement & the most artistic—would be the discovery by Dorothy after Rainham's death & just at the zenith of her husband's successful career (as e.g. on his being made a baronet by a government sensible of the claims of art—) of the actual state of

1. i.e. *A Comedy of Masks*.

the case & of the part which Rainham has played in her life. So—you see, the ironical idea at the bottom of the whole plot—would be clearly brought out at the end—& actually the pathos of Rainham's sacrifice would be only heightened by the suggestion left of its futility. That is about all I have to say I think now. I hope to get your synopsis at any rate ~~before~~ by Saturday & then will make a start somewhere at any rate. I am more taken with the novel than I was at first I must say. And I think conceivably we may work it out in a less pommadish spirit than I feared. The chief difficulty which presents itself to me now is as to the manner in which our heroine (Dorothy—Daisy—Mabel—Valentine—Violet—Iseult—Mildred—yes, why not Mildred?)—is to be introduced. Has Rainham known her since she was a child & does he introduce Chomondley to her?—Or does ~~has~~ Chomondley met her in Switzerland & does he bring Rainham to see her? Or is she a protégée of Lady Lowndes who wants to help her to go on the stage & does Rainham send C. to Lady L & then regret it because her Ladyship match-makes the marriage which from the first he rather dreads?—And again *shall* Rainham be a wharfinger or shall he also be in some artistic genre—or a man of leisure? And who is Olga to be if not the daughter of Rainham's manager? Or would it be better to make her Chomondley's model? Or would that wound the artistic sensibilities of your circle too much?—Well write soon. & mind you send me some more incidents & more characters. At present they stand in my mind subject to your approval as follows, (the names of course quite temporary). Andrew Rainham (a wharfinger). Laurence Chomondley—an artist. *Mr Oswin*—a painter with a French tradition painting masterpieces of brutality in the intervals of drunkenness for 2/6 a piece. Lady Lowndes, a grass widow with a bohemian-aesthetic salon in Brook St—Mrs Tressider & Mildred, her daughter. Bessie—a deceived maiden. Stubbins her lighterman avenger with an eye to blackmail.

Enough for the present: it should be a great book

always yrs   ERNEST DOWSON

103. *To Arthur Moore*

Tuesday [*17 June 1890*]

Bridge Dock

Chéri.

Shall expect you as soon after 6. as you can arrive. Have been struggling at Chap I. Shall probably not be in town myself—but *sans doute* you know your way by this time & there are trains galore.

Yrs   E D

104. *To Arthur Moore*

Saturday evening [*21 June 1890*]

Arts and Letters Club

Dear Collaborator.

Enclosed is the synopsis of "Masquerade" which is I think fairly complete. At least it represents some 8 hours solid manual labour. But I hope you will be able to emend it & expand it somewhat. It should be about that length I fancy, but as you will note, two or three chapters at least I have put down in great brevity & don't quite know how they will be filled up. The drowning episode as you will see I have omitted but it could be worked in if you think it would be best without materially altering the synopsis. The arrangement especially in the order of the first half dozen chapters is of course quite arbitrary & we must arrange at our next meeting what order to follow—besides having to make some distribution of the writing. The only new development is the character of Charles Sylvester. That, I think has the advantage of supplying a necessary sub plot which is besides subservient to & directly tending to the development of the main plot as arranged. The dénouement I am inclined to think should be pretty much as it is. The title "Masquerade" I am really beginning to be somewhat keen on: as also of the general idea of the novel. Of course a great deal more than I have suggested may be made out of Col. Lightmark. Oswyn you see in my synopsis has become an important character: also Mary Masters whose name, if it has not been used is entirely good—in fact the only name which really pleases me. For the present we had better stick to Rainham—though I don't altogether care for Laurence. Write as soon as you get this & have digested the synopsis—which please return with your emendments. ~~I will~~ My address after Monday will be

c/o Mrs Baker
The Cedars
Ramsbury.
nr Hungerford.

However if possible I will try & see you on Monday. I have already made a start on Chap I—& will put my whole energy into the work after this week. Mind & write

always yrs ERNEST DOWSON

105. *To Arthur Moore*
    [*25 June 1890*]

The Cedars, Ramsbury, Hungerford

Chéri Collaborateur.

Having half an hour on my hands after lunch I can hardly employ it better than in sending you a line & entreating you to write to me— soon—soon. This is a charming place & the weather is glorious but—I have an acute attack of nostalgia & I pine for the draughts of L.I.F and the delights of Sherwood St. Your letter will cheer me. At the bottom of the lawn here, runs the Kenneth in which I have been spinning for trout with minnows all the morning—unsuccessfully so far. But it appears to be chock full of them. I am now going to be driven over to Marlbro'. Let me know how your chap. proceeds & what you think of no I. At present I have done no more & may not till I return as I am chiefly out of doors. Also I require an inspiration other than trout and strawberries. You missed seeing a picture on Monday. My little Frauleinchen was quite too adorable in her pinkest pinafore, & a complexion of milk & roses. I hope to be back on Sat. perhaps I shall see you. *Mind & Write*

                              yrs ever   ERNEST DOWSON

106. *To Arthur Moore*
    Friday [*27 June 1890*]

Ramsbury

Mon cher—

Thanks many for your letter. I hope *very much* we may meet to-morrow & arrange a little the order of writing in the subsequent chapters. I have not been able to do anything more but will go away at it on my return. I shall leave Hungerford to-morrow at 1.40 & be at Paddington at 3.50. Could you meet the train & then when I have dis-embarassed myself of my impediments we could tea somewhere. Other-wise I will try & be at the Arts & Letters & shall expect you soon after 5.0.

No more now. Very pleased with Stanhopes frescoes in Marlbro' Coll. Chapel.[1]

                              yrs ever   ERNEST DOWSON

1. J. R. Spencer Stanhope (1829–1908). The frescoes are in the new chapel, completed in 1886.

107. *To Arthur Moore*
Tuesday night [*1 July 1890*]

Arts and Letters Club

Mon cher.

I got the novel all right. It's really excellent—notably chap II, & the Colonel in Chap III. I am not sure whether I would not have preferred Eve a little more ingénue somewhat more "Pansy" (Portrait of a Lady),[1] but that is of course only personal predilection. She is admirably described. The rain kept me away from you to-night. Also my severe physical disabilities consequent on having sat up the *whole* of last night with Lionel Johnson.[2] An extraordinary man who improves on acquaintance. I cant get on very well with Chap IV. Oswyn is a crux. Shall I see you on Thursday. I shall be staying in the Wood all this week. No more now. I am dead with sleepiness.

tout à toi ERNEST DOWSON

1. By Henry James, 1881.
2. Lionel Pigot Johnson (1867–1902) went up to New College from Winchester in 1886 and met Dowson at Oxford. On coming down in 1890 he lived in the Hobby Horse settlement in Fitzroy Street. He very soon became known as a critic, and published two volumes of verse, *Poems*, 1895, and *Ireland*, 1897. He was a close friend of W. B. Yeats and a leading member of the Rhymers' Club. He became a Roman Catholic in 1891.

108. *Postcard to Arthur Moore*
Tuesday [*Postmark 8 July 1890*]

Bridge Dock

I waited some time at the Corner yesterday but I suppose you had gone. To-day I shall be moving down to Woodford again & Wed & Thursday are I fear unavailable. Can you possibly manage a dinner on Friday?—when I hope to be able to bring you anot installment. Try & work it if you can as I am very full of engagements for the next ten days & may not be in town on Saturday. Let me know of the date of your début.[1] I shall try to be there of course. I was not damaged save by mud & bruises on Sat. I waited till nearly 4, & then drove away &

1. Moore was evidently engaged in amateur dramatics.

changed. Awfully sorry I have not managed to catch you for so long.
Au revoir. T à T.   E D

Will write. I fear I must abandon Chap iv. Can you have a try at it?

109. *To Arthur Moore*

Friday (thank the gods) [*18 July 1890*]

Bridge Dock

Mon cher Coquelin.

Schönes wetter! Absolutely the slackest day on record here. For
half an hour I have been vainly trying to proceed with *the* roman. But
they would not. In despair I will commence an epistle to you. I am
going to have a try at Chap vi or vii—(I haven't the syllabub here) in
which Rainham calls on the Sylvesters. But this sort of climate is
against composition. I have finally arranged in (default of your company) to proceed in about a fortnight's time with one A. C. Hillier, of
whom I have spoken to St Malo viâ Southampton, thence to Dol &
Rennes—& thence on foot anywhither as the mood may seize us. That
is to say *I* have decided to do that & Hillier has almost agreed to come
to. I now await his final decision. If he fails me—can't you *possibly*
manage it? It will cost extremely little & the return fare from London
to St Malo is only 40/- My people are all such wrecks that they absolutely decline to go out of reach of an English doctor. They will
probably be on the Broads again—or else on the Thames somewhere. I
go to a better land—& the only regret which enters into my departure
is that—unless you are haply at the 11th hour persuaded—you don't
go with me. Think of the notes we might make. Think of it—& *dont*
go to Oulton which is really a very pink little place.—If you are in
town to-morrow come & see me at the "A & L". I shall be there from
3 on till about 4.30. From 2 till 3 in Poland. If I don't see you then ~~or on~~
write me a Sunday special & console me for this evilest weather that
I know.

                         Yrs ever   ERNEST DOWSON

PS. Happy thought! Would the rabbit come think you to Britainy with
us? Shall I write?——

110. *To Arthur Moore*
[? *late July 1890*]

Arts and Letters Club

Dear Moore.

No signs of the Rabbit so far. Shall be in Poland if you will look in there here up till about 8.45. Will be here again at 9.0. But *come to Poland* if possible. Have left a note for him (the Brer Rab) if he calls. (P.T.O.) saying much the same.

Yrs

in haste   ED

PS. Should you by any chance see Smith or Davies[1] while calling here please be diplomatic. Keep my movements between now & 9.0 dark. (I have nominally gone to Paddington) & on *no account* bring either with you to Pologne—as I should obviously be convicted of culpable misrepresentation of my movements.

1. Charles Joseph Davies (b. 1864) went up to Queen's in 1883, but did not graduate until 1891. Dowson disliked him.

111. *To Arthur Moore*
Friday [*22 August 1890*]

Bridge Dock

Mon Cher Vieux.

Excuse this dilatoriness. I am still wearily working at Chap iv, & though I have nearly done it now I assure you it is greater pommade than you can conceive. You had better send me your chaps as soon as they are done—& I hope my contribution may be before you on Sunday. I had an evening with Johnson on Wednesday. He had just been to Newman's requiem Mass with Pater at the Oratory.[1] I see he has the lion's share of the Academy last week—(2 pages odd) with his review of *Michael Field*.[2] I went away from him with a "Counsel of Per-

1. Newman died on 11 August. A Requiem Mass was sung at the Brompton Oratory on 20 August.
2. Michael Field was the pseudonym used jointly by Katherine Bradley and her niece Edith Cooper; their poems are among the best of the period. Johnson's review of their verse play, *The Tragic Mary*, appeared on 16 August.

fection"[3] under my arm which I have since read. It's meritorious n'est-ce pas? And that a daughter of Kingsley the Intolerable[4] should have such very superior traditions is excellent! London is awful now. I envy you vastly. I leave for Bognor about the 1st.—but what is Bognor? And only for a week.

My people are all away at that delectable *plage* & I am eating my head off with ennui at Woodford alone.

Adelaide doesn't come home till next Wednesday.[5] In the meantime I dine in Poland desolately & listen to extracts from her letters. Then I go to the Club, fill myself with whiskey & play billiards, till about 11. Then I go home. It is very monotonous—but I hope when la chère petite comes back things will improve. Write to me soon, je te prie. I can make no suggestion about Ludovicus—unless it is that you may find a recitation of the office for excommunication in the Rituale Romanum to the Intention of all publishers rather soothing. The phrase "obscoenissima draco" occurs in it & is amongst other objurgations equally choice eminently fitting for these occasions.

I will refrain however. My liver seems as bad as it has ever been & my purse is even in worse case. I hope your health improves. Once more —Write

Yrs. ERNEST DOWSON

3. By Lucas Malet, 1888.
4. The Rev. Charles Kingsley (1819–1875) had begun the bitter controversy which impelled Newman to publish *Apologia Pro Vita Sua* in 1864.
5. She was hop-picking in Kent.

112. *To Arthur Moore*

Friday [*22 August 1890*] 12.30

Woodford

Mon très Cher.

Excuse my dashing you off another note—but I really must. Your instalment has arrived & I can not contain my congratulations. It has cheered me enormously. It is really quite wonderfully good—& the way in which you have made all the necessary points is most effective. The last chapter pleases me mightily especially & my only fear is that I shall not be able, to ~~keep~~ write up to you. I have been down here all this evening dutifully doing my Chap iv. I have just finished it & will copy it & send it you off to-morrow. But I am quite conscious how execrable it is.

I am then going to start on Chap V (iv in the original plan) bringing in Lady Garnett & Mary—then I suppose Chap vi—with Kitty which I confess I funk. Let me know what you are doing now.

I especially admire the very admirable way in which you have brought in the unfortunate Kitty. The only criticism I have to make otherwise is that as I feared you have not succeeded in making Eve a very distinct figure—& I certainly can not either. Our ingénues are certainly our weakest creations. Or are all ingénues so very much alike? You know them better than I do. And you have been at least "interested" in them from time to time—n'est ce pas?—whereas I have been interested in "young persons"—etc but *never* in ingénues. Couldn't she perhaps be a little more in the style of *Pansy*. She doesn't seem to me innocent enough—she seems to have too much the air of society considering that she is only just "out". We have got to bruise her you must remember, & make her suffer & this Eve of ours seems to me a sort of girl who would never suffer as long as she had a French milliner. I can't suggest anything however unless that we try & tone her down a little as we go on—develop her. By the way Rainham so far has been *Philip* not Laurence. Tell me when you answer this, which I hope will be soon—whether you have any definite idea for Chap xii & how the deuce are Chap x & xi to be filled up. Write soon,

always yrs   ERNEST DOWSON

113. *To Arthur Moore*

Wednesday night [*27 August 1890*] 10.30 p.m.

Woodford

Caro Arturo Mio.

I have just got down here & found your letter. I don't feel inclined for the next half hour to buckle to the roman so I will write you a short epistola to keep your courage up & assure you that Chap V is *almost* done & will reach you by Friday I hope—Sat. at the latest. I am getting very much interested in all our personages—especially in Rainham of your last chaps & in Mary Masters whose description I have just accomplished. If as I believe the Garnet ménage comes in at Lucerne in your chap—I may mention pro tem—that Lady G. is a French-woman by extraction (in my version) & that Mary her niece is aet 27, plain with good eyes & voice & a great command of the pianofe. *Please* emend Poland as much as you can.[1] I am *really* awfully disgusted with it & I only hope that the Chap I have in hand is not almost as bad. I

---

1. Chapter IV has a description of a restaurant, Brodonowski's, closely resembling 'Poland'.

have just returned from actual Poland where I have spent most of the evening. Missy came back all right looking rosy & prettier than ever & bringing a good scent of hops & roses with her. The effect of her entry was transfusing—we all with one accord became joyous (I have quite become one of the family you know now) and I observed a stolid German cousin who has been staying there for the last month, knitting in a perfectly torpid condition, smile for the first time. Die Kleine ~~is~~ more entirely ressembles a sunbeam than anything which I have ever come across. I am still mellow from the interlude. I could rhapsodize for many sheets but I will spare you. Only I feel it incumbent on me to let off a little of my exuberance on you on these rare carnivals of the spirit just as I have many times done before on the occasions of my exceptional heights of spleen. They may at least be documents of value if you are ever impelled to make a study of a barometric psychology. However I will wind up now as I shall certainly rhapsodize in spite of my intentions if I continue. I will even go back to Rainham & Mary Masters & all the other uninteresting adults one is foolish enough to write about. Why the deuce does any one write anything but books about children! ~~We~~ Quelle dommage that the world isnt composed entirely of little girls from 6–12. Well, well—you shall have chap V speedily. Send me yours. Don't trouble to answer this letter unless you are specially moved. Its purely ejaculatory

always yrs.   ERNEST DOWSON

Lucerne will do admirably—provided *you* describe it—or Interlaken just as you please. For Heaven's sake tell me what happens in Chaps x, xi?

114. *To Arthur Moore*
29 August 1890

Bridge Dock

Mon cher.

I am sending off chap V herewith. Observe that in the original syllabus it is summarized thus: "*Rainham calls on Lady G. Mary Masters. Enter Sylvesters. Charles & Eve.* (Charles in love with Mary. Eve talks of Lightmk. to Rainham: of the portrait)" As you will note after reading my *Chap* I have only done the portions underlined. The rest requires developping in another Chap I think—?—following on. Would you very much bar going on with the originally intervening Chap between the one I send you & your studio chap? As so far you have undertaken Kitty—in one chap especially which I have never seen—I think you had really better introduce her. Or if you like I will begin the chap with a little local colouring & send it on for you to finish. I *do funk Kitty* so awfully. I want to suggest also that in your subsequent portion somewhere you introduce a conversation between Charles & Lightmark in which the former opens his mind to the latter on the supposed iniquities of Rainham: suggests that he "fait la vie" somewhat. Lightmk. listens with suppressed mirth but not disputing the theory. Re: the picture fraud—the only suggestion I can make is a suggestion as to subject of the picture—an iron vessel docking at night —the flaring lamps—shadows & general murkiness of the thing—& sheen of the water. Oswin does it—L. cribs it & conventionalizes it? I hope you will be able to improve on this thought. Let me have a line by return on these matters. In the meantime I shall either work on the proposed intermediate Chap. or begin on Chap. V (original numbering). It's very cold here to-day. I had a card from Bouthors fr. Ostend. He was to arrive here yesterday. I had tea with Image & Horne yesterday —the latter is doing some charming designs for pew ends. You must go & see the altar which Image has decorated in St Mary's Soho when you come back. I go to Bognor Monday evening. Address from Monday.

Alpha House
Wood St
Bognor.

Send me your Park Chap & the rest—quam celerrime.

Yrs ever   ERNEST DOWSON

115. *To Victor Plarr*

[*6 September 1890*]

Alpha House, Wood St, Bognor

Mon bien Cher

Your letter is the bien venue this morning. I had been meditating an epistle for ages—though I too had a little fear that after Dr Johnson & my heresies you had abandoned me.[1] I am expiring to see you after such a period—& to give you my impressions of that most adorable country. Perhaps you have heard of them & of our ~~impressions~~ adventures from Hillier. My chiefest desire du reste is to make you return with me thither next year.[2] I have I fear to be another X days in this inexpressibly horrid *plage*—full of English Mlls[3] & Varsity men who

---

1. Dowson had earlier thought poorly of Dr. Johnson (see Letter 122).
2. Brittany. Plarr never went there with Dowson, but in 1892 he spent his honeymoon there following an itinerary drawn up for him by Dowson.
3. i.e. mesdemoiselles.

play cricket with them on the sands. The days hang heavy here, nom de Dieu!—& I shall beard the ogress[4] without a pang on my return. Will Walton be with you? I have been seeing a good deal of Johnson the 4tnight I was in Town alone. His first visit to me at the Dock was characteristic; he arrived there at 2-AM & departed at 6-AM. Have you begun the library yet[5]—and have you been writing much—and what?—and when oh when is that poem of a Violin coming out in "Atalanta"? And do We still continue ?[6]—One W. Hall[7] whose poems you saw at Sayle's turned up again just before I left town. I must bring him to see you as he is a charming person & properly a worshipper & devout follower of the most excellent cult of la Fillette. He has a great affection for Jepson[8] & told me things about him wh pleased me mightily. Bouthors is also returned though I did not see him. We must have a symposium shortly. I had a very charming letter from Sayle this morning without traces of that terrible coldness—& so with yours arriving too I am left exultant & pamé in sort of bath of forgiveness. Write again if you have time as je m'embête rudement ici. I am just going out to look at the charming children who swarm here & are the only compensation of these banal ressorts.

Au revoir à bientot

T à t.   ERNEST DOWSON

4. Plarr's fierce landlady, Mrs. Bach.
5. Plarr had been appointed librarian at King's College, London.
6. He means *The Critic*, which was merged with *Society* from 19 July 1890.
7. William Clarke Hall (1866–1932), barrister and later a distinguished metropolitan magistrate, knighted 1932. He published several volumes of religious verse.
8. Edgar Alfred Jepson (1864–1938) had been at Balliol 1883–1887, and had met Dowson briefly. From 1889 to 1893 was in Barbados: he then returned to London, earning his living as a schoolmaster and private coach. From 1893 to 1895 he was often in Dowson's company, and in his *Memories of a Victorian* he gives a vivid picture of Dowson at the time. He published more than fifty novels.

116. *To Arthur Moore*

Sunday [*7 September 1890*]

Bognor

Mon Cher.

Many thanks for your letter & appreciations of the beginning of Chap vi wh I fear is bad however. I will try & let you have Chap x. by Tuesday but I can't be sure as I find it much more difficult than I anticipated & am dissatisfied with the half doz. or so of pages I have already written. I met Lefroy the other day here over for a regatta & am going over to Littlehampton to lunch with him to-morrow. I am *du reste* getting awfully sick of this place, smoking & bathing & reading the English novels wh. circulate in *plages* and listening to the band on the pier of evenings. I shall be deuced glad to get back to town on Satur-day,—if I can possibly manage it. I have been reading Norris's "Mdlle de Mersac"[1] which is pretty eno': also again the "Mill on the Floss"[2] which one can always run through with pleasure. I apologize for this obscure writing but the only pen procurable is of the kind appointed by Providence to be used in post offices & I am afraid you will curse the result. Ludovicus *was* sent to me. I forgot to mention before. It's at Woodford. I saw the 1st no. of the "Whirlwind".[3] It is an amusing extravaganza. Thank the gods I have only seen one no. of the Society cum Critic. I can write nothing but banalités—& can only repeat that I find it enormously hard work to kill the days & shall be hugely de-lighted to see the red blinds of Poland again. So far I think we have got on pretty well with "Masquerade"—practically Vol I ought to be finished before we return to town. We must meet then at the earliest possible. I heard from Smith to-day who has been variously stalking grouse, deer & salmon for the last 2 months with Berridge in Ireland and comes to town on Friday—yesterday from Plarr who has just returned from Hastings—& from Sayle who was to start yesterday for Holland for 3 weeks so I hope town will be less desolate on our return than during the very embêtant week I had before coming here. Write soon

Tout à toi   ERNEST DOWSON

1. Published in 1880.
2. By George Eliot, published 1860.
3. An 'eccentric, original and indiscreet' weekly, which ran for twenty-six numbers, June–December 1890.

117. *To Arthur Moore*
[*c. 11 September 1890*]

Bognor

Mon cher.

Apologies for this delay in acknowledging the completion of Chap vi which is as excellent as it could be. I think we must have an inter-mediate Chap. between that & the Studio—which at present follows on rather abruptly. I am really awfully sorry that I am getting on so

slowly with Chap x. I am afraid I shall not have it done before Saturday
& I am not at all pleased with it. Thank goodness I shall be back on
Saturday & you I suppose are already returned. If you have nothing
better to do turn up on that afternoon at Victoria. I am anxious to press
your hand again after so long an abstinence. I am due at V. at *4.10*: I
shall drive thence (supposing you are invisible) to Poland. Let me see
you if possible somewhere before I resume the treadmill. I have had 2
quaint missives from Johnson this week—one of them asking me to
meet Ghose the Indian poet of Prima Vera.[1] I hope he will not be gone
on my return. I am sick to death of this place—& positively perish with
desire to be seated by a white table in some bright "unEnglish looking
room", in Leicester Sq. clinking glasses with you & observing your face
through a halo of cigar smoke & intoxication. I have just finished the
"Dean & His Daughter"[2] which has cheered me slightly. The ending is
A 1, & worthy of Stendhal himself. The amazing banality of these
places has really the most disastrous effect on my nerves & temper: it
quite undoes any good I derive from the ozone. I am exa[s]perated to the
last degree—I should like to fill myself with arack & run a-muck on the
Parade. Unless Poland has a soothing effect I am afraid I shall have to
go on the heavy rampage for a week when I return. Mon cher, be
advised by me & never while you have a fiole of laudanum or a razor
to save you go to an English sea resort. Drop a line Saturday to the
A & Letters if I am not to see you.

yrs ever   ERNEST DOWSON

1. Manmohan Ghose (1869–1924) went up to Christ Church in 1887. In 1890
   he published a volume of poems, *Primavera*, in collaboration with Stephen
   Phillips, Arthur Cripps and Laurence Binyon. He returned to India in
   1894 and became a professor at the Presidency College in Calcutta.
2. By F. C. Philips, 1887. A dramatized version was produced at the St.
   James's in 1888.

118. *To Arthur Moore*
    Tuesday night [*16–17 September 1890*]

Woodford

Mon Cher.
    I have just posted—or rather I posted some hours ago—Chap x: not
all of it but enough I think to enable you to copy the ensuing one. This
I hope you will do, not following my example but quam celerrime. I
have ~~been~~ to tell you that I expect my yachting will not after all occur.
I may go yet but it will not be this week—& as I should have to "join"

in France the question of "oof" will very likely stand in my way. Here follows a poem which please criticize—& if you can provide with a title.

> A gift of silence, Sweet
> Who may not ever hear,
> To lay down at ~~thy~~ your unobservant feet
> Is all the gift~~s~~ I bear!
>
> I have no songs to sing
> That you should heed or know:
> I have no lilies in full hands to fling
> Adown the path you go.
>
> I cast my flowers away,
> Blossoms unmeet for you,
> The garland I have gathered in my day
> My rosemary and rue.
>
> I watch you pass and pass
> Serene and cold; I lay
> My lips upon your daisied, trodden grass
> And turn my life away.
>
> Yea, for I ~~give~~ cast you, sweet,
> The one gift you shall take—
> Like ointment on your unobservant feet,
> My silence for your sake.[1]

Is "unobservant" legitimate? And where if anywhere, shall the above "nugae" go?

Now that I am booked for at least a week in London which is perhaps the best place to find oneself in after all, I trust you will contrive a dinner somewhere. And remember that in Poland at least, a dinner means two shillings at the most. Do you think also that some Sunday soon you can be available. I want you to meet the beautiful lotus-eyed Ghose & Sunday will be the best occasion. Write to me soon unless I see you & castrate & emend Chap x as much as you can. I am conscious of its many faults. All the same I am of opinion that "Masquerade" so far is a superior production. Yes write soon.

                    always yours   ERNEST DOWSON

Wed—Have definitely refused yachting invite.

---

1. Dated 16 September in Dowson's MS book. It appeared in *The Century Guild Hobby Horse*, October 1891, as *Amor Umbratilis*.

119. *To Arthur Moore*
   [*19 September 1890*]

Woodford

Caro Arturo Mio

   Delighted & surprised at your letter; the chapter satisfied me but very moderately, I suppose because it had been so long on hand. I will try & let you have those Chaps by Sat. I hope to do some to-night—I waited about 10 min. for you last night, but, I suppose, I was too late, or not late enough. I will try & see you to-morrow: will call for you by six. I was with Lionel until 7 of yesterday morning; any day next week except Sat. will suit him to dine with Money & ourselves, at the Aud[   ]¹ any day but Friday w[ill suit me, but] if possible let it be Th[ursday]. Fix it with Money: & let me [know]. I find Galton,² by the way, knows Money! I mentioned his name: he said—'Ah, yes, the man with the beautiful eyes: bring him round here'. This was new to me; but the Hobby is great in discovering unsuspected masculine beauties. Do you call Money 'Pindaric'?

   I went up & had "five o'cloque" with Missy, this afternoon: she was very charming: with much regret I had to refuse an invitation to a like ceremony at Mrs Shakespeare's³ yesterday (Johnson's beautiful cousin with filia pulchriore). They live in Porchester Sq: is it not somewhere near you? I will now go back to "Masquerade". Let me I [   ] you yesterday: perhaps if you are still [   ] you may be able "dissipere in Poloni[a"   ]

   Vale—

Yours ever   ERNEST DOWSON—

P.S. Johnson has sent my "Diary"⁴ to Pater!

1. A corner of the letter is torn off.
2. Rev. Arthur Galton (1852–1921) had been at Cambridge and became a Roman Catholic priest before going up to Oxford as an undergraduate in 1886. He was associated with *The Hobby Horse* and had also been a friend of Matthew Arnold, a volume of whose letters he edited.
3. Olivia Shakespear (d. 1938) published six novels between 1894 and 1910. She was a close friend of W. B. Yeats. Her daughter married Ezra Pound.
4. *The Diary of a Successful Man*, in *Macmillan's Magazine*, February 1890.

120. *To Arthur Moore*
[*9 October 1890*]

Bridge Dock

Mon Vieux.

How are you after our potations on Tuesday morning? I am a little decayed from that & subsequent up-sittings. I had a charming night again on Tuesday at Johnson's & at Horne's. Oscar[1] was on show and was quite charming, & in very good form: also Shannon,[2] (the artist & editor of The "Dial": that mad, strange art review (!): also the prototype of the artist in "Dorian".)—Ghose and Image. The week has been very full of delightful things: and damnable ones. Amongst the latter a sudden descent upon me here of the Social Pest of Took's Court & Cursitor St.[3] He was examining the accomodation of the Sunderland boat which starts from hard by: mercifully he has since departed by it. Worst of all a bomb shell yesterday morning from Bacon's[4] solicitors (Clement Cheese & Green in Pall Mall) inclosing an assignment notice of several of my debts total £22. 14. 6 to the said Bacon: demanding payment by Saturday or-- ! ---! I have answered it & told him that all I can offer is 10/- weekly until it is done: if he accepts that my oofless-ness will be terrible: if not—le déluge! Pray God—they serve the writ quietly & for some distant County Court. As a set off against these various ennuis complicated by neuralgia & heads—there has been first your visit—then Oscar—then the reading of a story[5] which Johnson has written & has sent me to peruse before he dispatches it anywhither. It's a thing quite perfect! a short story that Maupassant & James might have collaborated on & been proud of: a masterpiece of dreariness, strength & delicacy: and it leaves one as Maupassant's stories do quite bruised & overborne by the hopelessness of things. Yes—you will like it. Also among the delightful things an hour in Poland yesterday for "5. o'clocque." which I consumed in the salon au premier while Missy & a small French boy played duets very charmingly on two violins. I dined yesterday with Bouthors which was also pleasant. When shall I

---

1. Oscar Wilde (1854–1900) had scored a great success with his novel, *The Picture of Dorian Gray* published in *Lippincott's Magazine* in June 1890. At this time he was only slightly acquainted with Dowson; after his release from prison in 1897 Dowson was one of the few English writers who did not avoid him.
2. Charles Hazelwood Shannon (1863–1937), English painter and litho-grapher; life-long companion of Charles Ricketts, with whom he pro-duced *The Dial* (1889–1897) and issued numerous finely printed books from the Vale Press.
3. Herbert Williams.
4. Evidently a money-lender.
5. Probably *Tobacco Clouds*, published in *The Yellow Book*, October 1894.

LED–M

see you again—perhaps to-morrow. Alas if the Cheeses accept my liberal offer there will be few festivities for me for many a long day. Even dinners in Poland will have to be fewer. A year at least of dêche. Perhaps it will resolve my *paresse* & make me write.

always yours   ERNEST DOWSON

121. *To Arthur Moore*
[*10 October 1890*]

Woodford

Mon vieux.

The enemy has got the better of me altogether. My face has swollen up to twice the size of a plum pudding. I am shut in the house, support myself entirely on liquids—& at intervals the tusk rageth as per usual. I think in spite of my rooted aversion to the genre I shall have to call in a medicine-man. Write to me as soon as you can. I shall keep close all this week—until I am recognizable. So far the confounded swelling seems merely to increase.

yrs   ERNEST DOWSON

122. *To Arthur Moore*
[*11 October 1890*]

Woodford

Caro Aruro Mio.

Your letter has been my great consolation in this distress, which I fear is not yet over. I am in the hands of the medicine-man, & he speaks possibly of my leaving them early next week. The actual agony of tusk was not very long; but the swelling still remains though it has fallen from the size of an apple to a walnut; & I have only begun to-day to consume comparative solids. To return to your epistle: by all means bring Tweedy to Poland; & may I be there to meet him. Give him my Love. A man going to Chili is to be cultivated: if only for the pleasure of receiving letters from so far a part.[1] I have been too 'down' to tackle

---

1. Something of Dowson's story *The Statute of Limitations* may have been suggested by the circumstances of Tweedy's departure.

"Masqu:^{de}" or anything else in that way; but I hope to have a shot now, in my convalescence which palls on one down here. Cet affreux Woodford! By the way, I find old Waller must have lived here: in one of his poems he talks about

> "those cursed Essexian plains
> Where hasty death and pining sickness reigns."[2]

I have never run across an English lawyer anywhere abroad: a plethora of medicine-men; spiritual & physical; but not of "estate"! I have read a good many reviews of Mabel Robinson's[3] works; none of themselves: I gather she is a sort of George Moore & water; Vizetelly[4] publishes her. Would God, though, I had a novel, even of hers, to read! My people, meaning well doubtless, brought me a book of Marie Corelli's to read: But it was dedicated to "Wilson Barrett, whose Genius needs no Flattery" & I never got beyond that. You *mustn't* read Crawford![5] Indeed I have come to the conclusion that save Meredith, Hardy, Olive Schreiner & Lucas Malet it is safest to ignore English fiction; and the average of those careful craftsmen together is only about a work & a half a year—. These last days I have had to fall back on Boswell, which I am not sure is not more entertaining reading than *any* English novel. As a personality I think the Lexicographer grows upon one more than any other in literature. I started disliking him & I have come to love him as one does Montaigne & Charles Lamb—& who else? Hardly anyone—I think—unless it be Pepys: and no! he is too ridiculous. Let me hear from you again soon: I shall not see you before Tuesday, at the earliest. And if you go to Poland before me tell me all its news. I had a neat, charming little letter from Missie this morning, in answer to one I wrote her explaining my absence. But I suppose she will not write again: so an' you dine anywhere, dine there & tell me of her. Keep me informed also of Tweedy's motions: & write soon.

Le tout vostre   ERNEST DOWSON

PS. Have just received a note from Horne accepting my "Amor Umbratilis"; which pleases me mightily

---

2. *Upon the Death of My Lady Rich*, Edmund Waller (1605–1687).
3. Author of *Disenchantment* (1884) and *A Woman of the World* (1890).
4. Henry Vizetelly (1820–1894), who went to prison for publishing Zola's novels in England.
5. Francis Marion Crawford (1854–1909), a popular novelist of American origin.

123. *To Arthur Moore*
   [*19 October 1890*]

Woodford

Caro Arturo Mio

This is abominable behaviour of yours. Neither a letter nor a "personal interview" to quote C. . . I hoped at the Arts & Letters yesterday: but no: I hoped in Poland the other day when you were to bring Tweedy: but no. I hope now that it does not preface or intimate a recurrence of the old ill. Di meliora![1] Anyhow write, sir & justify yourself. I have little news: none of my story. Johnson [   ][2] been lodging in the same house with Blakelock[3] & that "Blakelock with flashing & excited spectacles is careering Romewards": & has made up his mind shortly to add S.J. after his name. Good! A somewhat similar piece of family news may slightly interest you. My absurd & rubicund cousin of Pembroke[4]—do you remember him?—has also joined the true Church and will shortly go to the Oratory: the second of my cousins who will be there.[5] Good also! Sayle will be received in Rome[6]—Smith may go any day—: this is charming! But I am quite sure that none of these people adore Catholicism more than Johnson & myself—who will nevertheless I believe, continue outside the portals for some time to come.[7] You ought to have come to N.D. de France[8] tonight. There was a procession after Vespers of the Enfants de Marie & I just managed to discern my special Enfant in spite of her veil, carrying a very big banner & looking as usual extremely self possessed & mistress of the situation. It was a wonderful & beautiful situation: the church—rather dark the smell of incense—the long line of graceful little girls all with their white veils over their heads—banners—: a few sad faced nuns— and last of all the priest carrying the Host, vested in white—censed by an acolyte who walked backwards—tossing his censer up "like a great gilt flower": and to come outside afterwards—London again—the sullen streets and the sordid people & Leicester Square! Really a most

1. See Virgil, *Georgics* III.513. Heaven grant a better fate.
2. The letter is damaged and a few words are missing.
3. R. B. S. Blakelock (b. 1867) went up to Queen's in 1886. He took his degree in 1890 and then read theology for a further year.
4. Apparently D. L. Secretan (b. 1871) who went up to Pembroke College, Oxford, in 1890. He graduated in 1894 and was Rector of Balcombe, Sussex 1909–1944.
5. This other cousin was Gerald Hoole.
6. Sayle was received in audience by the Pope on 7 April 1891.
7. Johnson made his submission on 22 June 1891 and Dowson followed him on 25 September.
8. The French Roman Catholic Church just off Leicester Square. Johnson wrote a poem on it, published in *Poems* (1895), which he dedicated to Dowson.

pictorial evening. Childrens voices in concert are wonderful! Children's voices exercised in the "Ave Maris Stella", are the most beautiful things in the world. What a monstrous thing a Protestant country is! I must go bedwards now. I hope I shall see you early this week: I have symptoms of tussis about me though O I cannot tell: To conclude let me inflict on your long suffering attention the last vapourings of my Muse.

AD DOMNULAM MEAM

Little lady of my heart,
   Just a little longer,
Love me: we will pass and part
   Ere this love grow stronger.

I have loved thee, Child, so well
   I can only leave thee:
Nay! my lips should never tell
   Any tale to grieve thee.

Little lady of my heart
   Just a little longer
I may love thee: we will part
   Ere my love grows stronger.

Soon thou leavest fairy-land,
   Darker grow thy tresses;
Soon no more of hand in hand,
   Soon no more caresses!

Little lady of my heart
   Just a little longer
Be a child: then we will part
   Ere this love grow stronger. [9]

A mere trifle—pardon it—who can have inspired it? Write soon or let me see you. I commend you to the Immaculate Heart of Our Lady!
               Always yours   ERNEST DOWSON

---

9. First printed in *The Book of the Rhymers' Club*, 1892. In Dowson's MS book it is dated 18 October.

124. *To Victor Plarr*
   [*26 October 1890*]

                            Woodford

Mon cher Vieux.
   Did you get our visiting card of occasion the other night when we (Johnson & I) violated the midnight silence of Gt Russell St. by shouting

your esteemed name. I think you must have been in bed & Walton reading: the light went out so suddenly. Forgive me if it was real & not an absinthe dream; as many things seem nowadays. Now you will have to come & see me. I shall never be able to face the infuriate Bac(c)h-(ante).[1] I have read your charming articles in the Globe & Macmillan respectively.[2] C'est de l'oeuvre. But I do hope I shall see you soon. Fetch me in Poland, either tomorrow Monday night, or Wednesday, at 8.45 or thereabouts; and we will go the Club, or, where you will! I dined austerely in that quaint refectory of 20 Fitzroy St.[3] on Friday: the bare clothless table is a stroke of genius. Yesterday I took my little Lady of Poland to Niagara[4] which is really rather wonderful. Today I have been lazy, torpid, motionless; getting up at 1 & sitting by the fire all day: du reste, reading Waller whom I think I prefer to the other 17th. century poets. I have only just mustered sufficient energy for letter writing. I hope everything prospers with you; and that I shall see you soon.

I am trying to write a Bréton story[5]—& to finish that interminable story[6] of which you saw the beginnings. If I fail to see you—write.

Yours ever   ERNEST DOWSON

1. Mrs. Bach, Plarr's landlady.
2. Most contributions to *The Globe* were unsigned and Plarr's article there cannot be traced. *Macmillan's Magazine* for October contains *The Shrine of the Fifth Monarchy* by him.
3. The *Hobby Horse* house; Plarr went to live there in 1891.
4. A panoramic show of the Falls, with stereoscopic views 'of all America', at York Street, Westminster.
5. *A Case of Conscience*, printed in *The Century Guild Hobby Horse*, April 1891.
6. *The Story of a Violin*.

125. *To Arthur Moore*
[*26 October 1890*]

Woodford

Vieux.

I have come to an arrangement with Clement Cheese:[1] practically what I suggested. But there are points I should like to consult you about before definitely closing; so prithee try & see me to-morrow (or is it to-day?)—Monday: I mean go not from the office before I arrive which

1. The solicitors collecting Dowson's debt to Bacon (see Letter 120).

I will surely do. Enough of such disagreables for the present. I hope I shall receive an edition de luxe to-morrow. I waited at the Club for you yesterday when I had returned Missie to her parents. Niagara was really not bad. I dined with the "Hobby" on Friday & of course spent the night there. We (Johnson & I) went out to a mass in the gray dawn after it. I have spent a very lazy day here: rising at one; sitting at the fire side & smoking; awaking sufficiently in the evening to complete Part 1 of my story, which I call "A Case of Conscience". I will get on with "Masquerade" directly that is finished & dispatched—to Mowbray Morris:[2] I must raise some argent now. Johnson was very furious the other night, having just been rejected by his "own familiar" tutor, Courtney[3] of "Murrays"—an ill omen for oneself in that quarter. I have made an endeavour to-day to read the Philoktetes; compassing about 50 lines; it's a distinct grind but I think necessary, if one is not altogether to lose the habit of Greek. Have you read "Wee Willie Winkie"?[4] etc? I am going through a course of Kipling directly. The Fitzroy St copies are all lent to the Ballet at present; but I shall follow on with them when they return. How is your health? The absinthe I consumed between nine and seven of the morning on Friday seems to have conquered my neuralgia, though at some cost to my general health yesterday. The curious bewilderment of one's mind after much absinthe! One's ineffectual endeavours to compass a busy crossing! The unreality of London to me! How wonderful it is!

However I think I will finish this scrawl now, since I shall see you to-morrow.

always yours   ERNEST DOWSON

2. 1847–1911; editor of *Macmillan's Magazine*.
3. W. L. Courtney (1850–1928), formerly Fellow of New College, now editor of *Murray's Magazine* and on the staff of the *Daily Telegraph*. Editor of *The Fortnightly Review* 1894–1928.
4. First published in 1888.

126. *To Herbert Horne*

Friday [?7 November 1890]

Bridge Dock

My dear Horne,

Your suggestion is most kind & I thank you for it. The story[1] is away at present, but when it returns, as it very probably will, I shall be

1. *A Case of Conscience.*

delighted to give you the next refusal of it. I am a little afraid however that even should it otherwise commend itself to you, you may find its length sufficient ground for rejection: anyhow I will send it you next.

Sincerely yours   ERNEST DOWSON

127. *To Arthur Moore*
    [*c. 25 November 1890*]

Bridge Dock

Caro Mio.

A million apologies for my remissness yesterday. It was impossible for me to reach you within a reasonable hour and too late, when the matter which prevented me, arrived to wire. I hope you did not wait long. I had the *Lucerne chap*: to bring you, but it was 6.30 before I had got further West than Cannon St. On further thoughts, I shall probably bring you nothing now till Sat: as the Park Chap, which I have done nothing to yet is in the same vol with that. I have also to finish up the other Chap in same book. Chap xiii shall be done by that day too & I hope Chap I Vol II which I have also in hand. Figure to yourself my consternation: on Monday, on the top of a bus, I met Williams! He was "numquam mutatus ab illo"[1] whom you know: insufferable, blatant, mendacious, fulsome—ugh! I also saw C. H. Swanton, last night, in Poland: his schemes seem falling through, but he is always sanguine.

By the way I hear that the Case of Conscience" has found favour in the sight of Horne, Image & Co & will appear in the next number. They have said some very pretty things about it. I am dining at home to-night and Friday. You must not wait for me: but perhaps I will call for you on Thursday; otherwise, at the A & Letters I hope on Saturday. I know I had other things to say to you: but I forget them. A riverderci!

yours   ERNEST DOWSON

1. cf. Virgil, *Aeneid* II. 274. Completely unchanged.

128. *To Charles Sayle*
   [*c. 25 November 1890*]

Bridge Dock

My dear Sayle.

I wonder whether you are still in England: or where? and if this will reach you. Anyhow it seems some time since I heard of your news & I will chance it: thanking you, to begin with, again for ~~your~~ the very kind letter, which I last had from you. I have been story-writing again: a Bréton piece, this time; which, having been refused, insultingly by Mowbray Morris & Temple Bar; has been taken by Horne, & will appear, probably, in the next "Hobby". I have been seeing a good deal of the people in Fitzroy St lately: chiefly of Lionel Johnson, who seems to me more wonderful & adorable the more I see of him. I have watched many nights with him; down here, until the morning broke over the gray river; and in Fitzroy St, in those charming rooms: each time I have come away more astonished at his extraordinary width of knowledge: at his Catholicity in every sense, including Zola & Newman. Another very charming person, of whom I am seeing much also, & whom doubtless you know is Ghose the Primavera poet: a divinely mad person! The climate here is less trying than usual at this season, though I should not be sorry to have the Channel & the most of France between me & it. Are you likely to be in town soon: you should run up, for the last time of the "Orfeo",[1] at Covent Garden next Saturday: if you are coming, I hope you will let me know & manage to see me. There is a good deal I want to converse of with you. I quite feel that one can do nothing but join the Church: but it is a great wrench & full of difficulties: for many reasons, I think it must wait till I am abroad. Let me hear from you when you have time: we had a symposium in my Poland, the other night at which Johnson, Plarr, Moore & my French friend Bouthors were present; you ought to have been with us. Please remember me very kindly to your mother.

always yrs.   ERNEST DOWSON

PS. I have also a poem coming out, some time, in the "Hobby Horse" which, I hope you will like.[2]

---

1. One of Covent Garden's few successes at this time. Giulia Ravogli in the title part won praise even from Shaw—a rare triumph for any singer. The last performance of the season was on 29 November.
2. *Amor Umbratilis.*

129. *To Arthur Moore*

Thursday night [*?4 December 1890*]

Woodford

Caro Mio.

I had hoped to see you to-night but I got to town, too late, to call for you: so I send you now a line, on my return, here, to remonstrate with you for not turning up at Fitzroy St last night. I hope I shall see you at the Club on Sat: but if not, write & let me hear of all things. I am going to take "Missie" to Mme Tussaud's (it will be my very first visit to that institution which seems incredible) on Sat afternoon & as I shall have to take her back to her parents (which will involve my five o'clocquing there) I may not get to the Club before 5.45 or so: perhaps you will call in at Poland: or dine there and in all probability meet Bouthors. What by the way of our symposium? Was it a success or not? I couldn't be quite sure. Or was the McLachlan[1] very much disgusted with the veal cutlet? If I don't see you, you must write & report on these things. And now let me make an act of contrition for my slackness in regard to the *opus*: it is partly the completion of Vol I which has temporarily afflicted my energy: partly, owing to the fact that I have been writing, and have nearly finished another *Nouvelle*;[2] which the editors, qui payent, really *shall* take: and also, mon cher, I have another story in my head, which must get itself written at once, "The Madness of Captain Max."[3]—a story in a different vein to my most: wild, fantastic, full of the sea, with a description of a death by drowning which I am keen on. But eheu editores! If these two and *Masquerade* fail, I seriously intend to give up writing, enter the Order of St Benedict and devote my life to editing the Fathers. Will you join me? We might collaborate, with advantage, on a commentary on St Alphonse Liguori! And we should look so charming in the Benedictine habit: not to mention the liqueur! I am reading a vol. of Hazlitt's essays: do you know them? They are surprisingly good: better than Leigh Hunt; and there are wonderful phrases every now & then. And have you read the Pater in the 4tnightly?[4] Do: it's full of marvellous sayings, and curiously bloody. I think the Master too,[5] is succumbing to the prevailing homicidal madness. We opened, by the way, a brand new bottle of absinthe for your & Money's benefit, last night: and you were not! It is a pity "Missie" is so coy in the presence of 'company'—you have hardly an opportunity of appreciating her.

1. i.e. W. M. Money.
2. Still *The Story of a Violin*.
3. There is no evidence that this was ever written.
4. On Mérimée. *The Fortnightly Review* for 1 December 1890.
5. The reference is still to Pater. Henry James had published nothing in England since *The Tragic Muse* in June 1890.

To-night she was more adorable and wonderful than ever before: if only you could come oftener, and let her get to know you, I believe you would worship her, as I do. However, la petite apart, is not the place an Institution? By the way, here is, as far as I recollect the roll of persons who have at different times dined or coffeed there with me, some of whom might form a Decameron, when the private room is started.— Yourself, Swanton, Smith, Tweedie, Berridge, Lefroy (Queens). Sayle, Johnson, Money (New) Plarr, Hillier (Worcester) Walton (Keeble) W. Hall, Ghose (Ch Ch) Bouthors, Noblet[6] (Paris). A noble collection and to be, let us hope, in time, judiciously increased. Good night. In beer, the only drink, I have been able to find, I propose a toast to you. Floreat Polonia.

Yours in saecula   ERNEST DOWSON

6. Probably the French journalist mentioned in Letter 98. He lived at Mons-par-Donnemarie, where Dowson went to see him in 1895.

130. *To Arthur Moore*

In fest John Lubbock [*26 December*] *1890*

Woodford

Caro Mio.

Your letter consoled me in the desolation of this hilarious season. I pity you & send you my sympathy for doubtless your festivities are longer & more constant than mine. I have been down here, drearily looking out at black trees, white, sorrowful snow, infinite cold, since Wednesday. To morrow I go back to civilization & comparative warmth: I gather from your note that I shall not see you. I have become a member of the "Grosvenor" since I saw you last so henceforward Albemarle St sees me no more. It's an improvement on the old place but, I fear, rather too conventional. I dined there on Tuesday with a Captain Rolleston,[1] who procured my election, Hillier; 2 more Irishmen. We were all very, very dull & banal: and après I was introduced to other people, tedious soldiers and pompous ecclesiastics, who seem to make a majority of the members. Only, there is a library of sorts, and the quarters are sumptuous. My pity for your task! I heard from Johnson, by the same post, which brought me yours, from his paternal mansion in Windsor Forest. He is pining for London and Absinthia

1. Probably Charles Ffranck Rolleston, Irish magistrate and Captain of Militia (1833–1913).

Taetra: I am pining for you both, and for Poland. Deo Gratias! this season is now fairly done with. My liver is all alive: or is it a last dying flutter? I know not where the early afternoon will find me, but I shall five o'clocque in Poland. My resources are at their Nadir and—£1 or 30/- are problematically distant. I sent Missie the works of the immortal 'Carrol':[2] & had a pretty card from her this morning. (This pen is hopeless: excuse it). I haven't succeeded in writing a page more of "Masquerade" or of anything during the holidays. I have read a good deal though in amends: chiefly French. The new 3 chaps of Zola's forthcoming "L'Argent" in a supplement of "Gil Blas" are promising.[3] But it is a weary and evil world. "Quand, oh, quand cela donc, finira t il? And the cold surpasses my experience: it withers, shrivels, consumes me. "Mittit Deus crystallum suum sicut bucellas: ante faciem frigoris ejus, quis sustinebit?"[4] Everybody is away except Smith, who, I expect, is rabidly furious with me for having avoided him these five days. Ma chè vuole? at a distance I admire & esteem him: but there is a certain lack in him, of subtility, or of tact; which is the outward & visible sign of an inward & spiritual subtilty; which at times reduces me to the last stage of abjectness— And this 3 months at Brighton[5] seems to have undone all the good civilizing effect of his year in town.

Well, I hope I shall see you to-morrow: or, at least, soon. Cura ut scribas: yes, write at once. Do read the "Pater" in the 4tnightly! and read Sir William Temple,[6] omnia quae extant. And read, when it appears, Galton's article in the Jan. Hobby—so topically, sweetly ironical, on the Parnell agitation, & the Rabelais raid, and the delicate wit of Dr Joseph Parker, that greasy pestilential fellow![7] O great, ineffably stupid beast the public! However "When all is done", says Temple, "human life is, at the greatest & the best, but like a froward child, that must be played with & humoured to keep it quiet, till it falls asleep; and then, the race is over"[8]

Vale et me ama.[9]   ERNEST DOWSON

---

2. Lewis Carroll published the two *Alices* in 1865 and 1872; and *Sylvie and Bruno* in 1889.
3. The novel appeared in 1891.
4. Psalm 147. The Vulgate was one of Dowson's favourite books.
5. Smith's first job as master in a preparatory school.
6. English diplomatist and essayist (1628–1699). Jonathan Swift was for a time his secretary.
7. This article by Galton, writing as 'Anthony Deane', was held over until the October 1892 issue of *The Century Guild Hobby Horse*. It was occasioned by the police raid on an exhibition of paintings illustrating Rabelais. This had come about at the instance of the Purity Society and its secretary, the Rev. Joseph Parker, who had long been notorious for his moral strictures on the theatre.
8. In the Essay on Poetry.
9. A friendly form of letter-ending, imitated from Cicero. 'Farewell, and keep your affection for me.'

131. *To Arthur Moore*

Friday [*2 January 1891*]

Grosvenor Club, 135 New Bond Street, W.

Carissimo Mio

Concerning to-morrow: do not come to Poland at lunch time; because I shall not be there: and a certain prophet[1] may be: but come to me here when you like, after 2.30. Or, if that is impossible, five o'cloque with me in Poland at 5.0: very likely there will be other company. In the evening I have to meet Oscar & a select assembly at Hornes:[2] and on Sunday— woe is me—to dance till 6.A.M, or not to dance, which is more probable at the Heresiarch's.[3]

No more: cura ut venias!

Amantissime   ERNEST DOWSON

1. Sam Smith.
2. This gathering was probably the first meeting of the reconstituted Rhymers' Club. Begun as a gathering of Irishmen living in London, it was now reorganized on a broader basis and met regularly during the next three years. The two collections of verse by its members (1892 and 1894) contain much that is characteristic of the decade.
3. The Rev. Stewart Headlam.

132. *To Samuel Smith*[1]

[*c. 1 February 1891*]

[Woodford]

. . . . Johnson yesterday: and that is all I think. I have just read through the VIth Aeneid; and am intoxicate with its adorable phrases. After all with all our labours of the file and chisel we can not approach these people, in this gross tongue.—"Sunt lacrimae rerum et mentem mortalia tangunt"—"Umbrarum hic locus est Somni Noctisque soporae,"—

Discedam, explebo numerum reddarque tenebris.
I, decus, i nostrum; melioribus utere fatis."

1. This fragment, written on the back of a manuscript of Dowson's poem *Vain Hope*, is all that Smith preserved of the letter. The dating is uncertain. See Letter 140, note 1.

On to the last couplet, by the way, I have tagged a sonnet:* which I will show you hereafter[2]—Write soon; pardon these meanderings and be critical and candid to the here to-before-appended.

Tuissimus   ERNEST DOWSON

* Entitled "To a Child growing out of Childhood: and Away!" (a real Hobby Horse title, I swear.

2. Dated 31 January in Dowson's notebook, and first published in *Poetical Works*, 1934.

133. *To Arthur Moore*

Monday evening
In fest Pur: Virg. [*2 February 1891*]

Grosvenor Club

Carissimo Mio.

I had hoped to see you on Saturday or to-night: but my movements were too vague to give you due notice of, on the first occasion: and to-day I came away too early to call for you. But perhaps on Wednesday? or Thursday?—The novel (Lud:) is now under consideration by the Editor of the "People". Lee[1] has promised, that it shall be read & his influence brought to bear. He is not the Editor, as I believed but assistant [ditto] & dramatic critic of the sheet. I hope for the best, but am not confident.

Thursday at Horne's was very entertaining: a most queer assembly of "Rhymers"; and a quaint collection of rhymes. Crane (Walter)[2] read a ballad: dull! one Ernest Radford,[3] some triolets & rondels of merit: "Dorian" Gray[4] some very beautiful & obscure versicles in the latest

1. Probably Edgar Lee (1851–1908), journalist and proprietor of the Universal Press Agency.
2. Book illustrator and poet (1845–1915).
3. Secretary of the Arts and Crafts Society, poet and editor (1857–1919). His first volume of verse, *Measured Steps*, appeared in 1884. He contributed to both the collections published by the Rhymers' Club.
4. John Gray (1866–1934) was at this time a librarian at the Foreign Office. In the next few years he became a distinguished poet and translator. He contributed essays, stories and poems to numerous periodicals and wrote plays in collaboration with his wealthy friend André Raffalovich. His friendship with Wilde and his good looks led to his nickname 'Dorian' and

manner of French Symbolism; and the tedious Todhunter[5] was tedious after his kind. Plarr and Johnson also read verses of great excellence; and the latter, also, read for me my "Amor Umbratilis": And Oscar arrived late looking more like his Whistlerian name,[6] in his voluminous dress clothes, than I have ever seen him.—

Have you perused the "Anti Jacobin"?[7] Johnson did the Newman letters & Ionica:[8] the latter review struck me as; well! as—! I have just been reading the extraordinary work by Professor Newman on or against his brother the Cardinal.[9] The Fliegende Blätter[10] is tame to it: it seems to be written by an ill bred school girl—for style, it is an insult to compare it with Ryder Haggard:[11] and for matter, it is so obviously silly as to become really funny. A work as laughable as "Rudder Grange".[12] Buy it: it would be cheap at a sovereign. Johnson is to castigate it for Greenwood,[13] but urbanely and with a smile.

I went to Hengler's[14] with Missie on Sat. Certainly a circus bores me less than pantomime. And yesterday at "Notre Dame de France" where I took Johnson, I had the pleasure of observing her, in procession, very charming and demure, & white veiled.

Let me hear from you soon. It is 7.0: & I go to Poland.

Amantissime   ERNEST DOWSON

the incorrect belief that he was the original of the character in Wilde's novel. In 1898 he gave up his previous life to study for the Roman Catholic priesthood. He was ordained in 1901 and the rest of his life was spent in Edinburgh, where, with the help of Raffalovich, he built St. Peter's, Falcon Avenue.

5. John Todhunter (1839–1916), Irish poet and playwright.
6. Mr. Mantalini. 'Never let me see you . . . in the combined costume of Kossuth and Mr. Mantalini,' the painter once said to him.
7. *Anti-Jacobin*, 31 January 1891. Johnson reviewed *Letters and Correspondence of John Henry Newman during his life in the English Church, with a brief autobiography.*
8. Poems by William Cory. Originally published anonymously in 1859 (second series, 1877), now reprinted with additional poems.
9. F. W. Newman (1805–1897), *Contributions Chiefly to the Early History of the Late Cardinal Newman* (1891).
10. A scurrilous weekly published in Munich, 1844–1935.
11. Rider Haggard made his name with *King Solomon's Mines* in 1886. *She* and *Allan Quatermain* appeared in the following year.
12. A novel by F. R. Stockton, 1879.
13. Frederick Greenwood, founder and editor of *The Pall Mall Gazette* and *St. James's Gazette*, and of *The Anti-Jacobin*.
14. Hengler's Grand Cirque was in Argyll Street, the building later being transformed into the Palladium.

134. *To Arthur Moore*
Edition de Dimanche [*7 February 1891*]

Woodford

Mon Cher Vieux.

I have a new, indelible pencil, which I propose to test on you, in the luxury of an arm chair. I thought I might see you yesterday: I had not time to acquaint you that I would be at the Grosvenor till 6: but I *was*: fideli cum Hillier, who also hoped to see you. Perhaps tomorrow, at the corner:[1] but, if I don't, write, and criticize the-on-the-other-side-appended-versicles which I wrote yesterday:[2] an experiment; the 3 first lines in Alexandrines, a favourite rhythm of Lionel's; but one in which at present my Muse is not quite at her ease. Today, mea culpa, mea maxima culpa, I have done nothing, neither "Masq[de]" nor my story: but a time will come, & please Mary, a place! Yes! I am reading Daudet's early novel "Jack", with some difficulty. Its too much like Dickens for my taste. Also I have run through "Silas Lapham" again: pace Lionel, who declares it finer than anything of James, I dont value it unius assis. Clever, very: banal equally—no, I don't mean that. Only what shows chiefly is an incomparable Talent for entering into the souls of vulgar people—and not in the judicial artist attitude of Flaubert & the Goncourts, but from their own point of view. Howells is provincial: Boston is really the standard by which he measures and weighs all things. He has no horizon, and then he writes in dialect, in Yankee and that's not realism (even Zola doesn't go so far) it's reportage. Thank God for James!

I am in risk of losing the post: cura ut scribas if I don't see you— Vale

Yrs ever ERNEST DOWSON

Non sum qualis eram bonae sub regno Cynarae!

HORACE Odes, IV, I, 3.

Last night, ah, yesternight, betwixt her lips and mine,
There fell thy shadow, Cynara! thy breath was shed
Upon my soul, between the kisses and the wine;
And I was desolate, and sick of an old passion,
    Yea, I was desolate and bowed my head:
I have been faithful to thee, Cynara, in my fashion.

1. Lincoln's Inn Fields.
2. Dowson's most famous poem. It is dated 7 February 1891 in his notebook and was first printed in *The Century Guild Hobby Horse*, April 1891.

All night, upon my breast, I felt her warm heart beat,
Night-long within mine arms in love and sleep she lay;
Surely the kisses of her bought, red mouth were sweet;
But I was desolate and sick of an old passion,
    When I awoke, and found the dawn was gray:
I have been faithful to thee, Cynara, in my fashion.

I have forgot much, Cynara, gone with the wind,
Flung roses, roses riotously, with the throng,
Dancing to put thy lost, pale lilies out of mind,
But I was desolate and sick of an old passion,
    Yea, desolate, because the dance was long:
I have been faithful to thee, Cynara, in my fashion.

I cried for madder music and for stronger wine,
But when the feast is finished and the lamps expire,
Then falls thy shadow, Cynara! the night is thine;
And I am desolate and sick of an old passion,
    Yea, hungry for the lips of my desire:
I have been faithful to thee, Cynara! in my fashion.

135. *To Victor Plarr*
    [*2 March 1891*]

                                    Bridge Dock

Mon Vieux.
    Seriously—what of my suggestion concerning the mutual-of-some-of-our-poems-presently-publication gewesen? If you don't mind!—At least if we can't do it now, we might select about twenty, ten of yours & ten of mine, arrange them, get a happy title—have them typed and discover what the cost would be. A thin little booklet of some twenty four pages would contain them—& ought not to cost more than £10. Perhaps Image would design us a cover. Give this your attention.[1]

                R O S E S   A N D   R U E
                by Two Authours.

Or Suaviola. or Vine leaves & Violets. or "Apple Blossom from Oxford" "Jean Thorel" who can't read English shall write us a French preface in the delightful French fashion stating how fine & large the poems are. You will be able to put in your "Disciple" sonnet: & reproduce those charming, idyllic verses which were wasted upon "Seafaring". I wish

---

1. This project came to nothing.

by the bye I might have a copy of those: I have lost that number which contained them.

Write to me if you have time: I shall not see you this week I expect unless it be on Saturday.

"Tout votre" ERNEST DOWSON

---

136. *To Arthur Moore*

[*4 March 1891*]

[Bridge Dock]

Dear Vieux.

Herewith I leave the long deferred "Hand".[1] and MSS of my last story—a typed version of which is now on its way to Mowbray Morris.[2] May he be merciful. Send me a criticism at your earliest—as no one has seen it so far & I feel nervous: although I have a sort of notion that it's the best I have done yet in point of style—as it is certainly the one (finished) which has caused me the most travail. I am all right enfin: & hoping to see you: but pretty full of engagements this week. Am dining with Horne to night: alone: formidable: & on Friday with Hillier—& his grandmama—: & yesterday with Ghose. To-morrow or Saturday will see you. Write anyhow, please, re. story.

alys yrs. ERNEST DOWSON

1. Probably Moore's *The Stolen Hand*.
2. Probably *Apple Blossom in Brittany*, published in *The Yellow Book*, October 1894.

---

137. *To Victor Plarr*

Thursday night [*5 March 1891*]

Woodford

Mon Cher Vieux.

Thanks for yours; the spirit in which you accept my suggestion is precisely my own: £10 is a chimerical sum to me; but let us prepare our garland for the day (surely it must come) when this impecunious tyranny is overworn.

Of the titles I like not much the Teutonic ones; they are quaint but not harmonious. Best seem Suaviola or Gossamer—as affording least handle to the banality of critics: better I like "Vineleaf & Violet"—& best perhaps "Rose & Pine"—both of which titles would certainly drive the same critics wild If the former of these two like you perhaps the appended perfectly meaningless verses would come in. It is the only poem that I ever wrote straight off in less than an hour. But *why* "Rose & Pine" and *why* "Vine Leaf & Violet"—? will the critics observe! I have been looking over my "Poesie Schublade" as represented by a small MSS book[1] and it will be with difficulty that I shall find ten worthy of the company of the least of yours. I will bring up about 15 if I can of the least bad & you shall reject five. Let me know if you will be in on Saturday afternoon: either this Sat: or next I go to Brighton; but if I am in town this next one, and you, I should like to see you. Horne was really exceedingly charming & kind last night: we had no one else not even the genial MacMurdo; and at 11.30 we strolled Alhambra-wards but were too late for his divinities so he accompanied me east-wards as far as St Mary le Strand. I was with Ghose on Tuesday: he is very anxious to meet you; therefore if you permit it, I will bring him round to you one evening next week. To morrow night I dine with Hillier at the Grandmaternal mansion: but he is I believe alone—I was in Poland to night: why did you not drop in to coffee? *Die Kleine* instead of changing, altering, repelling, as I $\left.\begin{array}{c}\text{hoped}\\\text{feared}\end{array}\right\}$ might happen, in the nature of things, seems to grow in grace & favour daily. What a terrible, lamentable thing growth is! It "makes me mad" to think that in a year or two at most the most perfect exquisite relation I have ever succeeded in making must naturally end. Yes, it makes me mad! One ought to be able to cease caring for anyone exactly when one wished; it's too diffi-cult: or one ought to be able to live entirely in the present. Something is distinctly rotten in the State of Denmark. Mon cher, I am afraid you have a very bad influence over me: you see I can't even write to you without becoming unreasonable. I shall have to read a sermon of But-ler's and a little Mill before I go to bed. One ought to be exactly as one should like to be, all at once and always! I should like to be a sort of combination of Mill & Newman with a little dash of Voltaire. And instead of that—pah! You will tell me I am either insane or insincere; probably both. Forgive me for inflicting these lengthy hieroglyphics on you & believe me.

always yours   ERNEST DOWSON

> Violets, and leaves of Vine,
> Into a frail fair wreath,
> We gather and entwine!

---

1. His MS notebook, now in the Morgan Library. For an analysis of its con-tents see *Poetical Works*.

A wreath for Love to wear,
Perfumed as his own breath,
To crown his brow divine,
                    night
All day till ~~eve~~ is near
Violets and leaves of Vine
We gather and entwine!

Violets and leaves of Vine
For Love that lives a day,
We gather and entwine!
All day till Love is dead,
Till Eve falls cold and gray,
                    blossoms
These ~~flowers of~~ yours and mine
Love wears upon his head!
Violets and leaves of Vine
We gather and entwine.

Violets and leaves of Vine,
For Love, when poor Love dies,
We gather and entwine!
This wreath that lives a day
Over
~~Upon~~ his cold pale eyes
Kissed shut by Proserpine
~~we sorrowfully~~
~~At fall of night~~
At set of sun we lay
Violets and leaves of Vine,
We gather and entwine.[2]

2. Dated 16 October 1890 in Dowson's notebook and first published in
Verses.

138. *To Victor Plarr*
    [*20 March 1891*]

Bridge Dock

Mon Cher.
    Thanks for the charming verses:[1] I like them, really, very much; a
great deal better indeed than that they treat of, whether supplied in the

1. *Burlesque*, included in Plarr's *In the Dorian Mood* (1896).

form of Alhambra, Gaiety or Pantomime. Yes, I admire the poem, the two last lines of the 5th stanza especially, and the ingenious rhymes, *partout.* You must give it to the "Rhymers".? & to "Violets & Vine Leaf" of course. It has given me the first intelligible notion of your, and the Fitzroyal, ballet worship which is vouchsafed me. I still am unable to join you; but I have, now, an impression of your temper; and respect it, as, at least, a form of intoxication.

I send you, in return, my latest Versicles:[2] the merest "symbolism", almost too slight for criticism! Its an attempt at mere sound verse, with scarcely the shadow of a sense in it: or hardly that so much as a vague, Verlainesque emotion. Its an inferior production. I hope we shall meet soon: if you are near the Club on Sat, would you mind calling for me on the chance? Very likely, I may not be there, however, so do not go out of your way for that. I have done nothing, seen nothing, nobody, the week. Simply sat here and otherwhere, "plumbing the depths of depression": in various bottomless, black pits of pessimism. And so I suppose I shall continue to do usque ad finem. Well: au revoir—à bientôt.

T.V.   ERNEST DOWSON

2. Probably *Vanitas*, which Dowson wrote on 19 March 1891.

139. *To Arthur Moore*
    [*20 March 1891*]

Bridge Dock

Caro Mio.

Your letter was the bien venu: for precisely that day, I was meditating an inroad on your corner. On Wednesday I dined at home. No, no, I cannot matinize: there is nothing I want to see, and if there were, such a weariness to the flesh of me has theatre going become that like enough, I should not go. I *must* go to the Museum though—but I know your aversion to it: still if you can compass it, you will find me there from 3–6, among the books. Endeavour: I know not whether it be the weather or what, but I have passed the week, in a consuming ennui, tristesse, spleen, and nostalgia of everything. Surely April must change this tyranny: if not, at least it will be April; and bring with it the rest of "The Pupil".[1] I have been writing verses, in the manner of the

1. By Henry James, in *Longman's Magazine*, March–April 1891.

French "symbolists": verses making for mere sound, & music, with just a suggestion of sense, or hardly that; a vague Verlainesque emotion. They are not successful enough to send you. Plarr has sent me a string of appreciative, impressionist verses on "Burlesque", which you will like. Johnson in to-morrow's "Anti Jacobin" is good with a burlesque of Swinburne's prose: "a papyrus from Putney".[2] Get it.

A white, monstrous, mist has come down over the river within the last ten minutes, obscuring everything; and the ships glide by in it like great, shameful moths. Why is not Oswyn here? A sense of perfect desolation about—damp, decay dreariness: incapacity to meet all possible events: one's mind grows as gray as the river! Quousque tandem, domine, quousque tandem? Cura ut scribas: Vale et me ama.

ERNEST DOWSON

2. 21 March 1891.

140. *To Samuel Smith*[1]
[*March 1891*]

Woodford

. . . I have seen the proofs of my 'Cynara' poem for the April Hobby. It looks less indecent in print, but I am still nervous! though I admire Horne's audacity. I read it, or rather Lionel did for me, at the last Rhymers . . . .

1. Text from Gawsworth, *The Dowson Legend* (1939). This fragment may be part of the incomplete letter 132. If so, the date for both is *c.* 23 March 1891.

141. *To Arthur Moore*
[*3 April 1891*]

Woodford

Caro Mio.
This silence, I know is inexcusable: yet, forgive it! for there are extenuating circumstances; though I have not been, as you might be-

lieve, in Haverford West,[1] and sustained its spell. I had a rheum of sorts, which kept me a prisoner, nearly until Good Friday:[2] and then I was at Brighton, a victim of circumstances, until Tuesday. And on Wednesday, did I not call for you, and did they not tell me that you were at Reading? And on Thursday, did not I receive your missive and did I not wait at the Cave of Aeolus[3] until 6.15: and you were not: and why should these things be? But alas! to-day I had to dine at home; and to-morrow I go down to Tonbridge to stay with Plarr: but haply I shall see you again on Monday, when, without fail, I am back again in Babylon: never I hope to depart, until I go in your company to Ploumariel. All this going to & fro has afflicted me with vicarious depressions; and my correspondence has accordingly suffered. Do not follow my bad example; but write to me, quam celerrime: and so will I emend my ways. Juriste, I have no news: except that I saw Swanton to-day. He is back again in London, and looking for rooms, in which, he may be able to read for the Bar, in convenient proximity to the Courts. Perhaps you will run across him? Yes! the "Pupil" is all that there is of most—! and "The Light that Failed"[4] (revised vers.) is far better—and Stevenson in "Black & White" with a South Sea story[5] is charming & leprous (in the strict sense of the word); though he is not by any means Pierre Loti.

I have done nought but compose a few inferior verses[6]—and meditate a good deal on *Masquerade*. By the way, would it not perhaps, after all, be expedient to drop that incident about the picture. I fear it is a melodramatic expedient: besides it is inconceivably difficult. Let me hear your views on this subject. I spent Monday at a Carthusian monastery in Sussex: Cowfold.[7] An adorable place, high up and away from everywhere. Beata Solitudo! Perpetual silence! It is an enchanting order: they scarcely live in community, having separate cells in which they live, eat, read & meditate: once a week, for an hour, they may mix with each other & converse. For the rest they see each other only at the various offices: and pass each other in the cloisters with a formal bow and a "memento mortis, frater!" Enchanting people! I hear that it is possible to go down and stay with them for two or three days: I shall try and work it.

Write soon.

Tuissimus   ERNEST DOWSON

1. The home of W. R. Thomas, notoriously bad at answering letters.
2. 27 March.
3. Lincoln's Inn Fields.
4. Kipling first published *The Light that Failed* in a shortened version with a happy ending in *Lippincott's Magazine*, 1890. The Macmillan edition of 1891 restored the original form of the book.
5. *The Bottle Imp* appeared in *Black and White*, 20 March and 3 April.
6. These have not survived; in his notebook there is nothing composed between March and 28 April.
7. A month later, on 27 May, Dowson wrote his poem on the Carthusians. See Letter 150, note 6.

142. *To Arthur Moore*
       Friday [*10 April 1891*]

Bridge Dock

Carissimo.

I have been meaning each day to see you: but a great, purple spleen has obscured my soul & I have not been able. And now, to-day, when for a while it is dissipated by this tardy sunshine, I have to go to tea with Plarr: & so I must even write to excuse myself. To morrow, may we not meet? At least look for me, if you do not matinize; at the Grosvenor; where, if brilliant weather does not tempt me, into the country, I shall surely be. Write if we miss each other! I have seen no one, done nothing, these many days: I picked up an edition of "Songs from the Dramatists" dirt cheap, in Charing Cross Rd: yesterday: & a Gray, containing the letters as well as the poems for 6d. Also, I have seen Smith, en route for Harrow: the unchangeable Smith! The "Hobby Horse" has not yet reached me: you will probably get yours before I do: I entreat you to confiscate it, lest it become anathema marantha to your house.[1] The sun is pouring down sublimely here, but it comes too late; the iron of this awful winter has entered into my soul. I am jaded, neurotic, dyspeptic: I have endeavoured to cut down my allowance of tobacco & the consequences are direful; sleepless nights only varied by frantic nightmares; & days of an appalling aridity the fruit of them. Let us put off the cares of office, quam celerrime, & fly as to the primeval forests. "Jam enim, hiems transit, imber abiit et recessit. Flores apparuerunt in terra nostra".[2]

                    Vale et me ama.   ERNEST DOWSON

1. The April number of *The Century Guild Hobby Horse* appeared a month late. Dowson's nervousness was due to the fact that it contained his *Cynara*.
2. Song of Solomon ii. 11–12.

143. *To Arthur Moore*
       Wednesday [*22 April 1891*]

Bridge Dock

Carissimo!

Your letter was a very excellent pendant to this late sunshine, more especially where you speak of your chances of flying Bretonwards in 2 months: I fully expected to have seen you before this: only, I have been getting away early: at four that is; and somehow, after having had tea in Poland, have not had the energy to drag my way Eastward again & pick you up. Yesterday I roamed in Regent's Park from 6- to 7. & appreciated the perfect desolation of it, at this such time of the day & year: & wished you were with me. To day I dine at home: tomorrow, if the Gods do not thwart me, I will come. Or was to-morrow the day you excepted? for, a curiously inapposite mutilation happened to your letter before it came to hand: and the "forbidden days" are clean clipped and gone, as it is with one's railway ticket, after many inspections. I will show it you: only, if Thursday was one of them, drop me a card *quam celerrime* to stay me. Perhaps on Saturday then? I shall be at the Grosvenor by 2.30: must fly at five: in the interim I await you. Malheureusement, that incorrigible idiot C. J. Davies, has made an appearance there. He takes up his abode in chambers, in Portman St: embarks in literature! It seems real ages since I saw you: or anybody: but indeed, I am parlous bad: only Ploumariel will restore me. I am taking to a diet of only eggs & vegetables: but cannot knock my smoke down to anything reasonable, without knowing it, painfully, in the fiendish dancing of my nerves. Have been reading nothing but Gray, & his contemporaries: letters chiefly. To-night I really intend to finish my present story:[1] then to-morrow it shall go to be typed by the Misses Duff; and so to the various editors. We celebrated the Natalia of "Missy",[2] last week; the thirteenth, I did not greatly care for the butterfly brooches: so found a cadeau, less ornamental. She has a charming, new toilette of which I entirely approve; dull slate blue with silver buttons: you must see it. I go to tea there now: so farewell: a rivederci!

Tuissimus   ERNEST DOWSON

P.S. Yes, by all means bring "Masquerade": when my "Violinist" is off my hands, I will settle down at it, I hope. But o for the summer, diligences, the Lyon d' Or,[3] trout, apple blossom & incense! I entreat you to bear these things in mind.

1. *The Story of a Violin.*
2. Adelaide was born on 13 April 1878.
3. The hotel at Le Faouet in Brittany, where trout was a speciality.

144. *To Arthur Moore*
    Mardi [*28 April 1891*]

Bridge Dock

Carissimo Mio.

I had hoped to see you yesterday, or I would have written: but there came a pressure of vessels here & I could not get away till six. Your letter came as a boon & a blessing; but, alas! I am not on the golden strand of Bordighera: nor is it at all certain that I may be, reasonably soon, or at all. It depends on the condition of my governor: and he is still vacillating and inclined to stay at home a good deal. I am rather less of a corpse than I was, but am still rudement mal. I was distressed not to see you on Saturday. I was at the Grosvenor and in Polonia: but you were not, you blighter: no, you were at a bad burlesque.

I have done a little more of Masquerade; but, very little: and my other story finishes itself; but very slowly and unsatisfactorily. I must see you soon: but where? When will you dine with me and discuss, or theatrize? To-night I dine at home: Saturday, I shall be with Missy all the afternoon; perhaps to-morrow I will see you, or on Thursday at the Corner: on the night of the last day, I go to meet a various crew, Oscar among them, at Hornes. The dilatory "Hobby" is still at the press. I will try & send you a copy as I shall have 2 or 3. How foolish of the Immortals to crown those impossible Scotchmen:[1] when the divine Albert[2] was there. By the way, I believe, Barabbas was a Scotchman. I dreamt a wild, weird dream last night. We were at Venice, you & I and Lionel, and we roamed round, not in a gondola but in a quaint phaselus like a Canadian canoe: the three of us sat in the stern with our portmanteaus and the boatman, who said that he had nursed Newman through a fever in Sicily: and we went on searching for an hotel, the bows very high in the air and the water coming in copiously—

Interruptions—enter captains, dry dockers, pilots, painters, shipowners. A German ship & an Italian steamer to be put in: then to tea in Poland.

Write if I don't see you.

                Tuissimus   ERNEST DOWSON

---

1. Scottish members of the Rhymers' Club. They were introduced by John Davidson, who insisted on their immediate election. But they were entirely unsuitable and a special meeting had to be convened to nullify the decision. See Yeats's *The Trembling of the Veil* (1922), p. 193.
2. Albert Moore had begun to write verse in 1887. He himself took it very seriously, but no one else would.

145. *To Arthur Moore*

In fest. Beat. J. P. Chanel[1] [*3 May 1891*]

Woodford

Carissimo.

My regret at not having seen you this past week is only equalled by the multitude of the reasons which prevented me. An unprecedented thing: I have been twice to the theatre. Once in the afternoon to "Hedda Gabler":[2] once in the evening, with Plarr, who had seats, to "L'Enfant Prodigue".[3] And on Saturday I was at Stockwell dining with Fallows. O! "Hedda" is magnificent: the "Dolls' House" is nowhere beside it, & Miss Robins, whoever she may be, is at least, as good as Miss Achurch: and Miss Marion Lea is most charming. O! it was perfectly well. If, as I am told, it goes into the evening bill, anywhere, prithee fix an early day & dine with me, in Polonia, & we will there together. I could see it many times.

"L'Enfant," also is good & Jane May most delicious: the week has been a success: but you must go to Ibsen—(This pen & paper be d——d). I have just returned now from Notre Dame de France: a function of sorts, very excellently done. I could not espy my 'Beata Beatrix' amongst the veiled Enfants de Marie: but I presume she was there.

But, I forget, you care for none of these things! Bien: when I have you in Brittany, I shall make it an occasion of putting you through a course of Catholic doctrine, & drive you to functions, with the relentlesness of college authorities in the matter of Chapels. Praise be to Mary—we are now in May. Cura ut assidue legas, ne forte ar......is![4] not that that last is credible. I glanced at the Ft.nightly this afternoon: a story by Hardy, extremely short, has points, & one by Wedmore is better:[5] Swinburne on Scott, that tedious hack! is irritating. Fallows yesterday, in his own rooms, impressed me more favourably than at the Grosvenor. His voice is improved, & he sang & played to me, for about an hour and a half, most excellently. I persist in liking him "in my fashion", although he is indefensible. To morrow shall I see you? I shall call at the corner if I do not get away early; when, I shall "five o'clocque"

---

1. Pierre Chanel (1803–1841), French missionary and martyr, beatified in 1889. Dowson had just attended celebrations of the anniversary of his death. Chanel was canonized in 1954.
2. By Ibsen, opened at the Vaudeville Theatre on 20 April.
3. By Michael Carré, music by Wormser; it opened at the Prince of Wales's Theatre on 31 March.
4. The incomplete last word must be *areris*. 'Read carefully so as not to be ploughed'; Moore's examination was coming in June.
5. *The Fortnightly Review* for 1 May contained Hardy's *The Midnight Baptism* and Frederick Wedmore's *A Chemist in the Suburbs*.

with 'Missy'—I am to take her, presently, to the Deutsch Exposition;[6] where I hope to be much instructed. They have promised to have her photographed soon: then I will convince you how curiously like she is to at least *two* photographs of Minnie.—I perceive I am being led into a topic which might run me into many tedious sheets. Pardonnez moi: & mine ever increasing absorption: & if, I see you not to-morrow, cura ut scribas, when & where, that may come to pass.

Tuissimus   ERNEST DOWSON

6. The German Exhibition at Earl's Court opened on 9 May.

146. *To Arthur Moore*
   [*8 May 1891*]

Bridge Dock

Carissimo.

I was grieved not to see you yesterday: but I had to dine at home; and tonight I suppose you will be going early. Tomorrow also, I fear, I shall not see you, as I go with my mother, in the afternoon, to Charles I.[1] Have you been there yet? Let me hear from you soon, as to your arrangements next week. I shall try & go to "Hedda" again then, probably on Tuesday: but like enough I shall not manage it. Tell me of Thomas & the rest: I presume you did not meet them all together.

I want to bring, or send you Frederick Wedmore's "*Pastorals of France*":[2] the first and third, I consider, quite charming: full of distinction, and of an almost Russian delicacy.

Lionel in the current "A.J' is excellent on the "Way of Writing".[3] Read him!

I have a severe cold & cough: I dose myself vigorously with ammoniated quinine etc: but I do not think, as yet, it is the Epidemic.[4] Are you keeping free of it? The May is at last exerting herself: let us hope this is a sample of what we are to have at Le Faouet, later on. Vale: and do not gamble.

Tuissimus   ERNEST DOWSON.

P.S. I have had a charming letter from Bouthors, from Heidelberg:

1. *Charles I* by W. G. Wills was revived by Irving at the Lyceum on 4 March 1891; Minnie Terry played Princess Elizabeth.
2. First published in 1877.
3. *The Anti-Jacobin* for 9 May.
4. There was a severe outbreak of Russian influenza in April.

147. *To Arthur Moore*
      Sunday [*10 May 1891*]

Woodford

Mon bien cher.

Forgive the paper & the pencil: but the languor of Sunday evening—
the aftermath of early dinner, that barbarous survival! is on me & I
cannot rise from mine easy chair: you may remember its alluringness.
Forgive me also that I write when I have nothing in the world to say.
We went to Carlos One yester noon: a charming piece, though the
"book" is beneath criticism.[1] I liked it, & Minnie was charming, though
greatly grown & with little to say. I have spent the day in great idlesse,
smoking Fieldcovitch & reading "The Mayor of Casterbridge":[2] at your
recommendation, I believe! which I greatly like. But I disbelieve in
Hardy's rustics.

I spent last evening with Plarr & Johnson in the formers room: he
was in the clutch of the epidemic, but in his usual excellent vein. The
"Hobby"[3] is here, or rather at Limehouse, in the seclusion of my desk.
Perhaps you have seen it: or has the MacMurdo, for once been discreet?
I like Shannon's monstrous illustration of the Canticle, with its curious
mixture of French technique & the mystique of Rossetti: a head of
Dante Gabriel on a nudity of Dégas? I have seen none of the picture
shows: Hillier "enthuses" to me over a portrait of T I G by T I G[4] at
the new: it was *not* Shannon's Miss Clough,[5] which I go for to see. I
shall hope to see you to-morrow or Tuesday: shall be in town, probably,
~~most~~ every days except Wednesday, when I dine here. Let me know
your programme. I can't finish my story;[6] it wants a matter of 10 lines
only, this 20 days: but alas! the right ones elude me. If this sterility
continues I shall devote my superabundant leisure at Bridge Dk: to
copying out the first volume of "Masquerade": then, by your leave,
we will submit it, either to Lionel or Hillier? Hy. James in the "New
Review"![7] have you read him? He strikes me for once, as scarcely less
dull than his fellows in the *Symposium* (alas! poor Πλάτων!) Lang &
Gosse. (These cigarettes are charming, but surely, as you say, drugged:

1. See Letter 146, note 1.
2. Published in 1886.
3. The long-awaited April number, containing *Cynara* and *A Case of Conscience*.
4. The reference is mysterious. The New Gallery exhibition contained
   nothing by a painter with these initials..
5. J. J. Shannon's portrait of Miss Clough, painted for Newnham College,
   Cambridge, was exhibited at the New Gallery.
6. His *Story of a Violin*.
7. James's contribution was *The Science of Criticism*, reprinted in *Essays
   in London and Elsewhere*, 1893.

I am inhaling them, slowly, these 3 hours & have a curious giddiness on me, not wholly unpleasant).

Horne's poems[8] appear in a day or two, from the "Chiswick Press". I suppose I must buy them. How do you proceed with Newman "on Miracles"?[9] It was an ill beginning: read the Catholic sermons, the volume on various occasions and that to mixed congregations: personally, I think them in the finest English I have yet met with outside Pater. I wrangled with Fallows the other day over "the great Cardinal": he took the contemptuous attitude, of the Broad Church—Kingsleian party, that impossible school! "a bounded superstition" etc. Putting aside the charm, quite special and apart in this detestable age, of his beautiful personality, isn't this view a little superficial? He strikes me not in the least as one of those, with a genius of conviction like St Paul or Pascal, but rather as of a temper essentially subtile & sceptical, resembling Butler's: & his Catholicism was the deliberate conclusion of a logical process, and not at all emotional or the issue of early prejudice: that is contradicted by his letters. His faith was not spontaneous & direct like Pascal's, but a reasoned state of mind conditioned on assent to certain intellectual propositions, which strike me, as at least, as worthy of serious consideration, as the flimsy and local claims of Anglicanismus & the Protestant sects. I am afraid I bore you with these desultory disquisitions! But I am so tired of Anglican condescension and Latitudinarian superiority; where Rome is in question. That, and the vulgarity of the dogmatic atheists, and the fatuous sentimentality of the Elesmere people et hoc genus omne! I am afraid, my dear, I am being driven to Rome in self defence. Vulgarity, sentimentality, crudity: isn't *there* an effectual, the *most* effectual protest against it all? I confess our Lady of the Seven Hills encroaches on me, in these latter days. I hope you won't mind, if I have to inform you, some time or other "Et vera incessu patuit Dea!"[10] In the meantime, with apologies: Vale et me ama! & write if I don't see you.

ERNEST DOWSON.

8. *Diversi Colores.*
9. *Two Essays on Miracles*, 1870.
10. *Aeneid* I. 405.

148. *To Arthur Moore*
[*18 May 1891*]

Woodford

Carissimo Mio!
Pardon this silence: I would have seen you on Thursday, but the gods were against me; and I might have seen you on Saturday, if I had

been certain beforehand that I should have been at the Grosvenor, which I was not. Let us hope for a rencontre this week. Praise Allah, the holidays are done:[1] I have spent them here, smoking & in bed, most languorously. Hillier dines with me here, on Wednesday: Saturday I go, weather permitting, with Missy, to the German:[2] other days I am at your service for the corner.

I am not sorry for this rain: it promises better for *our* August, the only season in which I am concerned. I am too lazy & consumed by too much *tussis* to write at length: I have been reading Hawthorne, whom Lionel worships & whom Henry James, as you know, rates high. I find his English; perfectly well: for the rest,—doubtless it is my own fault;—I am not carried away; he writes of things which do not in any great degree interest me—Puritans, Ghosts, New England, etc. Je m'en fiche!

But I am hopelessly slack: excuse these baubles & tell me your "dates".

Yours perpetually   ERNEST DOWSON.

PS. Thanks for calling my notice to the "Star":[3] I hadn't seen it: but find the person is Le Gallienne, Oscar's friend & a "rhymer".

1. Whit Sunday was 17 May.
2. The German Exhibition.
3. On 14 May *The Star* published a review of the April *Century Guild Hobby Horse*, singling out *Cynara* for particular mention; the review was signed 'Log Roller', the pseudonym used by Richard Le Gallienne for his weekly column. In the next few years Le Gallienne (1866–1947) became a highly influential reviewer and was literary adviser to Elkin Mathews and John Lane.

149. *To Arthur Moore*
     Tuesday [*26 May 1891*] 2 AM.

Woodford

Caro Mio.

When did I see you last? But never mind: this is a note of exhortation! "Hedda Gabler" is taken off on Saturday:[1] you have four more days, in which to avail yourself of an unique occasion. I have been

1. *Hedda Gabler* in fact ran from 20 April to 30 May.

tonight, for the third time, but if you can manage it, I shall be enchaunted to go with you any night you care, except to-morrow, when
I must be here. Wonderful, fascinating, sombre play: I have never seen
& never shall see, anything which can approach it. *Do* go! Even if it
must be without me. And it runs three weeks! and Sweet, simpering
Lavender,² & the absurd Profligate³ and Pinero's other silly pot pourris⁴
swell the exchequers nightly for aeons. O Philistia! O British Public!
"Nulla est in tam magno corpore, mica salis?"⁵ (And Pinero, all the
same, is by many degrees our least fatuous playwright).

My dear, send me your sympathies in my infinite dégout. Let us
give up writing & thinking and doing & hie us to Brittany with what
speed, we may, and there with cider and incense and a portmanteau full
of books, let us forget the infinite stupidity that prevails in this Protestant, respectable, democratic, hopelessly inartistic country. My
dear! I am full of spleen. Write to me.

Votre dévoué   ERNEST DOWSON

2. *Sweet Lavender*, first produced on 21 March 1888.
3. *The Profligate*, first produced on 24 March 1889.
4. *The Weaker Sex*, 1889; *The Cabinet Minister*, 1890; *Lady Bountiful*, 1891.
5. Catullus, 86; correctly 'Nulla in tam magno est corpore mica salis.'

150. *To Arthur Moore*
Friday [*29 May 1891*]

Bridge Dock

Carissimo.

My arrangements to-morrow are very much on the knees of the gods.
It is like this: my father being away, and the foreman, suffering from
The Complaint,¹ I have to pay the men to-morrow: and paying obdurate
& drunken iron men, all clamouring for more than their due, in the
absence of their proper time-checker, is a lengthy proceeding, which,
as a rule, terminates, in the ultimate intervention of men in blue. So
it may be 2.30, before I get away! Go, however to Hedda, to the pit:
and unless I receive word from you to the contrary, I will find you there,
if I can reach the theatre before 3. Or no! it is not worth wiring: if I
get away in time, in any case, I shall go there and so I will take my
chance of finding you: if I don't turn up, our meeting will be again post-

1. Influenza.

Minnie Terry
in 1889,
photographed for
The Theatre

Bridge Dock

Leonard Smith
and H. S. Nic

GROSVENOR CLUB,
BOND STREET. W.

6" July. 91

My dear Sayle.

I found your card here
today, on my return from
Bordeaux & Gascony. I was
so sorry to have missed you:
if you saw Johnson, you
doubtless heard, that I was
en voyage. It has been very
charming: deliciously sultry, real
meridional weather. Now I
am back again, until the

Autograph letter
to Charles Sayle
dated 6 July 1891

beginning of next month, when I
go to Brittany, with Moore.
It was charming of you to have
called: I hope you will make another
attempt, when you are next in
town, & that we shall have
more fortune. But why this
silence? I want to know if you
liked my story: and that you
did not very much mind
"Cynara". Try a good time
to send me a line.

Yours always
Ernest Dowson

The Hôtel Gloanec, Pont-Aven, now the Hôtel des Ajoncs d'Or

Charles Conder by William Rothenstein

poned, I fear, for I have an appointment at 5: and am dining at home. When shall this tyranny[2] be overpast: not till the middle of June, I presume?

I will write to Thomas,[3] and employ all the resources of my eloquence to lead him into the apple orchards of Faouet. But I think a personal interview might be more efficacious: shall I run up to Oxford on this worthy mission? or will you go who are, perhaps, in better odour than I, in those seats of learning? I called for you last night: but they told me, as usual, that you had gone! Have you the Anti-Jacobin? Lionel on "Pierre Loti"[4] seems to me, for the first time, in criticism, to have gone astray. D'abord, Loti is not a Bréton, nor of Bréton extraction! Whereby the article loses some force. And again, although I think Loti's prose, distinctly the most beautiful & caressing of prose, now made in France; I find it, as distinctly, lacking, in precisely those qualities, which he discovers in it: simplicity, strength! It's an exquisite, artificial, exotic, modern thing, like the writing of Pater: Maupassant, Flaubert, the Goncourts—these are the classical men! But read the article: and above all, read Loti himself—the Fleurs d'Ennui, Roman d'un Spahi, and the "Roman d'un Enfant" to begin.

I have just finished James study of Hawthorne,[5] which, I admit, with shame, I prefer to anything Hawthorne has done himself. Yet I am going to make another attempt on the 'Scarlet Letter'. I have done a set of verses on the "Carthusians" which I must show you: they are almost too lengthy to enclose: I hope Horne will take them, for a pendant to the 'Ursulines'.[6]

I met Arthur Symons[7] last night: do you know of him? He is a standing dish with the 'Academy' & knows his Paris well: but on the whole, I was not greatly impressed. I am to meet Le Gallienne next week: who gave me that anusing 'puff' in the Star. I believe, he is very charming. However it is unconscionable of me to scribble at such length, when I hope to see you so soon: put it down to the mellowness of the day, and the size of this impossible paper. À bientôt.

Tout à toi ERNEST DOWSON

2. Moore's legal examinations.
3. W. R. Thomas, who was still up at Queen's.
4. *Anti-Jacobin*, 30 May.
5. Published in 1879 in Macmillan's *English Men of Letters* series.
6. Dowson's poem on the Ursuline nuns appeared in the October *Century Guild Hobby Horse*, but *Carthusians* was not printed until 1899, when it appeared in *Decorations*.
7. English poet and critic (1865–1945). His first book, *An Introduction to the Study of Robert Browning*, appeared in 1886, and his poems, *Days and Nights*, in 1889. He was at this time an industrious reviewer with a special knowledge of modern French literature. In 1893 he was responsible for arranging Verlaine's visit to London. During 1896 he edited *The Savoy* and in 1900 published his article on Dowson, reprinted as the Introduction to the first collected edition of Dowson's *Poems* (1902).

151. *Postcard to Arthur Moore*
          Tuesday [*Postmark 9 June 1891*]

Bridge Dock

Have given up any hope of seeing you again, until this scholastic
horror is finished with. Are you sitting still "with vine leaves in your
hair"[1] reading those great law books? Write if you have time & re-
assure me that you are alive, at least. I have finished a story, called,
"An Orchestral Violin": which the Miss Duffs have typed, & which
goes immediately to Mowbray Morris.[2] Placeat! I have the draft of it,
which may have to read, if you care to, when you are again at liberty—
I have written to Thomas: but so far without result.
     Will you be at Lincoln's Inn to-morrow Wednesday about 5.45?

1. *Hedda Gabler*, Act II.
2. *The Story of a Violin* appeared in the August issue of *Macmillan's Magazine*. It was reprinted as *An Orchestral Violin* in *Dilemmas* (1895).

152. *To Victor Plarr*
          [*c. 9 June 1891*]

Bridge Dock

Mon Cher Victor
     I am grieved at this long absence of yours, but I hope it implies
nothing worse than convalescence, and that we shall soon have you
once more with us. In the mean time, I write to you, as an official
exponent of the sentiments of the "Rhymers" at their last meeting,
and at their request, to ask, if we can count on you, as a contributor to
"The Book of the Rhymers Club" which it is proposed to issue, in an
inexpensive manner in the autumn.[1] The Rhymers, to be represented
in it are, pretty much as follows:

Yeats
Greene
Johnson
Dowson

1. The book was published by Elkin Mathews in 1892 in an edition of 450
   copies. Dowson was represented by the permitted maximum of six poems.

Radford
Le Gallienne
Ellis
*Ghose
*Symons
*Rolleston
Todhunter
*Rhys[2]

NB. Those names with asterisks attached, are those of persons, who have not yet *definitely* promised to join in the scheme. May we add your name definitely to these? The expense will be *very small*, as it will be distributed amongst all in proportion to the pages given to each; and in view of their number, and the fact that the maximum of space allowed to any Rhymer is 6 pieces: it could not very well be any thing than inconsiderable; profits of course, if any, on the same scale. We count on your consent. Assuming it then, as given, I have to inform you that at the last meeting it was arranged, as to order of sending in & selecting rhymes, that Johnson should be, as a central person, intending to be in town, all the summer, appointed a sort of receiver of all the verses, although the selection is either to be made by the whole Club in council (wh. seems to me impracticable) or by a committee of 3 to be subsequently selected: 2nd that the maximum of pieces is to be 6 & the minimum 3 (probably). 3rd that each rhymer is exhorted to send in *double* the number of pieces he wishes inserted—say 12 for 6. 10 for 5 etc & that he may mark them in the preferential order he gives to them himself: & must state, where & when, if at all, they have been published. 4th. that the verses should be sent if possible to Johnson before the 26th inst: in order that they may be put before the House at the next meeting of the Rhymers & the book be got under way *quam celerrime.*

I have now, I think discharged my duty, in I hope a fashion not too obscure to be intelligible. We pray you to give your adherence to this notion & send your rhymes forthwith: or better still recover your health & come back to the Cheshire Cheese[3] before the 26th: this is our prayer. But I see the post goeth: please remember me very kindly to your people.

Yrs ever   ERNEST DOWSON

I have just finished a story which I have sent to Macmillan, & wh. will doubtless soon return.

2. The members who finally contributed to the book, besides Dowson, were Edwin J. Ellis, G. A. Greene, Lionel Johnson, Richard Le Gallienne, Victor Plarr, Ernest Radford, Ernest Rhys, T. W. Rolleston, Arthur Symons, John Todhunter and W. B. Yeats.
3. In Fleet Street, where the Rhymers' Club usually met.

153. *To Arthur Moore*
    [*c. 11 June 1891*]

Grosvenor Club

Carissimo.

My sympathies with you in this trying, laborious week. I won't
write at length, or attempt to see you until it be over. Let me have a
line *to the above*, before Sat: if I may hope to see you there, on Saturday
afternoon. If I hear I will be there till five: come then with "vine leaves
in your hair". I have many things to say to you.

Tuissimus   ERNEST DOWSON

PS. Do you remember my old, or rather young friend Mabel Vance?
I heard from her the other day.

154. *To Arthur Moore*
    Thursday night [*25 June 1891*]

Woodford

Carissimo Mio.

As you have probably surmised, I have burnt my boats, that is to
say, taken my berth and must depart at 1.0 tomorrow. Now, strange to
say, I have infinite shrinkings & would give much to feel that I was to
be one of those round your hospitable card-table to-morrow night. This
is to *entreat* you to let me find an epistle from you, at the Poste Restante,
Bordeaux, when I arrive on Monday: that is to say; write to me, of your
charity, not later than Saturday: for I shall not stay in the wine-town,
lest haply I fall, but go on to Perigueux or Agen, I know not which, &
haply light on another Faouet. You shall hear from me, from whichever
it be: but oh, write! I suppose it is that my nerves are in the last stage
of dilapidation, but I have suddenly generated an immense horror at
the notion of being solitary for 10 days. Would God it were the 8th
August,[1] a day to be ever marked, if it arrive, with a white stone. If
I find the Poste Restante full of letters, it may save me: or perhaps the
tonic spray of Biscay: but I am full of shudders & the solemnity of my
adieux in Poland almost reduced Adelaide to tears. She told me she
saw you: but to-night she had a new toilette & a new coiffure, & looked
precisely like a little child Marquise who had stepped out of a canvass

---

1. The day fixed for the start of Dowson's holiday with Moore in Brittany.

of Watteau. She is bound by solemn vows to write to me. Tell me, by the way, how you like the "Pastorals"?[2] I take "Marius", some Newman, Clough & Horace with me: I hope to pick up some bouquins at Bordeaux. I dare say it will be delightful. I feel already a sort of delight in feeling over the 5 franc pieces which I procured from Cook this morning: but I remain absurdly & unreasonably depressed.

Vale et me ama.

yrs affectly   ERNEST DOWSON

P.S. L.J. was received into the Church of Rome last Monday.[3] I have only had a brief intimation from him by letter, without stipulations as to secrecy: but perhaps you had better not mention it at present. It is a great piece of courage: his "first general confession" must have been extremely disagreeable.

2. Frederick Wedmore's *Pastorals of France.*
3. Lionel Johnson made his submission to the Roman Catholic Church on 22 June 1891.

155. *To Arthur Moore*

Tuesday 30 June [*and 1 July*] 1891

Hôtel des 5 Frères, St Médard d'Eyraux[1]

Mon cher.

Your letter consoled me greatly: I found it, on my arrival, yesterday, with one from Lionel and another from Missie. The passage out was enchaunting though alas! I weakly played "nap" with the Captain, an American, & a Cambridge man who almost broke the lot of us. Last night I came here, knowing nought of the place but its name & found as luck would have it a Rosière going on. In fact I hit, quite by chance, the great day of the year in this small, pretty, sleepy village. I went to the Fête Champêtre in the evening, & might have danced with la Rosière herself no doubt, had I not been incapacitated by intoxication. My landlord's son receives me en camarade & with a friend's assistance brought me eventually home. I blued much oof there somehow or other, & am fairly destitute unless substantial remittances arrive shortly. Perhaps that accounts for my not feeling quite as happy as I generally do in my fair France. I am beginning to think with the

1. A small village near Mont de Marsan in the Landes.

Scriptures, that it is not good for a man to be alone:[2] and I am positively appalled at the notion of spending 2 more days here: though it certainly is a pleasant country, this Gascony and the Gascons are as charming in their perfectly different way as the Brétons: and oh, the grand, sultry weather! I am glad you mistook Minnie Terry so: I always thought there was a strong likeness, & that is an excellent corroboration: but Adelaide must be taller.

Wednesday.

I am rather happier this morning, chiefly no doubt, because I found one of my despaired of louis under my bed where I supposed it rolled the night before last: you observe, I wear Eilert Lovbörg's vine leaves. At least, I have not, so far, visited the boudoir of Mlle. Diane. Di meliora. This is the queerest little auberge imaginable, quite *paysan*, but full of excellent folk. Madame, a fat old person, speaking only Gascon, has just been bandaging a burnt finger for me: I endeavoured to persuade her that as only one finger was damaged it was futile to elaborately oil the whole ten: but no! Madame assured me that so it "guérira mieux". I hope so: but in the meantime it is ennuyeux and does not improve my handwriting.

The weather remains meridional & charming, broken occasionally by grand thunder storms, or rather exhibitions of lightning, for there is no thunder. All the inhabitants of this village go about in shirt sleeves and in the evening we sit so for hours, four or five, on a banc; or rather, I am more elaborately vested, in a Pyjama jacket: and I expound on the products & agriculture of England; as to the whereabouts of it everybody is deliciously vague, and they evidently regard my assurance that in that country there is no conscription & no vines, as a mere Gasconade! But I am too solitary & I shall not be sorry to see my good friend Captn Randall again, although I shall steadfastly refuse to associate myself with penny nap & an unlimited Kittie. No more now: shall be at home on Monday: and will see you shortly: you must come down to Woodford: but write to Church End, mon gros Arthur.

Votre dévoué   ERNEST DOWSON

P.S. I flatter myself that is a signature perfectly French.

---

2. Genesis ii. 18.

156. *To Charles Sayle*
    6 July 1891

Grosvenor Club

My dear Sayle.

I found your card here to-day, on my return from Bordeaux & Gascony. I was so sorry to have missed you: if you saw Johnson, you doubtless heard, that I was *en voyage*. It has been very charming: deliciously sultry, real meridional weather. Now I am back again, until the beginning of next month, when I go to Brittany, with Moore. It was charming of you to have called: I hope you will make another attempt, when you are next in town, & that we shall have more fortune. But why this silence? I want to know if you liked my story:[1] and that you did not very much mind "Cynara". Try & find time to send me a line.

        Yours always   ERNEST DOWSON

1. *A Case of Conscience.*

157. *To Arthur Moore*
    [*20 July 1891*]

Bridge Dock

Carissime,

I grieved at reading your letter: I hope, by this time, you are sitting, with two less teeth & vine leaves in your hair, making itineraries. Let me hear from you, as I shall probably not see you this week. Fallows comes to me on Saturday. One day next week will you come Woodford-wards? It will be the last time, remember, for we definitely leave before Michael-mass. I should like to leave the day open for the present: send me a selection of days, which would suit you. I have been dining in Poland recently with a host of people—Swanton; W. Hall and Gray ("Dorian" Gray): also with one De Mattos,[1] a man whom I, & doubtless

1. Alexander Teixeira de Mattos (1865–1921) was born in Holland, but educated in England. He became the foremost translator of the day, editing the Lutetian Society's edition of Zola, to which Dowson contributed *La Terre*, and collaborating with Dowson in translating *Majesty* by Couperus, 1894.

you? have known by sight for years: a long, pale man with a hawk like nose, who was inveterate at the Arts & Letters. And Dorian, who is charming, returns frequently to the veal cutlet and the dingy green walls of my Eden: in fact he promises to be one of my most enthusiastic Polonais!

Try & get away on the 7th, if you can: I am more & more doubtful of the Saturday boat: & write soon and fully. I shall have a damnable spleen all this week: woe is me! Cura ut scribas. By the way, my people, who had almost taken a house in Chelsea (Poulton Square?)—have suddenly shifted to one in your neighbourhood, I believe: At least the station is Bishops Rd. The ~~place is~~ address Bristol Gardens: I have not seen the house, nor is the precise locality known to me. Perhaps it may be to you?

If we settle on it, which seems now almost decided, I shall count on you to smoke pipes with me, when the social claims are not too pressing. It will be charming to be near you: although I fear, it will be a long way from Poland: handy on the other side, for the Hobby House, where Plarr, also, takes up his abode in the autumn.

The other side, I send you the last vagary of my most modern Muse —of Montparnasse—or should I say Montmartre? Its obscurity, I may remark is designed.

                                        Tuissimus   ERNEST DOWSON

FLEUR DE 'LA LUNE

I would not alter thy cold eyes,
Nor trouble the calm fount of speech,
With aught of passion or surprise:
The heart of thee I cannot reach;
I would not ~~trouble~~ alter thy cold eyes.

I would not alter thy cold eyes,
Nor have thee smile, nor make thee weep:
Although my life droops down and dies,
Desiring thee, desiring sleep,
I would not alter thy cold eyes.

I would not alter thy cold eyes;
I would not change thee, if I might,
To whom my prayers, for incense rise:
Pale daughter of the lunar night,
I would not alter thy cold eyes!

I would not alter thy cold eyes,
With trouble of the human heart:
Within their glance my spirit lies,
A frozen thing, alone, apart;
I would not alter thy cold eyes.[2]

July 20/91

2. 'Fleur de la Lune' was printed in *The Century Guild Hobby Horse*, October 1891. It appears in *Verses* as 'Flos Lunae'.

158. *To Arthur Moore*
[*24 July 1891*]

Bridge Dock

Carissimo.

In the event of my not seeing you again this week, this is to ask, what day in the interior of the approaching week will suit you for dining with me at Woodford. Any day but Monday or Saturday will be equal to me: I will accommodate you with a couch; and we will go into our itinerary, elaborately, with maps, Murray & the Indicateur. I have Fallows with me, most probably, to-morrow: I shall not be sorry when the event is over. This weather looks promising for Faouet. I have been endeavouring from the first page of the Daily News to extract information as to the St Malo boats: but alone of Ry. Co's the S.W. Ry. seems not to advertize. If you can find out the *days*, inform me: the hours, I fear, we shall not be able to obtain until the 1st prox, when the monthly table is issued.

When you come down, I must show you my last year's bill from the Lion d'Or: you may then think it worth while, if you dislike the notion of binding yourself for a quinzaine to remain, simply from day to day, at a slightly higher charge, & move on, if weather or circumstances suggest it. I am becoming enamoured of our walking project. At present the following route seems feasible: tell me how you like it?
Dep. Waterloo. Sat. afternoon (probably) or Friday?
Ar St Malo. Sunday morning („ early).
dep „ „ „ ? 9. AM. or 12. AM.
ar Dol. 10 or 1.0 (lunch at Hotel Notre Dame, see town & dep. 3.0 P.M.)
ar *Lamballe* 5 or 6. PM. Sunday evening. Sleep.
awaking on Monday we put Pyjamas into a knapsack & dispatch our baggage by train to Loudéac, ourselves cutting across country to *Montcontour* (old & interesting with a ruined Castle) 10 miles further. There we sleep: & push on the next day to Loudéac about another 10: where we sleep again, regaining our baggage, and starting the next day by train to Pontivy (about ¾ hour) in time to catch the 1.0 o'clock diligence to Faouet where we should be landed by dinner time.

Otherwise, if you prefer it, we might make only 1 day's march out of the same route: & pass straight from Lamballe to Loudéac. These things we will talk of.

What contemplate you on Saturday? I greatly want to see Whistler's 2 pictures, the little girl, and his mother, at the English Portrait Painters:[1] will you come? If so, send word, where I may find you at 2.30: *not* at the Grosvenor, because of Davies! who is always there now. —Write, in any case!

---

1. *Miss Cicely Alexander*, now in the Tate Gallery, and *The Artist's Mother*, now in the Louvre.

Lamballe is an enchaunting place, at which I stayed last year & the hotel very excellent & cheap. Montcontour I only know from Murray: doubtless there are Hotels there. I have just remembered that we left Southampton last year, on FRIDAY: the Saturday boat, I fancy, is a cargo boat, carrying only a few passengers, which, if we could make sure of would be more comfortable.

Vale

Tuissimus   ERNEST DOWSON

159. *To Victor Plarr*
    Thursday [*30 July 1891*]

Bridge Dock

Mon cher Victor.

I hope you have not been misapprehending this long silence: only I have not been sure of your being able to read letters; and I felt pretty certain that you would not care to be writing them. Recent reports, however, have been more favourable, and so with no more preamble, I start on this epistolatory adventure. It is delightful to think that you are really to be roofed in Fitzroy St.[1] I hope I shall see much of you then, and that you will be perfectly, if you are not already, recovered. It will be nearer for me in a month: for I am thankful to say, we move into our new house (Bristol Gardens, Maida Hill) at the end of Aout. The station is Edgware Rd: which is a matter of a few minutes only from Portland Rd: you must often dine with us.

I suppose you have heard from Lionel of my Gascon adventures: it is a charming country, though not more so than Brittany, whither I go with Moore on Monday next. If it is not too bad for your eyes, you must let me find a letter from you there. Address me

Hotel du Lion d'or
    Le Faouet
        Morbihan.

We shall stay there for a 4tnight. Have you been able to write anything lately? And are you to be in our Booke of Rymes? I have a story, but not at all a satisfactory one in the current "Macmillan". It treats of Poland and Poles; Paris, Violins and Soho![2]

But I have been dreadfully lazy, and without any excuse for it. You are to be felicitated on your absence from London, which has been dreary and desolate to a degree. But I hope you will come back soon:

1. Plarr was going to live in the *Hobby Horse* house.
2. *The Story of a Violin.*

I hate it, when I am here; and go away anywhere, thankfully; but alas! such is my inconsistency, than when I have been but a little while from it, as says Johnson, that great lexicographer whom you blaspheme "I take the first convenient opportunity of returning to a place, where, if there is not much happiness, there is, at least such a diversity of good and evil, that slight vexations do not fix upon the heart."[3]

Please commend me to your people, who are well, I hope: and write, if you may.

Yours ever ERNEST DOWSON.

3. Letter of 20 July 1762 to Joseph Baretti of Milan (quoted by Boswell).

160. *To Arthur Moore*

In Fest. John Lubbock [*3 August 1891*]

Woodford

Caro Mio.

On this most dreary day, I found your letter with great relief, on my descent to the breakfast table at about 1.30. I wish you had suggested a rendezvous to-day, for truly these recurring festas are insupportable on the road to Epping. Yet to go to town, uncertain of seeing you, and certain of not seeing Missie—I have not the courage. It is better to sit and smoke and *s'ennuyer* in a reasonable temperature within reach of books, ink & paper. We have gone back to fires these se'en days: that is a slight advantage. Yes: come by all means to-morrow; of course I shall be there: but make it nearer 7.30 than 6.30, for I go in the afternoon with my mother, probably, to Bristol Gardens, shall have to reconduct her to Fenchurch St, and may be late in arriving in Poland. Also I expect I shall be able to dine chez vous before we go.

I suppose if there be a boat, you can depart on Saturday? If we can manage it, it will be greatly to my advantage, as would of course, Friday: because, my father goes yachting some time toward the end of August and of course I shall have to return before he departs. A couple of days saved now therefore are of importance, especially as ~~I have~~ Saturday and Sunday are no days here. Do you mind crossing in a Sat. cargo-boat if they will take us, and you can not catch the Friday boat? We will talk of these things however. I have been reading Loti's last work, "Le Livre de La Pitié et de la Mort".[1] It is wonderful and enchaunting, full of his best: only you must not read it until you know

1. Published in 1891.

at least 6 of his earlier books: for it is as, he says in the preface, the book, into which he has put most of himself; and without the rest of him it is unintelligible. Well, I have been up only 3 hours and I am already too sleepy to write. Come to Poland: This day last year I was at Ploërmel: did I not write to you therefrom? Macmillan has not yet paid me: peste! Au revoir.

Tuissimus   ERNEST DOWSON.

161. *To Arthur Moore*
Tuesday [*1 September 1891*]

Bridge Dock

Caro Mio.

I deeply grieve that you should have been afflicted with a gale of these dimensions: only I am beginning to persuade myself that you will have waited till to-morrow: when you shall have my prayers for a greater calm.

Write—or come & see me here if you are back. I am very sick & sorry & spleenful: the only ray of consolation that this returning had to me, was the prospect of seeing my dear damozel in Poland: but alas! she is away and does not come back till next week. So I shall probably not be in town before Saturday, when perhaps you will come to the Grosvenor: & talk Bréton-talk with Hillier, to whom I am just about to write.

Write me an account of your passage.

Tuissimus   ERNEST DOWSON

162. *To Arthur Moore*
Thursday [*3 September 1891*]

Bridge Dock

Caro Mio.

I was very glad to know you were in England again: come & see me if you can to-morrow. There is a tradition of scorpions, n'est ce pas, who sit in a fiery ring and sting themselves to death. It is what I am doing. In the interim I have nearly completed Chapter iv of the book: I rather like it, but it is quite unnecessarily dismal, & you may expunge what you will. My father hasn't yet joined his ship: in fact he has been laid up: but he may go any day when his condition improves. As he can't come to the Dock, it makes no difference in my returning: I should have had any way to return & take charge. Brittany was charming n'est-ce pas: unfortunately I feel just at present, as though everything that was at all charming and pleasant were entirely & irretrievably over. It makes me furious—but I must admit, that I am so unfortunately consituted as to allow small miseries almost to madden me. I have had a moral shock since yesterday, which has racked me ever since with an infinite horror that I may be misunderstood in the only thing that I really care about, by the only people to whom it matters. As ill luck would have it I came across the Star yesterday and read a most disgusting story of a disgusting person, which I suppose is a notorious scandal[1] that one has escaped by being in Brittany. The worst of it was, that it read like a sort of foul and abominable travesty of—pah, what is the good of hunting for phrases. You must know what I mean, and how I am writhing. I imagine all the comments & analogies which one's kind friends will draw, and unfortunately I can't help feeling that even her people—and mine, as far as that goes—might take alarm & suspect my motives. And yet I swear there never was a man more fanatically opposed to the corruption of innocence—even where women are concerned—than I am. Unfortunately the excellence of my conscience doesn't make any difference. This beastly thing has left a sort of slimy trail over my holy places.

I am sorry to bore you in this way: but I must cry out when I am hurt, and you are the most likely to understand. I don't expect consolations from you: I don't see that there are any. But come & see me or write to me, or dine with me, anywhere, to-morrow or Saturday for mercy's sake before I have gnawed out my vitals quite. I am simply stupid with disgust and anger at everything & everybody in this very gross world; and sick to death at the notion of things changing, and my one consolation being done away with. Certainly the gods are ironical: they always punish one for one's virtues rather than for one's sins.

Yours

de profundis   ERNEST DOWSON

1. See pp. 127–128.

163. *To John Gray*

Thursday [*3 September 1891*]

Bridge Dock

My dear Gray,

I was glad to hear from Poland (I think it must have been you they meant) that you are in England. I ought to apologise for not having written to you before, not for having omitted to answer your charming letter. That were impossible: but at least for having failed to write. But the gods have been tormenting me with a grievous neuralgia in France; and since I came back they have devized a peculiarly refined and indefinable form of moral torture, which on the whole is worse than the neuralgia. Hence this silence. Pardon me: and if you are not yet in Holland, come & see me: after the middle of next week I shall be in Poland to dinner generally.

Yours ever   ERNEST DOWSON

164. *To Herbert Horne*

[*Postmark 4 September 1891*]

Bridge Dock

My dear Horne.

I am sending you some verses[1] with this: please pardon the delay: but I waited for an inspiration which has not come; and this is all I can find!

I believe you have a MSS of the "Amor," but I include it in case it should have been mislaid. The "Ursulines" I have turned into "Carmelite Nuns": because I have made researches, and find that the other ladies do not perpetually adore. The other two pieces I put in, in case you should want anything more: but I neither care much for them myself, nor expect any one else to. The Sonnet, however, should you care to print it would go easily under a common title with the "Amor."

For a common title of the poems Lionel suggests "Umbratilia": in which case, as the "amor umbratilis" could not stand it might be called "Sola Beatudo" If you can devize a better title, however, which

---

1. Horne had already accepted *Amor Umbratilis*. Dowson now sent him the sonnet *Discedam, explebo, The Carmelite Nuns*, and *Fleur de la Lune*. The sonnet was not published till 1934, but the three other poems appeared in *The Century Guild Hobby Horse*, October 1891, under the joint title *In Praise of Solitude*.

should allow me to retain the original titles of the separate poems, I shall be exceedingly grateful.

This is a long letter about very little: excuse my diffuseness. & Believe me

Yours v sincerely   ERNEST DOWSON

165. *To Arthur Moore*
   [*8 September 1891*]

Bridge Dock

Caro Mio.

I fear I shall not be able to manage the "Sequel"[1] this week, as my father will be away & I must be down reasonably early. Can you send me another Chap. soon: the one I most require is the Chap in which Sylvester and Oswyn come together. In order to make anything of my next, I must see that first: in the meantime I am working on the next but one—the exposure. Send me all you can, as soon as you can. I will try and turn up at the corner one of these weary days soon. Let me hear from you if I don't manage it.

Yrs ever   ERNEST DOWSON

Here is an attempt to translate a thing of Verlaine: Of course it is a failure.

Il pleut doucement sur la ville.
RIMBAUD

Tears fall within mine heart
As rain upon the town:
Whence does this languor start,
Possessing all mine heart?

O sweet sound of the rain
Upon the earth and roofs!
Unto an heart in pain,
Ah music of the rain!

Tears that have no reason
Fall in my sorry heart;
What! there was no treason?
This grief hath no reason.

1. *The Sequel* by Louis Parker opened at the Vaudeville Theatre on 15 July 1891.

Nay! the more desolate
Because I know not why,
(Neither for love nor hate)
Mine heart is desolate.[2]

2. Dated 8 September 1891 in Dowson's notebook; published in *Decorations*.

166. *To Herbert Horne*
[*c. 16 September 1891*]

Bridge Dock

My dear Horne,[1]
   I have been meditating upon your account of Chamberlain's Paper:[2] I have even mustered the energy to read through the abortive "shocker"[3] by myself and another, of which I told you, the other day. It is really very sensational and the English, whilst not offending against grammar, is quite without distinction of any kind. Might it possibly do? If it would not be troubling you too much, both my collaborator, and myself, should be overwhelmed with gratitude, if you could put it before Chamberlain: or, at least, sound him, and break to him gently that two obscure "fictionists" contemplate sending him a MSS.
   I enclose a sort of testimonial which this work extracted from a notorious publisher, who refused it. Would it be of use to show him that? I am bound to add that the prophesies contained in that letter were not fulfilled.
   Forgive me for troubling you on this matter.
                    Yours sincerely,   ERNEST DOWSON

P.S. I have not received any proofs. I hope it be because you have not sent them, and not that the post has let them go astray.

1. Dowson appears to have sought Horne's advice in matters of literary business. He went to him again over the contract for *Dilemmas* (see p. 437) and Horne was responsible for the abortive arrangement that *Verses* should be published by Mathews.
2. Probably H. R. Chamberlain (1859–1912), at that time managing editor of the *Boston Journal*. In 1892 he became London correspondent of the *New York Sun* and remained in London for the rest of his life.
3. *Dr. Ludovicus*. The 'testimonial' came from Sampson Low (see Letter 48).

167. *To Herbert Horne*
[*Postmark 19 September 1891*]

Grosvenor Club

My dear Horne

Thanks exceedingly for your letter: and for the proofs, which I return corrected herewith. I am sending off your note with our parcel to Chamberlain at the same time. Did you by the way receive my letter on the subject? I am not sure whether your note is an answer, or written independently. And, as a letter, which I sent to a man, at the same time; and posted in the same box; has not reached him, I have a notion, that yours also may have gone astray. For the title, I am afraid I cannot suggest any great improvement upon "Tenebraria": unless you approve of "Laudes Solitudinis" which perhaps covers, in a different sense, the three poems.[1] Or that citation from one of the fathers, *nescio quem*, "Beata Solitudo: Sola Beatitudo."[2] Please do not accept my punctuation of these verses as final in any way: I should wish you indeed, if you will be so good, to revise it.

Hoping your health is progressing
    "Your obliged, obedient servant"   ERNEST DOWSON

1. Horne evidently liked *Laudes Solitudinis* well enough to translate the title into English for publication.
2. Attributed to St. Bernard of Clairvaux but now known to come from the work of the Dutch humanist, Cornelius Muys of Delft.

168. *To Arthur Moore*
[*22 September 1891*]

Bridge Dock

Mon Cher.

I am going to send you with this the little I have done of the Chapter you want with a brief skeleton at the end of how I purposed to finish it. Perhaps you will care to finish it yourself, or if not it may be enough to enable you to go ahead. I am awfully sorry that this is all I can do at present: but I have tried, and can only produce nonsense, even ungrammatical nonsense. You must not *m'en voulez*: I simply CAN'T do anything: for the present, I'm done, usé, as dry of any sense of words, or form, as dry of ideas as a sucked orange.

This thing is killing me. Since I came back, nothing has been the same: I've tried to persuade myself that I'm wrong, but I give it up.

LED–P

Her people are as kind & cordial as ever, there are no obvious differences made: only I can feel there is a difference and that it will become more apparent daily. C'est fini. I shouldn't have troubled you with the thing again, only I don't want you to curse me for neglecting Masq^de more than you can help. I daresay I shall be able to get to work at it soon: this sort of thing must end one way or another shortly. No more now.

Yours   ERNEST DOWSON

I liked those chapters you sent me, in spite of the bad things you said about them. I forget whether you said anything to me at the G. on Sat. about the completed chap. I expect it's bad enough.

We move this day week—to Maida Hill. It has the advantage of being near you, but I wish with all my heart it were Kensal Green.[1]

I sent off the MSS on Sat to Chamberlain. Did you find & post letter?

1. The cemetery.

169. *To Arthur Moore*
[*23 September 1891*]

Bridge Dock

Caro Mio.

A line to inform you how matters stand re: *Ludovicus*. Chamberlain has ~~seen it~~ glanced through it, but will not decide until to-morrow. In the meantime he ~~has~~ wishes us (Horne informs me) to say what we want for it. After discussing the matter with Horne (he said that they were thought in the matter of Miss Finley's novel[1] which the[y] bought for £70—they had been rather rushed, and it would be better not to frighten him.) ~~In the result~~ We agreed that Horne was to write and say we ~~consider~~ thought we ought to get £40—.— for the book. If he considered this excessive, Horne would then write again and ask what he would offer. There seems confusion of persons ~~here, but you will~~ in this hurried epistle of mine but I hope you will be able to make it out & let me know *by return* whether you approve or not. There was no time to communicate with you on the subject: so I acted to the best of my discretion.

1. Possibly *J. Reginald Cuttinghurst esq.* by Isabel Bowman Finley, published in *Harper's Weekly*, 25 July 1891.

Horne expects an answer to this communication to day and I am dining with him to-morrow & will let you know the result.

Yours ever   ERNEST DOWSON

PS. Of course Chamberlain only buys the newspaper rights—not copyright.

---

170. *To Charles Sayle*
  [*30 September 1891*]

15 Bristol Gardens, Maida Hill, W.

My dear Sayle.

It is a long time since I have heard of, or from you: but I think you will be interested to hear—that I was a few days ago received into the Church, by Father Sebastian Bowden, the Oratorian.[1] You will see from the address that we have moved into town at last; only since yesterday.

When we are settled down, we shall be delighted to give you a bed any time almost when you meditate a coming to town.

Ever yrs   ERNEST DOWSON.

1. Dowson was received at Brompton Oratory on 25 September 1891.

---

171. *To Arthur Moore*
  Friday [*16 October 1891*]

Bridge Dock

Caro Mio.

I ~~was~~ am sorry that fate has been against our meeting. Wednesday night I had to go to the Oratory, last night I called on my way from Poland & you were out; to night I go to the "Rhymers".

To morrow afternoon I go to the Oratory; as to to-morrow evening, I am vague, but would you mind calling on me at about 9.30 on the chance of my being in. Otherwise unless I hear to the contrary from

you, I will pay you an early-afternoon call on Sunday.
    Adios.
                              T à t.   ERNEST DOWSON
The Hobby is out. It contains an excellent paper by Image on Millet.[1]
which you must read.

1. Besides Dowson's *In Praise of Solitude.*

172. *To G. A. Greene*[1]
    [*c. December 1891*]

                                          15 Bristol Gardens

My dear Greene.
    I am sorry for delay, in returning these proofs,[2] but I have been out
of town. I hope the book is prospering. Is there to be a meeting of the
"Rhymers" soon?
                              yours truly   ERNEST DOWSON
G. A. Greene Esq.

1. Vice-Chairman of the Irish Literary Society, author and lecturer (1853–
   1921). He edited both the books published by the Rhymers' Club.
2. Of Dowson's contributions to *The Book of the Rhymers' Club.*

173. *To Arthur Moore*
    [*c. January 1892*]

                                          15 Bristol Gardens

Caro Mio.
    I find to-night a letter from my Professor fixing 9.30 to-morrow
night for seine Stunde—which is to take place here.[1] Can you try &
come round earlier then, from 8 until his arrival? If not I trust I shall
see you soon. In any case I will try & give you the Chap to-morrow. It
wants a matter of a page; and ten pages of copying. I will complete it,

1. Dowson was evidently taking German lessons, possibly from Dr. Oswald
   (see Letter 210).

and apologize for my slackness. If you could realize the immense temptation I have to retire like Roderick Hudson[2] to my sofa, and lie with my eyes shut smelling a rose,—you would wonder only that I have done so much as I have. In effect I am immensely distracted. I came away from Poland to-night with the sensation of my head having become a baloon. I went down to Brighton, after an evening there on Friday, with exactly the same sensation.

The issue of it all is, since I have not any longer a shadow of doubt that my condition is transparently obvious to everybody concerned, and that the Damozel perfectly understands the situation, and since it is merely an English ~~convention~~ tradition which assumes Heaven knows why? that a girl is not Amabilis when she is at her most amiable age— why should I delay in putting a rather untenable situation easily right? This is not folly as you will probably declare, but excellent reason. I mean that I should be quite content myself to possess myself my soul in patience, in recognition of a convention that I don't personally believe in, if it was required. Only when it is clear to me that by so doing I simply lose ground and ~~pass~~ my scrupulousness is only accounted to my indecision and lack of courage—I can't see the use of it. In fact the difficulties melt away: they are entirely social ones—*they* don't realize them and I have never understood them—and never shall. En voilà pour toujours. Therefore mon bien cher ami and esteemed collaborator, I have decided that when "Masquerade" is finished which should happen ~~shortly~~ on or before the 13th. April next which is also a Birthday—I will put an end to this absurd pretence of further consideration which deceives nobody and plainly declare myself.

And then if it is required of me, I will set to work to convince my people of what they ought already to be perfectly aware—that I will never be induced to do anything, or to refrain from doing anything, because it is conventionally desirable or impossible. I believe they will be reasonable. Well, forgive this lengthy scrawl, if it is only for the consideration that it will leave me freer for "Masquerade". I give you leave to call me a fool: I am not sure whether this is the last folly or the beginning of wisdom. Only be it folly or wisdom it is equally inevitable. I do not, at least change my point of view, as much as you may imagine. I do not believe in marriage in the abstract in the least. Only it is the price, perhaps a heavy one, which one is ordered to pay if one has an immense desire for a particular feminine society. In the present case, I would pay it ten times over, sooner than risk the possibility of some time or other regretting that I had let go irrevocably something which promised a good deal, which I have never had, & which is perhaps after all the best thing obtainable in this stupid world—simply out of lâcheté!

yrs ever   ERNEST DOWSON

---

2. The hero of Henry James's novel, published in 1873.

174. *To Victor Plarr*

    [? *January 1892*]

                                         Bridge Dock

Caro Mio.

    I return your letter with abundant thanks for the offer.[1] Alas! that it should be so, but my knowledge of German is so limited that I should be an encumbrance, rather than an aid, if I accepted it I could only translate Heine from French translations: and that is scarcely what your friend would desire. And where would appreciation of the Heinesque style come in? I am afraid you must pass on this attractive opportunity to some one more competent.

    I must try & see you one day this week. Let me know an evening when you will be chez toi. I must confess to you. Hélas, mon vieux, I am ready to make all the sentimental surrenders—even the last and most of all, when She is come to years of discretion. I haven't a shred of reason left in me.

    Don't despise me too much: but so it is. To think that I should have come to this. O shade of Sayle! Forgive my incoherency, give me your condolences & let all then be tacendum.

                         Tuissimus   ERNEST DOWSON

1. Plarr had passed to him a commission to translate Heine for an edition (published in 1897) being prepared by Professor C. A. Buchheim.

175. *To Victor Plarr*

    [*February 1892*]

                              [*15 Bristol Gardens*]

Mon Cher

    Toto meo corde I felicitate you.[1] I can't say how charmed and impressed I was. It was very good of you to have me; I hope I did not stay too long. Yes, mon cher, you and I are the only wise persons in a blind generation. What is then, this good, sweet, fresh aroma of the Lotiesque which the conventional culture of the drawing-room never produces? I think of my cousins—two very pretty, accomplished and amiable girls,

1. Plarr had just become engaged to Helen Marion Shaw.

as attractive as any girls istius generis whom I know, and at once I feel that they are without that curious indefinable charm which I recognized yesterday; and which makes the blood dance in my veins whenever She speaks or smiles or moves.

It seems to me that at last, by an affection of this kind one does really, in a life of shadows and dreams and nothings, set one's foot upon the absolute—the τὸ τί ἦν εἶναι.[2]

Adieu Floreas! Gaudeas in perpetuum.   ERNEST DOWSON

2. The innermost essence. See Aristotle, *Metaphysics* 1032 b.14.

176. *To John Gray*
   [*c. 8 February 1892*]

15 Bristol Gardens

My dear Gray.

Mes compliments upon your Paradox of Café concerts,[1] which was altogether admirable and charming: and my thanks for the ticket. I have not made a speech in my life, and I hope I never may: else would I have risen to express my pleasure and agreement.

I am quite of your advice, and hold that the artist should be too much absorbed in God, the Flesh and the Devil, to consider the World, quâ World, at all.

I drink to you, & to the memory of Master François Villon: and hope that you will pay me a visit some day, when you have time—in Prague!

I have been reading Maeterlinck,[2] am looking forward to Montanaro.[3]

Poignée de main   ERNEST DOWSON

John Gray Esq.

1. A reference to John Gray's lecture on *The Modern Actor* given to the Playgoers' Club on 7 February.
2. Probably *La Princesse Maleine*, 1889.
3. Gray had contributed a preface to J. T. Grein's translation of *In the Garden of Citrons* by the Spanish poet Emilio Montanaro.

177. *To Victor Plarr*

> [*c. 13 February 1892*]

> [*15 Bristol Gardens*]

Caro Mio,

Curiously enough I was meaning to write to you today (with an apology for having dispatched a flippant note to you, unwittingly, in the midst of your calamities), when I received your most welcome epistle. I hope both you and your mother are now very much better, and that someday, within a reasonable time, I shall see you again, either here or elsewhere.

I have not seen anyone very lately—until a few days ago, that is—not so much for any ailment as for a great lack of energy which has come over me, and my great absorption otherwise.

The situation in Poland remains virtually unchanged: except that, I think, a sort of tacit understanding establishes itself better and more securely every day. And for das Mädchen—she has never been more intimately charming: I become almost sanguine, although of course there are all the other difficulties still to be surmounted. It is useless to make plans however, it will arrange itself some way or other. But tell me of yourself, of your projects? Johnson spoke to me yesterday—we were coming from the Rhymers—and of your matter—is it then announced or did you reveal it to him?—in a tone which corroborated my opinion that he would be also my hostile critic. I confess, however, that I have long passed the point at which one is seriously moved by hostile criticism of anybody in these questions or can feel any more than a tolerant contempt for the point of view from which it is uttered. To take the world so seriously! Enfin c'est trop bête. God or the Flesh or the Devil—an artist may be in bondage to any one or other or all of these Powers and retain his self-respect—but the world mustn't, positively *must* not exist for him—or so much the worse for his art. Cher Poète je vous embrasse.

My mother has been very ill, is still unaccountably weak; after six weeks of the influenza with complications she can still scarcely walk across the room. These are parlous times. Would God we were all in Samoa[1] with others.

The Rhymers' Rhymes are out: and a copy for each poem of every contributor is at our disposal. Write to me soon, if you have time, and tell me when we may hope to see you. I will remember your rooms, and I wish I myself could take them: but it is a difficult house to recommend to persons, and one would have a delicatesse in recommending the person. Shall you never return to them?

With kind remembrances to your mother, and all my sympathies.

Tout à toi ERNEST DOWSON

---

1. Where R. L. Stevenson lived for the last four years of his life, 1890–94.

178. *To Victor Plarr*

[*c. 14 February 1892*]

Bridge Dock

Carissime,

Yes: there is a copy of the Book of Rhymes for each poem, which will mean, will it not, that there are five awaiting you somewhere. The person to apply to, I believe, is not Elkin Mathews,[1] but Greene of Pembroke Gardens, unless perhaps the two advance copies which were brought to each contributor, to the Cheshire, on the last meeting, and which are all I have at present, may have been handed on to Johnson to be forwarded to you.

The book is very good—better than I expected, on the whole, although the binding leaves much to be desired. And I still hold, that certain rejections amongst your poems are at least as charming as certain of the selected.

Your letter surprises me. Yes! it certainly surprises me. Please believe me also guiltless of any indiscretion: Johnson spoke first to me, and from his manner I assumed that you had yourself told him of these things, so that it is at any rate, a discussed subject in Fitzroy St.

That he should have fathomed me also is sufficiently overwhelming! You are wrong, however, in assuming that he differently damns us. No, we are bracketed—and I perceive now that his criticisms of your insanity are indirectly meant for mine—and I think it is not of vulgarity, of *banalité*, that he accuses us, so much as of being impracticable and foolish and irresponsible. As you say, however, what does it matter?—since to-morrow one dies! The criticisms of one's friends—'rumores senum severiorum.'[2] Allons donc! No—

> 'Non ego nunc tristes vereor, mea Cynthia, manes,
>   Nec moror extremo debita fata rogo:
> Sed ne forte tuo careat mihi funus amore,
>   Hic timor est ipsis durior exequiis.'[3]

Pardon these incoherencies and accept my gratitude for your charming sympathy.

Tout à toi,   ERNEST DOWSON.

P.S. The latest Rhymer is one Barlas, a charming poet and anarchist, who was lately run in for shooting the House of Commons.[4] And the latest news—that Gray, of whom I am seeing a good deal just at present, pursues the 'Star' for a libel asserting him to be 'the original Dorian of that name.'[5] This will be droll.

---

1. Elkin Mathews (1851–1921) was the publisher of the volume and of Dowson's volume of short stories, *Dilemmas*, in 1895.
2. Catullus, 5.   3. Propertius I. 19.
4. John Barlas (1860–1914) fired a revolver near the Speaker's residence on 31 December 1891 to show his contempt for the House of Commons.
5. The paper soon withdrew the offending remark and apologized.

179. *To John Gray*
>   Saturday [? *February 1892*][1]

>   15 Bristol Gardens

Poeta Optime.
    On the other side you will find a sonnet: I wrote it last night after consuming many whiskeys, & it presumably contained then some intention in it.
    This morning I found it, & it was absolutely unintelligible to me, & will remain so, I presume.

>   T à t.   ERNEST DOWSON

To His Lady: A Nocturne

Awhile we wandered, (thus it is I dream!)
    Through a long, sandy tract of no man's land,
    And only poppies grew amongst the sand,—
The which we plucking cast with scant esteem,
And ever sadlier, into the sad stream,
    Which followed us, as we went, hand in hand
Under the estrangèd stars a road unplanned
    Where all things grew the shadow of a dream.
And ever sadlier, as the stars expired
    We found the poppies rarer, till thine eyes
        Grown all my light, to light me were too tired,
And at their darkening, that no surmise,
    Might haunt me of the lost days we desired
After them all, I flung these memories.[2]

1. This letter cannot be precisely dated. It may have been written at any time between the date here suggested and the summer of 1893, when Dowson's family left Bristol Gardens.
2. First published in *Verses* as *Gray Nights* and there dedicated to Sayle.

180. *To Arthur Moore*
>   [*2 March 1892*]

>   Bridge Dock

Caro.
    I meant to catch you this morning, partly because I ~~had~~ left my umbrella in your room the other night: partly because I ~~am~~ wished to draw on you for 6/6: which amount I purpose handing over to Mme. F.

to-night, the new draw being on the 22nd. inst.[1] There is a Rhymers meeting to-night, but it is at Bedford Park, chez Todhunter, and I hardly think my energy will carry me so far. Therefore I will probably call in upon you on my way home: but do not wait in for me, as I am uncertain; only of your kindness instruct your domestic to hand me over my little blue and orange umbrella the lack of which is making my soul gray, gray, gray—and my hat pink. And forgive these baubles. I have been reading the D.C., Lang, Image, & the Black & White on the Rhymers. The edition is now absolutely épuisé, which is charming. I wonder if there will be a reprint & if so whether it will mean any personal profit. I wonder!

Let me remind you that that great work "Masqde" must positively appear in June, in order that we may run Brétonwards with easy minds, & that I wait for your chaps impatiently, in order to resume the thread of my narrative.

Fahrwohl! Let me see you soon.

On Friday I play whist with Hall in the Temple: therefore I shall dine at 6.0 Sat: you are burlesquing till 5: when I go to the Cult of Adelka.[2] ∴ unless I see you to-night or to-morrow we shall scarcely see one another before Sun.

~~I will Try therefore & communic~~ I will be therefore, if I miss you to-night to-morrow au Coq.[3] à 6.h. Try & come.

T à t   ERNEST DOWSON

1. Apparently a German sweepstake. See Letter 219.
2. i.e. Adelaide.
3. The Cock in Shaftesbury Avenue, one of Dowson's favourite rendezvous.

181. *To Victor Plarr*
   [*3 March 1892*]

Bridge Dock

My dear Victor.

Can you forgive me for this extremely unpardonable procrastination. I ought to have answered your kind invitation at once, but I was uncertain whether I would be able to come or not & what with one distraction & another, I let the psychological moment slip. I must try & come some Sunday soon, but while my people are ill, I find it impossible to make any fixtures. Thanks muchly for the cuttings & the letter which is most charming and polyglot: I return you all herewith save the Daily Chronicle, which I should like to keep as you have another, and the Daily News, which I will send you tomorrow, when I have shown it to my people. I am amused to find that my cursory acquaintance with the Anthology of Anthologies has made such a deep impression on my manner—or can it be that my reviewer does not know what the Gr. Anthology is about? I didn't go to the Rhymers last night, nor to the last meeting but one; chiefly because the meetings were in inaccessible places & the night was cold, & partly because I was in a condition too lyrical even for the society of poets. So I have not run across Greene: but you will be glad to hear that the edition is entirely exhausted. I have seen scarcely anyone lately but Gray & Hall; once for a short time Horne, & for a moment Image; & there have been accidental meetings. In effect I am become far too absorbed to do anything but sit, in Poland, & gather the exquisite moments. For—to quote mes derniers—

The wisdom of the world said unto me:
   'Go forth and run; the race is to the brave;
Perchance some honour tarrieth for thee!'
   'As tarrieth,' I said, 'for sure, the grave.'
     For I had pondered on a rune of roses,
     Which to her votaries the moon discloses.

The wisdom of the world said: *'There are bays:*
   'Go forth and run, for victory is good,
After the stress of the laborious days.'
   'Yet,' said I, 'shall I be the worms' sweet food,'
     As I went musing on a rune of roses,
     Which in her hour, the pale, soft moon discloses.

Then said my voices *'Wherefore strive or run,*
   On dusty highways ever, a vain race?
The long night cometh, starless, void of sun,
   What light shall serve thee like her golden face?'
     For I had pondered on a rune of roses,
     And knew some secrets which the moon discloses.

'Yea,' said I, 'for her eyes are pure and sweet
   As lilies, and the fragrance of her hair
Is many laurels; and it is not meet
   To run for shadows when the prize is here;'
     This said I, knowing all the rune of roses,
     Which in her hour the pale, soft moon discloses.[1]

I will write soon. I hope your Mother makes good progress

                      Ever yrs   ERNEST DOWSON

P.S. Dear Image! How charming his notice is: I had already obtained it.

---

1. Dated 19 February in Dowson's notebook; first published in *Verses*.

182. *To Victor Plarr*
  [*c. April 1892*]

15 Bristol Gardens

Caro Mio.

Can you come & have supper with us here, next Sunday, about 8? There is a certain Wilfrid Pollock,[1] of treasure Hunt fame, of Oxford & of Allahabad to be with us, whom my father thinks you might care to meet. Drop me a word by return, if you can come. Otherwise shall hope to ~~see you one~~ find you in one Evening soon. There is much to be said. I am down in Gehenna; I hope you are up in the clouds. In any case you have my sympathies. From every point of view this is a tedious world: unhappily rendered so perhaps, more than it need be, by foolish conventionalities and proprieties of ones relations and friends; and by the entire lack of charity in one's scandal loving acquaintances. No more.

Tuissimus   ERNEST DOWSON

Victor Plarr Esq.

---

1. Wilfred Douglas Pollock went up to Christ Church in 1878. He later became a journalist on the *Morning Post* and published *War and a Wheel*, 1897.

183. *To Samuel Smith*[1]
  [*April–May 1892*]

[*15 Bristol Gardens*]

I have been existing in a curiously tense state for the last month or so, and for the last week tense is scarcely the word. It is better than the old stagnation, but it is exhausting. Things are coming to a crisis, cher vieux! I go to have tête-à-tête teas with Madame! We talk intimately, we talk of Her—natürlich—and we are constantly on the verge of an understanding. Yesterday it was the nearest shave of all. She gave me an admirable occasion. I am sure she expected it. I was just coming out with a protestation, to the effect that my one object and desire in life was to be of service to her admirable daughter—when we were interrupted. We were both curiously moved! I went out and had a gin

---

1. Text from Gawsworth.

and bitters and poured it tremulously down my shirt, and passed a perfectly wide-awake night—damning the interruption. This morning I saw that it would have been foolish; but this afternoon I shall be in precisely the same state, and I feel certain that it is only a question of days now. To think that a little girl of barely fourteen should have so disorganized my spiritual economy.

I should like to see you and hear your advice, though of course unless it agreed with my own, however good it were, I shouldn't take it. It is a difficult case. If it were not for the complication of a foreign point of view and foreign traditions—I should be justified in waiting, in holding my tongue. Only when one remembers how very much earlier abroad these matters are arranged—and especially in Germany —the case is changed. An English mother would be scandalised at your proposing for the hand of her daughter before she were 16; a foreign mother might reasonably be equally scandalised if you were attentive to her daughter, without making your mind clear to her, at a much earlier age. But there are objections either way . . . I should like to see you, for verily, this matter grievously weighs me down.

184. *To Victor Plarr*
     [*April–May 1892*]

15 Bristol Gardens

Cher Vieux,

What must you think of me? It must be 3 weeks since I wrote you a ream of spleen, having incidentally to say, how grieved I was not to be able to join you & Hillier on a certain Sunday. And, a day or two ago, I found I had posted the letter in a pocket! I still hope that I may see you some day at Kings. I hope you and yours flourish. May we meet soon; in Valhalla at any rate, for after Götterdamerung, there is haply, Valhalla, & I think this is the twilight of the gods: but what I mean exactly, I could put more precisely in a sonnet, which might be found obscure. What are you doing? If you have a spare moment, write to me; your letters appeal to my τὸ τί ἦν εἶναι more than anything: or what are you not doing? Which is generally the most important form of action! I do nothing, live in a sort of dream, of nothing: and I have never before lived to such an exhausting extent. To find an irrational residuum in oneself, eluding one's last analysis, is by some strange freak, reasonably a consolation. Does not a great, personal passion become a whole metaphysic? At least an abstract, metaphysical notion, or a sacrament, or a mystery, or a miracle, in certain lights, becomes more credible than any material thing or appearance, one's mere going or doing, or talk or juxtaposition or the death one will die.

But I don't want to send you an essay on the absolute, & will conclude with a prayer for forgiveness, for these random impressions. But
I wanted to write a word to you;—and this by the way, because of all
the men I know you are the most likely to find me intelligible. Though
I have done, nor said, nor suffered anything tangible since I last saw or
wrote to you, I write as an *illuminato*: I seem to have seen mysteries, &
if I fail to be explicit, it is because my eyes are dazzled.

Ever yours   ERNEST DOWSON

185. *To Samuel Smith*[1]
[*Early May 1892*]

[*15 Bristol Gardens*]

I go on in precisely the same situation in Poland. I can't somehow
screw myself up to making a declaration of myself to *Madame*, although
I am convinced it is the most reasonable course. Any day however with
favourable omens it may arrive. She herself is sometimes very charming, sometimes not! But in the latter case it is merely my own abominably irritable temper which is to blame. I have had an interview of
abnormal length with Lionel, in which he argued with me most strenuously all night. He had been dining at my Uncle's (the Hooles) and
apparently this infatuation of mine was openly discussed the whole of
dinner-time *par tous ces gens*. So I do not see how it can go on much
longer without an understanding or a *fracas*—the latter I suppose will
be inevitable first—with my people. Altogether *Je m'embête horrible-
ment*; and my only consolation is that if it is so obvious to all my
friends and relatives it ought to be equally so to the Poles as well.
'Masquerade' is now under consideration with Bentley: the first publishers it has yet been to. If the result is favourable I really think I shall
be inspired to make the disagreeable necessary overtures in Poland.
Another year of the stress and tension and uncertainty of these last 6
months will leave me without a nerve in my composition and I am not
sure whether I have any now.

1. Text from Gawsworth.

186. *To Samuel Smith*

9 May 1892

Bridge Dock

Caro Mio,

I was so sorry to miss you last Wed: I had your message fr. Émile[1] & was on the point of writing to you, when your letter reached me. Unfortunately I have arranged to dine at home on Wednesday night next, having asked some men round. Can't you manage to join me there at 8. or thereabouts? You shall have some whist. Otherwise tomorrow and Thurs. I shall be dining in Poland & enchaunted to see you: but try and come on Wed. or if you are early enough over with the Academy, come & call for me in Poland at 6.0 & we might manage 50 up: before I wend my way home.

Missie has gone back to Mme. L. & is generally kept there till 8: So I do not amuse myself too much there nowadays. I have not been to the Academy yet, & look forward to doing so with much distaste: I intend to go; but I expect $\frac{1}{2}$ an hour at the New will be about as much as I shall manage. I have seen all our common acquaintance lately, except Swanton, I think, and Berridge. Johnson hoped you will come & see him whenever in town. Gerald[2] is away playing in various country towns in Kent and Surrey. Appended you will find the poem you speak of: I haven't yet contrived any title for it.

> By the sad waters of separation,
>   Where we have wandered by divers ways,
> I have but the shadow and imitation,
>   Of the old, memorial days.
>
> In music, I have no consolation;
>   No roses are pale enough for me:
> The sound of the waters of separation
>   Surpasseth roses and melody.
>
> By the sad waters of separation,
>   Dimly I hear, from an hidden place,
> The sigh of mine ancient adoration:
>   Hardly can I remember your face!
>
> You may be dead, and no proclamation
>   Sprang to me over the waste, gray sea:
> Living, the waters of separation
>   Sever, for ever, your soul from me.

1. Unidentified.
2. Dowson's cousin Gerald Hoole, who was an actor.

No man knoweth our desolation,
Memory pales of the old delight;
While the sad waters of separation
Bear us on to the ultimate night.[3]

ERNEST DOWSON

3. First published in *Verses* under the title *Exile*, and there dedicated to
Conal O'Riordan.

187. *To Herbert Horne*
[*Postmark 13 May 1892*]

15 Bristol Gardens

My dear Horne.

I am afraid I must defer my excursion with you to the Trocadéro,[1]
tomorrow: I have become the victim of the most stupendous cold
which has ever occurred to me, & fear that I shall spend tomorrow in
bed.

If I recover, I will let you know on what day next week I shall be
"at home" in Sherwood St—in the hope, that on one of them you may
manage to look in & drink a dish of coffee with me.

Ever yrs.   ERNEST DOWSON.

1. Music-hall in Shaftesbury Avenue; later the site of the Trocadero Restaurant, now a Bingo hall.

188. *To Victor Plarr*
19 [*actually 17*] May 1892

Bridge Dock

Mon cher Victor.

Why do I never see you now? Are you always away or am I, or
where are we? Mais où sont les neiges d'antan? I hear from Horne that
you of the Hobby House are all enrhumé; but I hope this does not
apply at all seriously to you? I myself have had one of the worst rheums

LED–Q

within my memory, but today I am recovered. On Wednesday (to-morrow) I shall dine at home: will you look in upon me? But perhaps I will call tonight at Fitzroy St; and, perhaps, I will see you? I hope all the affairs prosper. Mine do not flourish; or only by fits and starts; alternations which wear me out more than uniform frustration would do. I saw Hillier on Sunday: it seems agreed that the Rhymers should meet au Cheshire, on Friday, but nobody has arranged to send out the notices. Will you, or Johnson do this, as we have not the list of addresses? It is ages since I have managed to go to one; as a rule now I am too chronically irritated to go anywhere, except at rare, precarious intervals when there happens to be nowhere to go, and nothing to do. I am making rhymes in the meantime[1] and trying to write a short story.[2] Is your muse fertile just now? Or are you too fortunately occupied otherwhere to woo her? Well well! Au revoir.

T à t   ERNEST DOWSON

1. Probably *To One in Bedlam*, first published in *The Albemarle Review*, August 1892.
2. Probably *The Statute of Limitations*, published in *The Hobby Horse*, 1893.

189. *To Victor Plarr*[1]
    13 June 1892

Bridge Dock

Mon cher Victor,
    I hope you will consider the Breton journey seriously:[2] Moore, I am sure, would be very charmed. In case you decide upon it I send you a sort of itinerary which you may find useful, although you will very likely vary it.

[Plan of a tour]

I hope once more that you will think of it: I am sure that you would both of you be charmed with the country. The formal *table d'hôte* of Trouville, Cannes, Paris, Dinan, etc., is unknown . . . . I have a neuralgic disorder which swells my face abominably, so that unless there is a speedy improvement you will find me at home in the evening soon. A bientôt donc.

1. Text from Plarr.
2. Plarr was to be married in the summer and was planning his honeymoon. Dowson had already arranged to go to Brittany with Moore.

190. *Postcard to William Theodore Peters*[1]
   [*Postmark 23 June 1892*]

The Snuggeries, A public h——e, Charing X Rd.[2]

19 Sherwood Street

Can you dine with me at my restaurant on Friday the 24th inst. Gray will be there. In case you can't find my restaurant, address given above. I will wait for you from 6.30–7 in the Vestibule of the Café Monico, Regent St. The address on the right is not mine but that of the worthy publican from whose establishment I write. Mine you have I believe.

Yrs. ERNEST DOWSON

1. American-born poet and actor and 'permanent guest' of the Rhymers' Club. He had recently settled in London, and in 1896 published a volume of poems, *Posies out of Rings*. In the later 'nineties he lived in Paris, where he became a contributor to *Le Quartier Latin*. He died in 1904 or 1905.
2. Probably the Crown, another favourite rendezvous.

191. *To Charles Sayle*
   [*July 1892*]

15 Bristol Gardens

My dear Sayle.

We lunch at 1.30. But come to Mass with me first by all means; then I can show you the loved. I am afraid the Dominican Ch. Haverstock Hill would make us rather late. My usual Church is the Ch of Our Lady, Grove Rd. St John's Wood. That will not be far from you & is quite close to me.

Yes, we are near Maida Vale. Turn down the Street leading out (South) of that Vale which almost faces St John's Wood Rd. It is called, I believe, Clifton Gardens & it is almost straight, past a church called St Saviours.

I will wait outside the garden gate of Our Lady till 11.15 however on the chance of your coming there: if not hope you will find your way to us by 1.0

T à toi ERNEST DOWSON

192. *To Charles Sayle*
[*c. 10 July 1892*]

15 Bristol Gardens.

My dear Sayle.
To search for Barlas is like the search for the Sangreal: else had I answered you before.

His present address is unknown: a letter C/o H. H. Champion Esq[1] 142 Strand may find him; but he is not living there any more—Symons address is Fountain Court. Temple. No number is necessary, for there is only that house.

Thanks very much for the book & handkerchiefs. I wish I had seen more of you that little while you were in town. May we meet again soon.

I go to Brittany on the 23rd approximately.

T à toi   ERNEST DOWSON

1. 1859–1928. He was secretary of the Social Democratic Federation and had stood bail for Barlas (with Wilde). See Letter 178.

193. *Letter-card to William Theodore Peters*
[*Postmark 15 July 1892*]

15 Bristol Gardens

My dear Peters,
I feel terribly guilty after having given you three unembarrassed days to choose from at having, after all, to throw myself upon your mercy in the matter of tomorrow. Will you forgive me and give me another opportunity? The unfortunate truth is this: two ladies to whom I had pledged myself some time ago wrote to me yesterday to the effect that they had procured a box for "Lady Windermere"[1] tomorrow, & that they depended upon me. I am very much annoyed with them & with myself, & I don't want to see "Lady W" again in the least—but all the same I don't see how to get out of it. Hinc illae lacrimae. Please believe how sorry I am & give me another chance, before the 29th when I go to France.

Yrs very sincerely   ERNEST DOWSON

1. *Lady Windermere's Fan*, Wilde's first successful play, was produced by George Alexander at the St. James's Theatre on 20 February 1892.

194. *To William Theodore Peters*
    [*c. 18 July 1892*]

                              15 Bristol Gardens

My dear Peters,
    It is very charming of you to give me an opportunity of restoring my character for punctuality. This week I seem to be engaged. Next week on either Tuesday, Wednesday or Thursday, I should be delighted to dine with you: Tuesday would suit me best, & unless I hear to the contrary from you I will assume that that day will be convenient to you.
    Don't have any hesitation however in putting me off, if these days are occupied.
    If I have the energy to wrap it up I am sending you with this a copy of the "Hobby Horse",[1] ~~with~~ partly because there is something of mine in it, which I want you to see, partly because it is such an admirably arranged review that it seems a pity you should not know it, as I believe you do not.
    If I can't manage to post it, I will bring it with me.
                      Tout à vous   ERNEST DOWSON

1. The number for April 1891.

195. *To Victor Plarr*
    [*July 1892*]

                                Bridge Dock

Caro Vittorio mio. I have only just realized that you are finally departed; having been expecting daily to see you. Has your term at Kings also come to an end? And is one ever to see you again? At any rate let me hear from you speedily, & of your plans. I go to Brittany a week later than was arranged; on the 29th of this month. So there is all the more chance of our meeting. We shall not be more than a week at Le Faouet; whence we proceed into quite unexplored barbarisms on the extreme west of Finisterre: but we ought to run across each other, when we are returning. I wish I was going under your circumstances. However I must possess my soul in patience. Only write, if you have a moment to spare.
                    T à t   ERNEST DOWSON

P.S. Even if we happen to miss in Brétagne, you *must* visit Faouet: on the left hand side of the market place (looking south) from the Lion d'Or observe the house which whatever happen I intend to live in

196. *To William Theodore Peters*
   [*c. 28 July 1892*]

15 Bristol Gardens

Cher Poète,
   Herewith I send you the "Hobby" with "Cynara" & a charming lithograph of Shannon the Younger. I should like to know how the magazine strikes you. If you have time & inclination I should be delighted to hear from you. Hotel du Lion D'Or, Le Faouet, Morbihan, will find me some time or other within the next ten days.
   Thank you once more for a charming evening.
                                   Yours ever   ERNEST DOWSON

P.S. I should awfully like to go to Paris now, bearing your credentials, but I fear there is no chance of it. Perhaps it shall be in the spring.

197. *To Herbert Horne*
   [*Postmark 31 July 1892*]

Hôtel des Voyageurs, Plancoët.

My dear Horne,
   I entirely forgot to return you the enclosed proof.[1] Here it is with my apologies for the tardiness. I found it just before I left London & had no time to forward it before.
   As you will gather from the inscription, we are again in the land of apple blossom. Unhappily it has changed to cold & wet today although yesterday was charming. We move on in an hour or two, some where or other. Our destination is never settled until we reach the station.
   My compliments to the Cénacle which is to be: if you have any further developments to tell of, or require to communicate with me on any matter, my address for the next ten days—that is to say, an

---

1. Almost certainly of *Apple Blossom in Brittany*, though in the event it appeared in *The Yellow Book*.

address at which, some time or other within that time, letters will reach me—is

Hotel du Lion D'Or
Le Faouet
Morbihan.
Yrs very sincerely   ERNEST DOWSON

198. *To Victor Plarr*[1]

Minuit, Wednesday [*10 August 1892*]

Au Lion d'Or, Le Faouet

Carissime,

I am charmed to hear that you are in the sacred land. I also adore the granite and the cathedral of Dol. Alas! that we are just leaving for that direction. We hoped that you would arrive here before we left, but now you are not, and at 4.0 in the morning we depart for Pontivy, en route for Lamballe, etc. . . . I leave this note on the chance of your reaching here before we meet; but I hope that either at Lamballe or Dol we may rencounter. . . . If you come here let me entreat you to take a rough but most delightful walk up the hill opposite St Barbe. When you have seen the savage beauty of the view you get at about the end of the range, I hope you will be as devout a Faouettois as I am. No more now: we have but 3 hours' slumber.

Alas I shall be in London this day week. But I shall return and live here. Some day you must do likewise.

If you have time to send your impressions of this place to me, your letter will be to me even as the saving draught of water to the traveller in a thirsty land!

1. Text from Plarr.

199. *To William Theodore Peters*

Monday [*22 August 1892*]

15 Bristol Gardens

My dear Poet.

Many thanks for your note, which I found on my rentrée last week.
Can you look me up tomorrow evening about 9.0, here? I shall be at
home all the evening. I won't ask you to dine, as I am not sure of what
my people's plans are: but I can offer you some supper later on.

Don't trouble to write if you're engaged, as I shall be at home anyhow. If you don't turn up, I will try & arrange for another day—or will
you write & fix one yourself, when you can come round 8.30 or 9—
Friday? (I am only engaged on Wednesday & Saturday this week)—
giving me a day's notice. Or a third alternative come & see me any time
you like on Sunday afternoon, & have some supper: then I am sure of
being in.

In any case I am greatly hoping to meet you soon. I hope in another
few weeks sufficient Rhymers will be returned from wandering to make
a séance possible—when I shall hope to have you of the company. At
the present moment are we not almost the only persons in town?

I am just trying to finish off a short story for Macmillans'.[1]

Tout à vous ERNEST DOWSON

By the way there is a certain witty old lady of my acquaintance who is
anxious to meet you & who is at home precisely on Sunday.[2] Should you
come on that day, come before 5.0 & if you like, we might pay her a
call?

1. Probably *The Statute of Limitations*, later given to *The Hobby Horse*.
2. Miss Roberts. See Letter 16.

200. *To Arthur Moore*

Monday [*29 August 1892*]

Bridge Dock

Carissimo.

I am beginning to wonder, when I shall see you. Thanks muchly for
your letter; did you finally break that bank? Perhaps you are at
Monaco? If you are de rétour au contraire, will you come round to-night
I shall be in all the evening & I want to hear your further adventures. I

caught that Friday boat. I fully meant to write but postponed it, until it seemed doubtful whether a letter to Pontrieux would catch you. Pardonnez moi.

I am dining at home to-night, my father has gone off en yacht to Christiania. Can't you fetch me then in Poland on your way from office & we can go to Maida by the same courrier.

I will wait there till 6.15 for you: tâche à venir.

If not—à ce soir—n'est ce pas.

T à t   ERNEST DOWSON

201. *Postcard to William Theodore Peters*
[*5 September 1892*]

15 Bristol Gardens

Cher Poète,

As I find my mother will be quite alone tomorrow night (Tuesday) would you come here & dine with us, instead of my coming to you;—& bring your MSS with you. After dinner we shall have an uninterrupted tête à tête in which we may go through them. I hope you won't think this very rude of me: but you will understand the position. If you *can't* manage it, I can come to you on Thursday or Friday, but my mother joins with me in hoping you will. If prevented would you send me a wire before 1.0 addressed

Dowson, Limehouse.

202. *Postcard to William Theodore Peters*
[*Postmark 6 September 1892*]

[15 Bristol Gardens]

Forgot to say we dine at 7.30.

E D

203. *To Arthur Moore*
Thursday [*8 September 1892*]

Bridge Dock

Caro.

I called *en passant* for Chap v[1] this morning: it is *very, very good*, I feel sanguine of the ultimate prospect. Keep it up. My own chap. vi. progresses slowly:—but it will fall, I think into 2, the latter part of the last of which I shall hand over to you. I fear we shall not meet until Sat: will you call for me at Poland at 5.40 or thereabouts. To morrow I go to Greenwich early, to dine & sleep chez *les Plarr*. They returned on Sat, & on Tuesday I had tea with them in Image's studio. They looked very well, & Madame seems to have grown prettier. They were 8 days at Faouet & 3 at Scaer. Madame asked me if I knew Casimir. I said that we did! I dined yesterday with Peters & one Paul Emile Jenet, a cousin of Banville's (Théodore de)[2] Try & come on Saturday. Poignée de main. Missie is still away.

ERNEST DOWSON

Consider the development of Book II *en attendant* my instalment.

1. Of *Adrian Rome*, the novel he and Moore had begun as a successor to *A Comedy of Masks*. It was published in 1899.
2. French Symbolist poet (1823–1891).

204. *To William Theodore Peters*
Tuesday [?*27 September 1892*]

Bridge Dock

Cher Confrère,

I find since seeing you there is a Rhymer's meeting convened for Wednesday evening. Will you come to it, at the Cheshire Cheese, at 9.0? Otherwise, if you remember, I was coming to see you on that night. I fear I shall have to be dining & sleeping at Blackheath[1] on Thursday, & so cannot be of the suggested party. Mind & bring a rhyme with you: I fear I have none. My muse is frozen to death by these inclement days.

Ever yrs   E. DOWSON.

1. Where Plarr and his wife had taken a house.

205. *To Victor Plarr*
  [*c. 8 October 1892*]

15 Bristol Gardens

Cher Vieux.

I have had a great many tedious things to do; I have also had a cold: they are both now arranged to a certain extent, and I am able to do what I should have done before, thank you for the charming night you allowed me to spend at Midleton[1] last week. Were you at the Rhymers last night? I wish I could have managed to be of the party. I suppose it is settled that we are to hold the Laurelship as a corporate office, and present the butt of canary to the patron du Cheshire, as a composition for free drinks. I am sorry that Tennyson has crossed the bar:[2] if only, that it leaves us so much at the mercy of Sir Edwin, L.Morriss, Austin et Cie. But he was un grand poète, tout de même. Above all I love him because he did sacredly hate the mob—which whether it be the well dressed mob whom Browning pandered to, òr the evil smelling mob to which William Morris does now ~~still~~, to the detriment of his art and ~~the offence~~ of his own dignity still pander, I hold aliké to be damnable, unwholesome and obscene.

Write to me, as I suppose I shall not very often see you now; and send me anything you have written. My muse awoke from her torpor of many months yesterday, here is her feeble utterance, but she may run to another verse by and by.

IN AUTUMN

  Pale, amber sunlight falls across
    The reddening, September trees,
    That hardly move before a breeze
  As soft as summer: summer's loss
    Seems little, Dear! on days like these.

  Let misty autumn be our part!
    The twilight of the year is sweet:
    Where sunshine and the darkness meet,
  Our love, a twilight of the heart
    Eludes a little time's deceit.

  Are we not better and at home
    In dreamful autumn, we who deem
    No harvest joy is worth a dream?

1. Plarr's house.
2. Tennyson died at Haslemere on 6 October. There was no new Poet Laureate until 1896, when Alfred Austin was appointed.

A little while and night shall come,
A little while we have to dream.[3]

With very kind regards to your mother & Mme Victor

T à t   ERNEST DOWSON

---

3. First printed in *Verses*, where it is called *Autumnal* and duly has a fourth
stanza.

206. *To William Theodore Peters*
[*c. 18 October 1892*]

15 Bristol Gardens

My dear Peters,

Thanks very much for your kind invitation. I shall be charmed to
dine with you upon any evening you like next week, with the exception
of *Monday & Saturday* when I am engaged. Will you fix some day?

Sorry you could not come to the Rhymers: but on the whole you lost
little; we were all very tedious.

I was intending to write & ask you if I might bring my friend Gray
to call on you some evening; he is very anxious to meet you.

Now perhaps we shall be able to arrange a meeting.

Yrs v. sincerely   ERNEST DOWSON.

P.S. Shall I see you at the Independent Theatre on Friday?[1]

---

1. Performance of Webster's *The Duchess of Malfi* given by the Independent
Theatre at the Opera Comique on 21 October.

207. *Letter-card to William Theodore Peters*
    20 October 1892

[15 Bristol Gardens]

Cher Pierrot

Will you make my excuses to Bowkett[1] about the Rhymers: I forget if I told you—they meet not because of the Independent performance.

I have just accepted a seat in a box for that, so shall look out for you in the lobby during interludes.

          T à t   ERNEST DOWSON.

1. Sidney Bowkett, author of *A Snowstorm,* a curtain-raiser which was put on at the Gaiety Theatre on 1 October 1892.

208. *To William Theodore Peters*
    [?24 October 1892]

15 Bristol Gardens

My dear Pierrot,

When Lionel Johnson left me at 3.0 this morning I suddenly remembered that it was Sunday night, and the trains are eccentric then. I hope you got back comfortably, and that your throat has not suffered? I am starting on the play,[1] & will push on with it *quam cellerime.* But I find it excessively difficult and fear that with a limitation of two characters I can not attempt any dramatic effect. Is this required? Or will you be satisfied with a *folium rosae* which must depend entirely on its verses and the speaking of these to carry it through, with the help of the Pierrot's tradition? Would you by the way send me a line to say what you meant exactly with the extract of the fairy song you gave me?

Has music been made for that, and do you want to bring it in? Or is a lyric in that metre to fit the music suggested? Let me know of this. I should like to see you soon, to hear any suggestions you may have further.

          T à toi   ERNEST DOWSON

1. *The Pierrot of the Minute,* Dowson's short verse play, which Peters produced for the Primrose League at Chelsea Town Hall on 22 November 1892. It was published in 1897.

209. *To G. A. Greene*
[*?c. 24 October 1892*]

15 Bristol Gardens

My dear Greene.
Here is Hérédias unpublished sonnet. It seems to me very superb.
Shall I send out notices for Friday week or has it been arranged?
Yrs v sincerely   ERNEST DOWSON.

ANTOINE ET CLEOPÂTRE

Tous deux, ils regardaient de la haute terasse
L'Egypte s'endormi sous un ciel étouffant
Et le fleuve au travers du delta noir qu'il fend
Vers Bubaste ou Saïs rouler son onde grasse.
Et le Romain sentait sous sa lourde cuirasse
Soldat captif, berçant le sommeil d'un enfant
Ployer et défailler sur son coeur triomphant
Le corps voluptueux que son étreinte embrasse.
Tournant sa tête pâle entre ses cheveux bruns
Vers celui qu'enivraient d'invincibles parfums
Elle tendit sa bouche et ses prunelles claires,
Et sur elle courbé l'ardent impérator
Vit dans ses larges yeux qu'étoilaient des points d'or
Toute une mer immense où fuyaient des galères.[1]

1. Printed in *Les Trophées*, 1893.

210. *To Victor Plarr*
[*c. 26 October 1892*]

15 Bristol Gardens

Cher Vieux.
Your letter should have been answered before this: but I have been
frightfully busy, having rashly undertaken to make a little Pierrot play,
in verse for Peters which is to be played at Aldershot,[1] & afterwards at
the Chelsea Town Hall: the article to be delivered in a fortnight. So
until this period of severe mental agony be past, I can go nowhere. I
am looking forward to making you another visit. I searched for you at
the Independent Theatre the other night but you were not. Meeting
there, along with many other persons, the poet Green, I undertook to
send out notices for a Rhymers' meeting au Cheshire on Friday next
the   . Will you take this in lieu of a postcard and endeavour to come?
I have a quaint old German coming, Dr Eugene Oswald, the President

1. The performance at Aldershot was later put off till 5 December.

of the Carlyle Society,[2] whom you will appreciate.

L.J. was here on Sat. & slept here. he told me that your Chouan poem, which I like immeasurably, has been taken by Macmillan: my congratulations! I have a map of Morbihan, hanging up over me now: mine eyes water at the sight of it. Quousque tandem, Domine!

Very many thanks for remembering my Damozel, & collecting those journaux. I won't trouble you to send them by post, but will fetch them the next time I visit you: that will give me an excuse for inflicting myself upon you shortly. I would this play were done: half of it is completed & I have seven days more, but the second half is mightily oppressing me. And I am horribly afraid that when it is written I may be worried with rehearsals and enforced company with terrible South Kensington young ladies and fashionable Chelsea Mesdames. Have you heard that Horne is now in the Temple and the sacred house in Fitzroy St is full of men who know not Joseph? I must look you up at Kings' soon. Perhaps this afternoon. In the meanwhile a dyspeptic little poem, "to His Lady and His Friend".

Tout votre   ERNEST DOWSON

Every kind regard to your Mother & Mme. Victor.

IN TEMPORE SENECTUTIS
"Junior fui etenim senui!" Ps. 37.25.

When I am old,
   And sadly steal apart;
Into the dark and cold:
   Friend of my heart,
Remember if you can,
Not him who lingers but that other man,
Who loved and sang and had a beating heart,
   When I am old!

When I am old,
   And all Love's antient fire,
Is tremulous and cold.
   My heart's Desire;
Remember, if you may,
Nothing of you and me but yesterday,
When heart on heart we bade the years conspire
   To make us old!

2. Instructor in German at the Royal Naval College, Greenwich, author and translator of numerous books published between 1854 and 1911. His *Reminiscences of a Busy Life* (1911) has a brief reference to Dowson. 'I knew his father well; he was a neighbour of mine in Blomfield [?Bristol] Gardens, whom life had saddened. He had withdrawn from the poetical inspiration into the £ s. d. region, and not many of them. The son, also manifestly saddened, took no interest in public affairs.' He died in 1912.

When I am old,
   And all the stars above
Are pitiless and cold.
   My Life's one love,
Forbid me not to go:
Remember naught of me but long ago,
And not, at last, how Love & pity strove,
   When I was old![3]

24/10/92

3. First published in *Verses*.

211. *To William Theodore Peters*
   [*?27 October 1892*]

15 Bristol Gardens

Mon cher Pierrot,
   On further thought, I have come to the conclusion, that I shall not come with you on Saturday. Firstly, I seem to be abominably busy on that day, & might very likely be late. 2nd I have not been getting on very rapidly with the play & I can't hope to finish it in time to take it completed to Miss North tomorrow.[1] 3rd I should very much prefer, if it be necessary to read the play to Miss North, to read it her in a complete condition, than to make 2 'bites' of it. 4th I think it very much better that Miss North should have an opportunity of sampling it so to speak without being restrained in her criticism by the presence of the authour.
   I will endeavour therefore to let you have as much of the play as shall be written by tonight, in a fair copy, tomorrow afternoon. I will leave or send it to your house, some time before five p.m. Early next week the thing should be done: then I shall be at your disposal.
   Thanks for yor note: I quite agree with your criticism upon the "lost my heart & found my soul" line. I will expurgate it, & had thought of it, before hearing from you. I will bear in mind the "moonstones" but I confess I do not precisely like the "child Pierrot" phrase, although it

1. Ida North, who took the part of the Moon Maiden in *The Pierrot of the Minute*.

is better in French. I went over parts of it with Lionel Johnson last night: discussed certain lines I was not sure of, & accepted sundry of his emendations. The "sad music" line reads now "Why should I be so musical and sad?"[2]

Let me hear of your visit to Miss N: or see you on Sunday.

Tout à toi   ERNEST DOWSON.

2. Line 56.

212. Letter-card to William Theodore Peters
Monday [*Postmark 31 October 1892*]

15 Bristol Gardens

Caro mio.

Forgive my dilatoriness: I was literally done to death on Saturday, & quite unable to do any copying. I hope you are not very wroth: I couldn't get out of the private view of the British Artists,[1] where I was squashed into a jelly. The play wants about 100 lines (I think) to completion. I shall copy out most of the first part & bring it with me to 19 Sherwood St tonight, on the chance of your turning up there: shall be there 7–9. If not will leave it for you tomorrow. Let me know when I can see you. I am dining out one day this week but at present I am not certain which: shall be here tomorrow evening, if you could look in. I hope to have the whole finished (not copied) tomorrow.

Yours ever   ERNEST DOWSON

1. Winter exhibition of the Royal Society of British Artists, Suffolk Street, Pall Mall.

213. Letter-card to William Theodore Peters
[*Postmark 2 November 1892*]

15 Bristol Gardens

Dear Pierrot,

The play is done, I think: save only the song to your formula, which I will try & make before Saturday. I hope you will like my ending; but

LED–R

I am not quite sure about it. Will you not write an epilogue? I think that should be, after the excellent XVIIIth custom by a different hand to the play. My notion is that the birds twitter, Pierrot sinks back on his couch, She calls up music to be his mandragore; he sleeps. Then she says a speech over him, & retires: Pierrot is left sleeping; her escort of moon beams sing the song as yet unwritten, and the curtain falls, Pierrot lying asleep. A moment or two afterwards it goes up again, & Pierrot comes forward with his epilogue to the ladies, which I hope you will write.[1]

Ever yrs   E D.

P.S. If you have to wire to me about the Gaiety on Friday,[2] will you wire to 19 Sherwood St, as I am uncertain as to my movements on that day: but shall certainly be there at 5.0.

1. Peters adopted this suggestion. His epilogue is printed in Dowson's *Poetical Works*.
2. The 'second edition' of *Cinder-Ellen Up Too Late* by A. C. Torr and W. T. Vincent, with *A Snowstorm* as the curtain-raiser.

214. *Postcard to William Theodore Peters*
2.30 [*Postmark 4 November 1892*]

The Temple

As I was not sure about the tickets coming; I have promised to dine with a man tomorrow. Will you pardon me? I will be at the LC & DPG[1] books Temple 2.30 Sat punctually

E D

1. The abbreviation seems inexplicable. The next word is not clearly written and could be 'booking' or 'forks'.

215. *To William Theodore Peters*
   [*c. 5 November 1892*]

15 Bristol Gardens

My dear Pierrot
   Herewith the remainder of the play. I hoped to be able to do both
your copy & Miss North's in full, but as time pressed, in your copy I
have omitted the longer speeches of the Moon Maid, giving merely the
clues.
   Will you be careful therefore that Miss North gets the copy which is
marked for her.

In haste
Yrs   ERNEST DOWSON

216. *To William Theodore Peters*
   [*c. 8 November 1892*]

15 Bristol Gardens

My dear Pierrot,
   Your letter disturbed me greatly, & I devoted yesterday to making
a fair copy for His Censorship. Is it then necessary for the Primrose
League performance? I leave it with you herewith; as I know not how
one goes about such a thing.[1]
   Will you arrange about it.
   Tell me when your next rehearsals will be, as I should like to come to
one. I am engaged on Saturday, more or less all day; & in the evening.
But tomorrow morning or afternoon I think I could attend. I hope it
will be a success.
   I am feeling rather ill, though there seems to be nothing definite
the matter with me: the weather I suppose.

Ever yrs   ERNEST DOWSON

1. The Lord Chamberlain's licence for *The Pierrot of the Minute* was issued on
   16 November.

217. *To Arthur Moore*
   [*c. 10 November 1892*]

15 Bristol Gardens

Caro Mio.

I am beginning to realize, that the Hebrew word which has been translated "book" in the wish of Solomon, that his "enemy had written one"[1] should have been rendered "play". Oh, that mine enemy would write one, or that I had never been foolish enough to try. I shall hope to see you to-morrow at 5.45: one thing or another has prevented me all this week. The performance is fixed for the 22nd. next at Chelsea Town Hall—a bare fortnight from now. Very unreasonably as it seems to me, Peters & Mrs Hartshorn[2] have thrown the bother of seeing about the license upon me. I am rushing off now to see Texeira & find out how this is done, & what it costs. Peters suggests 'Somerset House'. Is that so? If T de M is out this afternoon, I ~~shall~~ will call & see you en revenant this evening at 9.30. If you are engaged or out, & *do* know anything of this procedure, could you send a note round explaining. I should think the time is rather short. I am afraid I shall have to give up such extravagances as billiards & cigarettes for the present. The fog yesterday *almost* killed me; and Peters is very indignant with me because I refuse to complete the catastrophe by running off to rehearsals at all hours of the day & night. Are you going to see the show? I am so awfully sick of it that I feel half inclined to take a week at Brighton until its done.

   Try & see me to-morrow.

                                    Yours desperately   ED

1. Not Solomon, but Job xxxi. 35.
2. The lady in charge of the arrangements for the Primrose League, which was presenting the play.

218. *To Herbert Horne*
   [*Date of receipt: 16 November 1892*]

15 Bristol Gardens

My dear Horne,

   Very many thanks. I do not feel at all sure that you will like the story;[1] it is only for very obscure reasons, that I do, myself. You shall

1. *The Statute of Limitations* which Horne printed late in 1893 in *The Hobby Horse* (successor to *The Century Guild Hobby Horse*, which came to an end with the number for October 1892).

have the refusal of it however with pleasure. I need not say how charmed I shall be, if you find it worthy to be shrined in the new Hobby.

Concerning the tea party: I am looking forward to it with anticipation, in the belief, that it is on Wednesday next. Is that right? Only, today, a sudden suspicion comes to me, that I am a week out; and, that it is today, I should have called for you. If that be so, my regrets and apologies! My play is for Tuesday evening, the 22nd Chelsea Town Hall. At present I know not, whether I shall have any tickets to give away; nor, where such are to be obtained. Of these things I will let you know, when I am, myself, further informed.

Ever yours   ERNEST DOWSON

I will send the story, today or tomorrow.

P.T.O.

Will you think me very tedious and frivolous, if I ask you whether you could put your hand upon the coloured picture representing the Polish arms, as Mdlle has asked me for them? Perhaps they have not survived your déménagement however.

E.D.

219. *To Arthur Moore*
Tuesday [*22 November 1892*]

15 Bristol Gardens

Caro Mio,

I have been so torn about by dress rehearsals & quarrels between my Company & Mrs Hartshorne that I couldn't see you yesterday. Will you do me the honour of attending to-night? It will I fear, involve dressing, & a hasty dinner, and as all the arrangements have been very badly managed, I can only give you & Hillier a ticket between the two of you. Do you mind taking him? I have hardly had any tickets given me & there were none, or almost none sold; it seeming to be very much confined to the actual Leaguites themselves.

Come & fetch me, *if you possibly can* in Poland as soon after 6. as may be, & tell me whether you will come, as otherwise I will give Johnson your ½ billet.

We have also, I may say, won our stake, a matter of 63 marks between us in the Braunsweigh business:[1] they have sent us another

1. See Letter 180.

ticket for the 2nd. part of the last draw but after consultation with Mme. F. who thinks most of the "big uns" are out, I propose with your sanction returning this, & asking for the "oof". Do you not prefer this? It seems useless to risk 63 marks for one draw only. Do try & come tonight if you can. Gray, Texeira, Horne, Symons & my people y' seront. I want your support. I went through scenes yesterday which would take ten years from a strong man's life. Pierrot looks more perfect even than Jane,[2] & more like a girl. He has borrowed a superb buckle from Lady Mount Temple,[3] part of the Palmerston diamonds; & looks dazzling. He acts well too, though in a big Hall, I fear he may be rather overheard than heard.

T a t   ED

If *absolutely impossible* for you to go, will you send me a wire *at once* to Poland?

2. Jane May, who had played Pierrot in *L'Enfant Prodigue*, which Dowson saw in 1891.
3. Lady Mount-Temple (1822–1901) was heir to Lord Palmerston through her husband. She was a friend of Oscar Wilde and a distant cousin of his wife's.

220. *To Herbert Horne*

6 pm. [?*23 November 1892*]

au Coq, Charing X Rd

Dear Horne,

Forgive my *défaillance*.

I hope you didn't wait long; most contrite. Was so seedy, that I couldn't manage the tea-party, & eluded the wedding. I fully intended to turn up however & found it to late to wire: will come round at 9.30 to you tonight, if convenient to go through MSS. Have no scruples about going out if engaged, in any case I come to the Temple.[1]

Ever yrs   E DOWSON

1. Horne had an office at 4 King's Bench Walk.

221. *To William Theodore Peters*

    [*c. 2 December 1892*]

15 Bristol Gardens

Dearest Pierrot,

Wie gehts? I ran off hurriedly the other day, because I felt that like a certain gentleman in Dickens, *nescio quem,* I was 'swellin' wisibly".[1] Since then I have been laid up; today am out, but still so unsightly, that I fear I may not summon up the courage to come on Monday.[2] However I will try my utmost to recover sufficiently.

My chief purpose in writing this is to tell you, that Harrington Bailey (the theatrical agent, manager, matinée promoter etc) who is a friend of my father's, is much interested in it, wishes to read it, & thinks it might be useful for drawing rooms etc; or as a front piece when he has some matinée to bring out. He knows Miss North & is, I believe, her agent. We must arrange some time for you to be introduced to him, & I think it very probable, that he would be able to secure an arrangement of this kind for the piece & its exponents—of course for a commission.

You might mention this to Miss North; but of course it is only an idea at present, so do not let us be sanguine; until he has read it.

Hoping you bear up well in view of Monday, & that I may see you then

Yrs ever   ERNEST DOWSON

Let me know by what train you go down on Monday, & where I shall see you.

1. *Pickwick Papers,* Chapter 33.
2. To the performance of *The Pierrot of the Minute* at Aldershot.

222. *To Herbert Horne*

    [*Postmark 2 December 1892*]

15 Bristol Gardens

My dear Horne.

Forgive my tardiness, in acknowledging the MS.[1] I have been laid up with complications, of chill & neuralgia, which only permitted me

1. Evidently *The Statute of Limitations.*

to go abroad today. Perhaps I had better send or leave the MS with you. A great many of your alterations I will adopt; some I should wish to on their intrinsic merits, but fear, that in doing so, I should undeniably destroy the rhythm; a few I do not quite care about.

I will try & let you have my corrections tomorrow; or I shall be in Poland at 8.30, then if you could come & fetch them.

I am anxious to see the Spinnet.[2]

The Hobby Horse is just come to me, with a curious effusion by Sayle.[3] Have you seen it?

Ever yours,   ERNEST DOWSON.

2. Horne was one of the first to become interested in old musical instruments. He printed articles on them in *The Century Guild Hobby Horse*, and his sister Beatrice was associated with the Dolmetsch concerts, some of which were given at the *Hobby Horse* house in Fitzroy Street.
3. The issue for October 1892. Sayle's effusion is an enthusiastic article entitled 'A New Poet' on John Gambril Nicholson's *Love in Earnest*.

223. *Postcard to William Theodore Peters*
[*Postmark 6 December 1892*]

[*Bridge Dock*]

I hope the show went off all right yesterday.[1] I intended to come, but the cold was so intense that my courage failed me, & I thought prudence was the better part of valour. I *do* hope all went well.

I am sorry to say that your P.C. did not come until the afternoon; so that it was too late to do anything with the Sp & D people.[2]

Let me know if there are any more notices, besides Ladies Pictl, Life, & Woman;[3] those I have seen. Hillier's is a charming paragraph. Come to Ellis'[4] house on Sat: he tells me you have a notice.

Ever thine   E D .

1. *The Pierrot of the Minute* was performed at the Officers' Club, Aldershot, on 5 December. Reviewing it the following month, *The Lady* reported, 'The stringed band of the Royal Horse Artillery played "The Moonlight Sonata" softly at intervals throughout.'
2. Alfred Dowson wrote to Peters on 2 December suggesting that *The Sporting and Dramatic News* should be asked to send a reporter.
3. Published on 3 December, 26 November and 30 November respectively. Hillier's paragraph was the one in *Life*.
4. Probably Edwin J. Ellis (1848–1918), poet, novelist, illustrator and member of the Rhymers' Club. His poems, *Fate in Arcadia*, appeared in 1892.

224. *To William Theodore Peters*
   [*?12 December 1892*]

Bridge Dock

My dear Peters,

I am so sorry you didn't come last night: we expected you until the rain came. You must try & manage next Sunday. I was coming to see you on Saturday afternoon, but I had to lunch out, & it was prolonged, until it left me no time to reach you, as I had a later engagement also.

My father is still confined to the house, but he says he will send the MSS. to Harrington Bailey. We must not be too sanguine however: for I fear HB's powers are rather limited.

I will let you know about Hillier: I expect it will be Friday.

Ever yrs   ERNEST DOWSON

225. *Postcard to William Theodore Peters*
   Thursday [*Postmark 15 December 1892*]

[*15 Bristol Gardens*]

Sorry cannot dine with you tomorrow: I will look you up, however, in the evening, if you are in, as soon after 9.0 as I can get to you.

ED.

226. *Postcard to William Theodore Peters*
   [*Postmark 17 December 1892*]

[*15 Bristol Gardens*]

I envy you your meeting with Pater: the finest artist now with us, & from all accounts the most wonderful in his personality.

Yes! tomorrow will suit me quite as well, even better. I may not be disengaged in the evening; I will try & look you up therefore in the afternoon, say about 3.0 or 2.30.

T à t.   ERNEST DOWSON

227. *Postcard to William Theodore Peters*
   [*Postmark 23 December 1892*]

15 Bristol Gardens

I do hope you are going on all right: it is cold, indeed. I have been hoping to round round & see you, but many things have intervened. Tomorrow Sat, I will try & look in & pass an hour with you—at about 2.30 if possible—but do not wait or expect me definitely, as I may be delayed.

ECD.

228. *To William Theodore Peters*
   [*30 December 1892*]

15 Bristol Gardens

Cher Confrère.
   Will you forgive me for putting you off tomorrow? In fixing Saturday, I forgot that the same was New Year's Eve, and that I was engaged for that evening. I shall be dining in Sherwood St, next week, upon all days, except Wednesday, & delighted to see you on one of them.
                                   Ever yrs   ERNEST DOWSON

Part III
1893-1895

E ARLY in 1893 Dowson made a serious effort to establish his financial independence. Bridge Dock by this time was providing an ever less certain livelihood; the property was heavily mortgaged, and his father was no doubt finding it difficult to pay him an adequate salary. Indeed, there was too little repair work to be had. The dock was small—287 feet long by 80 feet wide—and the size of ships coming up the river was increasing. Furthermore, to the irritation of both father and son, lax regulations in the Port of London now permitted shipowners to lie off in mid-stream instead of coming into dock as had always been the tradition. With this fall-off of work it is doubtful if the presence of both father and son as well as the foreman was necessary.

Another consideration, however, was probably decisive. For the last year he had been firmly resolved eventually to marry Adelaide Foltinowicz and the time was approaching when he would have to be in a position to support her and offer her a home if he were to expect his proposal to be accepted. So in February he put in for the office of librarian and secretary at Newington in south-east London. His application was supported by letters from Sayle and Plarr. But in spite of these testimonials from men already occupying responsible positions as librarians, he did not get the appointment. Had he succeeded, his life might have taken a different turn. He had worked conscientiously at Bridge Dock for over four years, and could have earned his living satisfactorily in a library. If he had done so and been accepted by Adelaide, he would have continued to enjoy the conditions of life under which all his best work was done—free from financial worry and the need to accept the hack-work which was to absorb most of his energies in the latter part of his life.

He was at this time as well received in society as among his theatrical and literary friends. He was always well dressed; yet even though almost a dandy, he had no concern for personal convenience, and it seems to have made no difference to him whether he passed a night in the comfort of his own bed or on the sofa in the sitting-room of a friend. If he missed the last train to Limehouse, he was likely to appear beneath someone's window and shout up, asking for hospitality. 'He had the cat's happy aptitude for sleeping where night found him', as it was put by Jepson, in whose Vauxhall lodgings he spent a number of nights curled up in the easy chair. One such occasion at this period yielded a happy result. The twenty-one-year-old William Rothenstein returned from Paris in 1893 and in the following year regularly shared Beardsley's studio in Pimlico. When Dowson shouted below the window Rothenstein admitted him on condition that he would sit for a portrait drawing before he left in the morning. The result is the best portrait of Dowson which is known. John Gray said particularly that the tint of the eyes is exact.[1] Rothenstein later in life was rather inclined to subscribe to Arthur Symons's discovery of *nostalgie de la boue* both in Dowson's poetry and in his conduct; but whatever may have happened later, such an element had no place in the poet's life at this time.

The disappointment at Newington was not the end of Dowson's endeavour to obtain regular employment. In the summer of 1893 we find him asking Peters to recommend him to an American theatrical company as secretary. This came to nothing, and in his endeavour to establish his independence by one means or another, he undertook in this same year the first of the numerous translations at which he was to work assiduously until his death. This was *La Terre*, which was to be included in a collected edition of Zola's novels published by the Lutetian Society. The editor of the project was Teixeira de Mattos, soon to become the most sought-after translator of his time, who later, in 1894, passed on to Dowson the task of translating *Majesty*, a novel by Couperus, which he himself had begun. The enthusiasm for Zola, which Dowson had felt since his Oxford days, and the prospect of contributing to an important undertaking were at first an inspiration; but before long the task palled and he is found writing impatiently of 'that tedious book *La Terre*'. None the less he carried out his undertaking conscientiously and laid the foundations of a good reputation as a translator; and his willingness to persist with work which he found uncongenial reflects his determination to make his living by literature.

Meanwhile affairs in 'Poland' continued to exert their depressing spell. In March 1893 Joseph Foltinowicz's health began to fail, and in the weeks which ensued until his death on 24 April the strain was almost unbearable. Dowson got a solicitor friend, W. B. Campbell, to come in and help Foltinowicz to draw up a will. Campbell was Irish and Catholic and towards the end was responsible for calling in a priest to set the dying man's soul at rest.[2]

[1] Statements to D.F. by Rothenstein and Gray.
[2] Statement by John Gray to D.F.

Dowson's resolution to bide his time with Adelaide broke down; he declared himself openly at the worst possible moment—when her father's life was despaired of—and achieved nothing. Adelaide, who was barely fifteen, temporized; and after her father's burial things reverted to their previous unsatisfactory state of indecision.

In Dowson's own home matters were worse still. His father's health was rapidly deteriorating as tuberculosis tightened its hold on him. In August 1893 the family moved from Maida Vale to Chadwell Heath, on the edge of Epping Forest, and thither late in the same month Dowson, who had made his home at Bridge Dock, had to go to recover from his own first recorded tubercular attack. It is noteworthy, to judge from Plarr's recollection of his visits to this rather dark house, that the serious state of health of Dowson's father did nothing to modify the genial hospitality for which he had always been well known. However, the family did not stay there long and within a year had moved to a flat, 7 Albert Mansions, near Battersea Park. This restlessness may have been caused partly by the progress of Alfred Dowson's illness and partly by the need to economize as the income from Bridge Dock steadily dwindled. Ernest continued to help his father in the administration, but the sad fact remained that sufficient work to keep the dock out of difficulties was not to be had. The economic situation was made worse by the severity of the winter of 1894–1895; the Thames froze over and such ships as required attention could not in any case make their way up to Bridge Dock. The only light relief was provided by Rowland Dowson, who used to bring his schoolboy friends down from Epping to climb over the ships when they were in.

Dowson meanwhile continued his own work steadily. *Terre Promise*, *Ad Manus Puellae*, *Mark the Day White* (for the birth of Plarr's child), the superb *Extreme Unction*, *Growth*, *A Requiem*, *The Garden of Shadow* and *Benedictio Domini* all date from 1893. His fifth short story, *The Statute of Limitations*, was published in *The Hobby Horse* and he was hard at work on his second published novel, *Adrian Rome*; the first, *A Comedy of Masks*, appeared in the autumn of the same year; Heinemann printed a first edition of five hundred copies and a further thousand as a second edition in 1894.

An important event late in 1893 was the visit of Verlaine. The great poet had always had a somewhat back-handed affection for England since the early days when he had been a schoolmaster in Bournemouth. William Rothenstein, who met everybody during his four years in Paris (Degas, when asked how this came about, said, 'Il était si petit qu'il est passé entre leurs jambes'), knew Verlaine and suggested to him that he should come to England to lecture. Symons and York Powell came into the project and an invitation was sent. Verlaine replied in October that he would be prepared to lecture on contemporary French poetry and to read from his own work. It was arranged. The poet arrived in the small hours one morning, was met by Symons bearing a packet of biscuits and a bottle of gin, and on 21 November gave his first lecture at Barnard's Inn, High Holborn. It was more successful than the lecture at Oxford which followed. Within that week Dowson had dinner with the poet, who returned to France with a not unreasonable sum of money which he and his mistress disposed of in the Gare du Nord buffet and other bars before he even got back to his home.

Alfred Dowson's life came to an end quite suddenly in August 1894. There was a widespread belief among Ernest's friends, and possibly his relatives as well, that his father had committed suicide. Writing as late as 1914, Plarr maintained a secretive silence on the subject and succeeded only in making it more mysterious. Mystery there may have been, but it is only proper to record that Alfred Dowson's death certificate makes no mention of any such possibility and gives only natural causes of death.[1] Six months later Ernest's mother died and here there is no doubt that she took her own life. All the photographs of her show a tragically sad face and there is evidence that she had always suffered from some degree of mental instability; it must have been the loss of her husband and the accumulation of financial worries that caused her in a fit of depression to hang herself. The complete silence on the matter in Dowson's correspondence at this time is a mute witness of the great distress which he must have felt. His younger brother, Rowland, went to live with relations and soon afterwards emigrated to the United States.

In the summer of 1895 Dowson gave up any hope of making a living out of the dock. He cleared out his office, gave one of his manuscripts to Richards the foreman as a parting gift, and left Limehouse.[2] He was to concern himself only once more with the dock's affairs, towards the end of his life. Thus within the space of a few months all his family ties had been severed and he found himself without home or job. He had taken a sharp buffeting and many of his contemporaries pictured him moving about in a tragic

[1] The decline of Alfred Dowson's fortunes is painfully shown by his will. Drawn up in 1890, this made provision for an annuity of £350 a year to Annie Dowson; Ernest was to get his income as joint manager of the dock with the foreman, J. Richards, but was to share with his brother the surplus accumulating after his mother's substantial annuity had been met. In fact, Alfred Dowson left £833 12s. 6d.

[2] Jepson helped him carry his possessions away; there was not a lot, mostly books, and they managed it easily between them.

mist of sorrow. For a while he certainly must have been too pre-occupied with practical affairs to have time to spend with those who had nothing to contribute to his well-being except an entirely unwelcome pity. But wretched though he must have been, his powers of recovery were considerable. He has left almost no record of his life in the year following his father's death; but the few clues which remain point, like the list of his publications, to the conclusion that he was by no means a broken man.

In 1894 he had a story in *The Yellow Book*; the *Second Book of the Rhymers' Club* appeared with six of his poems in its pages; the translation of *La Terre* was published; he completed his translation of *Majesty* and began work on Muther's *History of Modern Paint-ing*, a three-volume work, in collaboration with Greene and Hillier. During 1895 Dowson's volume of stories was published by Elkin Mathews under the title *Dilemmas*. The book had originally been offered two years earlier, while Mathews was still in partner-ship with Lane at the Bodley Head, and had then been read for the firm by Richard Le Gallienne, whose report read as follows:

Mr. Dowson applies very delicate literary treatment to some-what hackneyed themes—at least in the case of two of his stories, "The Souvenirs of an Egoist" and "The Story of a Violin". The great musical composer who started life as an organ-grinder, the second violin in an orchestra, poor and un-known, who was once the guardian and tutor of the fashionable prima donna (like little Bows in "Pendennis") are very old acquaintances in fiction. In Messrs. Dowson and Moore's "Comedy of Masks" one was struck with the concentration of theme and freshness of treatment. However, if these well-known types have been done before, they have seldom been done better. Of the other two, "A Case of Conscience" is very much in the manner of Mr. Wedmore's "Pastorals",—"A Last Love at Pornic" for example—delicate, vague, and generally "nice", but amounting to little. "The Diary of a Successful Man" is probably the most original—but the title should certainly be changed. It is a rough and ready label, with no true relation to the story. "The Story of a Violin" is also an unfortunate title, as nothing is more hackneyed than the conventional Stradiva-rius story the title will inevitably suggest. "Souvenirs of an Egoist" is a taking title, and so, I suppose, had better be left, but it suggests far more than the story fulfils.

On the whole, having regard to the delicacy of the treatment, *and the success of "A Comedy of Masks"* (which was not a con-sideration when I first read these stories) I would advise you to accept these as an instalment of a volume, (they are not big enough to make one themselves) with the promise that the stories to come should be more striking, more original in theme—not less so, not mere makeweights—than those under consideration.

In one of the last letters in this chapter Dowson mentions a new and advanced review shortly to appear—*The Savoy*. By the summer of 1895 *The Yellow Book*, after a year of barely deserved notoriety, was already in decline. Lane had published it largely as a medium for Beardsley's drawings. But amid the upheaval caused by Oscar Wilde's arrest and trial he lost his nerve and dismissed Beardsley in the hope of saving his magazine's reputation. This pusillanimous action received its deserts and *The Yellow Book* languished. It was at this point that the extraordinary figure of Leonard Smithers came upon the scene.

Smithers was born in Sheffield in 1861 and for a time practised there as a solicitor. About 1891 he came to London and joined H. S. Nichols as bookseller and publisher. His activities were various. He edited two volumes of French imitations of *The Arabian Nights* and collaborated with Sir Richard Burton in erudite and arcane editions of Catullus and the *Priapeia*. With Nichols he published and sold a considerable quantity of pornography in the guise of fine and rare editions, and by 1895 he had his own bookshop in Arundel Street, off the Strand. In the next few years his audacious and keen instinct made him the most celebrated publisher in London. The books he issued were distinguished by their excellent typography, paper and binding. He was willing and eager to publish the new, the dubious and even the outrageous: 'I will publish,' he said to Vincent O'Sullivan, 'anything the others are afraid of.' He was the only publisher after 1895 who would touch Wilde's work, which would undoubtedly have earned him a fortune if he had not gone bankrupt in 1899.

The best description of him was written by Wilde in 1897: 'He is usually in a large straw hat, has a blue tie delicately fastened with a diamond brooch of the impurest water—or perhaps wine, as he never touches water: it goes to his head at once. His face, clean-shaven as befits a priest who serves at the altar whose God is Literature, is wasted and pale—not with poetry, but with poets, who, he says, have wrecked his life by insisting on publishing with him. He loves first editions, especially of women: little girls are his passion. He is the most learned erotomaniac in Europe. He is also a delightful companion . . .'[1]

In 1895 Arthur Symons met Smithers and persuaded him to

[1] *The Letters of Oscar Wilde*, ed. Hart-Davis, p. 630.

start a new magazine to replace *The Yellow Book* as a vehicle for Beardsley. Thus *The Savoy* was conceived and by the time of its birth a few months later there had gathered round Smithers a group of the most original younger writers and artists of the 'nineties including, besides Symons and Beardsley, Dowson, Conder, Rothenstein, Max Beerbohm and W. B. Yeats. He himself was lavish in entertainment, in literary and artistic enthusiasm and in the large scope of his projects. Dowson was soon drawn into his circle, and amid the excitement of this new association must soon have lost the sense of desolation which had oppressed him earlier in the year. He undertook to contribute regularly to *The Savoy*, he accepted a commission to translate Balzac's *La Fille aux Yeux d'Or* which Conder was to illustrate, and was to follow this with a new translation of *La Pucelle* by Voltaire. Smithers, in fact, had promised to keep him supplied with work and to publish anything original he chose to do. Much had been achieved in the first half of the decade, but Dowson's prospects for the years to come must have seemed better still.

Little is known of Dowson's movements during the summer and early autumn of 1895, apart from the fact that he made several trips to Dieppe, which had become the resort of Beardsley, Symons, Conder, Rothenstein and others connected with *The Savoy*.

After leaving Bridge Dock he took rooms in a down-at-heel block of flats in Holborn, Featherstone Buildings. Something went badly wrong in 'Poland', and it seems likely that Adelaide declared firmly that she would not marry him. But if there was a quarrel, it was soon mended. Nevertheless London had become intolerable and at the first opportunity he left.

About the beginning of October he set off for a tour through Belgium with Conal O'Riordan. They went first to Bruges, and Dowson recorded their itinerary on the half-title of a copy of his collection of short stories, *Dilemmas*, which he carried with him for the rest of his life. They ended up in Paris, where Dowson took rooms in the rue Saint-Jacques, in the Quartier Latin. And here he remained until after the turn of the year.

NOTE

Letter 242 should be placed on p. 225 after No. 178. It is printed out of series in the position to which we mistakenly assigned it when we had only the fragmentary text printed in Miss Marion Plarr's *Cynara*. We obtained the text of the first paragraph, which fixed the date, too late to move the letter to its proper place.

229. *To William Theodore Peters*
Tuesday [?*17 January 1893*]

Bridge Dock

Dear Peters
   Forgive my procrastination: I should have written to apologize for
having failed to come the other day but I trusted to Hillier seeing you.
It appears he started but lost his way: I was unavoidably prevented.
The "Lady" is dated Jan. 5th. The 'Professional World' for Jan. (it
is a monthly thing) has a short notice.

Yrs in haste   ED.

230. *To Victor Plarr*
Tuesday [*17 January 1893*]

Bridge Dock

Dearest Vieux.
   It is I, who should apologize for taking leave of you so cavalierly. It
was a charming visit; my gratitude to you all, for the same. I handed
your note to ACM: doubtless you have since heard from him. Were you
at Headlam's? I was too sick & sorry to come. I fear my affairs will not
bear talking over, or writing about. They are like a Chinese puzzle; and
grow more confused and inextricable the closer one considers them. I
endeavour to possess my soul in patience, but the result is not so much
resignation, as a sort of sloth & tristitia, "which even monkish moral-
ists have held to be of the nature of a sin."[1] It is a vile and stupid world;
& it will be good to have done with it
                         in the meantime, ever yours   ERNEST DOWSON

P.T.O.
Appended the last effort of my Muse

TERRE PROMISE

Even now, the fragrance of her drooping hair
   Had brushed my cheek, and once in passing by
   Her hand upon my hand lay tranquilly:
Then what unsaid things trembled in the air!

   ~~Ah for~~ Always I know so little severs me
   From my heart's country that is yet so far;
   And must I lean, and long, across a bar,
That half a word would shatter utterly?

1. Quotation untraced.

Ah, might it be, that just by touch of hand,
Or speaking silence, shall the barrier fall;
And she will pass, with no vain words at all,
But droop into mine arms, and understand![2]

16/Jan/93

2. First published in *The Hobby Horse*, No. 3, 1894. In *Verses* it is dedicated to Horne.

231. *Letter-card to William Theodore Peters*
Friday [*Postmark 27 January 1893*] 10.30

Bridge Dock

Carissime,

This fog renders me somewhat uncertain of my plans today. I can't be certain yet, whether I shall dine en ville, or where. I will not ask you to turn out then for the uncertainty, but will call upon you tomorrow, *Sat afternoon*. Do not, however, alter any plans you may have made, or wait for me: as I have another call to make in South Kensington, and can go on there if you are out.

Amicissime,   ERNEST DOWSON.

232. *To Herbert Horne*
[*Postmark 5 February 1893*]

Bridge Dock

My dear Horne,

Many thanks for the revise:[1] I should have written before to acknowledge it, but I have been very busy. I shall always be delighted to see my verses enshrined in the "Hobby Horse. I will try and find something that may suit you: perhaps I had better send you two or three, in order that you may have scope for selection.[2]

1. Of *The Statute of Limitations*.
2. Dowson sent Horne *Terre Promise*, *A Requiem* and *Benedictio Domini*. They were published in *The Hobby Horse*, No. 3, 1894.

How goes the "Hobby" now? I suppose we may soon expect it.

Ever yours ERNEST DOWSON.

Have just received 1st batch of proofs[3] from Heinemann, so I suppose the novel will really be out in the autumn.

3. Of *A Comedy of Masks.*

233. *To Victor Plarr*
[*10 February 1893*]

Bridge Dock

Cher Vieux,

Yesterday an advt in the *Times* was sent me, for a librarian, in a Public Free Library (under the Public Library acts) at Newington, S.E.[1] I have been advised to apply for this, I fear, not very desirable post, & I thought that if you, with your official signature of Librarian at King's could give me a testimonial, I might stand some chance. Could you consider me then, in a short missive a competent person to hand out dime novels to transpontine shop boys? You might mention that I have knowledge of French & Italian; & in fact—make the most of me.

The office is really '*librarian & Secretary*': & not more than *three* testimonials are to be sent in. A proviso that some experience of a public library is required rather handicaps me, but it is worth while trying for—£160. & an unfurnished apartment on the premises. I write to Sayle for another testimony, & for my third shall try & secure a word from some city functionary as to my business capacities.

An early answer will oblige me enormously, as the limit of time allowed is not allowed.

I will try & see you at King's shortly.

T à t. ERNEST DOWSON

P.S. Alas! that I should have to write to you again so speedily & in such a matter: this is truly descent from the clouds. Ma chè vuole? one must exist

E D

1. The advertisement appeared on 8 February. Applications had to be in by 17 February.

234. *To Charles Sayle*
    [*10 February 1893*]

15 Bristol Gardens

My dear Sayle,

I am intending to send in an application for the post of librarian & secretary of a Free Public Library (under the Public Libraries Act) in South London. Would you mind, if you think you can say anything good of me, letting me have a testimonial? I shall be immensely obliged, if you can, as I fancy your titular dignities, properly set forth, & your connection with one & more of our 'seats of learning' should carry weight with the worthy burgesses of Newington who give this appointment.

I have to send in my testimonials in a few days, so that an immediate answer will be gratefully received.

I hope we may meet again soon somewhere.

        Yours ever   ERNEST DOWSON

235. *To Victor Plarr*[1]
    [*17 February 1893*]

[*15 Bristol Gardens*]

Very many thanks, indeed, for the testimony. I had your benevolent document with the others type-copied and sent them off yesterday, the latest possible day. I cut out a comment upon my German proficiency from yours, for alas! my knowledge of that difficult but dear tongue is too rudimentary to be mentioned. I do not, for the rest, attach very much importance to the matter, for I am afraid it is too substantial to be attainable. It is just worth applying for however, and in any result, I am infinitely obliged to you. . . . I cannot write a line of any kind just now: why, I know not.

1. Text from Plarr.

236. *To Charles Sayle*
     [*c. 19 February 1893*]

15 Bristol Gardens

My dear Sayle

Indeed, very many thanks: I have not ceased blushing since your letter came, & wish only that the vestrymen of Newington may be not too bitterly disillusioned should your kind recommendation induce them to elect me.

I do not suppose that there is any very real chance of obtaining this office, although Plarr, whom I saw yesterday tells me, that it is not a particularly high qualification which is necessary—as I should have said, indeed, myself. But it is just worth trying.

By the way, a post which it would certainly be fruitless for me to aim at, I see in the Athenaeum is vacant—the librarianship of the London Library—£400. Why do not you apply for this? Or are you grown too attached to Cambridge? I hear great accounts of you, and of music, absorbing you: & very likely you are right. But though I hate London more than the pains of Hell, I am kept here for a personal reason & must try to keep here, although almost any other place would suit me better. Do you know Norman Gale,[1] the man or his work? The last enchants me so much that I am anxious to meet the first. I should like to know what you think of my friend Gray's poems, which will appear immediately under the auspices of the good Lane,[2] if you come across them. I was in 'Atalanta' for this month, with a "Dead Child".[3]

Someday I hope we shall meet: in the mean time, with again many thanks

Ever affecty. yrs   ERNEST DOWSON

P.S. My family desires to be remembered to you; may I say the same to your mother.

---

1. English poet (1862–1942), author of *A Country Muse* (1892) and *Orchard Songs* (1893). His *Collected Poems* were published in 1914.
2. *Silverpoints* by John Gray was published in an edition of 250 copies by the Bodley Head. The book was designed by Ricketts and is one of the most exquisite productions of the 'nineties.
3. Reprinted in *Decorations*.

237. *To John Gray*
   [*c. 27 February 1893*]

Bridge Dock

My dear Poet,

Thanks, very many thanks indeed for the wonderful little book.[1] It is beyond my expectations even, in exquisiteness—a very solace of this dull and dismal day; a thing to dream of. Beyond my old acquaintances and admirations, the 'Desmoiselles', the 'deep in the dear dust poem, & others, I am especially enamoured of the second piece, of the nameless poem to E.M.G: which is wonderful & of a piece dedicated to one Edmunds.

The collocation, 'geranium, house leeks' gives me, I know not why, an extraordinary and subtile pleasure. That is, however, quite genuinely my impression of the whole book.

Once more very many thanks.

Ever yours   KIT DOWSON

It is so long since I saw you, that I can't resist appending my Muse's last offspring. Pardon it.

PUELLAE ⎱
AD MANUS DOMINAE ⎰

I was always a lover of ladies' hands!
   Or ever mine heart came here to tryst,
For the sake of your carved, white hands' commands;
   The tapering fingers, the dainty wrist,
   The hands of a girl were what I kissed.

I remember a hand like a fleur-de-lys
   When it slid from its silken sheath, her glove;
With its odours passing ambergris;
   And that was the empty husk of a love.
   Oh, how shall I kiss *your* hands enough?

They are pale with the pallour of ivories;
   But they blush to the tips like a curled sea shell:
What treasure in kingly treasuries,
   Of gold or spice for the thurible,
   Is sweet as her hands to hoard and tell?

---

1. *Silverpoints.* Gray inscribed Dowson's copy 'To Kit Dowson the master singer'. The book contained a poem, *The Crucifix*, dedicated to Dowson.

> I know not the way from your finger tips,
>   Nor how I shall gain the higher lands,
> The citadel of your sacred lips!
>   I am always in prison to their commands—
>   The hands of a girl, and most your hands.[2]

24/2/93

2. First published in *Verses*, where it is dedicated to Leonard Smithers.

238. *To William Theodore Peters*
    Tuesday [*?28 February 1893*]

Bridge Dock

My dear Peters,
    Many thanks for the notices,[1] they are just what is required, I should think. Have you sent any to any agent? I have heard nothing from Harrington Bailey, so I assume that he will be able to do nothing for us, which is very much what I anticipated & was led to believe. I hope your influenza is defeated; I am coming round one of these evenings to enquire after you, if I don't see you anywhere before.
    Have you seen Gray's book: I received it yesterday; it is indescribably dainty. I have seen only one review of it,—which was favourable.
    I shall be in Sherwood St all nights this week, save tomorrow when I go to the Irish Lit Society: if you are in the neighbourhood, *cura ut venias*. No more now.
                    Yours ever   ERNEST DOWSON

Is your station Sloane Sq: or S Kensington now? However I shall probably find an omnibus more direct.

P.S. I suppose you have noted a quaint misprint in your reprint of Hillier's notice: 'petting' for 'pelting'?[2]

1. A leaflet in which Peters reprinted the reviews of *The Pierrot of the Minute*.
2. The correct reading is: '[They] then begin to carry on a vigorous flirtation in rhymed heroic couplets and finally fall to pelting each other with love lyrics.'

239. *To William Theodore Peters*
Thursday night [*?2 March 1893*]

[*Fulham*]

Dear Peters,

Sorry to miss you but I could not get round before. Will you let me have a line *at once* if you have heard anything of the play. I sent it to Oscar[1] but have received no news. Another person has written to me about it from the Lyceum a stranger to me (Miss Vanburgh)[2] & I have been obliged to defer sending it to her until I hear the Haymarket decision. Shall be glad to hear from you therefore. I fear I cannot get round here again & am going out of town on Saturday until Tuesday. Awfully sorry to have so narrowly missed you last night, was there unprecedentedly late. As a rule I am not there ever after nine.

Tout à toi   ERNEST DOWSON

1. Presumably as a curtain-raiser to *A Woman of No Importance*, which was produced by Beerbohm Tree at the Haymarket Theatre on 19 April.
2. Violet Vanbrugh (1867–1942) was in Irving's company at the Lyceum, acting in *Henry VIII* and as understudy to Ellen Terry in *King Lear*. In July she appeared in *Love in Tandem* at Daly's Theatre and seems now to have been looking for a suitable curtain-raiser.

240. *To John Lane*[1]
[*?Early March 1893*]

15 Bristol Gardens

My dear Lane,

Appended I send you Verses which you were good enough to like:[2] I hope further consideration of them won't lead you to alter your opinion.

1. English publisher (1854–1925) and Elkin Mathews's partner in the Bodley Head, the most influential firm in the early 'nineties. Their list included Wilde, Beardsley, Rothenstein, Lionel Johnson, John Davidson, Le Gallienne, Horne, Alice Meynell, Francis Thompson and William Watson, *The Hobby Horse* and *The Yellow Book*. When the partnership was dissolved in 1894 they continued in business separately, Dowson leaving his *Dilemmas* with Mathews.
2. *Ad Manus Puellae* (see Letter 237).

Brodie Innes's[3] address, I find, is 14, Dublin Street, Edinburgh.

Yours v. sincerely   ERNEST DOWSON

3. John Brodie Innes (b. 1848), Scottish jurist and author and a member of
the Sette of Odd Volumes.

241. *Postcard to William Theodore Peters*
[*Postmark 3 March 1893*]

15 Bristol Gdns.

Did I leave a volume of Pater in your rooms last night? If it is there,
would you mind doing it up & leaving instructions with your landlady
that it may be given me, if I should call & you are out.

ED.

242. *To Victor Plarr*[1]
[*c. 23 February 1892*]

[*15 Bristol Gardens*]

Caro mio

Will you forgive a pencil scrawl, since I am lazy and the hour is late
and the ink remote? I have seen no reviews save only logrollers, which
quoted L.J. and Rhys at some length, and Symons!—damning the rest
of us with but the faintest praise. I am looking out however in many
journals for notices, and when I find them I will send you them. If you
have Lang's article, will you send it me, and I will return it promptly;
as it had not come to my knowledge. I see a morning paper rarely.
There was a Rhymers' meeting tonight, but I could not attend. To-
morrow Horne has another 17th Cent Concert which I am pledged to
attend, but it will be for a short time only, as at 10.45 I have to repair
to Charing Cross and meet the Club train from Calais which brings me a
pair of French *lune de mielistes*, who speak no English and require an
Hotel. I fear they will be considerably on my hands during their stay.
Would you were here to assist me in their entertainment. I should like
to run down and see you if the Sunday trains thither and hither are
serviceable—and Sunday suits you? But I had better postpone it perhaps until M. et Mdme Noblet have departed.

1. See Note on p. 265.

You ask after Her? She has been, I am glad to say, extraordinarily sweet for the last four weeks; so that in spite of my invincible pessimism I begin at last to think that there is, really, beneath her double perversity of enfant gâtée and jeune fille coquette a solid foundation of affection. She is growing up into a charming girl. Mdme who is also very much of a consolation to me, enquires often after you, and your eyesight, and your health generally.

I should like very much to reveal myself there entirely, especially insomuch as Monsieur's days are very obviously numbered, and before the changes and revolutions which this fact makes one anticipate, I should like to be firmly established. Not, poor man, that I have any ghoulish desires against his length of days. After all he is genial and harmless enough, and I have certainly been treated by him always with a great deal of consideration and I have hardly the right to reproach him with an undue love of alcohol. On the other hand it is useless to ignore facts.

It is terribly difficult to be explicit, cher ami! You were fortunate in that with you the family necessarily must come afterwards: with me of course it must be the first step. Explicitly I mean: because I am no longer in the least doubtful that to Her I am perfectly obvious.

Forgive me if I bore you: but you are absolutely the only person to whom I can turn for advice or sympathy in these matters: and as these matters now entirely absorb me, I neither write to nor see anybody else unless by accident, and a letter from you, and occasion of writing to you, is a godsend.

243. *To John Lane*
[*c. 22 March 1893*]

Bridge Dock

My dear Lane,
Would you care to see a performance of the play described in the enclosed prospectus—the printing, & *colour* & publication of which I am not responsible for. Peters has arranged to play it on Wednesday next, at 9.0 PM, in the studio of Miss Curtois, 5A Clareville Grove, Gloucester Rd. SW.[1]
We should both be delighted if you could turn up there.
If you are unable to come, would you let me have a line by return as on account of space, the audience is to be a limited one & I have to let the responsibilities know exactly how many people I have invited
Yours ever ERNEST DOWSON

1. This performance of *The Pierrot of the Minute* was given on 29 March.

244. *To William Theodore Peters*
    29 March 1893

Bridge Dock

My dear Peters,

    I hope everything goes smoothly & tonight will be a success. I shall be there if I am alive. I have been having terrible difficulty to secure my 8 visitors. "They all with one accord began to make excuse."

    I asked the Plarrs, they leave town today! My friend Miss Margaret Roberts & her publishing friend: somebody vient de mourir. Symons can't come: & so on. Last night, mercifully, Texeira turned up & dined in Sherwood St & I was able to secure him; he will bring Gray & Goodheart.[1] At present my list is composed as follows:

Paterson[2]	(i)
Teixeira de Mattos	(ii)
Gray	(iii)
Goodheart	(iv)
Moores (i)	
(ii)	(vi)

a cousin of mine an actor—Hoole   (vii)

    Image & Lane have not answered my invitation, whence, I assume they are out of town.

    Until this evening,

Yrs sympathetically   ERNEST DOWSON

1. Charles Goodhart, an actor living at this time with Swanton and de Mattos in the Temple. He committed suicide in 1917.
2. Unidentified.

245. *To Victor Plarr*[1]
    [early April 1893]

[Bridge Dock]

    I hope you will not be too surprised with my audacious wire. I was meaning to stay on in town until Sunday at any rate, but my foreman's youngest boy died here suddenly last night and the air is so depressing that I determined to go at once.[2] . . I *cannot* stay any longer in this atmosphere of dreariness and tears.

1. Text from Plarr.
2. Plarr had taken a house at Haslemere.

246. *To Victor Plarr*

[*April 1893*]

[*Bridge Dock*]

My dear Victor,

You will forgive my silence; all kinds of 'dragons' have been worrying me since I left you; and I could not even write to thank you for those charming days at Haslemere 'locum refugii, pacis et lucis'.

Foltinowicz is given up by the doctors, and sinks from day to day. You can imagine that in the rather strenuous atmosphere that prevails there I have been carried off my feet. I am afraid you will accuse me of great folly, but yesterday, last night, I declared myself. Do you blame me very much? I should like to know. I thought I had resolution enough to say nothing to her, until she was at least on her way to being seventeen. But we happened to be alone together, and we spoke of grave things and my resolution collapsed. She behaved with very much more discretion than I showed; she seemed to think that I ought to have waited till she was older, but she admitted that she was not surprised, and she was not angry. And then as they say in Parliament 'the matter dropped'. Have I ruined the whole thing, do you think? Advise me, prithee. I assure you that I had the most admirable intentions, the most exalted—and the result is that I feel as if I had made a hopeless, not very creditable fool of myself. What will be her attitude do you suppose? The understanding is that we should not allude to the thing any more for the present, but go on as before: do you think that is very possible? What ought I to say to her mother? What in the world shall I do? How long is this extraordinary cul de sac to last? I wish I could put the question before any woman: the mind of a girl, a girl of that age, is such an inexplicable country to oneself; but a woman might give one clues. Write, prithee, write to me. I am afraid I have been singularly indiscreet, but I assure you I meant it for the best.

Ever yours ERNEST DOWSON.

247. *To Samuel Smith*[1]

[*late April 1893*]

Bridge Dock

Cher Ami,

Let me preface this by saying that it is strictly private and confidential; and so proceed to inform you of certain recent developments in my

1. Text from Gawsworth.

affairs. I fancy, when I last saw you, must have been about the beginning of the rather distressful state of things which augmented itself later on. I daresay I was not very brilliant society then—(I don't remember frankly, much about our *rencontre*)—and certainly I have been too much absorbed to write letters ever since or I would have written to you. I suppose it will not surprise you very much to hear that I have at last unburdened myself. We were all in rather a stressful state of nerves—and Missie herself rather brought it about by her curious changes of mood—sometimes she was perfectly charming at others she would hardly speak to me. *Quid plura dicam?* Finally I was goaded into a declaration—of course it was rather an inopportune time, the father having been given up by the doctors—but on the other hand, I don't suppose except for the rather tense state we were in on this account, I should have been so precipitate. She took it with a great deal of dignity and self-possession; I don't think I have ever admired her more. She reminded me very properly that she was rather too young: but she proceeded to admit that she was not surprised at what I had told her, and that she was not angry. Of course I had asked her for no answer—I merely left her with no possible reason to doubt my seriousness in the matter. Finally I suggested that she should forget what I had said for the present—and that we should resume our ancient relation and be excellent friends—and nothing more. Upon this understanding we separated. The next day—after twelve of about as miserable hours as I hope to spend—it seemed to me that I had upset the whole arrangement—a conversation with *Madame* reassured me. Nothing could possibly exceed her extreme kindness and delicacy. She didn't in the least appear to resent, as she might very reasonably have resented, my proposing to her daughter, without her permission a couple of days before her 15th birthday; on the contrary she seemed rather pleased—in short, she was perfect. Moreover she gave me every hope—she said that Missie had told her she would like the idea in a year or two:—only just then she was naturally strung up and disordered by her father's state. According to *Madame* it will arrange itself. You may imagine how this pleased and touched me. All this was on or about the 15th; on Monday last Foltinowicz died[2]—yesterday I attended his funeral. I have seen Missie on or off pretty much as usual during this time—and I have not alluded to the important subject. We are both a little embarrassed—I more than she perhaps—and sometimes she drives me to despair by her coldness. At other times she is charming: *Madame* is always mercifully the same—I think on the whole, the most gentle and delicate minded lady whom I may hope to meet in this disagreeable world. And so, *mon cher ami*, it stands, my affair. Qu'en pensez-vous? I entreat you to write to me. I don't know how it will end—I hope at least that the embarrassment, the *géne* which I have produced, entirely through my own hastiness, will wear off. It has been an exhausting three weeks—I

2. Joseph Foltinowicz died on 24 April.

feel as if I had been travelling all the time, sleeping in my clothes, lacking beds and baths. On the whole it is a relief to me to have the air clear—at any rate *Madame* thoroughly understands the situation. For the rest I am not very sanguine; if she liked me less or had not known me so long, I believe, my chance would be much better. She has a very difficult character, but at the same time a very fine one; exceedingly fond of her as I have been, I was amazed to see her during the last diffi- cult week—that immensely trying time which has to elapse between a death and a burial—quite the cruellest part of death—she was intensely distressed and worn out, and perfectly composed. It was the same at the cemetery, when extraneous womankind were dissolved in tears, she stood like a little statue. At the same time I know that when she has been alone, she has had paroxysms of weeping, and this is a child of fifteen. I am afraid I am making large draughts upon your patience. But I may as well exhaust myself completely.

It is a very odd history—Heaven knows how it will end. In my more rational moments however, I am inclined to consider that that is of quite secondary importance; the important thing is that one should have, just once, experienced this mystery, an absolute absorption in one particular person. It reconciles all inconsistencies in the order of things, and above all it seems once and for all to reduce to utter absurdity any material explanation of itself or of the world. I will try and finish some verses I am working on and enclose upon this matter, to-night.[3] I wish you were down here; we must meet soon—but we might have an excel- lent symposium here, in this extraordinary place of silence, with only river sounds. When you come to Poland, not a word of this, but I hope you will not have anything unusual to notice, except the absence of *ce pauvre monsieur's* cap and coat. What an infinitely dreary thing by the way is a London funeral. We make death more hideous than it need be. As they treated the old Vikings we should be sent out into a stormy sea in a burning ship. That distressing delay, and wearisome *cortège*, and the pit-a-pat of earth on the coffin are cruelties which civilization should spare one. I suppose however that no amount of euphemism will affect the essential horror of the thing or make it a less inexplicable cruelty. I have been interested to note—I have had various occasions lately—the immediate revulsion of life against death, which occurs after the dis- posal of the body, amongst persons who have been weighed down by the sincerest grief: this is quite universal and well worth consideration. A sort of instinctive protest against the thought of death by healthy life: consciously justifying itself? Or may it not be really the result of a more generous instinct—that actually death is not an essential fact, but an accident of immortality—so that what seems such cruel dis- honour to a beloved person, all the corruption of death, is outside his interest or ours. I don't mean that this is rigidly apprehended—but is it not an innate feeling? You really must forgive me this prosing, I shall

3. Probably *Growth*, printed in *The Second Book of the Rhymers' Club*, 1894.

frighten you from my society. This letter is like *Tristan and Isolde*, it has nothing but love and death in it. I assure you there are still other things upon which I can discourse.

Au revoir,

Ever yours,   ERNEST DOWSON.

248. *To William Theodore Peters*
Thursday [*c. May 1893*]

Bridge Dock

Cher Pierrot,

You will be glad to hear that I have discovered the original draught of the Play & it is now being copied: I will send it off in time for Saturday's mail to Courtenay Thorpe[1] with a letter as we arranged. I am afraid it is no good my asking you down here tomorrow as I am uncertain whether I may not have to go up to town. In the evening I am engaged, but I shall be probably in Sherwood St. from 5.30 onwards, if you care to look in—or can dine there on Saturday when Moore also will be, I hope, in evidence.

This cold weather withers me up—if I were you, it is not Paris but to Nice or Naples that I should run.

Ever yours   ERNEST DOWSON

1. English actor (1854–1927).

249. *To William Theodore Peters*
[*early July 1893*]

Bridge Dock

My dear Peters,

Very many thanks for tickets; I have, however, such a lot of things to do, sorting, packing, & setting my house in order that I am afraid, much as I want to come, I shall not be able to manage it. I return them, & hope you will have time still to see they are not wasted. You oughtn't to have bothered about the order: of course I can't allow that. I daresay however I gave you rather a wrong impression the other night, I was so vexed at having cut it so fine, & having to expose my impecuniosity. N'en parlons plus—but come & see me again some time, & you shall do the same for me if you like. But Prithee, let us not send each other, disagreeable, blue, flimsy, official money orders, wherewith neither Pierrots nor Poets are concerned. I wish you *un grand succès* tomorrow. I should really come if I were not being worried to death with a host of corvées, connected with my move,[1] which will be next week. If I don't see you soon, let me hear how the recital went off: this address will be the most direct in future.

Yours ever   ERNEST DOWSON

P.S.   G. A. Greene's address:

21, Pembroke Gardens
Kensington, W.

What are the precise embroideries on your cherry coloured cloak—fruit or flowers?[2]

1. To Bridge Dock as his permanent home. His family went to live at Chadwell Heath, in Essex.
2. Peters had asked Dowson for a poem on his Italian cloak. It was first published in *Decorations*.

250. *To Victor Plarr*[1]
   [8 July 1893]

[Bridge Dock]

I have been a wreck of this hot weather and of this base city's outburst of snobbish sycophancy.[2] London on a gala day, when one thinks of what Paris and Florence can manage, makes me think of an ugly, fat, vulgar old woman putting on the graces of coquetry: one wants to hide one's face in one's hands. You are fortunate to be out of it. It is *not* all over, yesterday was as objectionable as Thursday. I daresay it will be all right on Monday, and then I may hope once more to be in a reasonably good temper: the last three days have severely tried it. I shall think of you filling your green book on a mossy bank, O founder of the

1. Text from Plarr.
2. The Duke of York (later King George V) married Princess Mary of Teck on 6 July 1893.

Haslemere school. Hillier ran down and lunched here t'other day on his way from the Lakes. . . . he has a cottage without a name in a pathless wood: so I fear we shall never see him again. ———— was very ebullient all the week, and yesterday evening was sober for the first time since they began to put up the decorations. . . If London increases in heat and aridity I suppose I shall have to retire from it for a brief space, but I *shall* hold on as long as I can. In [Poland] matters progress as well as I suppose they are likely to—I should think so probably if I had the great grace of patience; not possessing that, I die many deaths daily. Let me hear from you some day, and especially that you and your folk . . . are laying in copious stores of health. I shall probably bore you from time to time with my letters.

251. *To William Theodore Peters*
[*c. 10 July 1983*]

Bridge Dock

My dear Peters,
    I have hunted tremendously for the song,[1] but so far unsuccessfully; I have been in such a confusion of disorder since my move that I fear it is lost. Had I not better try & write another version? I will try my best to see you tomorrow evening, if only for twenty minutes. I will call about nine. Would you mind sending a complimentary ticket & a copy of the prospectus to

> John Lane Esq
> c/o Messrs Elkin Mathews & Lane
>   Publishers
> The Bodley Head,
> Vigo St. W.

    I will try & bring with me something in the shape of a song for your approval.
    I am sorry I have not been able to look you up before, but I have seen nobody, I have been suffering horribly from sleeplessness—although I try going to bed at 10 o'clock—and this makes me even in the day time fit company for nobody but myself.
    Until tomorrow then.

Poignée de main   ERNEST DOWSON

1. The Moon Maiden's song in *The Pierrot of the Minute*.

252. *To William Theodore Peters*
[*c. 20 July 1893*]

Bridge Dock

My dear Peters,

It was so wet and wretched yesterday that I thought you would forgive me my absence last night, especially as I have such a distance to get back. In default of that, I set myself to finish the verses you want & send you them herewith. I hope you will like them but I fear they are not worthy of their occasion. I go down to Brighton on Saturday until Tuesday: shall be back then & in town until the Sunday when I go to Birkhampstead to Hillier. Let us meet before you fly away to Homburg.

Ever yours ERNEST DOWSON

Let me know if you get the verses in the "Studio".

253. *To William Theodore Peters*
[*24 July 1893*]

Bridge Dock

My dear Peters,

I have had to postpone my visit to Hillier, for various reasons, & fear I shall not now be able to go to him, before he leaves on the 27th. I was at Chadwell Heath Sat & yesterday, the end of the world, where my mother stays at present. I can meet you almost any night you like this week—or will look you up on Saturday afternoon—or, if you have no engagement, & are still in town, will invite myself to lunch with you on Sunday next the 30th—as I am going to the Servite Ch:[1] in the morning & shall be in the neighbourhood. Command me when you will.

I am glad you like the Versicles: I wish they were more worthy of you.

Our N.Y. publisher, by the way is Appleton:[2] do you know aught of him?

In the hope of seeing you soon,

T à t. ERNEST DOWSON

1. Our Lady of Seven Dolours, Fulham Road.
2. Publisher of *A Comedy of Masks.*

254. *To William Theodore Peters*

[*Early August 1893*]

Bridge Dock

Herewith, my dear Peters, the dedicatory verses as amended. I like "silk & silver" better than "green etc"—but as you will notice I have suggested the apple leaves in verse one.[1] Do you think that so, it will do?

Should the poem commend itself to Gleeson White,[2] will you ask him to send me a proof of it here?

By the way—amongst your American friends of substance, you may possibly encounter one who requires a private secretary. In such an event would you bear me in mind and recommend me. I am rather anxious to obtain some such post, at any rate temporarily—until I find literature more profitable. Does the Bellew-Potter[3] combination, par exemple require a secretary? I know some companies carry one with them. I believe I could acquit myself in such an office successfully. In any case let me hear from you if you have time on your travels. Commend me to my ancestral Highlands[4]—which alas! I am not personally acquainted with—&

Believe me

always yours ERNEST DOWSON.

1. 'Ah! cunning flowers of silk and silver thread.' Verse 1 as printed makes no mention of apple leaves.
2. Poet and art critic (1851–1898) and editor of *The Studio* 1893–1894.
3. Kyrle Bellew was an English actor for many years in partnership with Cora Brown-Potter, the American actress and manageress.
4. Dowson's mother was of Scottish descent.

255. *To Arthur Moore*

[*August 1893*]

Bridge Dock

Caro Mio,

I have been bilious, choleraic etc since Saturday until yesterday. Yet I should have come round to you last night had not Goodhart enticed me away to sit on his house-roof—an occupation which the great heat commended to me.

What I have done—& very poor stuff it is, of the Chapter I will copy out & let you have before Sunday. I will post it, as I assume from your card we shall not meet to-morrow.

Let me hear from you, when we may meet before you go away as I am uncertain of what chap I am next to occupy myself on.

Yours

in a state of wreckage   E.D.

The stricture of proof sheets is unaccountable.[1] I see Norris' novel[2] is announced in a day or two.

1. Of *A Comedy of Masks.*
2. *The Countess Radna*, by W. E. Norris, published by Heinemann.

256. *To Arthur Moore*

    [Mid-August 1893]

Bridge Dock

Carissimo,

Are you cursing me very much in some secluded reach of what admirable river? I scribble a line to ask whither I am to send my abortive chapter?

The heat incommodes me damnably, & the quantity of gin and ginger beer with which I wrestle against it incommodes me more. I should like immensely to retire to Brittany for the rest of the month in your company, as I should like to have the wings of a dove, and the constitution of an ostrich, and various other equally impossible things.

Everyone is away now—& everyone has given up writing: the darkness of the unknown has swallowed up Hillier—unless he has really started with his adventurous *canotiers* to row to Constantinople. Let me hear of your movements, I pray you. I shall be here, at all events, until the middle of Sept.—not counting a few days at Chadwell Heath. I have had no proofs—& so gather, from your letter, that none are arriving. The emptiness of London is appalling: I can quite believe that Heinemann's staff have retired.

Above all things write to me soon.

Vale.   ERNEST DOWSON

I have discovered a book-making 'bacconist hereby—if you want to plank on gee-gees without sending to Vlissingen I can work it. His limit is 33–1.

257. *To Victor Plarr*

[*Mid-August 1893*]

Bridge Dock

Cher Vieux.

How are you all finding yourselves, and where; and when are we going to meet again? The whirlig[ig] of time has taken my people to the world's end, which is called by the sublunary Chadwell Heath—& there I suppose for the present I must pass penitential Sundays—with much regret for your ancient hospitable supper table. I suppose you are away from town: most people are, I think, now. I have had a prolonged epistolary paralysis or I would have afflicted you with a letter before. In fact I have only just reminded myself to-day that Greene's letter demanding rhymes[1] is still unanswered & likely to remain so. But I am trying to hunt up the necessary half dozen & will dispatch them: though I should think the Star Chamber will have decided by this time to dispense with me. The weather is—well, too damned hot to write about for fear of burning the paper with expletives. I imagine you in Devonshire, drinking cider, playing skittles & eating cream *du pays*. Write to me & assure me that this is so, or if not that you are at Midleton & will look in upon me here one afternoon. I am verily I believe "alone in London.[2] The darkness of the unknown has swallowed up Hillier, the provincial stage, Marmie.[3] Did you ever interview Lane,[4] and with what result? I called at his shop t'other day but like everyone else he was campaigning. I do not even attempt to write any longer, not even verses. My mental horizon doesn't extend beyond cooling drinks and cigarettes. Forgive this tedious letter.—It is too hot to write letters: but on the other hand they are the only literature that is light enough for one to read—so I may conclude with an apt enough citation from a prince of letter writers though a most vile poet—(*pace* Matthew Arnold:) "To be tiresome is the privilege of old age and absence; I avail myself of the latter and the former I have anticipated. If I do not speak to you of my own affairs, it is not from want of confidence, but to spare you and myself. My day is over—what then?—I have had it. To be sure I have shortened it; and if I had done as much by this letter, it would have been as well."[5]

Always yours   ERNEST DOWSON

1. For *The Second Book of the Rhymers' Club*.
2. Novel by 'the Author of *Jessica's First Prayer*' (i.e. Sarah Smith), published by the Religious Tract Society, 1869.
3. Marmaduke Langdale, an actor and close friend of Dowson's. He appears as 'Archie Longdale' in *Adrian Rome*.
4. About the publication of Plarr's poems *In the Dorian Mood*. The book came out in 1896.
5. Byron, letter to Thomas Moore, from Verona, 6 November 1816. We are grateful to Dr. Michael Slater for tracing this quotation.

258. *To G. A. Greene*

 [*c. 20 August 1893*]

Bridge Dock

My dear Greene,

Rhymers' Book

I owe you a thousand apologies for this unconscionable delay. I put off answering your letter until I could select some versicles to send with it—and the selection took time, & one thing & another intervened—& I hardly realized what an age it is since your letter came. Herewith, then (hoping I am not too late altogether) my Budget! I send a few more pieces than the required number in order that you may select: but I have marked them in the order in which I should wish personally to have them published. I suppose there is no likelihood of any Cheshire Cheese gathering before the Autumn?

Once more please forgive my epistolatory shortcomings.

Yours vy sincerely ERNEST DOWSON

List of Verses
1. "Cynara"
2. "To One in Bedlam"
3. "You would have understood me"
4. "Ad Manus"
5. "Benedictio Domini"[1]
6. "Love heeds no more".*[2]

Extras
Growth
Dead Child

* I will send you a title for this ED.

1. Dowson later withdrew *Benedictio Domini* (see Letter 271).
2. i.e. *The Garden of Shadow.*

259. *To Victor Plarr*[1]

[*c. 27 August 1893*]

[*Chadwell Heath*]

Caro Vecchio,

I am glad you have been to Greene, you will be able to make my peace with him. I sent off versicles of a sort to him before I left town—perhaps you saw them there—8 in all . . . I have been reading 'Many Inventions.'[2] Mulvaney's stories, above all 'Love o' Women,' like me most: après—'One View of the Question,' a beautiful piece of satire on English mob-worship . . . . We have received the last proofs of *Comedy of Masks*. I have seen no one—suppose every one away.

1. Text from Plarr.
2. By Kipling, 1893.

260. *To Arthur Moore*

Sunday [*27 August 1893*]

Chadwell Heath

Très Cher,

I have been down here since Friday, recruiting: I am better than I was but still far from well. Your letters & the rest of the proofs reached me here yesterday. It is a great thing to have the "Masks" off our hands. Your leniency in speaking of the embryo I sent you, in way of a chap is noble. I have brought down here vast quantities of virgin MSS, which is still tolerably intact—also "Many Inventions" & "Le Doc. Pascal".[1] The first with exception of a couple of stories "Love o' Women" & "My Lord the Elephant" is disappointing. Le Docteur" has faults but great power & beauty comme toujours. This is a dreary place; it just begins to rain. 'Missy' is at Southend from Friday till to-morrow or I could hardly have had the courage to stay here so long: I return to-morrow. I envy you your Yarmouth air & your landlady. I have half a mind to run down to you from Sat. to Sunday if she can cheaply accomodate me for a night. I will find out if a boat runs conveniently: let me know if you will still be there.

1. By Zola, 1893; the last of *Les Rougon-Macquart*.

I feel horridly vague as to the next few chaps of the *Opus*. By all the Saints we *must* go to Brittany together next year. The *roman* will be finished & we shall be able to concoct the bones of another. I hope this last work appears in Oct: does it not seem to you probable? Let me hear from you, above all if you can give me a few headings or points for my impending Chap. Hillier is returned, & Paterson is always with us—so I see prospect of some whist when you once more tread the grass grown ways of the Deserted Village.

I will send the proofs back tomorrow: here and now are no facilities for dispatch of parcels. I hope you are working like a house on fire—I fear I cannot sauce this precept with the spice of example. But I will emend. I really had a nasty jar on account of my lung. Adios! I hope to send you a MSS—or bring it. In the interim I hope to hear from you.

Tuissimus   ERNEST DOWSON

261. *To Arthur Moore*
[*2 September 1893*]

Bridge Dock

Caro,

Thanks for card. I am not altogether delighted at the date wh. Heinemann has fixed.[1] I think on the whole that Oct—the middle—would have pleased me more. Where are the reviewers now? And where are the supporters of Mudie? There may be some of them at Yarmouth, but I haven't seen any here lately. I have made one or two false starts with a new chapter. I can't do very much, however, until I know from you what has become of Lord Henry.[2] Has he accepted the Chiltern Hunds. or has there been a general election?

These things I would ask you at Yarmouth, but I fear I can not get away just now—so I shall live in the hope of seeing you immediately on your arrival. It is a great thing to have the proofs off our hands. I muchly wonder if the Transatlantic Edition is also due this month?

I am very much muddled about the present situation of ~~the~~ our characters: they seem to have got the better hand of me, and there are too many of them. I wish we could draw up a more detailed scheme—I am sure your chap is admirable as all yours have been, & mine afflict me with a rising despair. Are you going to bring me a pot of native bloaters? It renders me triste to think of you down there all this

1. Heinemann originally intended to publish *A Comedy of Masks* on 15 September. It came out on 22 September.
2. i.e. Lord Henry Minaret, in *Adrian Rome*.

time—by the bones of St Louis, not to mention Ste Barbe & St Fiacre, we will go to Faouet next year—

It is Saturday afternoon. I haven't the faintest idea what to do until five. I must go & play billiards with the marker au Marquis, whom occasionally I can beat. Par exemple it appears when one vanquishes the marker he does not charge for the game. At least that is the custom of this marker. Let us meet as soon as you can manage it after your return: I greatly desire to see you & to note the tonic effects of the brass bands & the bloaters on your countenance. Inform me of your plans.

T à t.   ERNEST DOWSON

262. *To Victor Plarr*[1]

[*c. 3 September 1893*]

Bridge Dock

Cressa ne careat alba Dies![2]

My dear Victor,

Your letter filled me with joy—with its double news. I send my very sincere congratulations, and all good wishes for the continued prosperity of the Bambina and the speedy recovery of the Donna.

The patronizing saint of Sept. 2 according to the Roman calendar is St Stephen of Hungary—(St Etienne)—of whom I know not much. But in a Milan calendar I find the day set apart to a certain San Mansueto—of whom I know less—that is nothing—but whose name is excellently propitious. My compliments then to Mdlle. Etienne-Mansueta Plarr. I append certain versicles pseudo 18th-cent. with which she has already inspired me: may she be provocative of many more.

> Mark the day white on which the Fates have smiled:
> Eugenio and Egeria have a child,
> On whom abundant grace kind Jove imparts
> If she but copy either parent's parts.
> Then, Muses! long devoted to her race
> Grant her Egeria's virtues and her face;
> Nor stay your bounty there, but add to it
> Eugenio's learning and Eugenio's wit![3]

1. Text from Plarr.
2. Horace, *Odes* I. 36. Plarr's daughter Marion was born on 2 September 1893. Her novel *Cynara, the Story of Ernest and Adelaide* (1933) quotes several of Dowson's letters to her father and is in several places the sole authority for the text.
3. First published in *Verses*.

Forgive this trifling: seriously I am very pleased. Also with the prospects of the 'Doric Moods'.[4] I will still maintain that they owe their good reception entirely to their merits and no whit to diplomacy of Johnson's or Le Gallienne. Our book is due for the 15th of this month. They have just sent us a suggested design for the cover—a tragic and comic mask with liberty to substitute what we like—within 5 days!! Of course in the time one can do nothing: otherwise perhaps Horne or Ricketts might have been requisitioned.

4. Acceptance of Plarr's poems by the Bodley Head.

263. *To Arthur Moore*
   [*c. 6 September 1893*]

Bridge Dock

Caro,
   Many thanks for the Synopsis: though I regret to see that you added to it no whit. I think I must send it you back again! However in the meantime I have started on Chap xvii, & am introducing a new character.[1] I will try & get on with it to the quickest of my ability: Shall I see you tomorrow? If not write or let me see you soon. I think I will do the whole of Chap xvii & if you w̶i̶l̶l̶ have any notion of the next one we will make that composite. In the meantime wire into that garden party: & let me know I pray thee when you have official confirmation of the proceedings in New York.
Tout à toi   ERNEST DOWSON

By the way, have you "Louvette".[2] If so will you send it me for Marmie.
   I have had another enquiry anent my play: this time from the provinces, via the "Professional World"

1. The new character is 'Archie Longdale'. Moore seems to have shrunk from describing the garden party, which is mentioned only in passing.
2. Novel (1891) in the series *Les Voluptueuses* by Jean Larocque.

264. *Letter-card to William Theodore Peters*
   [*Postmark 18 September 1893*]

Bridge Dock

Che Confrère,

Many thanks for note. I fear Tuesday may find me occupied. Shall we say Saturday next the 23rd when I am certain of being disengaged?

I fix this date also because I feel one of my periodic melancholies or spleens descending on me when I am bad company for myself & intolerable to my friends. By Saturday I shall be cured.

The "Comedy" appears—so it is finally decided on the 22nd.

I am anxious to hear your impressions of Oxford.

Tout votre   ERNEST DOWSON

265. *To Victor Plarr*
   [*c. 20 September 1893*]

Bridge Dock

Cher Vieux,

I was grieved, indeed, to miss you the other day: I had gone down to Chadwell rather early. You must give me another look in when you are returned from Devon, before you take up your abode in the Library. Let me hear how you fare there—& how the family are getting on. "The Comedy of Masks" appears on Friday—nominally—but I see no reason now why it should be actually any further delayed. You must command it from Mudies. I tremble at the prospect of being reviewed —I am painfully conscious of the innumerable blemishes & alas! the weakest points are in the first volume so that I fear sleep will overtake the reviewer before he reach any of of our less banal passages. What fools we are to write—or rather to publish! Mercifully Lionel does not review novels—and as to the opinion of the average novel-reviewing Le Gallienish animal—"we will not think of it." Peters has turned up in town again very redolent of the States and very enthusiastic over the Highlands.

Commend me to Walton if this should reach you in his neighbourhood.

Ever yours   ERNEST DOWSON

How shall you call la petite? This will be an exercise almost as difficult as the choice of a book title. En passant can you suggest a name for notre prochain roman—wh. is just half completed. 'A Misalliance" is I fear, bad English. "The Opportunist"—occurs to me, also "The Interlopers"—but none of these is good. Its better than "Masks" we both think but vindictive, savage, spleenful libellous almost, to the last degree. Heaven knows when it will be finished.

266. *To Victor Plarr*[1]
[*c. 25 September*]

[*Bridge Dock*]

The *Comedy* is out at last—very charming in its outward, visible aspect, and for the rest I hope no one will discover as many inward blemishes as I can. I am anxious to see the Infanta—her names are all pretty. Has she begun to show any literary tendencies yet?

1. Text from Plarr.

267. *To William Theodore Peters*
30 September 1893

Bridge Dock

My dear Peters,
 Just a line to tell you that I am going out of town this week & shall not be able to see you before Sunday—so could you *defer the portrait for the present*. I expect to be back by Saturday at the latest so if it is still convenient to you we will look upon our Sunday arrangements as a fixture—i.e. I will give myself the pleasure of lunching with you—& après will convoy you to Orchard St. Are you going to the Arts & Crafts[1] any time? Image gives a lecture one evening—I forget wh.— but you will find it in the catalogue.[2]
 Ever yrs   ERNEST DOWSON

1. The Arts and Crafts Exhibition opened at the New Gallery on 2 October.
2. On 16 November, with William Morris in the chair.

268. *To William Theodore Peters*
        Wednesday [*4 October 1893*]

Bridge Dock

Cher Peters,
    As usual my projects have collapsed—& my week of campagne reduces itself to being away for two evenings—last night & tomorrow. I was in Sherwood St till 6.0 yesterday when I went to Blackheath—& was sorry to miss you. Have you seen our reviews in yesterday's Daily Telegph. & todays Chronicle both far more favourable than we expected or perhaps deserved. These & I hope some more I will show you on Sunday, when I also hope to bring the MSS of "Pierrot" if Tree has by that time condescended to answer me.
                            Ever yours   ERNEST DOWSON

269. *To William Theodore Peters*
        [*October 1893*]

[*Fulham*]

Dear Peters—
    Have left "Comedy of Masks":—will you let me have it back as soon as possible as it is my only copy & I have to lend it again. Sorry to miss you: am dining out tomorrow night but will try & call on Saturday afternoon.
                            Ever yrs   E C DOWSON

270. *To Victor Plarr*
        [*c. 15 October 1893*]

Bridge Dock

Cher Vieux. What must you think of me for this ungrateful silence? But I have been so beset with inevitable correspondence that I have not possessed my soul since I saw you. I interviewed Warr on Sunday concerning l'affaire Williams & learnt from him what I heard in your letter of Monday that a musician was required.[1] But he was charming & I was glad to have met him. Also I believe secretly I was glad that the matter had fallen through for I have not the courage I fear, after all to absent myself from Sherwood St for so long.

You will have seen perhaps some of our reviews. Their benevolence has taken my breath away. The "Speaker", "Daily Chronicle", "Telegraph"—'Scotsman' all favourable, some of them gushing—& this weeks 'Graphic' wh. has just come to hand. So far the only downright bad one was in the "World".

I was staying with Teixeira last night in the Temple & sat up for long talking to Sherard[2] who is there & who came over with Zola & is writing a biography of him for Chatto & Windus. He is charming but the most morose & spleenful person I have yet encountered. His conversation is undiluted vitriol—like the man—nescio quem in "La Première Maitresse".[3] Also this morning Gray who is finally leaving the Temple—quantum mutatus ab isto—fat but friendly, I fear incurably given over to social things—& about to take up his abode in Park Lane![4] This is sad. May we meet soon—I have to return you your Spenser.

I send all my compliments to the family wh: I trust prospers,

Ever thine   ERNEST DOWSON

1. Plarr had given Dowson's name to Professor Warr of London University, who wanted someone to read German and play the violin to an invalid friend.
2. Robert Harborough Sherard (1861–1943), author and journalist, in whose cottage Dowson died in 1900. Zola was visiting London at the invitation of the Institute of Journalists.
3. Novel by Catulle Mendès, 1887.
4. Where André Raffalovich lived.

271. *To G. A. Greene*
    [*c. 15 October 1893*]

Bridge Dock

My dear Greene,

May I withdraw certain of the rhymes I have submitted for the 'Rhymers' new book, substituting others. I find that two or three of them wh: have been set up for the 'Hobby' are not likely to be out before the appearance of the Book. So if you could kindly return these to me I should be relieved—& will send you a further selection. The 'Hobby' pieces wh. I should like back are—"Benedictio Domini", a piece called, I believe, "Terre Promise"—beginning "Even now the fragrance of her trailing Hair"—&—if I sent it to you—wh. I can not remember a Requiem beginning "Neobule, being tired" etc.[1]

I may as well send you one of my alternative Versicles herewith. The rest later on.

Ever yours   ERNEST DOWSON

How do you like the new "Hobby" cover?
When do we have another Rhyming evening?
I saw you favourably reviewed in the 'Times' th' other day.[2]

1. When Dowson gave these poems to Horne in February 1893 he no doubt expected them to appear in the next number of *The Hobby Horse* well before publication of *The Second Book of the Rhymers' Club*. In fact, they were not published till late in 1894. The last two poems named were not, however, offered to the Rhymers' Club. The alternative poem sent with this letter cannot be identified. Dowson later submitted *Extreme Unction* in place of *Benedictio Domini*.
2. *The Times* reviewed Greene's *Italian Lyrists of To-day* on 13 October.

272. To Victor Plarr[1]

[*Late October 1893*]

[*Bridge Dock*]

Will you see the November *Bookman*? . . . they have made quite a creditable article of our meagre biographies, although it is news to me that I have been 'steadily making my way in literature.'[2] There is also a good review in it of *Masks* . . . Is the Infanta short petticoated yet? Or when does that interesting development take place? I went down to see Marmie play at Wimbledon the other day. He was an excellent Ralph Nickleby in a tedious play

I have seen no one much except the Temple folk lately and Sherard who camped out here one night after a peregrination with me in the East End during which, I am sorry to say, I contracted a frantic cold which is still harassing me. . . Shall you be aux Rhymers to-morrow?

1. Text from Plarr.
2. This article announced prematurely that a volume of Dowson's poems was to be published by the Bodley Head in 1894. In fact, *Verses* did not appear until 1896, and was published by Leonard Smithers.

Oscar Wilde after his release from prison

To E. Smithers   Octo 14.'97

Dear Smithers

    I to-day deposit with
you £45.0.0 of my money.
Please send Oscar Wilde
£10.0.0 , on a/c of what
I owe him, take £1.8.3 on
a/c of interest paid by you
for me & send me the balance
at £3 every Monday to
any address I may send you.
Do not send me more than
£3 each week.

        Yours truly.
        Ernest Dowson

Ernest Dowson

3·Soho Square·

London W.

1897			1897			
Oct 14	Cash	45.0.0	Oct 14	6. Wilde	10.0.0
1898			"	interest on pawn	1.8.3
Jan. 12	"	20.0.0	"	pawn & interest	6.16.6
			" 20	on a/c 1849	1.0.0
			" 23	"	2.0.0
			" 30	"	2.0.0
			Nov. 6	"	3.0.0
			" 13	"	2.0.0
			" 19	"	2.0.0
			" 26	"	2.0.0
			Dec. 3	"	2.0.0
			" 8	"	4.0.0
			" 16	"	2.0.0
			" 21	"	3.0.0
			" 28	"	3.0.0
			1898		
			Jan. 4		1.0.0
			" 6		7.0
			" 8		1.0.0
			" 12		5.0.0
			" 14	Peters	3.0.0
					56.11.9
				Balance	8.8.3
		65.0.0			65.0.0

Smithers's account with Dowson

Autograph letter to Leonard Smithers dated 14 October 1897

(above) John de Courcy MacDonnell, his wife and daughter
Eileen, in Limerick, in the mid-1890s

(below) 'Fairy Hill', Parteen, Limerick

273. *To William Theodore Peters*
     Sunday [*c. November 1893*]

                                              Bridge Dock

Dear Peters,
     I am sorry I was unable to come to you yesterday. I have a fearful cold, of the influenza type—& was unfit for society—am still indeed thoroughly wretched.
     I have written to the Signora however, to say that I will dine there on Tuesday—when I hope to be cured. Shall look forward to meeting you there.
                      Yours ever   ERNEST DOWSON

P.S. If you have finished "Wreckage"[1] wd. you mind bringing it on Tuesday?

1. A volume of short stories (1893) by Hubert Crackanthorpe (1870–1896), editor of *The Albemarle Review* and a friend of Dowson's.

274. *To G. A. Greene*
     [*c. 27 November 1893*]

                                              Bridge Dock

My dear Greene,
     Plarr has handed me the mss of the Rhymers which, I believe, I am to pass on to Johnson—& will do so today or tomorrow. I think your "Beyond" sonnet is about the finest thing in the collection, though I am also immensely taken with Plarr's "Ad Cinerarium, & Johnson's "Mystic & Cavalier. To discuss them in detail—your "Beyond" as I said before; & après—'They have taken away my Lord", Proserpine, Sugar Loaf, Lady Macbeth & Proserpine, & "Is it peace?" I put the latter last not critically but because of my general preference for short poems. Hillier's poems appeal to me in this order Memorial Garden, Midsummer Day, Opera Land, Orpheus, Brittany, In Excelsis—all of which I like—as I don't the "Witches Revel". Yeat's poems are always so good & his handwriting is so bad that I feel safe in recommending them all. Symon's budget being so small there seems no need for selection—I like 'Nora', the 'Variation on Love" & the "Song" particularly—& indeed all are better than the poems he was represented by in the 1st book.
    LED–U

I suppose all of Le Gallienne must be included, I like the London Ballad—but *not* the Ode to Spring. Could he be induced to withdraw the expression 'Shelley lark"?[1]

Johnson's are all fine, I like them in this order Mystic & Cavalier, Glories, to Marfydd, Dark Angel, Dorothy. Radford's own list puts his contributions in the same order which I should—except that I should prefer to see his 7th included at the loss of his 6th; if there is no objection to it on the score of its having been published in Mrs Radford's book.[2] I like it almost as much as the Labour poem wh. is certainly fine. I do not follow his theory however as set forth in the letter.[3] I shd. have said that Love & Death are almost more permanently with us than the Labour Movement & will probably survive it—& I don't quite see how the Radicals are going to abolish them. In the meantime as they interest me more than sociological questions I am afraid I shall continue to "use" them

Plarr's verses are all of them so charming & I know them so well that I find selection very difficult. Perhaps I shd arrange them as follows. (i) Ad Cinerarium (ii) Mejnun. (iii) Breton Beggar. (iv) Secret of the Sea. (v) Phantom Ship (vi) Death & Player—or Quatrain. I like "Eothen" the least.

Doctor Todhunter's budget is also very fine. My preferences are "Euthanasia"—the Memorial Poem to Tennyson & the "Isolt" song. Ellis' I should arrange (i) Venus. (ii) Rhyme on Rhymes. (iii) Green Leaf. iv A year on the River (v) St Anthony.

Rhys: (i) Olwen. (ii) House of Hendric (iii) Oranges. But both he & Rolleston give no occasion for selection. I don't care for Rolleston's "Cycling Song' so much as for his others. This disposes of all. With regard to my own I have substituted a poem on "Extreme Unction" for that on "Benediction" wh. I had to withdraw.[4] If people will accept the substitution I shall be glad as otherwise I shall not be represented by anything in that manner.

I must apologize for the length & abruptness of this letter. Plarr tells me that a meeting is to be convened shortly—if it is not this Friday, when I have to dine at the Odd Volumes I shall be there & shall hope to see you.

Very sincerely yours   ERNEST DOWSON.

---

1. Greene acted on most of these suggestions, though three of the poems by Plarr which Dowson favoured did not appear, while Le Gallienne's *Ode to Spring* did, complete with 'Shelley lark'.
2. Radford's *Heart and Home* was included in *A Light Load* by Dollie Radford, 1891.
3. Radford had written to Greene: 'Love being out of date and Religion a thing of the past, the hunting ground of our poets has become exceedingly small.'
4. *Extreme Unction* was duly included. It was reprinted in *Verses* and there dedicated to Lionel Johnson.

[*Postscript*] I congratulate you on the excellent reviews of your book & on your satisfactory rejoinder to Sharp in the Academy.[5]

5. William Sharp reviewed Greene's *Italian Lyrists of To-day* in *The Academy*, 18 November 1893, and accused him of plagiarism from earlier editors. Greene's reply appeared the following week.

275. *To Victor Plarr*

[*c. 28 November 1893*]

Bridge Dock

Cher Vieux.

Do you like the enclosed verses enough to include them in the Book in lieu of 'Benedictio Domini'? Johnson to whom I have conveyed the weighty packet seems to like them the best of my budget. He was very amiable & we drank much absinthe together. I voted for 6 of your poems with much difficulty for I liked all so much that I wished to see them all included. I placed the 'Cinerarium' Breton Beggar & Mejnun first—of LJ.'s I think I most admired the Cavalier & Mystic—Verlaine is after all still in London.[1] I am dining with Horne & Horne Père at the Constitutional tonight to meet him. So that if I have the courage I will even suggest to the Master that he should honour his disciples with a visit to the Cheese. À bientôt—with all amenities to Mesdames votre mère et votre femme et à cette chère Bébé

T à toi ERNEST DOWSON

NB Let me know what you think of Moore's story in Dec. Macmillan.[2]

EXTREME UNCTION

Upon the lips, the hands, the feet,
   On all the passages of sense,
The annealing oil is spread with sweet
   Renewal of lost innocence.

The roving feet that ran so fast
   To meet desire are soothly sealed:
The eyes that were so often cast
   On vanity, are touched and healed.

1. Verlaine had come to London to lecture at Barnard's Inn on 21 November. He returned to France about three weeks later after further lectures at Oxford and Salford.
2. *The Intermediary*, published anonymously.

From troublous sights and sounds set free,
    In such a twilight hour of breath,
Shall one retrace his life? or see
    Through shadows the true face of Death?

Vials of mercy! healing Oils!
    I know not where, nor when, I come
Nor through what wanderings and toils
    To crave of you, Viaticum.

Yet, when the walls of flesh grow weak,
    In such an hour it well may be,
Through mist and darkness, light shall break,
    And each anointed sense shall see.

276. *To John Lane*
    [*c. 28 November 1893*]

Bridge Dock

My dear Lane,
    Forgive my writing to you personally to enquire as to the fate of certain stories wh. I sent to you in your *corporate capacity* a month or two ago.[1]
    But not having heard any news I have latterly been getting rather nervous as to whether they ever arrived? And I believe the letter wh. I sent with them was included in the package.
    I shd. be very glad if you would let me know this—& assuming they reached you, what is your decision, & whether I shall come & fetch them away.
    Will you be at the Odd Volumes on the 1st?[2] I am dining there with Brodie Innes & shall look forward to seeing you.
                    Sincerely yours   ERNEST DOWSON

1. Dowson had sent Mathews and Lane the first four of his stories published in magazines. They were issued together with *The Statute of Limitations* as *Dilemmas*, 1895.
2. A literary and dining club which met monthly in London. Its secretary was John Todhunter. This is the only occasion on which Dowson is recorded as one of the guests.

277. *To Elkin Mathews and John Lane*
    [*c. 30 November 1893*]

Bridge Dock

Dear Sirs,
    I am obliged for your letter with reference to my stories. Would you kindly let me know, about how much more material you would require[1] to make up a volume uniform with 'Keynotes'?[2] There is a story of mine, recently published in the "Hobby Horse",[3] which I could include, if it should meet with your approval—and I have one story nearly completed, and another, unpublished,[4] which I could send you shortly.
    If this would not be sufficient, I am afraid I should not be able to add anything more until the summer, for I am at present engaged upon a translation,[5] which occupies, & will occupy, all my time until the beginning of May. If you would prefer the matter to stand over till then I could no doubt manage to add a few more. The two new stories, I propose sending you are both rather longer than the longest of those now in your hands. The story in the 'Hobby Horse', however, is not in more than 2,500 words.

Yours faithfully   ERNEST DOWSON

Messr. Elkin Mathews & John Lane.

1. Le Gallienne's report is printed on page 263.
2. A volume of stories by George Egerton published by Mathews and Lane in 1893, the first of a series named after it. The early volumes had title-pages designed by Aubrey Beardsley.
3. *The Statute of Limitations.*
4. Probably *Apple Blossom in Brittany*. The story nearly completed may be *The Eyes of Pride*.
5. Zola's *La Terre*, translated by Dowson for the Lutetian Society and published in 1894.

278. *To Victor Plarr*
    [*2 December 1893*]

Bridge Dock

Cher Vieux,
    Horne has asked me to write to you & let you know that there is to be another Verlaine lecture on Tuesday next, Barnard's Inn Hall at

8.0 by the clock.[1] Tickets 5/- on application to Horne or at the door. I shall try & go, & hope you will likewise do so—though I really think nous autres rimeurs should have been put on the Free list.

I had a charming evening at the Odd Vols last night. I sat opposite Todhunter who had 3 Irish guests (Rolleston, Percival Graves[2] & Standish O'Grady[3])—a charming Celt. My Lord Mayor[4] came with a gorgeous creature to wait on him—Lane had 3 editors & Le Gallienne one. There was no one else there whom I knew except—by sight only—York Powell.[5] Mes compliments to you all—in the hope of a meeting in the near future

Ever yours   ERNEST DOWSON

1. This projected lecture was cancelled.
2. 1846–1931, poet and Inspector of Schools; father of Mr. Robert Graves.
3. 1846–1928, Irish scholar and mythologist.
4. Sir George Tyler (1835–1897).
5. 1850–1904, Student of Christ Church and later Regius Professor of Modern History at Oxford. Verlaine had just been staying with him. Another guest on this occasion was Max Beerbohm, still an undergraduate at Merton College, Oxford, but he and Dowson never met.

279. *To Victor Plarr*[1]

[20 December 1893]

[Bridge Dock]

[He mentions a meeting with Jepson at a small Rhymers' Club gathering.]
Him I was delighted to see again although I did not recognise him, nor he me.[2]
[He thinks Jepson a good deal changed by his sojourn in the West Indies, and speaks of his own coming 'exile in Chalon-sur-Saône or Saumur-sur-Oise'.]

1. Text from Plarr.
2. They met at the Crown, Charing Cross Road. Jepson lunched with Dowson at Bridge Dock two days later.

280. *To Victor Plarr*[1]
  [*c. 15 March 1894*]

[*Bridge Dock*]

[In the spring of 1894, in an amusing letter excusing himself for having intruded upon us with Mr Jepson when we were entertaining a friend against whom I had warned him as not being sympathetic with poets, he speaks of retiring to Mr Hillier's 'cottage in the wood' for Easter with 'La Terre' in order to put in twenty pages a day of translation to make up arrears.]

1. Quoted from Plarr.

281. *To Samuel Smith*[1]
  Maundy Thursday [*22 March*] 1894

Bridge Dock

You are right, I fear, when you draw my horoscope. But the Ides are not yet. *Quod bene eveniat!* One lives and talks as if the making of many books were the end and aim of all things. I am afraid they are the straws one chews to cheat one's appetite. Whether the Ides come a little sooner or a little later, they must come this year. I always have a sort of feeling upon me that I am doing certain things for the last time. Therefore I am particularly anxious for you to come to Brittany with me this year . . . I must have one month more in Brittany before the Ides if only you could manage it. Noah must have had somewhat similar emotions to mine when he began to build his Ark. Out of what am I to build one? I am afraid I must trust to my swimming powers. In Poland there is no material alteration—perhaps we are a little troubled by the approach of anniversaries.[2]

1. Text from Gawsworth.
2. Of Joseph Foltinowicz's death on 24 April 1893.

282. *To G. A. Greene*
   [*c. 9 April 1894*]

Bridge Dock

My dear Greene,
   Thanks for the proofs,[1] wh I return herewith. As I suppose you will
not be sending out a revise, may I ask you to see, if the revise is sent
to you, that the alterations in "Extreme Unction" are duly inserted.
In the others there is not much to correct. I hope the book will be out
soon, & that we may have a meeting soon. At present I am working
tooth & nail to get a translation done of that wearisome work "La
Terre" at the stipulated time,

                         ever yours   ERNEST DOWSON

1. Of Dowson's poems in *The Second Book of the Rhymers' Club*.

283. *To Victor Plarr*
   [*c. 13 April 1894*]

Bridge Dock

Cher Vieux,
   Wie geht's? I have been so overwhelmed with Zola, & also disorganized by the sudden death of my housekeeper, & thrilled by other
things that I have deferred all writing. But I have wondered how it
fared with you & when we should meet. I have not done more than 340
pages.[1] Would you make my excuses to your mother, for not having
answered her note, and thank her for the symbolical stones according
to the Polish tradition. I am intensely interested in every kind of that
symbolism. I hope you are all flourishing: I suppose you are rurally at
your ease, now, so far as it is possible to be at your ease & translate Zola. I
have seen hardly anyone but Jepson, who dines with me almost daily, & I
fancy derives a good deal of satisfaction from studying my transparently imbecile condition. It is a great thing that so delightful a
person should at last have seen the absurdity of living in Barbadoes.
Are you going to the Yellow Book dinner?[2] I shall, I expect, but I feel that

1. Of *La Terre*. Plarr was translating *Nana* in the same series.
2. Mathews and Lane published the first number of *The Yellow Book* on 16
   April 1894. A dinner, which Dowson duly attended, was held that evening

I ought to go to no dinners until this pyramid is pulled down. I have had & returned my Rhymers' proofs. They have chucked my Lady's Hands, and my Terre Promise, in favour of 2 verses which I like less. Mine will be a very poor show: I hope they will bind the book decently this time. Are you by the way an astrologer? I begin to think that in my horoscope the first fortnight in April must be bound up with my fortunes very closely, critically or fatally, or perilously.

Let me hear from you! Are you at Blackheath next Sunday? But even, if you were, the chances are against my being able to leave my corvée.

These be parlous times

    & I am

Ever yours   ERNEST DOWSON

How do you like the appended?

'QUID NON SPEREMUS, AMANTES?'

Why is there in the least touch of her hands
    More grace than other women's lips bestow,
If love is but a slave, in fleshly bands
    Of flesh to flesh, wherever love may go?

Why choose vain grief and heavy-hearted hours,
    For her lost voice and dear, remembered hair,
If love may cull his honey from all flowers,
    And girls grow thick as violets, everywhere?

Nay! she is gone, and all things fall apart!
    Or she is cold, and vainly have we prayed,
And broken is the summer's splendid heart,
    And hope within a deep, dark grave is laid.

As man aspires and falls, yet a soul springs
    Out of the agony of flesh, at last;
So love, that flesh enthralls, shall rise on wings,
    Soul-centred when the rule of flesh is passed.

Then most high Lord! or crowned with myrtle sprays,
    Or crownless and forlorn, nor less a star,
Thee will I serve and follow, all my days,
    Whose thorns are sweet as never roses are![3]

9/4/94

at the Hotel d'Italie in Compton Street. Dowson's only contribution to *The Yellow Book* was his story *Apple Blossom in Brittany* in the number for October 1894.

3. First published in *Verses*.

284. *To G. A. Greene*

3 May 1894

Bridge Dock

My dear Greene,

Many thanks for the Rhymers' revise which I return herewith. They are all right—with the exception of one omitted full stop.

None of my pieces have been previously published excepting "Cynara" ("Hobby Horse") & "To one in Bedlam" wh appeared in Crackanthorpe's defunct "Albemarle Review". I have their permission to publish & will abide by your III stipulation.[1] Hoping we may meet soon at the Cheshire

yours ever   ERNEST DOWSON

1. This probably concerned republication.

285. *To Edgar Jepson*[1]

[*30 July 1894*]

Bridge Dock.

My dear Jepson,

How are you faring in Arcadia?[2]

We have had an awful time since you left, with Marie who had a relapse the day after your departure.[3] Then she improved to a certain extent and was persuaded to agree to go back and stay for two or three weeks with her sister. For two nights previously I had not been out of my clothes; Goodhart also had been up there all night. Last Friday—the day before her departure she came out and dined in Poland. She completely broke down there, and Missie made her go upstairs and lie down. We were in despair—Lennox[4] was due at the Elephant in the 'Cotton King'.

1. Text from Jepson, *Memories of an Edwardian*, 1937.
2. Jepson was on holiday at his parents' home in Kenilworth.
3. This episode is described by Jepson in *Memories of a Victorian*, 1933. The girl is there called Essie. She was brought to London by an actor in Benson's company, probably Lennox Pawle. She had taken an overdose of medicine and was critically ill for a fortnight with brain fever.
4. Lennox Pawle (1872–1936) was appearing in *The Cotton King* by Sutton Vane, which had opened at the Adelphi Theatre on 10 March 1894 and was now on tour. The first performance at Derby was on 30 July.

Finally Goodie arrived—we carried her down and got her into a four-wheeler and drove off with her. That night Goodie, Pawle and I were up till six. I was utterly worn out, so was Goodie. However, somehow or other Pawle and the Doctor got her off at ten the next morning—I was not there—but the accounts were graphic—Pawle had fainted twice during the night, and at the station even the Doctor added his contribution of tears to the ceremony. Goodhart and I wept bitterly when we said goodbye to her at six A.M., Marie of course was sobbing too. It was frightfully pathetic. In the evening Goodie and I went down to the Elephant with Pawle and a wire arrived to the effect that she had arrived safely, been met by her sister. We all waltzed around Pawle's dressing room and at the conclusion of the piece indulged so freely in liquor that happening to meet a friend in the Strand we annexed him boldly and carried him in triumph up to the 'Crown'. Later on we fell down and Goodhart and I tore our trousers. We slept anyhow (after having tried unsuccessfully to play whist) all about the place. So much for Saturday. Yesterday Pawle went off to join his Co. at Derby. Goodie and I met in the evening. He had a charming man with him, a twenty-ton opium eater, who had run away with his cousin and is now to marry her. We met at 7 and consumed 4 absinthes apiece in the Cock till 9. We then went and ate some kidneys—after which two absinthes apiece at the Crown. After which, one absinthe apiece at Goodie's Club. Total 7 absinthes. These had seriously affected us—but made little impression on the opium-eater. He took us back to the Temple in a cab. This morning Goodhart and I were twitching visibly. I feel rather indisposed; and in fact we decided that our grief is now sufficiently drowned, and we must spend a few days on nothing stronger than lemonade and strychnine. But the previous strain on our nerves had been terrible. I wish you had seen more of Marie. Her charm was really remarkable—it was not only men but women that it struck. She made an immediate conquest of Missie and her mother who didn't at all take to Hoole's or Marmie's irreproachable fiancées—in fact of everyone who came across her.

But I must say I'm deucedly glad she's gone.

Write and give me your nouvelles—and forgive any incoherences in this scrawl. My hand has a palsy of the first quality, and my head is full of noises.

Ever yours,   ERNEST DOWSON

286. *To John Lane*
   [*August–September 1894*]

Bridge Dock

My dear Lane,
   I have had my time so entirely taken up with correspondence and other business arising from my father's sudden death[1] that I am sure you will excuse me for not having communicated with you before, except by a hasty wire.
   I should very much like to see you when it is convenient to you with reference to my stories. Perhaps, if you are in town, or when you return to town, you will give me an appointment.
   I can call upon you any time in the afternoon except between 5 & 6, and almost any time after 6.30.
Yours sincerely, ERNEST DOWSON

John Lane Esq.

1. Alfred Dowson died on 15 August 1894.

287. *To John Lane*
   [*August–September 1894*]

Bridge Dock

My dear Lane,
   I felt rather seedy yesterday but hoped to be cured sufficiently to breakfast with you on Monday.
   To day however I have interviewed my doctor, & he threatens me with a quinzy unless I lie low, & look after my throat. So it is with much regret that I must again postpone our meeting,
Ever yours sincerely ERNEST DOWSON

288. *To Arthur Symons*[1]
 Thursday [*15 November 1894*]

               Bridge Dock

My dear Symons:
 Did I meet you the other night at the Temple or did I dream it? I am just going off to visit Elkin Mathews. I am wavering between 'Blind Alleys' and 'Sentimental Dilemmas' as a title for my stories.[2]
        Ever yours   ERNEST DOWSON

1. Text from Longaker. The date given there, 18 November 1894, is almost certainly in another hand—probably Symons's. We have accordingly dated the letter on the preceding Thursday.
2. The draft contract for the book is printed in Appendix B, p. 437.

289. *To Elkin Mathews*
 [*c. April 1895*]

               Bridge Dock

Dear Mr. Mathews
 Thanks for your note. The order of the stories will do very well as they are. It would certainly be not worth while changing them now.
 Would you please let me have a proof of the dedication,[1] as I should like to see the size of the type used etc.
       Yrs sincerely,   ELLKIN MATHEWS[2]

1. *Dilemmas* was dedicated to A.F. (Adelaide Foltinowicz).
2. Dowson must have been unusually abstracted to sign this letter with Mathews's name and misspell it.

290. *To Elkin Mathews*
  Tuesday [*9 July 1895*]

                 Bridge Dock

Dear Mr Mathews,
  Thank you very much for forwarding review in "Realm" of 'Dilemmas'.[1] I hope to call in shortly to see if you have any others, & to hear how it is going.
  If you could let me have a cheque this week for balance of royalties due on publication—I think it is £3—odd, I shd be much obliged.[2]
        Yours sincerely   ERNEST DOWSON
Elkin Mathews Esq

1. *The Realm* reviewed *Dilemmas* on 21 June 1895.
2. Endorsed by Mathews: 'Cheque £3. 10s. sent 10 July 95 making £7 10s. altogether.'

291. *To Edgar Jepson*
  Monday [*July–August 1895*]

                 Bridge Dock

My dear Jepson,
  I hope you did not expect me on Sat? Stupidly enough I did not realize until the morning of that day when I was on the point of setting out for you—that I had not the remotest notion of your address. I am sending this to Plarr asking him to forward it to you. May we meet soon. I must try & persuade you to visit me here when the climate moderates: at present it is cruelly uninviting.
        Ever yours   ERNEST DOWSON

Frid.
  This has hung about so long having been as usual posted in my pocket that I will add an additional word of apology.
  Are you likely to be in the neighbourhood of Picc. Circus any evening soon?
  If so & you would drop me a wire any day next week except Tuesday appointing a meeting at say 9.15 I should like to have an opportunity of meeting you & telling you of a new & very advanced Review[1] which

1. *The Savoy*, published by Leonard Smithers from January to December 1896. Plans for it were discussed from July 1895 onwards, often on expeditions to Dieppe, to which Dowson paid several visits at this time, usually with

is being founded & where perhaps some of your Barbadian Idylls—it wouldn't matter how swarthy they were—might be casé.

Should you wire to me after about 3. o'clock. 19 Sherwood St. Regent St finds me.

Charles Conder, William Rothenstein, Symons and Beardsley as well as Smithers himself. For the fate of Jepson's contribution see Letter 313.

292. *To Victor Plarr*[1]
[*c. September 1895*]

6 Featherstone Buildings, High Holborn[2]

[He writes of his 'abominable procrastination'.]
My excuse for not having come to you on the Sunday I daresay you will find equally inexcusable but it was simply because I was in such a state of nervous and physical disability that I had not the faintest recollection of having any engagement . . . I expect to be in this country, much as it tortures and maddens me, till Christmas or the New Year.[3]

1. Text from Plarr.
2. Dowson moved to this address after leaving Bridge Dock.
3. In fact he left in October.

293. *To an unidentified correspondent*[1]
[*1895*]

[*Bridge Dock*]

Dear Sir
In reply to your favour of yesterday with regard to our estimate for this steamer, we cannot see how the work can be done at the price you mention. As we are anxious to meet you and retain your business we will reduce our price to £35, which is the actual cost price of the work here.
Trusting

1. This draft letter, which cannot be more precisely dated, is the only relic of Dowson's career as a dock owner. It is written on the back of one sheet of the MS of his story *The Eyes of Pride*.

Part IV
1895-1896

DOWSON had a number of friends in Paris, including Henry Davray, Pierre Louÿs, Yvanhoé Rambosson, Jean de Tinan, Toulouse-Lautrec, Gabriel de Lautrec and Verlaine. Conder was living there and Smithers came over regularly, so that there was entertainment enough as well as sufficient work to keep Dowson happily occupied.

Another friend, or at least acquaintance, was an eccentric Bohemian who was Verlaine's general factotum, known as Bibi-la-Purée. Gabriel de Lautrec, known affectionately as 'le Prince des humoristes', records of this time:

> I heard that my friend Dowson, the English poet, had arrived in Paris, was staying at an hôtel in the quartier latin and was proposing to call upon me. As a matter of courtesy I decided to forestall him and set out to find his hôtel. I asked the number of his room; arriving on the right floor, I knocked and entered. But at the very moment that I crossed the threshold there was a blinding flash. It was Bibi who, probably lent by Verlaine, had taken it upon himself to revive the vestal flame for Dowson. Crouching in front of the hearth he was in the process of putting new life into the fire by rhythmically and liberally sprinkling it with a bottle of petrol, at the serious risk of setting the whole place alight. Meanwhile Dowson, while saying nothing and being ignorant of Parisian-Bibiesque ways of carrying on, nevertheless appeared somewhat daunted by this method of lighting a fire.[1]

Lautrec, who lived on the fourth floor of a building in a cul-de-sac near the Palais Royal, also recorded that Dowson's friend Rambosson used to go there for parties and poetry readings. Rambosson had some kind of connection with a woman who lived in a neighbouring apartment, and used to climb out of the window, work his way along the ledge, and knock at her window. She was never known to open up, but Rambosson would climb back apparently quite satisfied with this dangerous exercise.

At this particular time Dowson's trouble was lack of money.

[1] *Souvenirs des Jours Sans Souci, 1937.*

There was a considerable amount due to him from his parents' estates, but these were so encumbered by the complicated liabilities of Bridge Dock that payment was delayed for several years, during which Dowson had almost no income beyond advances and royalties from Smithers.

Dowson was ill in January, but had recovered by February, when Smithers came over and fixed up the publication of *Verses*. Dowson spent some time with Smithers, Lautrec and Beardsley— with the last named going to the first performance of Wilde's *Salomé* on 11 February. But in his straitened circumstances Paris was evidently too expensive; on the 12th he set out for the Breton village with which he is most closely associated, Pont-Aven.

Pont-Aven was one of the few prettily situated little towns in Southern Brittany and everything about it was guaranteed to attract the tourist, old houses, quaint streets, a small rushing river which ran through charming glades to the sea a few miles away, lovely old woods and shelter from coastal gales. The village attracted many painters, including Gauguin, who arrived in 1886. Renoir came in 1892 and stayed at the more expensive of the two hotels, the Villa Julia; while there he painted nothing but landscapes, because the only model in the village had abandoned posing for prostitution. Gauguin, who was still in Pont-Aven when Renoir arrived, lived at the Hôtel Gloanec. This was a more modest establishment run by Marie-Jeanne Gloanec with two maids, Marie and Louise; all three were characters, and Mme Gloanec had the additional virtue of liking artists of all kinds and not pressing for payment of their bills. Until quite recently many of the villagers owned paintings left behind by artists in settlement of their debts.

Dowson arrived at the Gloanec on the 14th and remained there, with only one short break, for six months, even though his health was deteriorating and the climate did not suit him. He was no longer the dandy of his London days, and he became an object of concern to English-speaking visitors. Among these were Gertrude Atherton, the American novelist, who came with Horace Annesley Vachell. Vachell, an extremely fastidious man, was shocked to find that Dowson's clothes were dirty and his teeth were bad. But it is probable that the accounts which these more respectable acquaintances left at this time were greatly exaggerated. He was certainly still capable of enjoying himself. At one point during his stay he conceived a passion for the wife of the local baker and late one night was indiscreet enough to knock on her door, loudly demanding admittance. The door was opened by the baker, a large man, who promptly knocked him flat.[1]

[1] The procès-verbal will be found in Appendix C.

In June, Dowson's collection of poems, with the modest title *Verses*, was published. The edition consisted of three hundred copies on hand-made paper and thirty on Japanese vellum: Smithers had made it one of the finest of the many fine books of the 'nineties. There was a preface 'For Adelaide' in which Dowson wrote: 'To you, who are my verses, as on some very future day, if you ever care to read them, you will understand, would it not be somewhat trivial to dedicate any one verse, as I may do, in all humility, to my friends? . . . I need not write your name for you at least to know that this and all my work is made for you in the first place . . .' The dedication of single poems to friends was copied from Verlaine, and a number were inscribed to his friends in Paris: *To One in Bedlam* to Henry Davray, *Amor Profanus* to Gabriel de Lautrec, *Flos Lunae* to Yvanhoé Rambosson, as well as others to O'Sullivan, O'Riordan, Smithers and Beardsley. *The Times* in reviewing the book commented on this and added that it was rather alarming to come upon *Extreme Unction. For Lionel Johnson* and *A Requiem. For John Gray* 'when there is no reason to believe that the gentlemen in question are anything but alive and well'.

Throughout the summer Dowson continued to work on *La Pucelle* which he was now editing rather than translating—combining two earlier English versions and rewriting them only in a few places. From time to time he returned to *Adrian Rome* and throughout the year he contributed stories and poems to *The Savoy*. Much of his best work was already behind him, but his talent was certainly not spent. It was at Pont-Aven that he wrote the finest of his short stories, *The Dying of Francis Donne*, and a number of poems which show him working in a new manner in response to the life and landscape of the Breton countryside.

During July and August several friends came to visit Dowson at Pont-Aven, among them Smithers, Moore, Fallows and Lugné-Poe. He also made the acquaintance of a young man named Michael Holland, who travelled with him to Rennes, where they entertained a party of French cavalry officers at their hotel. On this occasion Dowson made the only speech he is ever known to have made in his life, addressing the officers in French in enthusiastic support of Anglo-French alliance.

In the August *Savoy* Arthur Symons discussed *Verses* and fabricated for the first time his Dowson myth—'that curious love of the sordid, so common an affectation of the modern decadent, and with him so expressively genuine, grew upon him . . . and now, indifferent to most things, in the ship-wrecked quietude of a sort of self-exile, he is living, I believe, somewhere on a remote foreign sea-coast'. He sent the proofs of his review to Dowson, whose response was merely to suggest a few minor changes in order to spare some of his older friends any alarm about him. Otherwise he was content to let Symons write as he wished, though he must have smiled at some of the more exaggerated touches. It needed a highly coloured imagination to convert Pont-Aven, that picturesque but civilized resort, no farther from London than is Edinburgh, into 'somewhere on a remote foreign sea-coast'; and much of the article was written in the same key.

The reasons for Dowson's six months' stay in Brittany were far less romantic than Symons suggested. They were simply economy and quiet in which to work. By the end of the summer, however, the solitude of the place outweighed these advantages. His friends had all gone, and he decided to go too. He returned, after a year's absence, to London.

294. *Postcard*[1] *to Leonard Smithers*[2]

[*Postmark 2 October 1895*]

[*Ypres*][3]

Have you wondered what has become of us? We found Bruges crammed with English and came here: perfectly quiet place . . . but

---

1. Text from *Two Hundred Books from the Library of Richard Butler Glaenzer* (New York, 1911).
2. Leonard Charles Smithers (1861–1907) settled in London about 1890. For five years he was in partnership with H. S. Nichols in a bookselling and publishing firm (whose list included Burton's translation of *The Arabian Nights*.) In 1895 he set up in business on his own. His first book was Symons's *London Nights*, published in June 1895, and it was through Symons that he was able to recruit Beardsley, who had recently been dismissed from *The Yellow Book*, to be principal illustrator for *The Savoy*. He published a number of finely produced editions of standard classics as well as books by Dowson, Symons, Vincent O'Sullivan and Max Beerbohm's *Caricatures of Twenty-five Gentlemen*, but his business depended chiefly on the sale of rare books and erotica until 1898, when he scored a popular success with Wilde's *The Ballad of Reading Gaol*. He became bankrupt in 1899, and thereafter scraped a living by issuing pirated editions of Wilde and 'proofs' of Beardsley drawings.
3. Dowson had left London to travel through Belgium with Conal Holmes O'Connell O'Riordan, Irish actor and novelist (under the name F. Norreys Connell) (1874–1948), whose first novel, *The House of Strange*

owing to a great demand for lodgings by officiers and sous-officiers, we found it . . . impossible to find what we wanted. Are bearing therefore in the direction of France. E.D.

[Added in O'Riordan's hand: Peut-être à Dieppe à la mode Dowson.]
Not if I know it! E.D.

> *Women*, was published in 1895. His next book, *The Fool and His Heart* (1896), was dedicated to Dowson. In 1910 he succeeded Synge as Director of the Abbey Theatre, Dublin.

295. *Postcard to Charles Conder*[1]
[*Postmark 12 October 1895*]

Hôtel des Médicis, 214 Rue Saint-Jacques, Paris

Dear Conder

So sorry to have missed you the other day. I dropped a card in an obscure receptacle, so obscure that I doubt your finding it & therefore write this line to let you know that I have taken up my abode here for the present. Write & let me know when & where we may meet. I am working very hard & contemplate an exile of years—though not here I think if it grows much colder. It is beastly cold here on the Boulevard des Capucines where I write this. Mind & write

Ever yrs. ERNEST DOWSON

1. English artist (1868–1909) famous for his designs for fans and his water-colours painted on silk. He had been commissioned by Smithers to make the wood-cut illustrations for Balzac's *La Fille aux Yeux d'Or*, which Dowson was translating.

296. *To Arthur Moore*
[*c. 15 October 1895*]

214 Rue Saint-Jacques.

Mon cher Vieux,

Here we are, established, after some wanderings (Connell[1] & I)—in fact we have been here a week to-day We tried Ypres but found it impossible to get rooms unless we took them for about 9 months wh.

1. i.e. O'Riordan.

was too awful to think of. Came on to Lille but had something of the
same difficulty in establishing ourselves so finally pushed on in desperation here. We have taken these rooms here in the Quartier for a month
definitely but find it almost impossible to keep it on. The rooms are
cheap enough & one can eat cheap enough but it is impossible to live
in Paris without sitting in cafés & they mount up. We have therefore
determined to move on after a month to Brittany & I am writing to ask
you to let me have by return the name of your cheap pension at
(Pontaven?) in order that I may write & ask what terms they will take
us for. I have written to Le Faouet but fear that Mme Mitouard may
be too dear. I want to work it including rooms for about 100 francs a
month—at most 180 a head We can just do that here but with infinite
discomfort & privation: i.e. Connell smokes & drinks nothing in order
to have his two square meals & I tighten my belt in order to allow myself
a sufficiency of cigarettes & absinthe. As for women . . . we dare not
even look at them.

Therefore I think the sooner we can shift to a village where food
is plentiful & cider sufficient the better.

I hope everything goes on well in London; I feel as if I had ~~not~~ left
it for years. I have been working hard but can not proceed to the novel[2]
until I have knocked off La Fille wh. should be this week. Mind & write
by return. With love to all

T à t   ED THE EXILE

P.S. Have kept this open till the post came in. Could you possibly
manage to let me have a fiver by return also? Some money which we
were expecting has apparently gone to Lille & there may be some
delay in getting it. I can let you have it shortly—as some is due to me
from Smithers next week.   ED

2. The long-neglected *Adrian Rome.*

297. *Postcard to Henry Davray*[1]
[*Postmark 24 October 1895*]

214 Rue Saint-Jacques

My dear Davray,

I hardly expected that the first letter I should ever write to you
would be dated from your own street in your own town. I came here,

1. French author and journalist (1873–1944), for many years principal reviewer of English books for *Le Mercure de France* and a distinguished
translator.

more or less by accident from Belge & expect to be here until Nov. I
called on you, but heard you were in London still—a city which I hope
not to revisit for years—and that you would not be back for a quinzaine. That has nearly passed. Let me know when you are once more
chez vous and we will meet, I hope.

Tout à vous   ERNEST DOWSON

298. *To Edgar Jepson*
   [*c. 13 November 1895*]

214 Rue Saint-Jacques

My dear Jepson
    It was charming to hear from you, and I ought to have written
before but Connell had written to you (he does most of our correspondence) only a day or two before I received your letter, so that I gathered
you had news of me.[1] My own news is of the scantiest; beyond the
obvious fact that I am, and have been for some 5 weeks in Paris, and
that j'y probablement resterai. That is to say unless you feel inclined
to try Brittany with me in another month. The Hotel Gloanec, Pont-
aven, Finisterre, (recommended strongly by Moore and sundry Parisian
painters I have met) offers board and lodging, including cider for 85
francs a month. I should be strongly tempted to try this for 2 or 3
months in company; therefore think it over. I doubt if I could stand it
alone. Connell has made arrangements with a married couple[2] to whom
I have introduced him who live about 2 hours from Paris, to be taken
in as a boarder, and I think he will be more comfortable there than he
has been here. He leaves me in a 4tnight. For we have rooms in a *hotel
meublé* where nothing can be got in the house and Connell's notion of
comfort is as deeply rooted in a sense of being able to eat and drink
entirely on his own premises as mine is in the opposite facility.
    Failing a companion, therefore, to the Breton shore, I shall probably
remain in Paris which suits me excellently. I know a heap of persons
and get as many cards for private views as if I were a celebrity.
    I was uneasy at first over your remarks on the Symons libel action.[3]
He is (*don't show this to anyone*)—a silly b——r. But I should think he
must get a verdict, and even if he doesn't, Smithers is so little dis-

---

1. O'Riordan wrote to Jepson on 30 October. His letter is in the Redpath
   Library, McGill University.
2. The Noblets at Mons-par-Donnemarie.
3. There is no record of these proceedings, which presumably were settled or
   withdrawn before reaching the courts.

turbed about it, that he has inspired in me something of his own security.

In any case I doubt if the "Savoy" will be materially affected. I have sent off my story to it,[4] and am tolerably satisfied with it—in fact it is the best I have done—except perhaps that in the "Yellow Book". By the way, Harland[5] has been in Paris and we met curiously enough at Bullier's, on the very day on which both he and Smithers had arrived in Paris. I introduced the rivals and for the rest of their common sojourn here we foregathered and got on famously. Teixeira also turned up here and called on me. I have heard news of you and frequently of Edwards,[6] from Davray who is now de retour. Write to me soon and tell me London news and if it would not bother you too much send me an occasional *Daily Chronicle*. I have not seen a single English paper since I left England—how many years ago? Also, if you have Smith's address would you send him mine and ask him to write to me—or send him this letter. I have lost his but I should like to write to him.

I find I can do considerably more work here than in town and if I am to keep it up and do not find it too expensive would prefer to remain here than hibernate in the country. If I had been alone, indeed, I should have come away here straight, and avoided our useless and expensive Belgian campaign of which doubtless you have heard from Connell. I have run across Verlaine, quite by chance, and am going to call on him next week. Also Vaughan[7] and Conder are living here. Although one never quite escapes from the "horror of life" one avoids it better here. No more now: write soon—by return if you are not too busy—and tell me how things move, and if there is any chance of your joining me. If you see Moore tell him that I am writing tout de suite—but I am really working very hard and find almost every moment occupied. Remember me affectionately to all the brethren.

Tout à toi   ERNEST DOWSON

---

4. *The Eyes of Pride*, begun before he left Bridge Dock and published in *The Savoy*, January 1896.
5. Henry Harland (1861–1905), American novelist and editor of *The Yellow Book*.
6. Osman Edwards, master at St. Paul's School and contributor to *The Savoy* (1864–1936).
7. Possibly William Wyamar Vaughan (1865–1938), who had been at New College and the University of Paris. He married (1898) Margaret, third daughter of John Addington Symonds. He was Headmaster of Rugby 1921–1931.

299. *To Samuel Smith*[1]

　[*c. 20 November 1895*]

[*214 Rue Saint-Jacques*]

　　You mustn't imagine, as I gather from your letter you perhaps did, that my 'crisis' was sentimental. God forbid. I have just answered my *damigella's* last letter and we are on the most affectionate terms—at least I think so—that we have been on for years. You must go and see her when you are in London—*please* do that, and speak of me as freely as you like, *only do not* speak of my exile as being so prolonged as I presume it will be. I always write to her with the intention of returning in a month or two—and so I may—*for a fortnight!* but I doubt if ever I shall make my home in England again. My great desire is that the Foltinowiczs will carry out their long-conceived idea of returning to Germany. Then I would go there and join them. But I have taken a great dislike to London. I really came away on a sort of mad impulse— which I have not since regretted—because I was financially broke and . . . somewhat sensationally I admit, but not in the state of desperation which I believe is rumoured about me. *Par exemple*, dear Marmie, who has written me letters full of the most noble offers and sentiments writes to me in his last, received two days ago: 'I have created a sort of mist of trouble, vague as ghosts in a dream, with which I surround you. It forms a sort of halo of sorrow for you and excites the tears and sympathy of those who live and admire you from afar!!!'

　　Do tell him (don't show him this letter) *do* suggest to him, without hurting his feelings, for I know he has really a great affection for me, and it pleases him to give me an 'atmosphere', that I don't want no halo of this kind and extremely object to being wept over, I am not remarkably prosperous nor particularly happy—who is? But I *do not* go about in Paris with a halo of ghosts and tears, having been gifted by God with a sense—common to you and myself but to how many of our other friends?—of humour! I occasionally smile, and even in Paris, at a late hour of the night, and Paris is later than London, have been known to laugh.

　　Write soon, *mon très cher*, I implore you. And if you see Missie, tell her to write to me often, and if you could convey to her, not *from* me, but as an expression of your own personal opinion that to get a letter from her is my chiefest pleasure in life, you will be doing me a favour, and falling short of the extreme truth which perhaps it is not yet seasonable to say.

---

1. Text from Gawsworth.

300. *To Conal O'Riordan*
   Tuesday [*? 26 November 1895*]

Café d'Harcourt

Cher Vieux,

I have been lunching here, money having arrived, & must send you a line to wish you an happy inauguration in your new home. I was very seedy all yesterday—lit my fire & stayed at home, drowsing, all day until 8, when I went dined at a very decent place in the Boul. Miche. which I found, for 1.25. Then I came back, went to bed, had, for once in my life, a fairly decent night, & actually rose & breakfasted at our Crémerie at 8 AM. I then went for a walk to the Gare Montparnasse, looked at the hole in the station[1] & returned to find Smithers' letter.

I have bought a conical hat—black—& think of having my hair cropped very short so that it will suit me better. I feel much better today except for my specific disease which increases by leaps & starts.

Have heard no news of my fracas with the Snailmer-chant:[2] so trust it is all happily over.

I saw Léopold[3] in here just now, but he has received "a little money from Petersburg" so has gone off to the races. Write me a line to say how you are getting on, if you have not done so already—or even if you have & remember me "mes meilleurs amitiés" to the Noblet. I hope you lunched to-day as well as I did.

Tout à toi   ERNEST DOWSON

1. On 22 October 1895 an express train from Granville crashed through the barriers and the station wall; the engine and one coach fell fifty feet into the Place de Rennes.
2. He clearly means snail-merchant, but the reading given in the text is undoubtedly the correct one and there may be some further allusion.
3. Leopold Nelken, a Polish medical student and Dowson's closest friend in Paris, dedicatee of *My Lady April* in *Verses*.

301. *To Conal O'Riordan*
   [*late November 1895*]

214 Rue Saint-Jacques

My dear Connell,

By some oversight you have run away with the key of No 15.[1] The proprietor has asked me to write to you & remind you of this: I feel that

1. O'Riordan's room in the Hôtel des Médicis.

with my natural propensity to put off, unless I write at once I shall get into trouble with my proprietor. This must be my excuse for writing shortly. Further news at a more convenient season,

T à t.   ERNEST DOWSON

Brasserie des Femmes-en-Rut

302. *To Conal O'Riordan*
Heure d'apéritif [*early December 1895*]

Café d'Harcourt

Dear Exile,

Your letter agreably to hand. I am sorry the Mons-par-Donnemarie food is not all that it should be, but I had my suspicion that the déjeuner we partook of was a sample to inspire confidence. (Par exemple, don't leave this letter about—) I rather emmerde myself since your departure. Was seedy yesterday & stayed in bed & sent for the ordinary litre of milk. To day got up early, took the steam train from the Odéon to Bourge-la-Reine & had a charming walk to Antony where I lunched, returning by the train to the Gay-Lussac station. The country was charming, but the trees more decayed than at Donnemarie. I have had a letter at last from my young lady. She tells me that there is a "Trilby boom"[1] in London now—everything, hats, collars, coats & mantles à la Trilby. It is also on at the theatre quelque part. I have also had an ennuyeux letter from Horne: Jepson has, I fear, successfully embroiled me with everybody.[2] I have just written to ask what the devil he means by it! Have received a line from Smithers & the proofs of my story. He says he is simply waiting for money to come over. Léopold, for whom I am now waiting, received certain roubles from Russia, the day before yesterday & promptly got extremely drunk here & retired with a most exceptionally ordinary woman to whom he probably gave £100. By the way there is an amusing paragraph, dealing with us, inserted by Rambosson, in the "Nouvelle France" & I am told also in the Écho de Paris describing an imaginary reception by "M. Henri Davray l'orientaliste dans son appartement superbe aux glaces, Rue Fleurus, pour fêter les poètes anglais Ernest Dowsog et O'Connell Norreys" at which

---

1. George du Maurier's novel *Trilby* (1894), dramatized by Paul Potter, was produced by Beerbohm Tree at the Haymarket Theatre on 30 October 1895. It led to a brief fashion-craze (often satirized in *Punch*) whose lasting legacy is the trilby hat.
2. See Letter 307.

assisted X. . . Y. . . Z. . . . et Marcel Schwob, Gabriel de Lautrec, Yvanhoé Rambosson, le Docteur Charrier (I put down the names I remember, but there were many more). The honours were done by "Madame D. Davray resplendissante dans une robe noire et or." And music was played by the "pianiste anglaise bien connue Miss Ethel Jepson et le compositeur Ruschoff Bey". I will send you the paper— show it to Noblet, but let him take it au sérieux. He will probably realize what great men we are & either give you decent food or reduce your pension.

I ran across Lautrec[3] the other night & am going to lunch with him on Sunday.

I have no other news that I can think of to consummate this page. Write me a letter by return. I am consumed with ennui, & start for Auvergne at the end of the month.

By the way I am devoutly thankful, much as I miss you that I was not idiot enough to ~~come to~~ share your rustication except for one thing which your letter informs me of—your visit to the Curé. It is hard lines after all my efforts and ambitions, that you should be moving—you who probably don't appreciate it—in the best ecclesiastical society while I do not even know a seminarist. I feel towards you, as you would towards me if I had dined with the General Saussier[4] & he had talked to me for hours on the art of fortification & sent me a MSS on "The right employment of cavalry in a siege"

Write at once, dear Rusticus, & I am,

always yours,   ERNEST DOWSON

3. Gabriel de Lautrec, French author and journalist (1867–1938); at this time a leading contributor to *Le Courrier Français*; dedicatee of *Amor Profanus* in *Verses*.

4. Félix Gustave Saussier, French soldier and politician (1828–1905), was Military Governor of Paris 1884–1886.

303. *To John Gray*

[*December 1895*]

214 Rue Saint-Jacques

My dear Gray,

It is many years since I heard from, or, indeed, of, you at any length, but the news has just come to me of an approaching volume of your verse.[1] If you have a copy to spare, do not forget me: if you have not,

1. *Spiritual Poems*, 1896.

let me know the publisher & if it is published by anyone else than John Lane, I will procure it, if it be procurable, Via Mathews. At any rate I must have it: I have your last book—one of the very few books that I carry about with me on my travels, & I was only wondering a few days ago when you would once more throw out a volume.

Mine will be out shortly, & I will send you a copy.

Do you know this place from which I write?[2] Six years ago—(but certainly it was in the summer) I thought it the prettiest place in the world. Now the Palace looks to me like a barrack, the church is the very image of a half-bred dachshund & the terrace—well, I did not go on the terrace; I shivered when I looked through the grille. And yet I have lunched exceedingly well, & the petite femme, who lunched with me, is exceedingly pretty, . . . and the weather is remarkably fine for December . . and what a thing it is to have been young!

However, send me, or tell me where I may procure your poems. I move soon, East or West or South, if I have the energy, but the above address will find me, and in any case I shall remain there till the end of the year.

By the way I have dined once or twice lately with Pierre Louÿs,[3] who asks constantly after you. Have you seen the delightfully scabrous roman which he brings out now in the Mercure de France? I have a story in the forthcoming new "Savoy" which I should like you to read, also a poem,[4] but that is rather pommade.

Write to me if you have either time or inclination,

Tout Votre   ERNEST DOWSON

2. This letter is written on the paper of the Hôtel Colbert, Saint Germain-en-Laye.
3. French novelist and poet (1870–1925) who had met Gray in 1892 when they were both in Wilde's entourage. The 'scabrous roman' is *Esclavage*, which began serialization in August 1895. It was published in book form as *Aphrodite* in 1896.
4. *Impenitentia Ultima*, reprinted in *Verses*.

304. *To Conal O'Riordan*

Monday [*9 December 1895*]

214 Rue Saint-Jacques

Very dear Gossip,

Delighted to receive your letter. Here too, the cold—but only yesterday & today has been biting, and a high N.N.E. wind has prevailed. I am in an awful state of penury & unless Smithers or someone else (a debtor) to whom I appealed on Sat. respond by tomorrow I know not how I shall exist. I dined en famille ~~yes~~ on Saturday with the Davrays, & ~~on S~~ yesterday called on the most noble Vicomte de Lautrec, who insisted on my staying to dine with him. It was a most charming & original dinner; his younger brother shares his apartment, & cooks & apparently does all the house work. The other guests were, the poet Wattein,[1] an anonymous poet, & an elderly professor at the Lycée, of which Lautrec is also a professor. After dinner which was most creditable to Henri de Lautrec's culinary talent we drank rum & worked hankey-pankey with planchette at which Lautrec & the professor are adepts. We got a message from Satan but he appeared to have nothing of the slightest importance to say. We then took haschish, & eventually all, with the exception of the elderly Professor, slept on sofas & mattresses at Lautrec's. A charming evening, but today I have felt a little worn & weary. You will like Lautrec extremely though, & I am sorry we had not enough energy to seek him out before you left. But Passy is a hell of a way off. I write this at the D'Harcourt & Leopold has just entered, so I must cut it short. If he asks me to dine I shall not refuse, for I have just 1.50 in the world. I hope & pray money arrives tomorrow: if not & you have any spare cash would you send me 10 francs. Do this unless I wire to you: I will wire if money reaches me. Au revoir, carissime Rustice. Write—write—write. It is not in my disposition to write letters but see how voluminous I get.

T à t.   ERNEST DOWSON
of Paris

I will send you a most amusing Caran d'Ache[2] "Journal" with a military story in it if you will not mind after perusing it sending it on to

> Arthur Moore Esq.
> 5 Loudoun Rd
> London N.W

He adores Caran d'Ache.

(Continuation).

Leopold was called away by a friend so I have returned chez moi to dine on the most frugal scale that I have yet contrived—I don't count my litre of milk days when I lie in bed. My dinner is one longish roll 5c. one Brie cheese 20c. ½ bottle red wine 50c. I had an absinthe at the D'Harcourt & have spent something on tobacco & cigarette papers. And curiously enough I do not feel depressed at this meal in my room, although I would sooner be dining at the D'Harcourt. I have a splendid

---

1. Not identified.
2. Eminent French cartoonist (1858–1909); a frequent contributor to *Le Journal* and *Figaro*.

fire, twopence in the world, & only complain—(but Heaven or Smithers send me some money tomorrow!) that I am in such bad company—the only company I can not stand—my own! I feel like working too. Curiously enough also & secondly the exact opposite in the matter of my hours & habits to what I anticipated after your departure has happened. It is probably owing to the fact that when you were with me I depended on you for all knowledge of the time of day & knew you would call me when you were ready for déjeuner, whereas now I am utterly at sea when I awake as to whether it is 8 or 12—but the fact remains, I am almost invariably up & out by nine o'clock now. This is not an economy to me, because it means that after a petit déjeuner at the Crémerie I get hungry again & have to indulge in a 1.15 déjeuner at 1.0. But I will pause, (this descriptive passage has reminded me that I must dine)—when I have finished my sumptuous repast I will continue.

[Sketch of meal on table, the items numbered and listed below: 1. Bread. 2. Cheese 3. Tooth-Glass 4. ½ Bot. 5. Various literary effects.]

Wednesday night [*11 December 1895*]

I did not send this letter because no money came—the gales in the channell having disorganized the postal service—& I preferred to spend my two pence on bread, rather than on a three sou stamp. I confess I did not enjoy yesterday!!!! But I had philosophy enough yesterday, even yesterday!—and can you imagine from my previous Monday's beginning, what yesterday was like? to quote in anticipation "Forsan et haec olim meminisse juvabit." . . . . And this morning lo there was a letter & £1—. & I went out with tears of gratitude in my eyes & had an absinthe & afterwards a breakfast à 1.25 at my recently discovered rest[nt]. My seclusion of yesterday had given me a sort of letch of adventure, so I took a return ticket to Sceaux (80c., & the third class carriages are sumptuous!) & walked thence some kilos to Fontenay-aux-Roses: is it not an adorable name? And the place too is adorable: I felt inclined to look about for lodgings. The East wind of yesterday had utterly gone; except that the trees were a little worn & weary, it might have been a very fine day in spring. And I drank my beer outside a rural café & wrote a letter, & concocted verses[3] and generally basked for an hour or so: then strolled back to Sceaux & so back to Paris to dine. One has one's fortunate days sometimes—do you remember "Marius"?[4]—so that after my expansion of the afternoon I was not surprised that I should strike quite by accident on the most attractive of cheap restaurants that I have yet encountered—a little place in the Place St André

3. Possibly *Soli cantare periti Arcades*, first published in *Verses*.
4. The phrase itself does not occur in *Marius the Epicurean*, but there are others like it in Chapters XVII, XIX and XX.

des Arts, near the Place St. Michel. The cuisine was wonderful: it was
à la carte, & including coffee my bill reached the sum of f1.75. When
you come back—you must run up for a day soon, we will dine there.
Après, I fell in such a Christian mood—even towards my relations,
(because it suddenly struck me that however prosperous & well conditioned they may be, their malice & meanness, even from a purely
pagan point of view hurts them far more than it can ever me) après I
took an omnibus to the Bourse and got into Notre Dame des Victoires
just at the fag end of the sermon before Benediction. I had never been
to the church before,—only know of it from Huysman's marvelous
novel,[5] which, by the way, you should posess, if your own novel deals
with a reconciliation to Catholicism. But I was immensely impressed
by the sort of wave of devotion which thrills through the whole crowded
congregation,—I had fancied Huysmans had exaggerated it—: but the
reality exceeds his description & I can imagine no other church in
Paris, no other church anywhere, perhaps, except Lourdes, where one
may have the same experience. It makes me afraid to go back there,
for fear it should move me too much. Because—although I know sooner
or later I must put on the dust & ashes, there are things I care about
so much, which I want to do first. And I am afraid, or rather certain,
that after all this long time of abstinence, when I once do bring myself to the point of reconciliation, it will be so horribly serious, and
it will be all up with my work and so on . . . However, let us return to
our muttons. I am writing this very unnecessary scrawl, which I hope
won't bore you too much, in an arm chair, by a noble fire, in No 14,
my paper being supported by an exercise book on my knee & this fact,
& the uncertain light must excuse sundry blots & uncertainties in the
writing. It is not very late for I came straight back here from N.D. de
V. but I suppose it is the middle of the night with you. I wish you were
back here. My plans are utterly vague, but probably after Smithers'
visit, which he tells me in his letter that arrived today, may be at any
moment, I shall decide something. I don't think I shall stay here; I
may go to Florence; I may get a room like this at some convenient
suburb—the suburbs here are not in the least like anything within
thirty miles of London—such as St Germain, Chantillon, Sceaux or
Fontenay; I may go to Cannes where I am told I can get a room for
about f40–50. If you get tired of Mons after your month or arrange
definitely to get tired of it by the end of Dec. I will go to Brittany with
you & postpone my other projects: but I can not face it alone. Of these
things we will talk after Smithers' visit. Write soon, not to say immediately: I quite realized Noblet was economical as it is only in the
nature of the bourgeois French to be—I told you so in Paris—& I can
see with my own eyes how he waters the ink. But send me a sample
menu of déj. & dinner. It will be instructive. And also describe to me

5. *En Route* (1895).

your personal relations with "Mons, Madame et Bébé" not to mention the dogs.

Always yours   ERNEST DOWSON

As this letter-journal extends over several days, I number it for your convenience.[6]   ED

6. Most of this letter is written on small scraps of paper and each piece is numbered.

305. *To Arthur Moore*

[*11 December 1895*]

214 Rue Saint Jacques

Mon cher Vieux,

You cannot imagine with what delight I received your letter. I began to fancy that everyone had abandoned me; for my letters are few & far between & even the faithful Marmie has not written to me for a fortnight. My many thanks for the Balzac: it is very useful, but I fear I shall have to consult (when I have an entrée) the Bibliothèque du Panthéon which is close by me, before I can complete my preface.[1] I am quite alone now, Connell having departed to live en famille with my old friend Noblet in the country some two hours & a half from here. He writes me amusing, semi-despairing letters about the food which they give him & the discomforting economies which they practise, but as he suffers from asthma from time to time, he prefers Mons-par-Donnemarie with all its discomforts, to Paris, in our hotel meublé, where if one is indisposed one lies in bed & starves until one recovers sufficiently to crawl out & eat at the nearest place of comestibles. I have extreme moments of depression, however, since he has retired—so much so that unless I realized how impossible it would be for me to live *en famille*, as he does, with not particularly interesting provincial French folk, I should take a ticket & join him. Therefore, write to me, mon cher, as often as you can, if it is only a line, & you will be doing more charity than you can conceive of. Indeed, my only regular communication with England comes from Effingham House[2] & Sherwood St. I don't know that I have much news of my doings to recount to you. I

1. To his translation of *La Fille aux Yeux d'Or.*
2. Smithers's office in Arundel Street, Strand.

have lunched & dined with Pierre Louÿs once or twice—(it was to him
if you remember, to whom Oscar dedicated Salomé[3]). I also ran across
Lautrec—I forget if you met him with me in town? this summer? &
dined with him t'other day & took haschish with him & a select party
without much result. He is very much interested in nous autres litérateurs anglais, & reads English greatly, so that I have promised to send
him our roman. Would you mind writing to Heinemann & asking him
to send a copy? I have already done so in the case of Pierre Louÿs, &
I don't want to bother him again. Of course when you get an account
in again—I suppose there will be one in March—you will deduct from
anything due to me the charge made for these copies: (there was one to
Mrs. Wilde.[4]) But if you don't mind sending a card to Heinemann in
this case I shall be obliged. The address is

> M. le Vicomte de Lautrec,
> 38, Rue Desbordes-Valmore,
> Passy, Paris.

I have been out for a day in the country all to-day, walking, loung-
ing & writing verses in rustic cabarets. The environs of Paris are certainly most charming: in half an hour one is in as perfectly rural a
place—going South—as one would be in two hours starting from
London. And the weather is marvellous. There has been a little rain
(no fog) & yesterday & Sunday were sharp from the N.E. wind, but to
day has been perfect. At Fontenay-aux-Roses I drank my bock, basking
outside the café, & except for the decrepitude of the trees—although
they are still, many of them, in foliage—I had fancied myself in a very
precocious end of April. And, only once, since I have been in Paris,
have I carried a *pardessus*. I am keeping the roman until Smithers
returns: he writes me to-day that I may expect him at any moment. He
shall bear it back to you. And I hope to proceed à grands sauts: for certainly I can work far better here than in London. I can not understand
about your story[5] for I know Symons was keen on having it. I will ask
Smithers—who is practically ~~its~~ editor—about it on his arrival. Have
you seen the prospectus? Write soon, I implore you, even if you have
nothing to say. I am in a pleasant hour to-day, but I wallow constantly
in blackest sloughs of despond, when even the sight of your handwriting on a blank post-card would cheer me.

always yours   ERNEST DOWSON

I am sending you a "Journal" with an intensely funny Caran d'Ache—

---

3. The original French edition of 1893. The English version (1894) was
   dedicated to Lord Alfred Douglas.
4. Dowson had visited Wilde in May 1895 when he was on bail before his
   final trial, and in February 1896 he again took the trouble to write to
   Mrs. Wilde, who was now living in Italy.
5. For *The Savoy*. It did not appear.

but *don't* open it en famille, for it is a little coarse. I sent you the other one for the Nayve[6] evidence: it struck me as exquisitely humourous. *Do* send me a Chronicle. I have had one "Truth" & one "Star" since leaving England.

6. On 5 November, after a long and sensational trial at Bourges, the Marquis de Nayve was acquitted on the charge brought by his wife that he had murdered her illegitimate son.

306. *To Conal O'Riordan*
[*? 13 December 1895*]

214 Rue Saint-Jacques

My dear Conal,

You must be thinking me a fearful brute, but I did not get your letter until yesterday, having been seedy & in bed and yesterday also I was a prisoner in my chamber. Rambosson[1] came to see me & I gave him my letter—a long one—to post wh. probably has reached you. To day I am all right again & I enclose a *mandat* for 20f. I have kept the balance of 5f. to buy the guides, which I will do tomorrow or on Monday. I hope this involuntary delay on my part hasn't seriously inconvenienced you, but if so you have all my sympathy (moi qui sait la dèche)—at any rate you have had your food, but I during the 24 hours which—if Rambosson posted my letter—you will dimly imagine from the ". . . . . . ." was practically foodless.

By the way I hope you will succeed in cashing the enclosed document in less time than it took me to obtain it. ~~I am~~ It is the first time I have ever "dealt" with a French postal order & I took *half an hour* without exaggeration getting it: and I signed enough documents to have set me up in London for some years in a promising Chancery suit. Write soon.

T à t.   ERNEST

I don't write at length now for fear of missing the post. I dined with Strong[2] last night, & tonight go to dine with Lautrec.

1. Yvanhoé Rambosson (b. 1872), French poet, whose first book, *Le Verger Doré*, appeared in 1895; dedicatee of *Flos Lunae* in *Verses*.
2. Rowland Strong (1865–1924), Paris correspondent of *The Observer*. He later played a prominent part in the Dreyfus affair by publishing an alleged confession by Major Esterhazy in September 1898.

307. *To Arthur Moore*
   [*c. 13 December 1895*]

214 Rue Saint-Jacques

Mon cher Vieux,

My many, many thanks for the 'Chronicle': but why not a specimen of your handwriting my most unworthy & malingering collaborator? I am writing this while I wait for the English train which should, according to latest dispatches, bring the person of the publisher of the "Savoy". It is due here at 7.P.M. but I gather from the news of gales & tempests in the Channel that it may arrive at any time between now & ten. Have you heard of the fuss about the picture on the prospectus— alleged to be indecent?[1] I hear Jepson was especially asinine about it— as he joined in a ~~protest~~ threat with Geo. Moore[2] & others to withdraw his contribution unless the prospectus was changed, and I hear made more fuss than all the rest put together—whereas—and this is richly humourous—his own contribution is a story so confessedly indecent that he is afraid & has refused to *sign it,* for fear it should damage him scholastically. I wish by the way, if you see Jepson, you would tactfully convey to him that I am not particularly gratified by his constituting himself a sort of emissary between myself & Mathews in the matter of my poems.[3] Before I left town I was speaking of trying to get some definite offer from Mathews for the poems & he offered to go & see him on the matter—he did not even *know* Mathews mind you. I told him definitely to do nothing of the kind & said that anything of that sort I was not able to negotiate myself by letter, I should ask *you* to arrange for me. There the matter rested until I received a letter from Jepson the other day, offering terms, advising acceptance of same & generally writing as a recognized go-between between Mathews & myself. I thought it so impertinent that I have not troubled to answer it. Will you, mon cher, therefore as delicately or as *forcibly* as you like, suggest to Jepson on the first occasion, that by interfering in my affairs he is not assisting me but on the contrary seriously compromising me both in my relations with Mathews & Horne. By doing this, cher vieux, if you don't mind, you will be doing me a great favour & saving me from the necessity of writing in rather strong terms to Jepson himself. By word of mouth this sort of hint can be conveyed more pleasantly than by writing. But if you have *any* objection in the least to conveying my

1. Beardsley's design, a portly John Bull, contained a slight but unmistakable indecency, which was easily expurgated.
2. Irish novelist (1852–1933). His only contribution to *The Savoy* was a translation from Mallarmé, published in the number for July 1896.
3. Mathews had been advertising Dowson's poems for several months as a volume in the *Diversi Colores* series edited by Horne. Dowson had by now almost decided to give the book to Smithers. See Letters 311 and 320.

meaning, let me know, if you will, quam celerrime, for the one thing I am determined on is to make it quite plain to Jepson that there shall be no more of this interference.

Enough of a disagreeable subject. I have some rather charming Caran d'Aches in the Journal to send you toute à l'heure. Let me hear from you soon. I will send back the chapters of the roman to you by Smithers. No more now. I go to the station

Tout à toi   ERNEST DOWSON

308. *To Conal O'Riordan*
    [*c. 16 December 1895*]

214 Rue Saint-Jacques

My dear Connell,

Forgive my tardiness: but you must know by this time how in-grained & incurable is my habit of procrastination. I got your letter last night—or rather this morning for I entered after a night with notre Léonard at 7. AM. The storm of which you send so graphic a description must have coincided with the one which conveyed Smithers from England. You will have heard of his arrival here. I am writing this in the Rue Druout while he deals with a bookseller across the street. The "Savoy" business was very foolish "much ado etc" but I gather from a letter reaching me today from Jepson that he & the other objectors believed themselves entirely in the right. I have conveyed to them my own opinion in the frankest terms: viz that they are a parcel of idiots. We have pursued our usual courses since Smithers arrived—varied by a visit to a prison to call on his friend who is confined in St. Pélagie. We go & *lunch* with the said prisoner tomorrow: is it not a charming idea? I shall certainly write an article on it.[1] Nothing could be more pleasant than the surroundings of the captives of that grisly dungeon. Except that two rather sleepy gaolers sit at a little table by the door & object to our friend's leaving he is entirely free apparently to wander where he wills. His room is one for which one would pay 60 francs at the Hotel de Médicis: he gets it free. His meals are provided by the state and are sent in from a restaurant. He is apparently free to ask his friends to lunch. He is not stinted in society—for instance when we called yesterday his three children, his mother-in-law & his wife were sitting with him. There is a library in the gaol & a benevolent govern-ment provides him with *12* newspapers daily! (This is *literally true* although it seems incredible) And a climax which will especially appeal

_____

1. He appears not to have done so.

to you, he burns wood logs in his stove & has a pile of them enough to
stock a fortress. He can smoke also—not only in his room—but about
the establishment. Why, oh why am I not a prisoner of Saint-Pélagie?
I thought of Oscar & marvelled at the quaintness of this adorable
country.

No more now—I must join Smithers. Write soon. I will write again
tout de suite. Love to the Noblets.

T à t.   E D

PS. I suppose it was owing to the improper overtures which you made
to Maxime that the poor boy was sacked? If it had been a chamber
maid it would have been only excusable.

309. *To Conal O'Riordan*
[*22 December 1895*]

214 Rue Saint-Jacques

My dear Conal,

I enclose this line in a letter answering Noblet's ~~letter~~ invitation
which of course I have gladly accepted. I was thinking of asking you to
come up here for Xmas, but it will be just as well *chez vous*—not that I
approve as a rule of celebrating that fête, à l'Anglais—it should rather
be celebrated, at least in my case, & perhaps with you, as the *jour des
morts*—All Souls Day. But it struck me that we two might seasonably
spend it together. I haven't heard from you, but your key has arrived.
Smithers, Leopold & myself had a very gay evening together before he
left last Friday, & our two friends got very friendly; even, Smithers
accepted a loan of twenty francs from Leopold, as he had run short.
To day, when I was in bed, who should arrive but John-Paul-Emmanuel
Ashworth,[1] very drunk,—the Newhaven–Dieppe boat having taken
nine hours instead of four in crossing & J. P. E. Ashworth having spent
the extra five hours in standing whiskey to the crew & himself. John
Paul Emmanuel was commissioned by Smithers to repay ~~him~~ Leopold
his twenty francs & we consequently called there. J.P.E.A. repaid the
debt, & told Leopold thirteen times at intervals of three minutes that
he was "one of the best"; he also told him that Smithers was "one of
the best" & that ~~he (Leopold)~~ I was "one of the best". We then went
out & had drinks at the D'Harcourt & elsewhere & at ten fifteen I succeeded in taking Jean-Paul-Emmanuel-Ashworth back to the Hotel
d'Athênes & putting him to bed.

---

1. J. H. Ashworth, art dealer and collector, at this time helping Smithers
with the production of *The Savoy*.

I then, feeling responsibility was over—for Ashworth was really so drunk that I was in terror of a row—came back here—the German beer café in the Rue Soufflot & had a *demie* & wrote these letters.

I will turn up, as Noblet suggests on the 24th.—that is if I have the money for my fare.

The "Fille aux Yeux D'Or" is now in the printers' hands. I spent an entire night in writing the preface (from midnight–8.30 AM) & Pierre Louys has allowed it to be dedicated to him as the greatest authority in Europe on Lesbianism except myself. Why, by the way, did you bugger up Smithers so much about me over your lunch the other day? We are both fond (unduly) of "fire water" & you know that, but the result was that I had to spend the rest of the day in defending you on the ground of your being, as I believe you are, really one of my best friends, & explaining your remarks away as an indiscretion of friendship. And, *seriously* you were wrong in talking like that, because I might easily have interpreted what you said as a sort of treachery, & resented it; & with anybody else except Smithers you might have done me serious harm. As it was, I refused to regard you as a sort of (Jepson + Teixeira)², put down your animadversions as kindly meant, & as Smithers declared your conversation had given him a thirst we drank that day more heavily than ever. Of course I should not write like this unless I knew you were really a friend of mine—one whom I look forward to meeting in a day or two. Jepson's interference I have satisfactorily dealt with. I have not answered his last two letters but I have written to Moore (my collaborator) who sees him every now & then & asked him to give him (Jepson) a hint. He answers me that he will give him the "hint". He puts it with the quotation marks. I forget if you know Moore, but he has the most polished manner & can be more infernally rude in an urbane way than any man I have ever known in my life. As Jepson, with all his faults is subtile, & Moore dislikes him personally, apart from my own resentment with him—I gather Mr. Jepson & I have made a happy consummation of our correspondence. His last letter was most impudently familiar . . . But enough of an unpleasant subject. The students have invaded this café & are beginning to "sing". Therefore it is time for me to go. Until the 24th,

Tout à toi,   ERNEST DOWSON

310. *To Arthur Moore*
    [*22 and 27 December 1895*]

214 Rue Saint-Jacques

Cher Vieux,

Scanty as was your letter I was glad to get it. Perhaps you had better leave the matter alone, upon which I wrote to you in the flush of my indignation. The simplest thing, after all, is merely to take no notice of such interventions, &, in dealing directly with the worthy Mathews, to ignore them entirely.

I was not able to send the cahiers back by Smithers, as he was so chocked up with books that he had bought here, that he had even to leave many of his own with me to forward him gradually through the post. I will therefore send you the *cahiers* by degrees. Will you once more tell me the precise numbers you require, as I have mislaid your letter, & I have a number which I am sure are already type-written. By the way, Missie tells me in her last letter that she is learning that excellent art—of type writing. But I doubt if her proficiency is yet equal to our needs. I had a very pleasant week while Smithers was here, & am consequently somewhat depressed & solitary since his departure. The weather is damp & unpleasant, but it has only once or twice been cold enough to wear a paletot.

I think of starting for Pontaven at the end of this month, but I am very vague, & I have a second string to my bow in the shape of Annecy & Aix-les-Bains, both places which I know (in Savoy), of which the climate would suit me better than Brittany, & where I could live, if not as cheaply as at Pontaven, at least as cheaply as here. Lautrec received the *roman* very promptly, & is now reading it. I am dining with Stuart Merrill[1] to-morrow. I suppose you have heard of the abortive petition which he started among French litérateurs for the grace of Oscar?

I did not send the Caran d'Ache. I will send a "Journal" however to-morrow with an amusing thing of Prévost's[2] in it.

Enough for the present. I wish you would write oftener—I am so entirely isolated from everybody that I look forward to the post with the same sort of excitement every morning as I knew in my early youth. Write soon. I am just going back to work.

T à t   <small>ERNEST DOWSON</small>

Look in at Sherwood St some day & take a cup of tea. They are wondering what has become of all my cénacle. Also there are two large folio volumes with which I presented you, which you have never removed.

<small>ED.</small>

Yes look in at Sherwood St & tell Missie to write to me. This letter is a week or so old now. Christmas is over: I spent it at Donnemarie with Connell & the Noblets. Ashworth, Smither's coadjutor has been over here for the last week buying books, & he brought over with him an

---

1. American-born French poet (1863–1915). Wilde's sentence of two years' imprisonment in May 1895 had caused indignation in Paris, but six months later Merrill was unable to obtain the support of any prominent French man of letters for this petition.
2. A series of *Lettres de Femmes* by Marcel Prévost (1862–1940) appearing in *Le Journal* and published in book form in 1897.

advance copy of the Savoy which appears on Jan 6. It is really very
excellent, I believe your story is being reserved for No. 2. For type &
excellence of reproduction it licks the "Yellow Book" hollow & no
expense has been spared in reproducing the illustrations. Also Beardsley[3] is at his best & his literary contributions although I scarcely like
them are really abominably clever.

I spoke of Pontaven above but my energy slips away & I see myself
staying here indefinitely. I have made one great friend here, a Russian
—or rather a Pole—though his people live at Petersburg—by name
Leopold Nelken—a most charming fellow studying medicine here. Like
all Russians he has been everywhere & speaks all languages & like the
best kind of Russian he has that sort of indefinable 'Varsity quality
which is lacking in most of my French acquaintances—those who have
most talent. I started to write a letter to you the other day from Saint-
Germain-en-Laye which you will remember, like a good student of
James, was the place where the young American met Madame de
Mauve:[4] but I did not complete it. I have heard & received a little
book of ~~carol~~ quaint ~~me~~ *fin de siècle* mediaeval hymns from John
Gray.[5] I have finished my Fille aux Yeux D'Or & am dedicating it by
permission—or request—to Pierre Louys—a connoisseur on the subject—to whom the original Salomé was dedicated. Instead of translating the Pucelle[6] as originally arranged I am merely revising an old
English translation. This will give me more time for the novel at which
I will seriously work now. I have also promised another story for No 2
of the Savoy[7] but so far have no idea of what it will be about—but I
suppose the scene must be in or about Paris. Smith is in town now, I
hope you will see him. Thanks very much for the Chronicles, send me
more when you can. I will send you any French papers which strike me
as having any interest for you

Do write soon & at length. I get most frightfully blue at times. And
of course I need not mention the good wishes I wish you pour l'année
qui arrive. May we arrive together—but the road is un peu long.

Tout à toi　　ERNEST DOWSON

3. Audrey Beardsley (1872–1898), the foremost illustrator of the time, was
   now effectively Art Editor of *The Savoy*. The first number contained eleven
   of his drawings as well as a poem and the opening chapters of his story
   Under the Hill.
4. *Madame de Mauves* is one of the stories in *The Madonna of the Future*, 1879.
5. *The Blue Calendar*, 1896, a small pamphlet of poems in a series sent out by
   Gray to his friends every New Year 1895–1898.
6. Voltaire's mock-epic on Joan of Arc. Dowson's edition, published by
   Smithers in 1899, combined the translations of W. H. Ireland and the
   Countess of Charleville. His own contributions are generally confined to
   short linking passages.
7. *Countess Marie of the Angels*, published in *The Savoy*, April 1896.

311. *To John Gray*

[*Postmark 27 December 1895*]

214 Rue Saint-Jacques

My dear Gray,

It is most remiss of me not to have acknowledged the adorable little blue-book before. But I have been in the country for Christmas, keeping melancholy festivity in a barren house which all the fires of Hell would never warm.

I can't tell you how delighted I am with the Calendar: it is something quite apart, rare, audacious, successful—admirable in a word. And it reminds me of the deliciously quaint sign of a cabaret in Montmartre "Le Moyen-Age-fin-de siècle".

It makes me look forward to your hymns with an increased anticipation.

My own poems I will send you as soon as they are out. At present the delay is due chiefly to the fact that I am unable to make up my mind with whom to publish them. I do not feel particularly bound to Mathews, as the arrangement was made, so long ago, & not directly with me, & he could have published them two years ago if he had wished, but he professes to be very anxious now to have them. And the fact of his having advertized them makes it difficult for me to give them to Smithers, as I should like to do, as besides offering me most magnificent terms, he is one of my most intimate friends.

I must, however, make up my mind soon, I suppose.

Pierre Louys when I last saw him was armed with a modern Greek dictionary & was leaving the next day for Athens, where he is still. His Paris address now is 11 Rue de Chateaubriand. Do you know a friend of his Jean de Tinan[1] who has just sent me one of his books?

It is so long since I sent you a verse that I adjoin my latest—which was chiefly written at the place whence I first wrote to you. Forgive me boring you with so long & barren an epistle, but this vie de café & the freedom of writing paper leads me into correspondence imperceptibly.

Tout votre   ERNEST DOWSON

SAINT GERMAIN-EN-LAYE

(1887–95)

Through the green boughs I hardly saw thy face
They twined so close; the sun was in mine eyes;
And now the ~~barren~~ sullen trees in sombre lace
Stand bare beneath the sinister, sad skies.

---

1. Symbolist author (1875–1899). The book was probably *Un Document sur l'Impuissance d'Aimer*, 1895.

O sun and summer! Say, in what far night,
The gold and green, the glory of thine head,
Of bough and branch have fallen? Oh, the white
Gaunt ghosts that flutter where thy feet have sped

Across the terrace, that is desolate,
And rang then with thy laughter: ghost of thee
That holds its shroud up with most delicate,
Dead fingers; and behind, the ghost of me,

Tripping fantastic with a mouth that jeers
At ~~ruddy~~ roseal flowers of youth the turbid streams
Have tossed and torn, through all the barren years
To death, the host of all our golden dreams.[2]

Saint Germain-en-Laye
Dec. 1895

2. Published in *The Savoy*, April 1896.

312. *To Conal O'Riordan*
[*31 December 1895*]

214 Rue Saint-Jacques

Mon bon Vieux,
    I must send a line to wish you all my good wishes for the year which opens tomorrow. It can easily be more prosperous to you & to me than this one which is over.
    Vincent O'Sullivan[1] ~~has~~ is over here now, has called on me, & been banqueting me at the Café de Paris. He is a very nice fellow & improves on acquaintance. I hope you are better than you were when I left. Convey my necessary compliments to the Noblets. Write soon: I have but a moment or two to catch the post & am besides, too profoundly triste to write at length.
                    Poignée de main,   ERNEST DOWSON

1. American-born poet, novelist and writer of short stories (1868–1940). He went up to Exeter College, Oxford, in 1892 and from 1894 to 1897 was on the editorial board of *The Senate*. In 1896 he published *Poems* and *A Book of Bargains*. His *Aspects of Wilde* (1936) gives many interesting details about Dowson and Smithers. The latter part of his life was spent in France and he died there during the German occupation.

313. *To Arthur Moore*

    [*c. 12 January 1896*]

214 Rue Saint-Jacques

Mon cher Vieux,

I have just risen from a bed of sickness, incomparably uncomfortable, as in my *hotel garni*, one is reduced under such circumstances to living entirely on milk the only nourishment that one can procure. That is my only excuse for not having written before to thank you for your prompt remittance for which I am deeply grateful. I will endeavour to liquidate the debt at the earliest possible moment. The frightful extent to which the giving of *étrennes* is carried here ruined me entirely. *Dieu merci* the back of the New Year is at last broken. —I was very glad indeed to hear from you. I should write to Symons, if I were you, about the story. Smithers knew nothing of it when last over here. I think the "Savoy" from what I hear, should be a success & a permanent apparition. Jepson, by the way, did *not* withdraw his story. He was one of the people who went and embêtéd Smithers & Symons most about the wretched prospectus, & as the story which was in question, was one that he had refused to sign, for fear of compromising himself, his objection seemed so grotesque that they were, I think perfectly right in sending his story back to him. Image & Geo. Moore, who had signed their articles were of course entirely within their rights in protesting— although personally I think the picture a most harmless one—but the position of an anonymous contributor—anonymous at his own request is different. But I am perhaps prejudiced, as for more reasons than one, I am acquiring the most profound distrust of Jepson. I will do as you suggest about the *roman* & forward it in instalments, it is perhaps better than sending it by an intermediary. It is possible—though not probable—that I may have to run over for a week or so to England myself. If so I will bring it you. There are days when I somewhat hunger once more for the *brouillards* of your Village & the lamps of Piccadilly. Did Verlaine's death[1] excite much interest over yonder? It was a great event here. I saw him about a month ago & thought at the time that he was at about the end of his tether. I hear terrible accounts of snow & frost with you, & also in the Midi: here to-day it is mild & wet to discomfort, but there has been no snow thus far.

Write soon, mon cher! I hope to have some money shortly. In the meantime once more, my extremest thanks for the £2.—

T à toi,   ERNEST DOWSON

---

1. Verlaine died on 8 January 1896.

314. *To Conal O'Riordan*
     [*mid-January 1896*]

214 Rue Saint-Jacques

My dear Connell,
    I hope you have not *m'en voulu* for my silence, and that your own is
not due to the same reason as my own—that is to say to persistent &
increasing lack of health. Make my excuses to Noblet for not answering
his letter & tell him that I will send him the papers he wants & the
addresses in a day or two. For the last ten days I have been more or less
decrepit—sometimes well enough when pricked by the stings of starva-
tion to get out of doors, as to-day, but never of sufficient robustness to
~~get out of doors~~ cross the river & reach the kiosques whereat I can buy
the papers he wants. Write & tell me how you get on & when I may
expect you here? I have arranged to leave at the end of my term i.e. by
the 5th. Feb. but I may go before. I merely wait to see Smithers who
may arrive any day & when he leaves I leave also—for *Brittany*, not for
Aix-les-Bains as I had intended—but in Brittany certain people have
promised to come & see me, & my horror of my own company increases
with my infirmities. I hope you will turn up here, however, before I go.
I would come down to see you if it were possible, but I am saving myself for the journey to Pontaven, which I begin to think will be my last
journey. *En effet* you who have known me when hélas I was *plus gai et
plus brillant* will hardly believe that now a walk from the Hotel des
Médicis to the Place St. Michel is an adventure which knocks me up for
two days.
    What, however, more I think than my physical collapse is really
killing me is the ~~feeling~~ conviction that has come to me—justified by
the news I get from England of how my affairs are going—of the
monstrous way in which I have been exploited and swindled and ruined
by the very people who, from their near kinship to me, I had thought
I could depend on—at least *not* to rob me too flagrantly—I never
expected justice or generosity from them. But you can have no conception of how I have been exploited: I have only recently realized it
myself. And, as perhaps you will understand, this feeling (multiplied by
my temperament) lights up a sort of intense flame of hatred and loathing
which destroys the peace of my days, & the sleep of my nights & deprives me of any chance that remains to me of getting cured. For I have
been told particularly that my one chance depends on my ability to
avoid any strong emotion or excitement. But this thing grows on me,
though I know that even if I had the money I should not have the
energy to take the necessary legal proceedings to make the blood-
suckers disgorge.
    Forgive me for boring you with these allusions to my personal
affairs; but I am acquiring such a profound distrust for everyone—the
result of my unhappy experiences—that except Smithers and yourself

I can think of nobody to whom I can speak of these matters without fear of treachery. Even Langdale, who, I know means me very well, ~~writes to me about~~ & who has been profuse in his offers to serve me, writes to me about an uncle of mine, whom he knows, as if it was a sort of testimonial to me that the said uncle speaks "kindly" of me, & is anxious to do anything in his power for me. I told Langdale in reply that it was quite indifferent to me whether my uncle was kind or unkind, but that he (my uncle) should feel intensely grateful to me for having recognized the fact that he was only weak & not *méchant*, and so having refrained from prosecuting him for culpable negligence.

Keep this letter, my dear Connell, & send it, at a future date, to persons whose address will be given you. I am settling up my affairs just now & am making you—if you don't mind—& Smithers my executors.[1] Give all the necessary compliments (& don't tell him how very little I want to meet his friends) to Noblet. I *will* deliver that card of introduction to the deaf & dumb however, when I am in better health. At present, I avoid everybody, except Leopold Nelken, who is awfully nice to me; & write soon.

Tout à toi,   ERNEST DOWSON

1. This arrangement was not put into effect. Dowson died intestate, and probate was granted to his uncle, Stanley Hoole.

315. *To Henry Davray*
[*Postmark 14 February 1896*]

Hôtel Gloanec,[1] Pont-Aven, Finistère

My dear Davray,
Me voici at the World's end (finis-terrae) at last. I am so sorry that I could not come & say au revoir (not good-bye) to you but I was in such a rush getting off. I have left your books & also one of Lautrec's with my Russian friend Léopold & have asked him to send them round to you. This is an adorable little town all shut in by hills except where an estuary of the sea runs up. The weather is glorious & yesterday at Quimperlé, I took my coffee in an arbour in a garden. Write to me, I will also write shortly. Shall be here for at least a month.

Ever yours,   ERNEST DOWSON

1. Now the Hôtel des Ajoncs d'Or.

316. *To Arthur Moore*
  [*c. 20 February 1896*]

Pont-Aven

Cher Vieux,

I was so glad to get your letter. Yes—here I am established at Pont-Aven, a place which is full of your aroma. For instance, I discovered an admirable sentiment of yours in the Book of Gloanec, when I was asked to write in it by Jourdin,[1] a French painter whom perhaps you know. The place is charming, the people less so. In fact the people are bête à faire mourir d'ennui. By this mean the people living at Gloanec —English, French, American, & the English—painters I believe but of the worst Jamesonian[2] type who are at Julia's[3] & who are playing billiards whilst I write. Robertson[4] has been gone a long time, but of course he is well remembered. I have had a drink—several indeed—at Marie-Joseph's. I am working fairly regularly here, but I am afraid I must get rid of my arrears of hack-work, which accumulated in Paris, & on which my bread & butter depends before I touch on Adrian. But in a week or so I will try & send you off isolated cahiers. My poems are now in the press. Smithers is publishing them, printing them at the Chiswick press, & I believe Mathews is advertizing them. So there will probably be ructions. But Smithers was so very keen about them, & I was so anxious to do anything I could for him in return for the innumerable services he has done me, that I could not but *poser* the good Mathews *en lapin*. But it was ~~not~~ purely a matter of friendship & not of commercial instinct as I have no doubt Jepson is kind enough to say. You will of course, duly receive a copy when it appears.

I wish there was some immediate prospect of seeing you, cher vieux. I shall stay here for a period varying from 3–5 months. If I have done as much work as I hope by the middle of May I shall return to Paris & probably spend the summer at St Germain or some other charming suburb of that beloved city. Otherwise, I may stay on here till June

---

1. Emile Jourdan (1865–1931) was born at Vannes and spent his life in Brittany. He was an associate of Gauguin, whom he first met in 1888 and saw frequently on his later visits to Pont-Aven.
2. The abortive raid led by Dr. Jameson, the Administrator of Matabeleland, into the territory of the Transvaal Republic on 29 December 1895 ended in his recall to England, where he arrived amid great patriotic excitement on 23 February 1896. He was charged with offences under the Foreign Enlistment Act, tried in June and sentenced to fifteen months' imprisonment, but released in December 1896 on grounds of ill health.
3. The Villa Julia, opposite the Hôtel Gloanec, and a less bohemian establishment.
4. Eric Forbes-Robertson (1865–1935), English painter, a younger brother of Johnston Forbes-Robertson, the actor and manager.

—for I don't fancy Pont-aven in the "season" & then go to Ushant which I have had a glowing account of—from my point of view—from a sailor-aubergiste, & which one reaches by boat from Brest. There or in some other Breton solitude, perhaps we may meet? But my original hatred of the English grows gradually to an almost insane pitch. And I have not the remotest intention of ever visiting London. Therefore you must come over here. Write to me soon, mon vieux, & *send me an occasional* "Daily Chronicle". I am abonné to the "Journal"—but otherwise most literatureless. Was there anything in the English papers about the representation of Oscar's "Salomé" at the Théâtre de l'Oeuvre?[5] I went there with Beardsley & I wrote a long account of the enthusiasm with which it was received to Mrs Wilde. It is astonishing how different the feeling about him is in Paris to what it is in London.

I saw Conder, a day or two before I left: he speaks of returning to England. Connell, who started to foreign parts with me originally, has also made the great retreat & returned to that sâle pays. Do you know an American painter, a great drunkard, Fordham,[6] who has lived here —near the Quai, & been a pensionnaire of the Mère Gloanec for 4 years? He does not know you by name but seems to have come across you. I wish you would send me a copy of "Tomorrow"[7]—published by Henry & Co. I first heard of it in a letter from Paris, from Davray: & am anxious to see it.

Once more, write soon.

T à t.   ERNEST DOWSON

5. Produced by Lugné-Poe at the Théâtre de l'Oeuvre on 11 February 1896.
6. Unidentified.
7. Published monthly under the editorship of J. T. Grein 1896–1898. Shaw and Max Beerbohm contributed occasionally, but it was otherwise rather unenterprising.

317. *Postcard to Victor Plarr*

Thursday [*20 February; postmark 21 February 1896*]

Pont-Aven

Mon cher Vieux,

Many months have I meant to write to you & give you of my wandering news. But arriving here, after passing through these Breton lands which are so associated with you makes it incumbent on me to send at least a post card, I will follow it up with a letter when I am settled down but write to me in the meantime. I shall stay here at least a month. I wish you could come too & leave your fogs to bask in baking sunshine as I did this afternoon, taking my coffee in an arboir in a garden of my hotel at Quimperlé. I feel I shall do much work here: it is an adorable place, & much as I love Paris where I have lived now some time I felt rested & restored to some prospect of reasonable health directly I came here.

Write & believe me in spite of all my shortcomings as a correspondent always yrs.

                                                    ERNEST DOWSON

318. *Postcard to John Gray*
   [*Postmark 23 February 1896*]

                                                    Pont-Aven

My dear Gray,

Forgive me boring you: but if you happen to have a poem of mine on Saint-Germain-en-Laye, I should be awfully obliged if you would not mind sending it me. I have no copy of it & I can not remember it, but I have promised it for the next "Savoy" & they want their stuff in at once. Therefore if you have these verses & would not mind copying them & forwarding me them here my mind will be relieved.

I expect to stay here for a month or so, if the weather remains good, but my plans are variable. My volume of poems is now in the press & I will send you a copy when it emerges therefrom.

                    Ever yours   ERNEST DOWSON

319. *To Henry Davray*
   [*c. 15 March 1896*]

                                                    Pont-Aven

Mon cher Davray,

(Mais pourquoi—should I write to you in bad French when you understand so well English?)—I was very glad to hear from you, & that you have got back the books which you were kind enough to lend me.

I am also much obliged for your offer of papers. I should be very grateful if you will send me from time to time any French or English paper which is likely to interest me. (*Except* the "Journal" to which I am *abonné*.) Here in this pastoral place I can get no papers except the "Petit Journal" which is not inspiring though I can forsee that if I stay here long, I shall begin to take an absorbing interest in all the accidents at Dijon and in the intrigues of M. Xavier de Montépins[1] feuilleton.

Could you without much trouble procure me 2 Exemplaires of the Courrier Français, in which was Lautrec's article on the Savoy?[2] I enclose a mandat for the price & postage, & shall be much obliged if you can get them & post them here.

I am glad to be here, I am working fairly hard, & find the people pleasant—chiefly painters, French & American. But there are moments when I have a very strong desire to take the next train back to Paris. Have you seen Beardsley? I hear he has returned to Paris & will stay there for two or three months. If you have not yet met him I will, as soon as I get his address—put you into communication with him. He was very amusing on my last Sunday at Paris. We went to see Lautrec, & Beardsley took some haschish for the first time. There was no result for some hours: then suddenly, while we were dining with Smithers at Margery's the haschish began to work very powerfully. Luckily we were in a *cabinet* or I think we would have been turned out—for Beardsley's laughter was so tumultuous that it infected the rest of us—who had *not* taken haschish & we all behaved like imbeciles. I am glad you have come across Leopold Nelken. C'est un charmant garcon; with a particularly suave & gentle manner, which I find essentially Russian.

My poems are now in the press. I will send you the volume when it appears. Write to me when you have time, & commend me to our friends, Ramsbosson, Lautrec etc & to Madame Davray.[3] O'Sullivan is likely to be in Paris soon, after which he intends to join me here.

Tout votre,   ERNEST DOWSON

1. Prolific French novelist and dramatist (1826–1902). He regularly issued his books in the *Feuilletons* of *Le Petit Journal*, the current one being *Les Demoiselles du Château*, which appeared in 203 parts, 1895–1897.
2. The number for 2 February 1896.
3. Davray's mother.

320. *To Herbert Horne*
     19 March 1896

Pont-Aven

My dear Horne,

Forgive my long and inexcusable silence. That of Paris was due to a certain extent to my ignorance of your address, but that, since your

LED–Z

last letter was forwarded me here, must be put down to the natural indolence of this remote village, & my wish to make the most of superb summer weather, when by all rights, one should be shivering; a little also to a great press of work. You will see from my address that I am more remote from the hubbub of things even than yourself.[1] As for Virtue—Dio Mio! (as I have no doubt, you now habitually remark) here, one is virtuous perforce. For the virtue of the womankind of this department, is only equalled by their ugliness.

However, it is a refreshing change after Paris and the Quartier, "the gold nights and the scented ways" (Vide: Symons).[2] Of course, I knew Marcelle—even two of them—and three Margots, and Germaines and Yvonnes and Gabrielles into the bargain. More than *ces dames*, I regret the hosts of interesting persons with whom I forgathered, & whose company really kept me there so long, & so put Florence out of the question. I *may* possibly be in Paris again in May, but it depends a good deal on my health, which for the last two months has been persistently and incorrigibly bad: although I believe I have recruited a little since I came here, where I have already spent six weeks. Vincent O'Sullivan is to visit me in a few days: he also is *en route* for Paris, where Beardsley —who was there *en visite* when I left—is now more or less permanently established. Have you seen the "Savoy", & do you like it? At least, I think it "knocks the wind" out of the "Yellow Book."

To come to your letter before this one which I am now answering: I am afraid it *is* too late. I am afraid you will think me, to put it mildly, vacillating & unreliable. I had always intended to publish my poems with Mathews—even without question of terms—and I am more sorry than I can say, that I shall not appear in your series. But I was so *intensely* irritated by a most unaccountable *démarche* of Jepson's, (who went to Mathews—entirely without my authority or wish—and appears to have tried to extract terms out of him, on my behalf,) that in my annoyance I promptly told Smithers, who was always anxious to have them, that he could publish them on what terms he liked. This was, perhaps, hasty, but it is too late now, as they are already in the press. What made me more wrathful was that, when I was in London, I mentioned to Jepson that I thought of asking Mathews to give me a certain royalty, and when he offered to approach Mathews for me—an absurd offer, considering he was not even acquainted with Mathews— I *expressly* begged him to do nothing of the kind. When I got his letter then, you can imagine my surprise. I thought it was not only a most impertinent interference with my business, but a gross breach of confidence. And since then I have heard from Smithers, further details, which I can thoroughly appreciate of Jepson's double-dealing.

1. Horne had settled in Florence, where he was working on the life of Botticelli. His house is maintained by the Municipality as the Museo Horne, Via de' Benci.
2. A line from *Paris* in *London Nights*, 1895.

Enough of a disagreeable subject. I do hope sincerely that you will not *m'en vouloir* for this arrangement, and also that it will not involve you in any disagreement with Mathews. It need not, I should think, because as I shall inevitably be hopelessly *embrouillé* with him, you can put the onus of the misdoing entirely on me. No more now: write soon, if it be only a line of pardon for my various misdemeanours. With Beardsley, the night before I left Paris, I saw a triumphant performance of Oscar's Salomé at the Théatre d'Oeuvre.

I had a very kind letter from Image in Paris, & heard here, today, from Symons: of or from Johnson, no word. O'Sullivan is an admirable correspondent & keeps me supplied with what news I receive.

always yours,   ERNEST DOWSON

321. *To Henry Davray*
    [*Postmark 22 March 1896*]

Pont-Aven

Just a line to thank you very much for the various reviews & mags. O'Sullivan had already sent me the *Senate*[1] with excellent portraits of Verlaine. Thank you also immensely for your offer to write of my poems in the "Hermitage".[2] You shall have them as soon as they are out. I have finished a *nouvelle* for the "Savoy" but fear it may arrive too late for the forthcoming number. I had a letter from Symons a day or two ago, also from Horne, from Florence. He—Horne will be in Paris about May. I expect Vincent O'Sullivan here in about a week. When he leaves me, which I hope will not be soon, he also goes to Paris. Go and see Beardsley at the Hotel St Romain, Rue St Roche. Smithers was also there last week. I will write at greater length shortly. The "cuttings" are admirable. Quel fou ce Buchanan.[3] Mes amitiés à Mme., à toute la bande et à toi-même.

ERNEST DOWSON

1. Published monthly 1894–1897. O'Sullivan was a regular contributor. The wreath it sent to Verlaine's funeral caused a sensation among the general public attending, who thought it had come from the (French) Senate.
2. *L'Ermitage* was published monthly from 1890 to 1906. Davray contributed an article on *The Savoy* (singling out Dowson as 'le délicieux poète') to it in October 1896, but his review of *Verses* appeared in *Le Mercure de France*, August 1896.
3. Robert Buchanan (1840–1901), poet, playwright and journalist notorious for his attack on Rossetti in *The Fleshly School of Poetry*, originally published (under the pseudonym Thomas Maitland) in *The Contemporary Review*, 1871. His article on *The Savoy* has not been traced.

322. *To Arthur Moore*

   [*22 March 1896*]

Pont-Aven

Cher Vieux,

   It was charming to get your letter. Our previous ones had, I think
crossed. Yes, I am quite acclimatized to the place & know its beauties
by heart. None of the people you mention are here except God—
Fordham whom I perceive you know. The man I chiefly consort with,
you may have seen, although he more often than not retires in the
summer. He lives with a Breton mistress above Marie-Joseph's—
Jourdin a French impressionist painter. There is a very charming child,
whom must also have been here in your time, & with whom I am on terms
of great intimacy. She is the adopted Italian child (natural daughter of
a conspirator) of an English socialist-anarchist woman of the Mrs
Besant[1] type—one Mrs Henry.[2] They are going to England shortly. I
shall look forward to seeing you & Chilcott & Co[3] here one of these days.
It is very likely that I may stay right on here—or in the department—
till October. But if I can afford it, I may spend May & June in Paris
& return here for Aug. & September. I enclose you my last month's
bill from which you will see how moderately one may live here. Would
you mind returning it to me when you write next. I am grieved about
your story. Is it the same one you sent to the "Savoy"? I have just sent
off a story I have succeeded in finishing here to that notorious publication. It is supposed to appear in the forthcoming number, but my
delay may have rendered that too late. It is called "Comtesse Marie of
the Angels" & the maiden name of its heroine is Marie-Joseph Angèle de
la Tour de Boiserie! Good old Faubourg St. Germain!

   I am constantly ailing here, with more various & trying complaints
than I care to think of. On the whole I think I was really better in
Paris. But the place is very soothing. I miss you, however, enormously.
Come what may we must certainly meet *somewhere* this summer. There
will be a poem of mine[4]—written here—in the next Savoy, which I
hope you will like. I heard recently from John Gray, who is editing
17th century things,[5] & from Horne in Florence. Take in, without fail,

---

1. Socialist, campaigner for birth control and later president of the Theoso-
   phical Society (1847–1933).
2. Almost certainly Agnes Henry, author of *The Probable Evolution of British
   Socialism*, published in *To-Morrow*, September 1896.
3. Possibly friends from the office of R. H. Chillcott, a solicitor in Chancery
   Lane.
4. *In a Breton Cemetery*, first published in *The Pageant*, 1897, after being
   passed over by Symons in favour of *St. Germain-en-Laye*. See Letter 323.
5. Gray's editions of *Fifty Songs* by Campion and Drayton's *Nymphidia* were
   published by the Vale Press in 1896.

the "Senate". It is far the best weekly review I know—& why not send your story there. One of its most frequent contributors, who writes very gruesome but striking stories in it, (Kipling + Poe)[2], Vincent O'Sullivan, is to visit me here next week. As he persists in crossing by Calais, and comes to me from Amiens "*on his way*" to Paris, I look upon him as a man of great nobility. I should like to give him a letter of introduction to you. He is an American but without any trace of Americanism—Oxford has suppressed it in him—except his disregard of distances and his habit of always living in Hotels: un charmant garcon!

Write to me soon, mon cher: & *send* me a Chronicle however dull it be. I want to see the folly, which I gather is being written, about this monstrous man Jameson. Thanks for "To Morrow" but it was the *third* copy of the same number which I had received, one of them hailing from a Parisian in Paris! I agree with you as to its demerits.

I hear from my Damigella that Poland is a thing of the past: the restaurant is disposed of & she and her mother live in seclusion in upper chambers, at which she is considerably bored. Indeed London would now be a place of shadows & unreality to me, if I were ever, by any remote chance to return to it. Smithers wrote me yesterday from Paris, en route for Bruxelles. Beardsley has taken up his abode there. Really the "Savoy" is grown as much a Parisian organ as a Londonian.

always yours,   ERNEST DOWSON.

323. *To John Gray*
[*c. 22 March 1896*]

Pont-Aven

My dear Gray,

a thousand pardons for not having written before to thank you for your prompt attention to my rather unreasonable request. My poem in your hand-writing pleases me, as it did not before, & I think of having it framed. I have sent it to Symons—but with an alternative— so that I do not know which of the two will appear.

I may be here for months, as the place suits my dilapidated health; on the other hand, I may return to Paris in the month of May. But I will keep you informed, as, who is it says? of my movements, in the hope of having your book. You will, I hope, receive mine, in a week or so.

I envy you your period of edition, the more so because I am editing the most tedious & uncongenial work which I have read.[1] I have,

1. *La Pucelle.*

however, succeeded in finishing a story, I hope in time for the forthcoming "Savoy" which the kindly critic will, I am sure declare, as
"seeking to conceal a (more than usual) poverty of thought beneath a
(more than usual) preciousness of language"; but which I hope you
will like.

My heroine's maiden name is Marie-Joseph Angèle de la Tour de
Boiserie.

I am sorry for you just now, that you should be in London, in the
flood of all the vicious nonsense that is, no doubt, being talked and
written *ad nauseam* about this ridiculous apothecary—Jameson. I wish
you could be here.

　　　　　　　　　　　　Ever yours　　　ERNEST DOWSON

I append a versicle du pays; & you need have no fear of receiving, for
unlike the other it is duly copied & preserved.

IN A BRETON CEMETERY

They sleep well here,
　　These fisher-folk, who passed their anxious days,
　　In fierce Atlantic ways;
And found not there,
　　Beneath the long, curled wave
　　So quiet a grave.

And they sleep well,
　　These peasant-folk, who told their lives away
　　From day to market day;
As who should tell,
　　Dimly, interminably
　　The same poor rosary.

And now night falls;
　　Me, tempest-tossed and driven from pillar to post,
　　A poor worn ghost,
This quiet pasture calls;
　　And dear dead people with pale hands
　　Beckon me to their lands.

Pont Aven
March/96

324. *To Samuel Smith*
[*c. 24 March 1896*]

　　　　　　　　　　　　　　　　　　　　[*Pont-Aven*]

I sent off a story, written here, the other day to it, but it may not be
in time for the forthcoming number. In any case it will include the

following—or another poem—for I have given them a choice of two.

[*In a Breton Cemetery*, dated Feb./Pont/Aven/96/]

Yes: I deeply regret that I shall not be in Paris to receive you; but let us hope it is only the post-ponement of a réunion which we will have there. How did you like doing the "Lysistrata"?[1] Smithers offered it to me, but I funked it. I hope you get on with him: he is, all round, the best fellow I know, & it is astonishing to me how many people fail to see this, or seeing it temporarily—(instance Conder, Rothenstein inter alios) succeed in quarrelling with him. I had a delightful few days of "wind-up", before I left Paris, with Beardsley, himself & a girl from the "Thalia"[2] who travelled with them. Once more, write soon.

Tout à toi, ERNEST DOWSON

P.S. *Par example*, a simpler way of conveying my letter of introduction is to go to the Café d'Harcourt at the hour of apéritif, ask for a *garçon* called Paul, who knows me, & ask him to convey the letter to "Monsieur Léopold"[3]—by the *chasseur* if he is not in the café. The same Paul will then point you out to the said Leopold on his arrival.

1. Smith translated Aristophanes's play for Smithers, who issued it in the autumn of 1896 in a privately printed edition with illustrations by Beardsley.
2. A supper club (i.e. night club) in Great Chapel Street, Oxford Street. Smithers was a member and often took Dowson and Beardsley. Jepson recalled that he found it rather dismal and for a long time was under the impression that its name was The Failure.
3. i.e. Nelken.

325. *To Leonard Smithers*
  [*c. 7 April 1896*]

Pont-Aven

My dear Smithers,
  Many thanks for your letter, the 50 francs, and the news of Miss Potter's birth[1] (By the way "The Birth of Miss Potter" is a good name for a story in my manner). Do not be intrigued at the arrival of a rug. It belongs to Langdale, he has begged me to send it to him, & as an amiable English lady was leaving here for London, I imposed it on her,

1. Apparently (but not certainly) an illegitimate child.

with a shilling, to forward to your care viâ Carter Paterson & Co. This
I did partly because Langdale was out of town, partly from malice, to
give him an occasion for calling upon you. I hope its custody will not
bother you. The Circus was stupendous. I took a small girl there—the
adopted daughter, Italian, of the English anarchist lady above referred
to, and she wept copiously at the appearance of the cerf, who turned
out to be a rein-deer. "Ce n'est pas que j'ai peur" she said, "*mais*, il a
l'air si MECHANT!" This charming child, I regret to say has now left
us; she was by far the most intelligent person in the Hotel. There have
been various other shifts & changes in our ménagerie; & the said
changes give the persons who are left occasion to remark to me, who
am looked upon as an independent witness, on the iniquities of the
persons who have left. We are divided upon other points; we are agreed
upon the character of the departed—(at least, I never contradict anybody) and in our contempt and loathing for the *pensionnaires* of the
rival hotel, because the *pension* there is some twenty francs a month
dearer. I am in somewhat evil odour, because as now, I sometimes visit
this establishment to write letters, or play billiards with a French
painter of its inmates.

I duly note your requirements & will do my best to fulfil them. The
story is already under weigh.[2] My studies have been interrupted the
last day or two by the Easter festivities[3]—& fair—when this town is
en fête it is terribly difficult to work, and the arrival of a Parisian
acquaintance,[4] with an introduction from Jean de Tinan.

No more for the moment. I will send "Pucelle" tomorrow, I hope, &
the proofs[5] by return when they arrive.

I hope you will call Miss Potter Yvonne or Ysabeau, good Breton
names, & will bring her up in the True Faith, and I am,

always yours,   ERNEST DOWSON

2. *The Dying of Francis Donne*, published in *The Savoy*, August 1896.
3. Easter Day fell on 5 April.
4. Maurice Cremnitz. See following letters.
5. Of his contributions to *The Savoy*, April 1896.

326. *To Leonard Smithers*
[*c. 9 April 1896*]

Pont-Aven

My dear Smithers,
Just a line to ask you not to *forget me & to send a hundred francs* if
you have not done so already. I missed the post with the 'Pucelle', but

you will receive it before this letter & also the proof of story.

I have done a poem ~~in a~~ in my Breton manner[1] which I will send you when I have worked it up a little, & am getting on, though slowly, with my story & the "Pucelle".

But I am working regularly & only drinking just enough to keep me in reasonable spirits. Have been feeling better than usual the last two days, having had three good nights; yesterday got a boat which I took down the river (with Cremnitz—Jean de Tinan's friend in it) nearly to the sea. Missed the tide, or forgot about it, & had to scull up four miles, unaided—Cremnitz being ignorant of the art of rowing—against a tide of seventeen horse-power. With the result that to-day my legs are so stiff that I can barely move. But the exercise was no doubt salutory.

Ever yours,   ERNEST DOWSON

---

1. Probably *Breton Afternoon*, published in *The Savoy*, July 1896.

327. *Postcard to Leonard Smithers*
Mardi [*Postmark 14 April 1896*]

Pont-Aven

Un mot d'urgence avant que le courrier part. Envoyez moi cinquante francs, de grace, tout de suite. Serai sans un sou.

J'entends d'O'Sullivan, qui lui-même est malade à Paris que Beardsley est assez malade à Bruxelles.[1] Écrirai une lettre ce soir avec les épreuves.

Bien à vous,   ED.

---

1. Beardsley had suffered a severe tubercular attack. He remained an invalid for the rest of his life.

328. *To Arthur Moore*
[*c. 19 April 1896*]

Pont-Aven

Mon cher Vieux,

What becomes of you all this time? I am grieved at your slackness. I am truly grieved. I have been honestly very seedy lately & only just able to get through with the necessary work for Smithers. But once I have worked off these arrears—heigh ho for Adrian! I have almost made up my mind to stay here—or at Faouet, or in Ushant, for the summer & return & winter in Paris or Brussels when the weather gets cold. In that case I look forward greatly to seeing you here in the summer; & we might then make much progress. A friend of mine from Paris one Maurice Cremnitz has just left after passing a 4tnight here. He introduced me to a very charming painter Loizeau[1] who has recently arrived & with whom I foregather. The "Savoy II" should be out by the time you receive this; I hope you will like my story. My poems will be out in a fortnight: one of them is associated with your name.[2]

I was much amused, and a trifle annoyed, to hear from Connell (O'Riordan) that when he first entered the "Crown" for the first time after his return to England, Jennings, the manager, greeted him with much empressement, and added in a mysterious undertone, "And Lord Alfred[3]—and Mr Dowson, I hope you left them quite well, Sir!"

Write soon, mon cher, I get horribly blue here, when no one writes. The Smithers—Rothenstein process was amusing.[4] Do you remember a dinner—I think you were at it—not so very long ago at the Comedy, when plaintiff, defendant and council for the defence were all present & on the best of terms. Jepson, also, if I mistake not was one of the party, Jepson with whom I am now on terms of extreme hostility. What revolutions!

Beardsley is at Brussels, ill, being nursed by his sister; Smith, as you probably know, in Paris.

The weather is wonderful here at times, but changes most rapidly, no one day being like the next. To-day has been a fête, with a charming procession of children who have made their first communion this morning. It is certainly a lovely place, but I don't think it quite agrees with me. It is enervating, & I sleep far worse here than in Paris; and I am certain it is a less healthy place by far than Faouet.

Once more write soon,

Ton bien dévoué,   ERNEST DOWSON

1. Gustave Loiseau, French painter (1865–1930), who had been at Pont-Aven with Gauguin six years earlier.
2. In *Verses*, *Quid non Speremus, Amantes?* is dedicated to Moore.
3. Lord Alfred Douglas, poet and later editor of *The Academy* (1870–1945). He left England at the time of the Wilde scandal, in which he figured prominently, and was now in Paris.
4. Proceedings brought by William Rothenstein at Westminster County Court on 26 March 1896 to recover payment for his etching, *La Pucelle*, reproduced in *The Savoy*, January 1896. Smithers defended the action on the ground that Rothenstein was in breach of a contract to deliver a second etching, but Rothenstein was given judgement and costs.

329. *To Henry Davray*
   [*c. 24 April 1896*]

Pont-Aven

My dear Davray,

I had been long meaning to write to you when your welcome letter came to "hurry me" up. I heard of Osman Edward's visit to you from Smith who was in Paris and ran across you at Bullier's I believe.

Beardsley as, perhaps, you have heard has been *very seriously* ill at Bruxelles. He went to see Smithers off at the Gare du Nord & quite in the spirit with which we used to retire to Dieppe last summer decided at *the station* to go with him. There he was attacked with congestion of the lungs & has been nursed by his sister and the good Smithers. From this last who is once more in England I hear that he is now getting better.

I am doing a fair amount of work now, chiefly stories & the interminable "Pucelle". I am daily expecting the volume of my poems to arrive, & you will receive one at the same time as the *Mercure de France*. It is charming of you to write about me in your series. Any "documents" you may require I shall be delighted to send you. I have also sent a copy to Lautrec.

Life is very charming here & I feel no inclination to move. A friend of Jean de Tinan, le *nommé* Cremnitz was here for a quinzaine. There are also some half a dozen painters, French & English, very excellent fellows—especially Louiseau, whom I knew before slightly, & whose work is exquisite. Séguin[1] is expected & perhaps Goguain;[2] also later on some of our English comrades. Smithers, however, is very anxious that I should meet him in Paris, so that I may *possibly* come for ten days in May, when he will be there: in which case I shall hasten joyfully to press your hand. But in any case I shall return here for the summer & remain here till October. Then—heigh ho for Paris—or perhaps Bruxelles, & perhaps—very much perhaps, for it involves the question d'argent, Alger, et les jolies femmes arabesques. Here, I have no petites Amies. C'est la vieille Armorique et pas la jeune qui me retient ici.

I was delighted to hear of Louÿs' success:[3] I have written to him.

1. Armand Séguin (1869–1903), French painter and illustrator, who had been a pupil of Gauguin. He was born in Brittany and spent most of his life in and around Pont-Aven.
2. Paul Gauguin (1848–1903) had last been at Pont-Aven in 1894. The following year he left Europe for Tahiti.
3. *Aphrodite*, now published in book form. François Coppée (1842–1907), despite his friendship with Verlaine, was regarded as a highly orthodox writer, and his enthusiastic review in *Le Journal*, which assured the success of the book, came as a surprise.

Imagine Coppée!! Je viens de lire un livre d'Edouard Rod.[4] "Dernier Refuge" qui me semble très bien écrit mais assez fade et fatiguant.

The "Savoy" ought to be "out" today. I have a story and a poem in it, & am busy with a story for No. III. Symons has sent me his new book,[5] which *entre nous*, I find disappointing. Connell O'Riordan's new roman "A Fool & his Heart"[6] will appear in a day or two. I believe he has dedicated it to me. Tell me how I can get into communication with "Jean Thorel" (Bouthors), who I see has just produced a play at the Odéon.[7] Five years ago, he sent me a book of his published by Vannier "La Complainte Humaine", & his brother Louis Bouthors was, when he was in England, for a year my most intimate friend. When I last wrote to him at Dresden my letter came back by the post & I should like to find out from his brother what has become of him. Would a letter to the Odéon reach Thorel?

Of Horne I have had no news for a month. O'Sullivan was in Bruxelles with Beardsley, and in Paris for one day, en route for Pont-Aven. But in Paris he became alarmed about his health and returned to London; since which time I have received no news of him. Alas! We are a degenerate and *maladive* race. My own health is of the worst. The life and the early hours are no doubt good for me, but the actual climate suits me less well than at Paris.

Write soon & tell me all the news. Do you ever see Leopold Nelken? My friend Smith seems to have had a most debauched and frivolous quinzaine under his ciceronage.

Commend me to Rambosson and all our connaissance.

Votre bien dévoué   ERNEST DOWSON

I have not yet had time to write anything for "Tomorrow" but when Louys sends me "Aphrodite" I hope to write an appreciation upon it there.[8]

---

4. Swiss novelist (1857–1910).
5. *Silhouettes*. This was the second edition (the first appeared in 1892) but contained nineteen new poems.
6. Published by Smithers.
7. *Deux Soeurs*, which opened on 23 April 1896.
8. Dowson did not contribute to *To-Morrow*.

330. *To Leonard Smithers*
 [*c. 25 April 1896*]

Pont-Aven

My dear Smithers,
 Many thanks for the two volumes of verse (Symons and Miall)[1] & the "Savoy". I ~~like~~ think it better than the first number, as far as its literature, but Beardsley is not so good, & your new man Horton,[2] I do not care for; but Shannon's things are superb. Is the Rothenstein the disputed picture?[3] I have not written because I have been ill (for two days, rather seriously) & am still shaky. Am still seedy & depressed and contemplate leaving here & trying Faouet for a month. But I am able to start working again & will send you story & more "Pucelle" in a day or two. One of these days I will live at Bruges. In the meantime, I hunger greatly to see you in Paris. You asked me the other day about payment of poems. I think a royalty of 1/- you once offered me. May I suggest that instead of that you should give me a royalty of 3d or 6d as it works out, and a tenner ~~down which will~~ down, or rather when you next go to Paris, which I will then come and spend with you there, returning here, when you return to England. If this suggestion appeals to you let me know.
 There has been a bad bicycle accident at Quimperlé. A man I met here, an Englishman fractured his skull & is lying there in a precarious state. There is a wedding here today & the air is loud with bag-pipes. I do not much care for your "New Writer".[4] He is clever but too smart. Conal has written to me, & seems to be getting work.
 Will you send me Alfred Douglas' address. I here he is in Paris. I will send him a copy of my volume. I think you were ~~write to~~ right not to publish him, but I am sick of the monstrous bêtise of the people who make it unwise for you to do so.
 Yes, I will go to Faouet; and perhaps, if *really* you & Symons will visit me, to Bruges.
 I see you have a dialogue by Mrs Crackanthorpe:[5] why do you not

---

1. *Silhouettes* and A. Bernard Miall's *Nocturnes and Pastorals*, both just published by Smithers.
2. W. T. Horton (1864–1919), English black-and-white artist who contributed several drawings to *The Savoy*.
3. *Two Ladies*. Rothenstein had been dissatisfied with the picture and tried to withdraw it.
4. Mrs. Clara Savile Clark, contributor of a story, *A Mere Man*, over the signature 'A New Writer'.
5. *The Love of the Poor*, a poem in dramatic form by Leila MacDonald. Smithers adopted Dowson's suggestion and printed *Anthony Garstin's Courtship* by Hubert Crackanthorpe in *The Savoy*, July 1896.

get a story from Hubert, her husband. No more now. I will write again & send you the book by this post.

O'Sullivan's poems are fine[6]—finer than I realized. He also as you no doubt know, has been seriously ill. What a maladive and wretched generation we are. My story or study[7] rather will not be too long for one number. Tell me, how you like my "Countess M etc".

Ever yours,   ERNEST DOWSON.

6. *Poems*, just published by Elkin Mathews.
7. *The Dying of Francis Donne.*

331. *To Samuel Smith*[1]

[*c. 25 April 1896*]

[*Pont-Aven*]

I hope the dedication of my poems will be understood of her and accepted—as, although there is no name, nor intials even, it will doubtless be understood of others—who will not, I hope, think it extravagant.[2] It is very literally true.

1. Text from Gawsworth.
2. Most of the poems in *Verses* are individually dedicated to Dowson's friends. His original intention was to dedicate the book as a whole to Adelaide by means of a dedicatory letter, though without printing her name. Shortly before publication he changed his mind and put in the heading 'In Preface: for Adelaide'. The dedication ends with a quotation from Flaubert's *Education Sentimentale*: 'Quelquefois vos paroles me reviennent comme un écho lointain, comme le son d'une cloche apporté par le vent; et il me semble que vous êtes là quand je lis des passages d'amour dans les livres. . . . Tout ce qu'on y blâme d'exagéré, vous me l'avez fait ressentir.'

332. *To John Gray*
    [*c. 25 April 1896*]

Pont-Aven

My dear Gray,

Your poem[1] was exquisite & I am looking forward eagerly to the "Hymn-book". Send it to me here. I may go to Paris for ten days in May, but I shall return here in any case. This is to tell you that my volume is, or will be, sent to you; it should be out by this time. I am afraid I have written an indiscreet "preface", although it seems to me very exquisite:—indiscreet, I mean, in that it will give an handle to the little yapping puppies of the press to *émender* me. Tell me how it strikes you. I am afraid, but afraid! of committing a Legallienism.[2]

Has the fame of Louÿs new book reached London? It has obtained a succès épatant, & I think very justly. One writes to me yesterday, from Paris, that he has just seen, at the Mercure, the last 15 copies being handed over to a bookseller, and that 5,000 more, most of which will be taken up at once, are in preparation. When one thinks of the sale of his previous books & of those of most of the other jeunes de Mercure, this takes one's breath away.

I suppose you will not come to Brittany or to Pont-Aven, this summer? I grow more enamoured of it daily. I love especially the primitive insouciance of its officials. For three weeks I have been unsuccessfully "stalking" the Mayor, to witness a document for me. I see him daily, playing *manille* or billiards in divers places; if I make a pilgrimage to a neighbouring village where there is a fair, I see him there, the life of the company—and the Captain of Douanes, the receiver of indirect contributions, the juge de paix and the inspector of roads are usually with him. But in his official capacity I cannot reach him, although I call daily at the mairie & at his house; so that my signature is like to go unwitnessed. Let me hear from you one of these days.

Ever yours,   ERNEST DOWSON

1. *The Forge*, printed in *The Savoy*, April 1896. The 'hymn-book' is *Spiritual Poems*.
2. Le Gallienne was notorious for the gushing sentimentality of his dedications.

333. *To Arthur Moore*
    [*c. 25 April 1896*]

Pont-Aven

Mon cher Vieux,

    Many thanks for the postal orders. I may possibly have to return them to you & ask you to send me a *money order* instead as they are not easy to change here. But I am told that Julia may possibly be able to get them changed for me ~~at~~ through her banker. I forgot to tell you when I last wrote that a sort of demi-semi uncle of yours is here with his wife, Mr Bollans,[1] a very genial & jolly old boy. I have been for a drive with him & his wife & consumed considerable quantities of scotch whisky with him at Julias. They are great friends of a painter Hunt[2] who has been at Julia's on & off for about 6 years, & are going on probably to Arcachon.

    I am very seedy now, & may go any day to Faouet for change of air.

    I have received the 2nd. Savoy; it is in some ways a better number, but in some ways a worse. *Write soon.*

T à t,   ERNEST DOWSON

1. Edward Bollans, brother of Elizabeth Moore (see Letter 84).
2. Herbert S. Hunt, English portrait and landscape painter, who worked chiefly at Concarneau, near Pont-Aven.

334. *To Samuel Smith*[1]
    [*April–May 1896*]

[*Pont-Aven*]

    I have asked Smithers to give you a copy of 'Verses' which may be out by the time this reaches you. Let me know how you find them, and if you think the 'Preface' is indiscreet.

1. Text from Gawsworth.

335. *To Victor Plarr*[1]
  [*May 1896*]

Le Faouet

My dear Victor,

I am ashamed of myself for not having long ago answered your charming letter, from Pont-Aven, but constant ill health and depression of spirits have made me a sorry correspondent. At least, I will not go away from this place, with which we both have had pleasant associations, without putting myself in touch with you. You will remember the room (salle à manger) in which I am writing. This visit of mine has not been a success; I came up from Pont-Aven only two days ago, to see if the change of air—from Pont-Aven to Faouet is really an enormous change, though it may sound ridiculous to you—would do me any good, and to spend a fortnight. But the ineffable *tristesse* of the place is too much for me and I am returning to what is more or less my permanent home and address (Hotel Gloanec, Pont-Aven, Finistère) tomorrow. Faouet is charming in the daytime. One can work without interruption, and, tired of work, one can bask in the blazing sunshine by Sainte-Barbe. But the evenings, the cold, bleak desolation of the evenings! Perhaps Pont-Aven, where I know everybody, and have many friends, French, English and Breton, has spoilt me; perhaps Le Faouet has changed, more likely I have. But I have not the courage to stay here by myself. It is more beautiful, however, now than in the full summer. There is no one in either hotel. Our old friend Jeanne has retired and Madame Mitouard (who asks to be remembered to you) is shaky on her pins. Marie-Joseph has gone to Paris. Miss or Meese Rose, who spoke English, is post-mistress or tobacconist at Vannes. The two little twins, whom Moore and I admired much at the *billiard*, are grown into ugly and *farouches* girls of twelve. And the two trees, whom (? which) Moore christened the 'Sisters Limejuice', are cut down. Eheu fugaces! But it is probably I, who have changed, more than Faouet, and doubtless if I was here with you and Moore I should love the place again. But in my sick and sorry old age I begin to be dependent on society: so I am off to Pont-Aven *après demain*, and there I hope you will write to me.

I hope you and yours prosper. It is long since I have heard news of you. My poems will be out in a day or two—perhaps are out now. You must forgive the freedom I have taken with yours and your wife's name in my inscription to my poem on Marion.[2] I am full up with work of various kinds and I suppose I ought to be satisfied with myself, for it

1. Text from Plarr.
2. See Letter 262. In *Verses* the poem is headed 'On the Birth of a Friend's Child: For Victor and Nellie Plarr'.

LED–A[1]

is all work that pays. But as I have no lungs left to speak of, an apology for a liver, and a broken heart I may be permitted to rail a little sometimes.

Write to me soon, mon Vieux. I shall be at Pont-Aven for two or three months and winter probably in Paris. Smith, Smithers and Moore are my only regular correspondents. Johnson sends me messages, with promises of speedy letters, but has not written as yet since I started on my wanderings. With Jepson I have seriously quarrelled; and I am afraid Horne is annoyed with me because I have published my verses out of the series. Missie[3] writes to me fairly often, *friendly* letters, which give me sleepless nights and cause me to shed morbid and puerile tears. But she is very kind. With all remembrances to all,

affectionately yours,   ERNEST DOWSON

3. In Plarr's text the names of Jepson and Horne are represented by initials only, and for 'Missie' there is a dash.

336. *To Leonard Smithers*[1]

[*May 1896*]

[*Pont-Aven*]

. . . Pierre Louÿs has sent me his *Aphrodite* . . . the copy he gives me belongs to the 12th [thousand] . . . I should like to translate it, but I suppose it would mean our joining Oscar in his gardening operations in Reading Gaol[2] . . .

1. Text from *Books from the Library of John Lane* (Dulau, 1928).
2. Wilde was transferred from Wandsworth to Reading Gaol in November 1895. After his release he said of the Governor: 'Such a delightful man, and his wife is charming. I spent happy hours in their garden, and they asked me to spend the summer with them. They thought I was the gardener.'

337. *To Leonard Smithers*
    [*c. 25 May 1896*]

Pont-Aven

My dear Smithers,

Your letter gratefully received & the 50 francs; but I am truly grieved to hear that you also have fallen a victim to treachery of the skin. You are welcome to pass it on to me if you like, for one more malady, more or less, makes no difference in my museum of ailments. It is a fête again today—curse these fêtes which seem to occur every other day—& in consequence I have found the post shut after déjeuner & am unable to send you my story which is ready, until tomorrow. I hope it will reach in time. In any case, I fear it has spun out to too great a length for one number, especially, as I presume the Savoy, having taken to menstruation,[1] will be less in volume than of old.

It is a great & admirable institution the "Savoy", & held in high esteem here as elsewhere. I hope it will succeed as well in its monthly aspect as I presume it has as a quarterly. May the hair of John Lane grow green with envy! When may I expect my verses? I am grieved about "Lot's Daughters".[2] I have mislaid both my manuscript & the original but I will have a search this afternoon amongst the mass of letters, proofs & manuscript which have accumulated in my room. I am quite resigned to spending my life at Pont-Aven like the other exiles who have drifted here: except that I want to see your classically sin-stained countenance, I should not even think of a week in Paris.

In its monthly shape will the "Savoy" take chronical notice of literary events. If so I should like to write a short notice say a couple of pages on the three most notable recent publications in Paris, Louÿs' "Aphrodite", Zola's "Rome" & Tinan's "Erythrée".[3]

I have no more to say, except that I hope my "study" will satisfy you & that I will now resume the "Pucelle" like a Trojan.

On the 10th of the ensuing month, unless I am with you in Paris, I shall be let in for my landlord's wedding, which will be an infernal nuisance as it occurs some 15 miles from here, & a Breton wedding is kept up for two days,—two days of riotous gaiety & compulsory drinking, which finishes up with a ball at our Hotel! Write soon.

Always yours,   ERNEST DOWSON

I have sent you a little book.

1. In *The Savoy*, April 1896, Smithers announced that from July onwards the magazine would appear monthly.
2. Apparently *Une Fille de Loth*, a novel by Charles Legrand, 1887. No translation of it by Dowson has come to light.
3. This suggestion was not adopted, though Symons discussed *Rome* in *The Savoy*, July 1896.

338. *To Leonard Smithers*
     [*Postmark 30 May 1896*]

Pont-Aven

My dear Smithers,

Write to me soon with news of your recovery to good health, with a fifty franc note, s'il vous plait, & with acknowledgment of a little French book, my story & Canto V. all of which must have come to hand. I will send Canto VI this week.

I am still *très souffrant*; but so far as the malady is concerned I have driven it off my hand & am able to go about without a glove—for the first time since I left Paris. I want much to see you in Paris & there give you the power-of-attorney; as if I can raise the £60. or say 1500 francs, I have an idea of buying, living in, & doing much excellent work in, a gipsy-cart. My good friend Louiseau will join me in the adventure & paint excellent pictures. He will also do the cuisine, I charging myself with care of the horse; also I calculate that once the initial expense of horse & carriage undergone, an expense we should halve—we can live most independently, the 3 of us Loiseau, myself & the horse, at a cost of 4 francs a day, including wine or cider. I think he underrates the eating capacity of the steed, even the sort of old screw we should buy for 100 francs—& we have been offered a horse for 50 francs! But putting it at 6 francs it is not dear, & I have no doubt that a book of selections from the diary of our journeying would be a success.

Of this I will talk to you when I see you.

I have been sitting to Loiseau for my portrait.[1] He has made an excellent picture of me, but being an impressionist he finds my dominant colour violet & brick red, so that I am unable to discern any likeness in it—mercifully for he has distinctly depicted me as a sort of person one would be sorry to meet on a lonely road of nights. I have begged him, if it goes to the "Salon" to inscribe it as the "Portrait of a Murderer" not of "Ernest Dowson". Write to me soon. And what about the Verses? I am daily expecting copies. And tell me how Beardsley marches?

Always yours   ERNEST DOWSON

I will send you "Aphrodite", or, if there is any likelhood of you going to Paris soon, bring it for you, as also the Du Puygaudeau[2] picture.

---

1. This portrait has not been traced.
2. Fernand de Puigaudeau (1864–1930), self-taught French painter. He was a friend of Monet, Renoir and Degas, had been at Pont-Aven with Gauguin in 1888, and after some years of travel settled at Kervaudu in Brittany.

339. *To Leonard Smithers*[1]
[*early June 1896*]

[*Pont-Aven*]

. . . [Thanks him for 50 francs and for the two volumes of his own poems.]

My compliments and thanks for the luxury with which you have encadré my lucubrations.[2] The cover is really very beautiful: and I congratulate Beardsley if, as I gather, his is the design.

[Asks for a list of those to whom the book has been sent, and for reviews. Also for news of the safe receipt of Canto V of the *Pucelle*. He is writing on *Aphrodite*.]

I trust that you are cured. I am worse than ever, *really* I believe on my last legs.

1. Text from Catalogue No. 93, Elkin Mathews & Co.
2. *Verses* was bound in white Japanese vellum, with Beardsley's cover design printed in gold.

340. *To Leonard Smithers*
[*c. 4 June 1896*]

Pont-Aven

My dear Smithers,

My very many thanks for your long letter, which has thrown me into quite a flutter of delight. So there is actually hope of seeing you here! I am more glad even than if the Paris arrangement was maintained. You will already have received my brief acknowledgement of the poems. I am more delighted with their appearance than I can say. Beardsley's binding block is admirable—*simplex munditiis*,[1] & yet most sumptuous. I am only afraid the reviewers will think the contents unworthy of such display. I have given one of the two small paper copies to Du Puygaudeau. I will content myself therefore with only *one* l.p. copy; but shall be glad if you can send me three or four more of the small paper, as I want to dispatch copies myself to Pierre Louÿs & André Lebey.[2] Yes, please give a copy to Connell Holmes.[3] I think

1. Horace, *Odes* I. 5. 'Plain in thy neatness' (Milton's translation).
2. French poet (b. 1878) associated with Davray, Lautrec, Louÿs and *les jeunes* of *Le Mercure de France*; dedicatee of *Sapientia Lunae* in *Verses*.
3. i.e. O'Riordan, to whom *Exile* is dedicated in *Verses*.

there is no one else in England to whom I need send copies. You will not of course forget the large paper copy to Adelaide. I am writing a brief notice of "Aphrodite" which I will shortly dispatch, & will also do a poem.[4] Will not the story I sent you do for No. IV? In any case, however, I will start another story in the intervals of my "Pucelage".

My extremest thanks for looking after & redeeming my pawn tickets. I had no idea the amount was so high.

I suppose when you come here you will come viâ Southampton & St Malo. It is the cheapest & least tiring route.

I heard to day from Teixeira & Symons, & a few days ago from O'Sullivan. I have had no news for ages from Conal, but I presume he is at Plowden Buildings. You do not tell me where Beardsley is.[5] I am glad he is mending. The weather here has been very hot & heavy, which perhaps accounts for my objectionable symptoms; but it promises a change today.

Our hotel is very full now; in fact several people are living out in the town; and people arrive daily; most of them, however, birds of passage.

O'Sullivan wrote to me that if we were going to Paris he would join us there. Perhaps, when you are decided upon your coming, he will journey with you. Write soon & keep me *au courant* with the adventures of my Muse. I am particularly anxious to see what the Chronicle will say, & what Le Gallienne in the "Star".[6] The latter is generally very complimentary to me.

Ever yours   E.D.

4. Probably *Venite Descendamus*, published in *The Savoy*, August 1896. The review of *Aphrodite* did not appear.
5. Beardsley returned from Brussels to London on 4 May 1896. He spent the rest of the year at Crowborough, Epsom and Bournemouth.
6. The *Daily Chronicle* reported receiving *Verses* on 3 June, but published no review. Le Gallienne's review in *The Star* of 2 July 1896 was very favourable.

341. *To Samuel Smith*[1]

[*c. 4 June 1896*]

Pont-Aven

I am glad you like the volume. Do you like Aubrey Beardsley's binding-block? I am very pleased with it. There are no reviews yet, but

1. Text from Gawsworth.

I have had very charming letters from Gray, Teixeira and Symons, the last of whom, as also Yeats, are going to write about it.[2] Perhaps you are right in your remarks about my preface. Conal is dedicating to me his new novel 'A Fool and His Heart' and I fear the dedication is appropriate. But it is too late to convert me now; I am idolatrous for the rest of my days. Idolatrous to the extent that Keats was when he wrote from Rome to his friend Browne: 'the lining which she put in my travelling cap *scalds* my head',[3]—and like Keats I can not open her letters for a day or so after they reach me. There is nothing in the universe which you can do, which will give me more pleasure than to pay the visit of which you speak. I have not yet sent her the volume, as the large-paper copies will not be bound for another week . . .

Well, enough: it grows near post-time. Go and see my Missie I beseech you: and tell me how she takes my 'Preface'—if she reads it. I only ask that she does not *m'en vouloir* for it, and that is a little thing to ask for as absolute an adoration as any girl or woman has ever had from anyone.

2. Yeats did not review *Verses*; for Symons's article see Letter 345.
3. Letter to Charles Brown, written from Naples, 1 December 1820.

342. *Letter-card to Henry Davray*
      [*Postmark 7 June 1896*]

                                                 Pont-Aven

My dear Friend,
   Many thanks for your long & charming letter. I will write at greater length shortly. For the moment I am very busy & this is but a line to commend my book of "Verses" to you, which Smithers will have sent you before now. I have had very nice letters about it, from Symons, etc; both he & Yeats are to write about it but have had no reviews yet. I shall be very glad & flattered if you care to make me one of your series in *L'Hermitage*;—as I said before, in a letter which I think may not have reached you, I shall be glad to give you any "documents" you may require.[1] Pierre Louÿs has sent me "Aphrodite", & I am writing upon it for the next "Savoy"; also upon Tinan's "Erythrée", which—*entre nous*—I do not much appreciate. *Aphrodite* is superb! I am in

1. See Letter 329.

wretched health, with continual blood-spitting (alas! that Lebaudy is dead, & I cannot sell my *crachats!*)[2] but am doing much work, verse especially. Mes compliments à Madame Jeanne, Rambosson et Cie.

Tout votre ERNEST DOWSON

2. Max Lebaudy was a millionaire who died of typhoid on 24 December 1895 at the age of twenty-three while a conscript in the French Army. He had attempted to evade military service by the claim that he was consumptive, but the authorities, sensitive to criticism from the Left, had not dared to release him. Instead he had been moved from one hospital to another until he had almost inevitably picked up the fatal infection. After his death it came out that he had been pursued by a gang of blackmailers threatening *inter alia* to reveal that they had supplied him wi : diseased *crachats* for submission to the medical authorities in place of his own healthy ones. Their trial, and the subsequent acquittal of all but two in the face of overwhelming evidence of their guilt, had been the chief scandal of March 1896.

343. *To Arthur Moore*
[*June 1896*]

Pont-Aven

Mon cher Vieux,

Forgive my lengthy silence, & my neglect of your commands. But my poor, harassed brain grows worse & I have not yet extricated your letter from my mass of papers, your letter which gives me the numbers of the MS volumes you require. This I will do shortly. I am also muddled as to whom, I have or have not sent copies of my "Verses"—a very dainty little white book which should have been sent you. Let me know if you have not received a copy, & it is an error which I will rectify. I trust your own worries & ailments ameliorate. For me, I am as usual, dégoûté de la vie et de tout. The prospect of meeting you at Faouet, or here, in August, alone, gives me glimpses of happiness, though I am keenly looking forward to the visit of Smithers which I am expecting daily. Fallows expects to come here in July, & Smith also announces an intention of arriving. I am compensated so by the attachment of my friends for the venomous hatred which I bear towards my relations, with whom (as Sherard would say) I have "no further dealings".

There are—or have been, alas! many charming people here. I deeply regretted the departure of your genial old uncle, whose stories of travel over Julia's whiskey were a perpetual joy to me. There have also been sundry pretty & gracious—I mean *gracieuses* English & American women here[1] who have been very attentive to me in my character of poet, & with whom I have drunk far too much afternoon tea in Julia's wood, & Hunt's studio. Hunt—the brother of your "lean fisher of trout", an excellent fellow left yesterday for Beg-Mail, where he passes the summer, to escape the crowd here. It is reached by boat ~~by~~ from Concarneau a place I visited for the first time yesterday, ~~when~~ I driving over his dog & luggage, while he accompanied me *en bicyclette*.

It is a "pleasant" place Pont-Aven & I quite understand now the difficulty which so many people ~~have~~ find in leaving it—as Hunt for example a 6 year old with intervals, the big Englishman Smith, a ten year old, at Julia's—you *must* have met him, Donaldson,[2] the painter, who has a house at Moelan, & Penfold,[3] the American painter, one of the pioneers of the place, who has returned this year after ten years absence. In situation I vastly prefer Le Faouet, but I could never settle down there, alone, as I have practically done here. Also Mme. Mitouard with all her qualities is by no means so entirely delicious as are Julia & Marie-Jeanne[4] with both of whom, greatly as they detest each other, I am on the most intimate terms.

It is awfully stuffy to-night, not a breath of air, & I am writing nothings to you, chiefly, because it is too close to think, & the impossibility of ~~turning~~ sleeping is obvious. I have had very little news from England: a letter from Johnson to-day, nothing recently from Smith or Langdale. You mentioned once hearing from Miss Roberts. I should *greatly* like to know what she said about me, for I am ashamed to say I have never communicated with her since I left England. Douglas, I am glad to say, has been persuaded *not* to publish his poems,[5] which is vastly better both for his own sake & Oscar's, if that poor victim of English hypocrisy ever lives through his torture. Conder, I hear is in London again. Have you seen him? Nous nous sommes un peu brouillés à propos de rien. I should like to come across him again, however & see his trousers. My Missie is well; they have resumed their restaurant again but are trying to sell it outright. There is nothing in the world which you could do for me, for which I should be more grateful, than to go & see them, & write to me of them. I have broken my heart over her, but she remains, none the less, my sole interest in life. In any case, write soon. You can not imagine what a letter is to an exile.

Ever yours   ERNEST DOWSON OF PONT-AVEN

---

1. Among them the American novelist Gertrude Atherton, who published her recollections of Dowson in *Adventures of a Novelist* (1932).
2. Probably J. B. Donaldson, landscape painter (b. 1853).
3. Frank C. Penfold, one of whose paintings is at the Musée Municipal, Brest. He had returned to teach in the *Académie* held in the Villa Julia during the winter season.
4. The *patronnes* of the two hotels at Pont-Aven.
5. Douglas did, in fact, publish his *Poems* in Paris late in 1896 but omitted the projected dedication to Wilde.

344. *To Henry Davray*
[*late June 1896*]

Pont-Aven

Mon cher Davray,

Many thanks for your charming letter and the most flattering things you say of my little book. I have heard from Soulages[1] and am replying to him to the effect that I shall be delighted to let him publish any translation of my verse that you may care to translate; but that I would rather leave it for you to decide which piece is most "traduisible".[2]

With regard to the phrases which you mention as not having understood—*posies*—is à peu près "bouquets"—and "scentless wisps of straw" "des brins de paille—sans odeur—a rather fantastic image (I imagine the madman (fou) making imaginary bouquets of roses out of the straw which lines his cage.

In the other poem "runes" were an ancient form of picture or symbol-writing used in Druidical times before writing was invented. As I use it, it ~~means~~ is little more than an archaic form of *oracle*. Mon idée peut être assez bien traduite par "oracles des roses".

I congratulate you on having finished your études for the time being, and I wish there was some ~~occasion~~ chance of seeing you here. I had meant to visit Paris this month to visit Smithers—but as he has decided to visit me here instead, and I am now daily expecting him, I have renounced the project, but hope to see you there in October.

Vincent O'Sullivan has been ill & is now in a monastery in Wales. Beardsley is still *dangerously* ill. I am in my usual state, worn out with insomnia. Have you seen the "Savoy" in its new, monthly guise? It promises to keep me very busy.

I shall be greatly obliged, if you will tell me in which number of the "Mercure" you will write of my book, in order that I may obtain it. Write to me again soon, when you have time, & remember me to our friends & to Madame.

Tout à toi de coeur   ERNEST DOWSON

1. Publisher of *La Revue Sentimentale*.
2. Davray published translations of *My Lady April* and *Villanelle of Marguerites* in *La Revue Sentimentale*, July 1896. The phrases Dowson explains here come from *To One in Bedlam* and *Sapientia Lunae*.

345. *To Arthur Symons*

le 5 Juliet 1896

Pont-Aven

My dear Symons,

My thanks for your charming letter & the article, à propos of myself & my work.[1] You are right in assuming my complete indifference as
to what things may be said of me over yonder, & I am content to be
found of sufficient interest personally, to be the subject of your
chronique. Would you, however, mind, toning down certain ~~sentences~~
phrases on the 3rd page of your proof which I return forthwith to you
—sentences which would—if the veil of your article ~~is~~ were penetrated
—give an erroneous & too lurid account of me: for ~~am~~ have I not been
peacefully rusticating these five months en pleine campagne? The sentence "Abroad in the *shadier* quarters of foreign cities etc down to
"Gay" to him" is the one which I have in my mind & suggests the too
hopelessly disreputable. *Could you, without spoiling your article,* change
that sentence into an expression of the fact that my wanderings in
foreign cities are a result of my chronic restlessness—for indeed I have
long since outgrown mine old "curious love of the sordid", & am grown
the most pastoral of men? I should be grateful if you would do this, not
so much for my own feeling, as for the benefit of sundry of my friends,
who might otherwise be needlessly pained (as for instance Image, who
heard exaggerated rumours of my life in Paris & was at the pains to
write a most kind grieved and paternal letter.).

If at the same time you would suppress a too alcoholic reference to
the cabman's shelter—(for the "refused admittance was to outsiders
generally & not personal) substitute "readier means of oblivion" or
some such phrase for "oblivion of alcohole", & if you *could* possibly
find a less ignoble word than "very dilapidated", there is nothing in
your article which I have any objection to your publishing.

It is always of curious interest to get any genuine idea of the manner
in which others see you, & I am fortunate in my chronicler. I am
especially charmed with the sympathy & tact with which you touch on
what you rightly call my "supreme sensation". And for your conclusion ~~the~~ I take off my hat to the compliment—the "genius" is perhaps
too partial & beaucoup trop flatteur, but, as no one is better aware
than myself, I have ~~alas!~~ always had, alas! too much of that "swift,

---

1. The reference is to Symons's *Literary Causerie* printed in *The Savoy*,
August 1896. The article does not name Dowson, but gives a recognizable
and highly lurid account of him. Before publication Symons made some
changes in two of the offending sentences, but retained 'That curious love
of the sordid, so common an affectation of the modern decadent, and with
him so expressively genuine, grew upon him, and dragged him into yet
more sorry corners of a life which was never exactly "gay" to him.
'Very dilapidated' became 'an appearance somewhat dilapidated'.

disastrous & suicidal energy" which destroyed our dear & incomparable Verlaine.

You will, probably, have seen some of my reviews. I foresee that I am to dispute the honour with you of being the most abused versifier in England, and I am flattered at the position. It is curious how uniformly the average reviewer will complain of your offering him violets because they are not cream-cheese, when doubtless if you bring him cream-cheese, he clamours for violets. And I hope you read the egregious remarks of the Daily Courier,[2] who complained that I did not write patriotic platitudes which did not scan. Yet they have always their Austin, & his praise of *filibustiers*.[3] But these reviews are really a joy to me.

I am daily expecting the announcement of Smithers' voyage here; perhaps, you will come with him. There have been charming people, & pretty & agreeable women here, but lately they have thinned out a little. It will be only too full, however, in a week or two. Have you seen the "Centaure", a new French review which my friends Pierre Louys & Jean de Tinan have inaugurated with Henri de Regnier[4] on the model of the "Savoy"? Davray, as you ~~know~~ doubtless know, is writing about ourselves, Yeats & Johnson in various places.[5] The latest review *des jeunes* "La Revue Sentimentale" is to publish a translation of one of my poems. I will send you the no. when it appears.

John Gray has sent me his new book "Spiritual Poems". I can not determine whether his mysticism is sincere or merely a pose—but I begin to think it is the former. I am glad you like my "Donne" study. I read & admired your "Lucy Newcome"[6] but, frankly, found it a little cold & impersonal. Your work which with your poems, fascinates me the most are those little studies & sketches, such as "Dieppe" & "Bertha"[7] which are always exquisite & always personal, which in fact nobody but yourself can write. Let me hear from you when you have time.

Always Yours   ERNEST DOWSON

2. 26 June 1896.
3. Alfred Austin's appointment as Poet Laureate was announced in the New Year Honours List for 1896. On 11 January he covered himself in ridicule by publishing in *The Times* a set of doggerel patriotic verses called *Jameson's Ride*, which were promptly parodied in the other papers and in the music-halls.
4. Henri de Régnier, French poet and novelist (1864–1936), author of *Les Lendemains* (1885) and eleven other volumes of verse before this date. The editorial board of *Le Centaure* also included the names of André Lebey, André Gide and (posthumously) 'P.V.' (i.e. Verlaine).
5. As well as *Verses* Davray reviewed *The Savoy*, Yeats's *Celtic Twilight* and Johnson's *Poems* in *Le Mercure de France*, August 1896. He contributed an article on Yeats to *L'Ermitage* for the same month and discussed Symons in 'Les Plus Récents Poètes Anglais', *ibidem*, July 1897.
6. 'Pages from the Life of Lucy Newcome', *The Savoy*, April 1896.
7. *Dieppe* appeared in *The Savoy* in January and *Bertha at the Fair* anonymously in July 1896.

346. *To Henry Davray*
    27 October 1896

Hôtel de l'Univers, St. Malo

Mon cher Ami,

Il faut que je te demande mille pardons pour cette longue silence; mais j'ai toujours, de jour à jour eu l'intention de t'écrire et de te remercier pour la traduction si charmante de mes vers dans la "Revue Sentimentale" et pour les choses si flatteuses que tu as dit de moi dans le "Mercure", dont j'ai reçu un exemplaire de Lugné-Poe[1] qui a passé quelque temps à Pont-Aven . . . mais continuons en Anglais—I have been staying here for the last five or six days *en route* for London, where I leave tomorrow, Wednesday, & where I shall stay four or five days. Afterwards I may return to Brittany, to Pont-Aven, or to some southern & sun-favoured part of Europe. In any case I shall try & pass through Paris *en revenant* & shall hasten, need I say it, to press your hand.

I am sorry indeed that I shall not probably see you in London, for doubtlessly you are returned to Paris. I received the announcement of your marriage, & I feel ashamed of myself for not having sent you my congratulations before. Will you convey my apologies to any of our common friends, in Paris, who have written letters to me which I should have long ago answered, & explain to them, as I hope you will understand yourself, that my remissness has been due to persistent ill health nervous & other disorders, which increase and increase—and not to forgetfulness or rudeness. Merci encore, mon cher ami, pour ton article sur mon livre; mon hommage à ta femme, mes amitiés à toi même et à tout le monde qui m'en garde le souvenir,

Tout à toi   ERNEST DOWSON.

Very, very vague as to my movements, except in so far as I sail tomorrow for Southampton. But letters either to Pont-Aven or c/o Leonard Smithers Esq will always find me.

1. A. M. Lugné-Poe (1869–1940) was Director of the Théâtre de l'Oeuvre, where he had produced *Salomé* in February.

347. *To Conal O'Riordan*

[*Postmark 4 November 1896*]

c/o S. Smith, Esq. 46 Preston St, Faversham, Kent.

Private

My dear Conal,

Behold me here in England again, for how long I know not, but for longer, I fear than I had hoped when I arrived. I am staying for the next day or two with Smith. Forgive my asking you, and don't my dear old chap inconvenience yourself if you are in evil case, (for I know nothing of how you are situated) *but* if you could let me have a sovereign & send it here as soon as possible I should be very grateful. Smithers has not abandoned me but I have to get back to town, & I am anxious not to have to ask him for money immediately. If you would not mind writing by return I shall be relieved.

I am anxious to see you again but am too busy at present to arrange a meeting or make any plans: nor am I quite certain where you are.

Affectionately   ERNEST DOWSON

P.S. Please treat this as confidential.

348. *To Conal O'Riordan*

[*late November 1896*]

6 Featherstone Buildings

My dear Conal,

I am dreadfully remiss: I wrote to thank you for the very acceptable sovran, but in my oblivion did not post the letter, nor did I call at Royal Arcade[1] & find your letter till yesterday. Note my address & let me know when & how I may see you. I am starting on a new & monumental translation for Smithers,[2] which may necessitate my staying in London, & have many other schemes of work in my head. I have seldom felt in more industrious mood; & seldom felt more pessimistic or

1. 4 and 5 Royal Arcade, Old Bond Street, Smithers's office and shop since August.
2. Of *Les Liaisons Dangereuses* by Choderlos de Laclos (1782). Smithers planned an edition illustrated by Beardsley, but the latter, after an enthusiastic start, became too ill to continue the work, and Dowson's translation was published in 1898 without illustrations.

unsociable. But I should greatly like to see you again, if you can come to town.

Ever yours,   ERNEST DOWSON

349. *To More Adey*[1]

[*Postmark 4 December 1896*]

6 Featherstone Buildings

Dear Mr Adey,

Forgive this delay, but I myself had mislaid Lugné-Poe's address & only found it to-day after much search. It is:

15 Monte-Christo Mansions,
Newington Green,
Green Lane, N.

Is there any truth in a rumour I hear to-day that Oscar has been released?[2] It seems too good to be true.

Yours very sincerely   ERNEST DOWSON

1. Author and art critic (1858–1942). He was a close friend of Wilde's and together with Robert Ross, was looking after his affairs during his imprisonment.
2. Wilde had now served eighteen months of his two years' sentence and had recently submitted a petition for release without success. Adey had also approached the Home Office on Wilde's behalf.

Part V
1897-1899

EARLY in 1897 Dowson moved from Featherstone Buildings and took a room above the Foltinowicz restaurant in Sherwood Street. Nothing could have been worse for his peace of mind. Adelaide was there but out of his reach, for she was now at least unofficially engaged to Augustus Noelte, the son of a tailor who had at one time acted as waiter in the restaurant but had now reverted to his father's trade at the same address.

One old acquaintance who saw him at this time was Charles Sayle who recorded in his diary that he visited him on 19 April with Lionel Johnson.[1] Dowson was also still in touch with O'Riordan and Moore, but there were many friends whom he chose to avoid. The decline in his health, reluctance to inflict himself in his dilapidated state on people who would find it offensive, and the need to keep his energy for the translation of *Les Liaisons Dangereuses* combined to make him a semi-recluse.

In April however he roused himself to leave and travelled with Charles Conder to Arques-la-Bataille, the little village near Dieppe where Beardsley had stayed in the summer of 1895. They had been there for some six weeks when Oscar Wilde, just released from prison, came over to Dieppe on 20 May and six days later moved to the Hôtel de la Plage at Berneval-sur-Mer, five miles along the coast.

Dowson had known Wilde only slightly in the great days before the crash of 1895, but he was one of the few friends who had visited him at Lady Wilde's house in Oakley Street in the grim period when he was out on bail before his final trial. He now renewed the friendship and soon the two were frequently spending their days together in Dieppe. On 3 June Wilde wrote to Lord Alfred Douglas:

'Ernest Dowson, Conder and Dal Young[2]—what a name—are coming out to dine and sleep; at least I know they dine, but I believe they don't sleep.' They arrived that afternoon and stayed

---

[1] Sayle gives the address as Sheffield Street, but this is clearly a slip for Sherwood Street.

[2] Dalhousie Young (1866–1921), a composer and pianist. Although unknown to Wilde at the time, he published in 1895 a pamphlet entitled *Apologia pro Oscar Wilde*.

up talking until three o'clock in the morning. On the 5th Wilde wrote to Dowson: 'Cher Monsieur le Poète, It was most kind of you coming to see me, and I thank you very sincerely and gratefully for your pleasant companionship and the many gentle ways by which you recalled to me that, once at any rate, I was a Lord of Language and had myself the soul of a poet. Of course I am lonely after the departure of my three good friends—Le Poète, le Philosophe and le Peintre—but I have no mourning-suit, so all I can do is to wear my red tie "with a difference"!'

On the 15th Wilde was at Arques breakfasting with Dowson, after which they returned to Berneval, where Dowson spent the night. The friendship between them, two lonely people, had deepened suddenly, and Wilde wrote, 'Had I stayed at Arques I should have given up all hopes of ever separating from you. Why are you so persistently and perversely wonderful?' They continued to meet regularly. On the 28th Wilde sent a postcard: 'Dear Ernest, I must see you; so I propose to breakfast at St Martin l'Eglise tomorrow at *11.30* and you *must* come: take a *voiture* and be there. I want to have a poet to talk to, as I have had lots of bad news since you left me . . .' And after the meeting: 'I write a little line . . . to tell you how charming you are . . . Tonight I am going to read your poems—your lovely lyrics—words with wings *you* write always. It is an exquisite gift, and fortunately rare in an age whose prose is more poetic than its poetry.'

In August, Dowson returned to England and Wilde lent him money for the journey. A few weeks later Wilde sent on Dowson's mail and added, 'I hope you will be able to send me what you owe me in a few days, as I have no money. Your bill with Monsieur Bonnet[1] was £11, and then in Dieppe of course there were huge expenses, and I also lent you money. It comes to £19, which I hope to receive within a week, as I cannot pay Monsieur Bonnet and he is becoming offensively tedious.' Unfortunately Dowson was slow to pay back his debt and did not send any money until October.

It took some courage for anyone to be seen with Wilde in 1897; most of the friends who had been proud to know the eminent author in his successful days now coldly ignored his existence. Dowson was one of the few who did not abandon him, and his action in seeking out the ostracized poet is evidence of that generosity and charm to which all his friends have borne witness. Wilde's friendship was the best possible thing for Dowson, and their visits to each other and their expeditions to Dieppe provided an excellent cure for low spirits.

From London, Dowson went to Ireland to stay with a friend, J.

[1] Owner of the Hôtel de la Plage at Berneval.

de Courcy MacDonnell, at Fairy Hill, Parteen, County Limerick.
MacDonnell was not a writer, but was intensely interested in
literature. He spent some time in Dieppe and it would seem probable that he and Dowson met there. At any rate, there was a
mutual attraction, and MacDonnell, who died while serving in the
Gordon Highlanders in the First World War, always 'thought a
lot of E.D.'[1] Dowson remained at Fairy Hill, a handsome house on
the banks of the Shannon, until October, when he passed through
London and returned to Paris. On 30 September, while he was still
in Ireland, Adelaide was married in the Bavarian Chapel, Westminster. Symons's assertion that Dowson fled to avoid being in
London at the time is almost certainly without foundation. Moore
attended the wedding on Dowson's behalf and also took his
present. That Dowson's days were now numbered was in one sense
fortunate, since it is difficult to imagine the distress he would have
felt at Adelaide's death, from septicaemia following an abortion,
which occurred three years after his own.[2]

Early in 1898 Dowson returned to London and made one more
attempt to clear up the affairs of Bridge Dock. The family solicitors were careful administrators and needed considerable per-
suasion before they could be brought to pay Dowson the smallest
sum on account of an eventual sale; indeed, the firm was not
finally wound up until 1902. As a result Dowson spent the last five
years of his life in repeatedly disappointed expectation, in varying
circumstances, depending on his income from writing, and died
penniless, yet after his death was found to be the owner of an
estate valued at over £1,000.

Smithers helped him when he could, but he too was short of
money and after the summer of 1897 could make only small pay-

---

[1] Statement to D.F. by Miss Eileen de Courcy MacDonnell, J. de C.
MacDonnell's daughter.

[2] Adelaide Helen, to give her her full name, had two children, both girls,
by her husband, whose full name in turn was Carl Frederick Augustus
Noelte. The first, Amelia Adelaide Winifred, was born at 30 Comeragh Road,
Hammersmith, on 5 August 1900. The second, Catherine, was born at 19
Sherwood Street on 15 December 1902. What led to the tragedy a year later
will probably never be known. Adelaide died at 19 Sherwood Street on
13 December 1903. At the inquest reported in the *News of the World* on
10 January 1904 a verdict of manslaughter was brought against the abor-
tionist, Bertha Baudach, who was a German midwife. Evidence was given
that the abortion had been performed during the previous summer. Thus
Adelaide's health must have steadily given way over a period of months as
a result of the abortion. Considerable suspicion was attached to Joseph
Kaiser, a German who boarded with the Noeltes; he stayed on to the end to
give Adelaide her medicine when she was not fit to be left alone, but was
dismissed by the Coroner for lack of any evidence of complicity.

ments for instalments of translations as Dowson delivered them: translations which when completed Smithers in some instances had not the capital to publish. He has so often been accused of dishonesty that it is right to state here that in his dealings with Dowson he was the one man to whom Dowson was content to entrust what little money he had. One of Smithers's accounts has survived, together with Dowson's letter of instruction (see illustration after page 296 and Letter 364). It shows that in October 1897 Dowson deposited £45 of his own money, presumably extracted from the family solicitors as he passed through London on his way from Ireland to Paris; further income was £20, which may have been a further instalment from the solicitors or a payment for work delivered, in the following January. On the debit side, Dowson wished to receive regular weekly payments of £3; £10 was to be sent to Wilde, and later £3 to William Theodore Peters. No one, even considering the value of money and the low cost of living in Paris at that time, could grow fat on £3 a week; but there must have been hundreds of artists and men of letters in the city who managed to subsist on a good deal less.

He made one new friend at this time, M. P. Shiel. Having been an interpreter at the International Congress of Hygiene and Demography, Shiel was beginning to make a name as a writer. He stayed with Dowson in his lodgings in Guilford Place (which he described in his novel, *The Weird o' It*, 1902) and they used to dine together frequently at the Dîner Français. There was also a visitor from Austria, the poet Rainer Maria Rilke, whose friend Verwey had been in London and sent such an enthusiastic account of Dowson's poetry that Rilke promptly came over to London in order to meet Dowson.

Apart from a second visit to Limerick in the summer, Dowson spent 1898 in London. He edited the text of Ben Jonson's *Volpone* for Smithers's new edition, *Adrian Rome* was at last completed and he was at work on his translation of *The Memoirs of Cardinal Dubois*, which Smithers published in 1899. He was in touch with Horne, Moore, Lionel Johnson and O'Riordan, but saw few of his other old friends. Guy Thorne (pseudonym of Ranger Gull, a friend of Smithers) has left an account of him at about this time:[1]

He seemed a lost creature, a youthful ghost strayed amongst the haunts of men, an object of pity. Pale, emaciated, in clothes that were almost ragged, poor Ernest flittered from bar to bar in search of someone with whom to talk. When he found a friend, his face would light up with a singular and penetrating

[1] *TP's Weekly*, July 1913.

sweetness that made one forget his untidiness—to use no other word—which verged on offence. He was never penniless, was always the first to pay for others, and when the drink was served he would sometimes furtively take a little gold cross from his waistcoat pocket and dip it in the glass before he drank. Someone who did not know the circumstances said, "Ernest, were you ever in love?" The poet answered in the words of Voltaire. "Vous me demandez si j'ai aimé: oui! c'est une histoire singulière et terrible." While I live I shall never forget the wan smile, the haunted look in the poor fellow's eyes.

A possible explanation of Dowson's remoteness from his older and more respectable friends at this time may be guessed from a letter from Wilde to Smithers of 18 February 1898. Wilde was now in Paris after five months in Italy, and Smithers had proposed bringing Dowson over to visit him. He appears also to have intended to bring another visitor, but in the end decided to go by himself, for Wilde writes: 'I am so glad you are coming over *alone*. I don't want to be bored with *Mrs* Dowson. Ernest is charming, but I would sooner be with you alone, or with him along with you.' It is clear from this that Dowson had acquired a regular mistress and may have installed her in his lodgings.

The relationship, if there was one, did not last much over a year. Early in 1899 Dowson was back in Paris by himself, and with his departure from London the series of his letters to Smithers was resumed. He was now busy translating the Goncourts' *Confidantes of a King*, which occupied him till the summer. Another project was his second volume of poems, *Decorations*, published at the end of 1899, a year which had also seen the appearance of *Adrian Rome*, *La Pucelle* and the Dubois memoirs. With this record of industry before them, his friends in London may perhaps be forgiven for not realizing the seriousness of his situation. His health was rapidly declining and he had not the money, or perhaps the inclination, to buy those comforts which might have at least prolonged his life. He did manage to get away for a change—to St. Germain, and to La Roche Guyon.

To the latter, a picturesque small town on the Seine, where Richard Coeur de Lion died and in 1944 Rommel made his headquarters, he went in March with Conder. It is probable that Conder suggested it, for he had been there before on a visit so enjoyable that, he said to D. S. McColl, it was 'like something that never happened'. But within a few days Conder wrote to Rothenstein: 'Dowson was taken very ill on Saturday and wanted one's whole attention. He had a fit in the morning which left his mind in a

most confused state and with a most extraordinary series of hallucinations. I left him there as he refused to come to Paris—has
promised to let me know if he gets any worse.' And on the last day
of the month he wrote once more: 'Dowson is all right again, but I
haven't seen him for a couple of weeks.'[1]

Even Smithers, who saw him several times during the year, did
not realize his desperate situation and remarked rather callously
à propos the death of Jean Tinan: 'Damned puny Frenchmen.
They can't stand anything. Look at Dowson, is he dead?'

Robert Harborough Sherard alone saw that Dowson needed
help, and did what he could by giving him a bed for a week or two
during the summer in Paris. He was probably a poor host and
Dowson's comment on this episode[2] leaves an impression very
different from that conveyed by Sherard in his *Twenty Years in
Paris*: none the less Dowson must have been glad of Sherard's
company and care, for he would otherwise not have contemplated
accepting it again, as he did a few months later.

[1] Quoted in J. Rothenstein, *The Life and Death of Conder* (1938).
[2] See Letter 399.

350. *To Elkin Mathews*[1]

8 *February 1897*

[*London*]

I think it is nearly a year since I last heard from you re *Dilemmas*. I
should be much obliged if you would let me know how it has been
going, and whether any further royalties are due to me.

1. Text from *Books from the Library of John Lane* (Dulau, 1928).

351. *To Samuel Smith*[1]

[*April 1897*]

19 Sherwood Street

I know that you must think me a fool, but I am suffering the torture of the damned. I ought to have drowned myself at Pont Aven, or having come back to London I ought to have had the strength of mind to have kept away. Now, if I change my rooms or go to the Arctic Pole it is only an increased intolerable Hell, and except yourself, and slightly, Morse,[2] there is not a person I come across who realizes that I am being scorched daily, or does not put down my behaviour to sheer ill humour. *Quousque tandem, Domine, quousque tandem?*

1. Text from Gawsworth.
2. A slip for 'Moore'.

352. *To Conal O'Riordan*

[*Date of receipt 21 April 1897*]

19 Sherwood Street

Private

My dear Conal,

Your letter reached me today. Forgive my flippancy & don't imagine that it—(or Dolly) is, at all, chronic. We were three—& you know her ways of talking about common acquaintances, & her passion for correspondence—& my slackness in the morning. For Heaven's sake, don't ask me to lunch with her, & *don't* for the sake of my whole happiness give her my address. I enclose two letters, which will show you how your own came to me. *Please burn them both & this one also.*

I am devoutly thankful she has anexed your postal order as I should have had to send her somewhat more. I too (except for an expedition to Bruges, & the brief night of intoxication which led to my letter to you) am working furiously at present. I shall be here for the next month or so: i.e. I want to get away before Mrs Guelf's decorations & crowds begin to loom too near,[1] & shall hope to see you one of these days. Should you call on me & take me by surprise, remember not a word

1. Queen Victoria's Diamond Jubilee was celebrated on 22 June 1897.

about Dolly & such like follies. *Vraiment,* it is only the third occasion since I returned to this sad country that I have dealt with a whore.

Affectly. yours   ERNEST DOWSON

N.B. *Please* burn all this "packet" instantaneously.

This should have been posted before, but I forgot it
Have been at Arques la Bataille ruralizing with C.C.[2] who remains there Am crossing back tonight & expect a hurricane.

2. Conder.

353. *To Henry Davray*
[*May 1897*]

Hôtel du Château d'Arques, Arques-la-Bataille, Seine-Inférieure.

Mon cher Ami,

Je suis ici pendant quelque temps en train de reposer après le train de Londres. Conder est également ici et nous travaillons tous les deux. Il a déjà fait plusieurs charmants eventails et un tableau—et moi je traduis comme un moulin. Par exemple, voulez-vous être assez aimable de me faire une faveur. C'est de me procurer et m'expédier ici un exemplaire, n'importe quel—pourvu que ça ne coute pas trop cher des "Liaisons Dangereuses". J'aurai fini demain le travail que j'ai apporté ici,[1] et je voudrais continuer ma traduction des "Liaisons". Si vous voulez faire ça pour moi vous m'obligerez beaucoup. Je crois qu'il doit être une édition moderne à 2. ou 3.50—mais vous me direz le prix et je vous enverrai un mandat.

Je suis tres faché de ne vous avoir pas vu encore pendant votre séjour à Londres, mais j'ai parti tout d'un coup pour voir cet endroit et quan[d] j'étais à Londres je vous ai cru parti.

Un de ces jours, peutêtre, je viendrai serrer votre main à Paris, mais pour le moment je n'ai ni le temps ni l'argent. Mes compliments a Madame Davray.

Tout votre   ERNEST DOWSON

Conder "sends his remembrances to you".

1. Probably the revision of *La Pucelle*.

354. *To Conal O'Riordan*
　　[*c. 10 June 1897*]

Arques-la-Bataille

My dear Conal,

　　Have you balm in Gilead for me? I write in a grand désespoir to beg you for old days' sake to sound Siemons[1] to see if he is open to any suggestion of work for me. For the hour has come, which I have long foreseen when Smithers' & my arrangement has ended. Perhaps, it is a good thing for me, in some ways; or will be, rather, if I can get a little money to go along with. Conder was with me here for long, in similar terrible straights, & then I bore up. But a good Samaritan, Dal Young came to his rescue, bought a picture which enabled him to pay his Hotel bill & took him back to England. The same Young, who is a marvel of good nature is busying himself with selling or mortgaging through his solicitor a small share of mine in an East India Ry. which brings me in £18—a year & on which he is sanguine of raising £300. But he has not written today, & it will take time, & my credit will expire & I shall not have the money for tobacco & stamps, & I feel as if all the world have abandoned me—& Crackanthorpe's ghost is calling to me from the other side of Styx.[2] Write to me by return, mon cher ami; send me a little money if you can, but *write, write*. Siemens once asked me to write a short novel & hinted that he would finance me to some extent while writing it. If he were of the same mind today, & would advance me something on it, I would write one in a month. I have the idea, but in this state of worry & distress, how can one write? If once this £300 reaches me, I shall take a little house for about 500 francs in the country, pay my debts, a years rent in advance & make the balance last me for at least a couple of years, while I write, write, write But this waiting kills me. I write this dismal appeal in an enchanting garden, on an enchanting day—et j'ai envie de pleurer. And it angers me to think that I have never felt so physically well, or so morally fit to work & not to drink as I do at present. The other day I met Oscar & dined with him at his seaside retreat; I had some difficulty in suppressing my own sourness & attuning myself to his enormous joy in life just at this moment—but I hope I left him with the impression that I had not a care in the world. He was in wonderful form, but has changed a good deal—he seems of much broader sympathies, much more human & simple. And his delight in the country, in walking, in the simplicities of life is enchanting. When Conder had left he described, by the way, Conder's delightfully inconsequent mind & manner of con-

---

1. Not identified, but perhaps a member of the firm of Henry and Co. for whom O'Riordan was working.
2. Hubert Crackanthorpe drowned himself in the Seine in December 1896.

versation, which you will remember to perfection. Conder's conversation, he said "is like a beautiful sea-mist." N'est ce pas, que c'est le trait?

Adieu, my dear friend; writing to you has somewhat cheered me, but all my misères will return in a moment. *Please* do not delay to write.

affectionately   ERNEST DOWSON

By the way, I need not say that Oscar does not want his retreat generally known; nor his pseudonym.[3]

Enclosure written later

Dear Conal,

Since writing this long & lugubrious scrawl—I have had a letter to cheer me. I am saved; although it may be a week or so before I have any money. Dal Young writes to me, after interviewing my solicitor as follows: "You have no need to be anxious in the least. He (Nairne)[4] spoke very nicely about you & absolutely assured me that there was no difficulty in getting some money on your East India Ry property. He wanted to know the exact amount you wanted as, apparently £300 w^d not quite exhaust the whole value of your share. If £200 w^d do for you now, for instance, you could leave the rest to be realized at some future time." Of course I wrote to Young to say that £200 *would* do & I await in hope for a letter from Nairne. Meanwhile as I have but a few francs left I should be immensely grateful if you could produce a pound or so —or a few shillings even & send me the same here. As you will gather from the quotation from Young's letter there is no hitch about the money, I am sure to be able to repay it to you within a week or ten days.

I am going to take a house near Rouen.

I am so poor that I hope you wont mind posting enclosed letter to Moore. 2½^d a letter is awful—& yet I am rich!!!

Adieu, cher vieux.

3. Wilde was now living at Berneval-sur-Mer under the name Sebastian Melmoth.
4. Partner in the firm of Baker and Nairne.

355. *Postcard to Henry Davray*
    [*Postmark 11 June 1897*]

Même addresse

My dear Friend, Will you forgive me for having waited so long without thanking you for your kindness in procuring me the Liaisons? But I have been very busy & have not a sou for the moment. My solicitor promises to send me £200—in about a week, in which case I propose to take a *maison meublée* for a year somewhere on the Seine, near Rouen— & I shall try & come to Paris for a day or two, (not more) for I am going to be excessively serious & work "like a nigger".—plus de ces traductions! Conder has returned to London. Yes, it is true about O.W. *mais il ne faut pas le dire, sauf aux amis.* Conder & I went & dined & stayed with him about ten kilomètres from here, & he is coming over to déjeuner with me here next week. He is in splendid health & spirits, toujours plein d'esprit, but unlike he was of old in the extreme joy he takes in the country & in simple things. He is delighted to see his friends, but anxious that his address & pseudonym should not be in the Journals. Forgive this card: I will write in a day or two.

Ever yours   ERNEST DOWSON

Tinan m'a envoyé son nouveau livre que je trouve fort bien.[1]

1. *Penses-tu Réussir?*

356. *To Henry Davray*
[*16 June 1897*]

Arques-la-Bataille

Mon cher Ami,

Je viens de recevoir votre charmante lettre, étant justement de retour de chez Oscar Wilde. Il est venu déjeuner avec moi et m'a ramené après pour diner. J'ai un rendezvous avec lui demain (Jeudi) a Dieppe, quand je lui communiquerai votre lettre, qui, je suis sur, le touchera beaucoup. Je suis sur qu'il sera vraiment charmé d'être mis en rapport avec vous, et très reconnaissant à vous et aux auteurs des livres dont vous parlez. C'est une seule formalité donc, qui me fait attendre jusqu'à demain, quand je l'aurai vu, avant de vous envoyer son adresse et le pseudonym très Oscaresque sous lequel il croit cacher son identité—comme si ça fût possible—!

I will write tomorrow then, if he does not write to you himself, which is most likely as any mark of sympathy moves him greatly. He is in excellent health & spirits, & has such a wonderful vitality & joie de vivre that after some hours of his society even a pessimist like myself is infected by it.

I hope I shall see you soon & I wish it might be here or hereabouts. I remain at any rate until the Jubilation in London is dead & buried. If I succeed in taking a house on the Seine near Rouen as I hope, you must come & stay with me this summer. In the meantime, my dear friend, all my *amitiés* to Madame Davray & yourself & all your charming circle.

always yours   ERNEST DOWSON

The ink of this hotel is not beautiful—*ma chè vuole?*

357. *To Conal O'Riordan*

[*Postmark 16 June 1897*]

Arques-la-Bataille

My dear Conal,

My most hearty thanks for the 50 francs received today & your letter yesterday. I hope things will soon right themselves, although since I wrote to you with my usual luck it turns out that one of the trustees of the fund, my share of which my solicitor is to realize for me, is *non compos mentis*, so that an order of the Court (? of Chancery) will have to be got. This I fear means delay. I am writing, however, to see if I can not obtain an interim advance of £50 while this is being done. I hope to get a small house somewhere near Rouen, which is not too far from London to enable me to treat with publishers & stay there for a year, paying a year's rent in advance & living of course most frugally. The MacDonnels of Fairy Hill, Limerick[1] have sent me a truly Irish invitation to come & stay all the summer with them & fish salmon; but although this is tempting, I fear lest Irish hospitality should be too little conducive of the hard work I propose for myself.

Oscar came over & lunched with me the other day & carried me back with him to Berneval. His gorgeous spirits cheered me mightily. I was amused by the unconscious contrast between his present talk about his changed position & his notions of economy & his practise, which is perversely extravagant. He does not realize in the least that nobody except himself *could* manage to spend the money he does in a *petit trou de campagne*. He is a wonderful man.

You tell me nothing of your own doings: I hope they are rosy. I saw Rothenstein the other day, on his return from a pilgrimage to Berneval, & he told me that Teixeira is leaving Henry's? I hope this is not true, or that he is doing it merely to "better himself". Once more, my many thanks. I hope you will write soon, as I don't hope to escape from

---

1. J. de Courcy MacDonnell was Librarian at Marsh's, Dublin.

Arques for another ten days & shall have sundry relapses into the blues until something is settled.

Affectly yours,   ERNEST DOWSON.

Moore highly approves my idea of taking a house over here. Thanks for the review:[2] it is charming. Do you know who wrote it? You have, doubtless, heard that Beardsley has become a papist[3] & is living surrounded by images & crucifixes at St Germain.

2. Probably of *The Pierrot of the Minute*, published by Smithers earlier in the year.
3. Beardsley was received into the Roman Catholic Church on 31 March 1897 shortly before leaving England for the last time.

358. *To Henry Davray*
    Jeudi [*17 June 1897*]

Café des Tribunaux, Dieppe

Mon cher Ami,
    Je vous écris un mot comme j'ai promis. J'ai communiqué votre lettre à M. Oscar Wilde, qui se trouve avec moi à ce moment, et qui m'a chargé de vous dire comme il est touché des signes d'intérêt et d'amitié que vous avez temoigné. Il sera très content de recevoir les livres et les revues dont vous parlez & il me prie de vous présenter sa carte, que vous trouverez ci-jointe. Vous comprendrez bien, n'est-ce pas, que c'est le nom merveilleux qu'il porte à ce moment. C'est un nom de famille (littéraire) car son grand-oncle a été l'auteur du roman celèbre de "Melmoth", auquel Balzac a ajouté le dernier mot.[1] Je n'ai pas besoin de vous prévenir, vous qui savez ce que sont les "reporters", que ce nom aussi que cette adresse ne doivent pas être répandus.
    Au revoir donc, mon cher ami; je reste encore dix jours à Arques; n'oubliez pas de me prévenir de votre nouvelle adresse. Je vous salue bien amicalement et Madame Davray aussi.

Votre bien dévoué,   ERNEST DOWSON

1. *Melmoth the Wanderer* by C. R. Maturin, 1820. Balzac's 'étude philosophique', *Melmoth Réconcilié*, appeared in 1835.

359. *To Elkin Mathews*
    [*August 1897*]

    c/o J De Courcy MacDonnell Esq, Fairy Hill, Limerick, Ireland

Dear Mr Mathews,
    I shall be much obliged if you will send a copy of "*Dilemmas*" to the above address.
    I should be glad also if you would let me have an account at your earliest convenience as to how the book has gone as it is now more than 18 months since I heard any news from you about it—
                         Yours truly   ERNEST DOWSON

Elkin Mathews Esq

360. *To Victor Plarr*
    [*September 1897*]

                                      Limerick

My dear Victor,
    I have been meaning for weeks to write and tell you of my arrival here & to thank you & your wife for your kind reception of me on my passage through London, but the lazy Irish climate has laid hold of me entirely & I have hardly written a line. I hope you enjoyed your Norman tour. Let me know all about it. I left the day after yourself & am expecting to sojourn here until I go to Paris in November or Oct. It is a sweet place, on the Shannon, but my host like most of his compeers having been ruined entirely, has let it go to pieces. Personally, I rather like the aspect of decayed grandeur. The climate is rather trying & utterly destructive of all energy. But it is a dear country, although I fear we consume considerably too much whiskey. I quite understand Johnson's enthusiasm[1] & if I wasn't already so much wedded to France I should feel inclined to take up my abode in it. However, I begin to pine already sometimes for the Gallic tongue & as I have said I go to Paris for the winter. I have heard no news of anyone for the last month. Are you still controverting with Jepson[2] or has that duel yet come off? Tell me of these things.

1. Yeats had converted Johnson to enthusiastic Irish Nationalism.
2. Jepson's article *The Norse Renascence* in *To-Morrow*, May 1897, had praised the new 'nordic' spirit of Kipling, Henley and Shaw at the expense of the 'celtic' Yeats and Johnson. Plarr replied in June and was answered by an abusive letter from Jepson in the issue for July.

I shall only stay a day or two in Town but I will come & see you on the first of them. I hope you are all well & that your new appointment fits you.[3] Embrace Marion for me & tell her to send me her photograph. There are five children of tender years in this house & they have just invaded the room so I will perforce conclude. With my best volontés to you all.

T à t   ERNEST DOWSON

3. Plarr had been appointed librarian of the Royal College of Surgeons.

361. *To Conal O'Riordan*
[*Date of receipt: 13 September 1897*]

Limerick

My dear Conal,

How wags the world with you, Sir? I gather from some journal or other that you have retired to some country estate of yours to write a very readable work.[1] I have been staying here with the MacDonnells for the last month for the same end, & am to stay here until October when I hope fortune will allow me to proceed to Paris for the winter. I interviewed my solicitor on my way through London & expect to get £300 out of him shortly. I will send you the £2 you so kindly lent me the moment I have it. At present, I am utterly stony. I am trying to write sundry things but this is a terribly lazy though very charming place. I was staying with Oscar for some time before I left France. I introduced Smithers to him, who had turned up at Dieppe, & they have struck up an alliance. Conder & Beardsley, the Dal Youngs etc were also at Dieppe; it lacked only you & Symons to reproduce the former occasion.[2] Only some of us being wrecks & some of us ruined a good deal of the joy of life had departed.

Let me hear soon of your news. Are you a member of the "Authors' Club"?[3] If so I will ask you to put me up later on as a foreign member as I want a London address. I am going to take an apartment in Paris & furnish it. I have given up the idea of the house at Pont de l'Arche.

1. O'Riordan's next novel was *How Soldiers Fight*, published in 1899.
2. In August 1895, when plans for *The Savoy* were being made.
3. Founded by Sir Walter Besant in 1891 and housed at this time in a private hotel in St. James's Place. Early members included Symons, Le Gallienne and Harland, but not apparently O'Riordan.

I was only in London two days en route here. I dined with O'Sullivan, saw Johnson & stayed with the Victor Plarrs. They were in a mighty fury over a letter of Jepson's in "Tomorrow", which you doubtless saw. I suppose that man of sin still flourishes? Tell me what has become of Teixeira? *Do* write soon

Tout à toi   ERNEST DOWSON

Who is the editor of *Pearson's*?[4]

4. *Pearson's Magazine* was edited by the publisher, C. Arthur Pearson. During the latter part of 1896 it ran a series of articles by Sherard under the title *The White Slaves of England*.

362. *To Henry Davray*

[*September 1897*]

Limerick

Mon cher Ami,

I wonder if you are still in Paris. I have been staying with friends here for the last six weeks & remain some time longer. It is a charming place & a very wild country & as there is little society I have plenty of time for work. I am writing now to ask if you would mind putting me in communication with the Mercure de France, as I shall not be in Paris myself for another month, perhaps. I enclose a letter which Pierre Louÿs sent me respecting a translation of "Aphrodite". I wrote to him telling him I would undertake the translation with pleasure but I have not heard any more from him. I should be much obliged then if you would tell Vallette[1] that I am ready to translate the book at once. Perhaps, you would advise me as to the "conditions" I should propose, or obtain an offer for me from Vallette. However, any "conditions" could stand over until I come to Paris, if I can obtain an assurance that my translation will be published. I hope this is not troubling you overmuch but I know you are often at the Mercure de France & I have only met Vallette once. I am anxious to do the book even if the "conditions" are not good. Oscar Wilde thinks a translation by me ought to do well.[2]

1. Alfred Vallette (1858–1935), founder and publisher of *Le Mercure de France*.
2. Wilde had written on 18 August 'I think your translating *Aphrodite* a capital idea, I do hope you will get someone to make good terms for you.'

My own plans are only vague in the matter of dates. But I expect to come to Paris in October or November & shall take an appartement for a year & furnish it, although I do not intend to spend all the winter there. It will be charming if you & your wife, to whom convey all my compliments will assist me in the matter of furnishing. Autrement je serai sur d'acheter rien que des choses absolument inutiles.

I hope to have two volumes (roman & nouvelles) in the press by the beginning of next year.[3] I trust you are both well & that I may see you soon. I stayed with Victor Plarr whilst in London. He & his wife were delighted at having met you.

Bien à toi   ERNEST DOWSON

3. *Adrian Rome* was finished in October 1897, and Dowson was planning a new volume of short stories, but this project came to nothing.

363. *To Leonard Smithers*
  30 September 1897

Limerick

My dear Smithers,
  I am sorry that you have to find fault with my translation of the "Liaisons Dangereuses". I can only hope that as you read further you will find your first impression is a wrong one. I did it to the best of my ability. *In any case*, I should be most reluctant that it should go to press without my having seen proofs. If you will send me them here I will return them to you by the following post; but if the whole copy has not gone to press I should be quite ready to go through the whole MSS myself, if you care to send it to me. I could easily do that in a couple of days.

In that case, I should ask you to be kind enough to send me also a copy of the ordinary 3 franc edition of the original. The text is precisely the same as that of the contemporary editions,

With regard to the *memoirs*,[1] I can only repeat what I said at Dieppe. I sincerely hope that your alarm about another contemplated edition is premature. It can't be more vexatious to you than it is to me to feel that the books are with my other things at Arques. I am making every possible effort to get the necessary money to pay my bill there & immediately I do so I will secure my things, & return you the books. You

1. *The Memoirs of Cardinal Dubois*. Dowson's translation was published in 1899.

Ypres.
Lille.

Ernest Dowson
Bruges 1895

Bruges. 1897.

Dieppe. 1897.
Arques. " "

TO

MISSIE

(A. F.)

le Faouet.
Pont. Aven.
Pouldu
St Malo.

Paris.
1895-6.

London. 1597.

Limerick 1898

Paris 1899

London 1898.   La Roche-Guyon. 1855.

St Germain 1855.

Dedication page of Dowson's copy of *Dilemmas,* which he carried
with him and dated

(above) Ernest Dowson. A drawing by Charles Conder

(below) R. H. Sherard

56 Sandhurst Gardens
Catford

My dear Conal,

I was going to write & say how grieved I was at the news in your 1st letter when the second came to relieve my mind. Of course my dear old chap nothing you said hurt me & when I get to you I can't say how much I want to I shall ask my uncle to come & see me. I am deeply grateful for the sums you can send me as medicines are so dear & I accept them with less reluctance as I had better news from my col—r the other day & fancy that my money is now within measurable dist of coming — at anyrate I have con—

The last letter

—sented to an arrangement which avoids the necessity of lunatic proceedings & think the whole affair is now so settled that one of my uncles will at any rate advance me something.
Come over & see us soon, we all wish it.
Yrs
Ernest Dowson

N.B. Probably the last letter he ever wrote C. (1/4/00)

IN MEMORY
— OF —

ERNEST CHRISTOPHER
DOWSON,
WHO DIED 23ᴿᴰ FEBRUARY 1900,
AGED 32.

Ernest Dowson's grave in Ladywell Cemetery, Lewisham

must surely know that it is not from lack of endeavour on my part that I have not yet been able to raise the money. In another week I have every expectation of being in a position to send for the books. I hope I may be in town myself by the time they arrive there when of course I will bring them to you. But if, for any reason, I am longer delayed here I will have them sent to you direct.

But I hope to see you very shortly in London & will write before I start.

Yours sincerely   ERNEST DOWSON.

364. *To Leonard Smithers*

14 October 1897

[*London*]

Dear Smithers

I to-day deposit with you £45. 0. 0. of my money. Please send Oscar Wilde £10. 0. 0, on a/c of what I owe him,[1] take £1. 8. 3 on a/c of interest paid by you for me & send me the balance at £3 every Monday to any address I may send you. Do not send me more than £3 each week.[2]

Yours truly   ERNEST DOWSON.

1. Dowson owed Wilde, who was now living at Posilippo, near Naples. £19. Smithers sent this payment of £10 promptly, but it was delayed in the post, and Wilde was desperate for money for several days before it reached him. See *The Letters of Oscar Wilde* (1962) pp. 662–667.
2. Dowson's account with Smithers for the next three months is reproduced following p. 296.

365. *To Leonard Smithers*

[*c. 18 October 1897*]

214 Rue Saint-Jacques, Paris

My dear Smithers,

Here I am installed in my old quarters, in a very bad room at present but shortly I hope to be changed for a better. I have also a new proprietor. I found the consigne shut on my arrival at Dieppe, so was obliged to write to the chef de gare to forward me my things here. They arrived this evening and I will send you your books to-morrow.

LED–C[1]

I am very much obliged to you for having thought of your salutary scheme for my preservation against my improvidence. I think you might send me £1 on receipt of this—a postal order & I will then ask you to forward my money to me at the rate of £2- a week, not £3 unless I specially require it. Time is what I chiefly want & then I believe I can make some money. I have an appointment with Vallette to-morrow & hope I shall be able to arrange something. I have seen Beardsley who looks better than he did at Dieppe,[1] also Davray, Smith etc.

I have received OW's telegram[2] & have written to him c/o Cook, which was the only address he gave. I wish you would send me the proofs of *Les Liaisons Dangereuses* as they come in. There are always certain corrections one can make when matter is printed & I will certainly return them to you promptly. I forgot to ask you when we met in London whether you would like me to write a preface. I had thought of writing an article on the book.[3] Would you object to this, if I could arrange to secure its appearance in some magazine about the time of the appearance of your edition? I am very glad to be in Paris again & feel much better than I have been for a long time.

Sincerely yours,   ERNEST DOWSON.

1. Beardsley was at Dieppe from July to September 1897. He then returned to Paris and stayed at the Hôtel Foyot.
2. Wilde was by now writing and telegraphing frantically for the payment of Dowson's debt.
3. There is no record of Dowson's having written this article. See Letter 373.

366. *To Henry Davray*
  [*c. 21 October 1897*]

214 Rue Saint-Jacques

Cher Ami,

Je ne pouvais venir hier vous voir un ami étant venu ici. L'adresse d'Oscar est Villa Giudice, Posilippo, Napoli. Ce qu'il m'a chargé de vous dire c'est qu'il n'a reçu aucun dessein de Hermann[1] et par conséquence se trouve forcé de faire paraître son poème *sans* dessein comme il ne veut pas trop attendre.

Je n'ai pas encore eu le courage d'aller voir Vallette. Si vous devez

1. Paul Herrmann (b. 1864), a German artist living in Paris. He had been introduced to Wilde by Davray and had offered to illustrate *The Ballad of Reading Gaol*, which was now in Smithers's hands waiting to be printed.

y aller quelque matin ou après midi et m'amèneriez je prefererais ça. Laissez moi un mot

Votre bien dévoué ERNEST DOWSON

Savez vous si Choderlos de Laclos a écrit autre chose que les *Liaisons*? Je veux faire un article sur lui mais à Londres je n'ai pas pu trouver des renseignements.

367. *To William Theodore Peters*
[*Late October 1897*]

214 Rue Saint-Jacques

My dear Peters,

I was detained this morning by sundry *courses* I had to *faire* across the river. I write this line in case I miss you to beg your forgiveness. We must arrange another meeting. I have moved into my new room which is not too bad. You will find me there any mornings—or I will look you up of an afternoon.

Tout à toi, ERNEST DOWSON

368. *To Leonard Smithers*
[*5 November 1897*][1]

214 Rue Saint-Jacques

My dear Smithers,

Will you send me £3= tomorrow instead of £2- as I want to give my landlord some money & I may possibly move somewhere else. I have been looking at other rooms in other quarters & I am not sure that I should not find cheaper & more comfortable installations elsewhere. In fact, whether that I have changed or the quartier has, I know not, but I am coming round to your opinion of it, that it is a somewhat squalid & noisy & uncomfortable place. The other side of the Luxembourg is better but it is very dear.

I hope you are well & flourishing. It has turned very cold here & I

---

1. The date has been inserted by someone else, probably Smithers's secretary.

am somewhat enrhumé & have been obliged to send to Arques for my pardessus.

Don't forget about the money: I shall really require the supplément.

Bien à Vous   ERNEST DOWSON

369. *To William Theodore Peters*
Sunday night [? *7 November 1897*]

214 Rue Saint-Jacques

Dear Will,

Forgive my non-appearance this afternoon. I had a bad night & an excruciating day of neuralgia & did not leave my room until hunger drove me out about 8 P.M. Come & see me tomorrow afternoon, if you can. I want you to tell me where I can get some buttons sewn on a pardessus. Also, I have spent tonight reading through & destroying old letters, & am in the bottomless pit of depression. So come & see me— morning or afternoon.

Tout à toi de coeur   ERNEST DOWSON

370. *To Henry Davray*
[*c. 13 November 1897*]

214 Rue Saint-Jacques

Mon cher Ami,

Many thanks for your note about Choderlos de Laclos. I waited in for you on the Sunday before last but you did not come. On Tuesday, I was obliged to go out in the afternoon. I hope I did not miss you, but I did not hear of any one calling on me.

Come & see me soon. I am thinking of shortly taking up my abode at Fontenay-aux-Roses where I have found a cheap & comfortable hotel.

Ever yours sincerely   ERNEST DOWSON.

371. *To Leonard Smithers*
   [? *14 November 1897*]

214 Rue Saint-Jacques

My dear Smithers,

   Thanks for cheque. I am going to stir up my solicitor & will arrange
to have the money lodged with you & draw it weekly. I hope you will
come over here soon. It is lovely now & I always take my déjeuner in
the open air. But I am beginning to hanker after the flesh pots of
Egypt. I am afraid my simple tastes have been corrupted! A dirty, or
no table-cloth has come to distress me & I often hanker for a good
dinner with you chez Foyot & the taste of decent wine. I am thinking
of moving out of Paris shortly to Fontenay aux Roses. I have found a
very cheap and comfortable place there & as I should be the only
pensionnaire & no one ever goes there except on Sundays I should be
undisturbed. My landlord, however, may stick out for his pound of
flesh: i.e. his next fortnight which I have encroached on. If he does not
I shall wire to you to send me £2. I shall not wire until I have arranged
to leave the following day so do not fail me, I pray you as I shall want
money for my deménagement & will try to do without anything further
the week following.

   My neuralgia has gone I am glad to say, but I am quite worn out
with want of sleep. Your remedy is more appetizing than mine—but I
fear the brandy. Excellent stout is to be had for 40 centimes at the
American bar in the rue Soufflot & I often sample it.

   There is a rumour that Douglas is in Paris:[1] somebody saw him in
the Bois. I suppose that this is not true. I have only seen Aubrey
twice. I gather he is rather *lié* with Whibley[2] whom I greatly dislike &
do not want to meet. Is O'Sullivan coming to Paris soon?

Votre bien dévoué   ERNEST DOWSON

Fontenay is about half an hour from Paris from the Luxembourg
Station. There is a last train about 12.50 so that I shall be able to pass
an occasional evening here.

1. Douglas was living with Wilde at Posilippo, but was under pressure from
   his family to leave him. This he did early in December, when he went to
   the French Riviera.
2. Charles Whibley (1859–1930), English journalist and critic; collaborator
   of W. E. Henley.

372. *To Leonard Smithers*
     [*c. 20 November 1897*]

214 Rue Saint-Jacques

My dear Smithers,

Many thanks for cheque. I had to wire as my finances were disorganized by the presence of a bad 5 franc piece in my pocket. I think it must have originated from the Café de la Paix which I visited a few days ago.

I called at Belin's[1] this afternoon "on my own". The publication is "Paris Dansant" I presume? He tells me some of the large plates are "tirés" but that Willette works very slowly & the thing will certainly not be published *before* March. Is this what you want to know?

Aubrey is just off in time,[2] if he is really off, as we are starting very raucous fogs nowadays. I have had several good nights since I have taken to drinking nothing ~~except milk~~ after dinner except milk or red wine (of the most ordinary I need not say) but I have a very bad cold and, doubtless owing to the milk, expectorate for an hour or so every morning like a German Jew.

Yours very sincerely   ERNEST DOWSON

1. Bookseller and publisher on the Quai Voltaire. In 1898 he brought out an elaborate volume, *Paris Dansant* by Georges Montorgueil, with illustrations by A. L. Willette (1857–1926), the distinguished painter and caricaturist.
2. Beardsley left Paris on 19 November for Menton, where he died on 16 March 1898.

373. *To Leonard Smithers*
     [*1 December: date of receipt 2 December 1897*]

214 Rue Saint-Jacques

My dear Smithers,

Thanks for the cheque & also for O'Sullivan's new book.[1] I think it is one of Beardsley's most charming covers—altogether one of the prettiest of the many pretty books you have published.

Would you care to have *Le Rire* album of the monarchs of Europe,

1. *The Houses of Sin*, O'Sullivan's second volume of poems, just published by Smithers.

1 f. 50? It contains the highly flattering & most amusing caricature of the Queen which caused the seizure in England of the number of the *Rire* in which it appeared.[2] Some of the other caricatures are also rather waggish.

I am feeling the cold a good deal here; it has been bitter. The Cork Herald has asked me to send them Paris letters.[3] I have started them but there has been no arrangement about terms & I fancy the Irish papers—even the leading ones—are rather hard to tap. I don't want to put them off, however—so my idea is to wait until they have printed a certain amount & then send in a bill. What is your idea?

Will you send me £2= tomorrow. Last week, your letter did not come till Saturday night so that I was somewhat embarrassed during the Saturday & Sunday.

I am really surprised at what you tell me of the *Liaisons*. When shall I see the proofs? I have discovered all that there is to be discovered about Choderlos de Laclos but the facts are so meagre that I despair of making an article of them. I have had no news from Oscar for some time. There was a paragraph in the Journal the other day which I hope was exaggerated.[4]

Yours sincerely   ERNEST DOWSON

2. The cover of *Le Rire*, 11 June 1897, was an unflattering portrait of Queen Victoria by C. Léandre.
3. The *Cork Herald* printed no 'Paris Letters'.
4. A report that Wilde was starving to death in Naples. He was, in fact, very short of money, but certainly not destitute.

374. *To Leonard Smithers*

[*c. 4 December 1897*]

214 Rue Saint-Jacques

My dear Smithers,

Thanks for cheque & letter. I am in correspondence about the money but I *expect* I shall have to come over to London about it and as I am afraid of ~~being~~ its running on to Xmas I have pretty well decided to come over at once & try & settle it.

I can get put up by Swanton, Plowden Buildings, until the 14th which will save expense.

Will you do your best to send me £5[1]—so that I can get it on *Friday*

1. Dowson's deposit of £45 was not yet exhausted, but Smithers himself was short of money at this time, and was finding it difficult to pay his printers and blockmakers.

on which day I shall probably start. (Pawn the ring if ~~possible~~ neces-sary—or *sell* it which would be preferable—but send something as I shall have to give a sop to my landlord even if I don't pay him off & bring all my baggage with me.

If anything turns up in the interval which authorizes me in staying on here I shall not want the usual money next week—but send a fiver in any case if you can.

Tout à vous   ERNEST DOWSON.

375. *To William Theodore Peters*
Tuesday [? *7 December 1897*]

214 Rue Saint-Jacques

My dear Will,

I haven't yet gone to London but *may* go in a day or two. I have written to Lautrec & to Lebey about your révue.[1] Perhaps, you would do well to write to the former yourself in a few days if you have not yet received an answer from him. His address is: M. le Vcte. Gabriel de Lautrec, 37, Rue Desbordes Valmore, Passy. I am feeling very ill in body & remorseful in mind after my stupid vaudrouille of the other night & my subsequent monstrous invasion of you. Please forgive me the latter & believe me

Ever yrs affectly   ERNEST

1. Probably *Le Quartier Latin*, published in Paris and London. Peters was a regular contributor.

376. *To Leonard Smithers*
[*c. 13 December 1897*]

214 Rue Saint-Jacques

My dear Smithers,

Thank you for the cheque (£4-) which I got on Saturday. I haven't yet been able to leave partly because I am still (and shall be till Friday) expecting a letter from Mr. Nairne re: my affairs & also partly because my bill for the month which has just turned up was very much larger than I expected. Will you try & send me all you possibly can by Friday or Saturday as on that day or Sunday at the latest, I propose to return. I am very anxious if possible to get the thing settled by Xmas which is now painfully near. After that, I shall get a room here, or perhaps, a little apartment just to put my things in for I have a great disgust of my hotel. I had déjeuner at a place in the Rue Jacob & met Mr Symes[1] today. His speech takes longer to come out of him than ever. Please write by return: it is very urgent.

Yours,   ERNEST DOWSON

1. Unidentified.

377. *To Leonard Smithers*
Christmas [*25 December 1897*]

214 Rue Saint-Jacques

My dear Smithers,
Thank you for your cheque
I wish you many wishes for this season which I have passed almost entirely in bed with a swollen face which reminded me very much of the national plum pudding.

I am pretty square with my landlord—don't owe him more than about 10 francs. As he has retired for ten days I shall have no difficulty in getting away with a valise at any rate! No—I have not taken literature as an amusement; I have tried to live by it. There I join issue with you. But if that were true, there is all the more reason for my abandoning it now while I have still a small capital which might be turned to account. I will discuss all that with you, however, when I see you, and when this same money is realised. My idea, however, is to leave £200 with you (or any further sum which may accrue to me beyond the £100 I shall reserve for my expenses) and go to Johannisberg. I have a friend out there who edits a paper & who does pretty well & if nothing else turns up which I could work "on my own", I should be sure of getting a berth on his journal. But there are lots of other openings which I should try in preference. I can get to the Cape (intermediate) for a very few pounds & something might be done there, *en route*. If, according to a pamphlet I remember ~~seeing~~ hearing of, you can start as a tobacconist with £20—surely with a few hundreds I can get a better crutch than literature in some of our numerous colonies. I want to discuss all this with you, and I need not say I shall give your advice much weight. I haven't got quite enough for my fare, or would come over to England this evening. But I suppose Nairne is still digesting his plum pudding & I lose nothing by waiting a day or two. My landlord gets nothing more

until I have entered into my inheritance. Send me only the fare over &
I start at once; and I depend on you to help me to deal with this thing
promptly.

Once more wishing you all the seasonable wishes.

yours very sincerely   ERNEST DOWSON.

378. *To William Theodore Peters*

14 January 1898

4 & 5 Royal Arcade, Old Bond Street, London W.

Dear Will,

Thanks awfully for your wire received today. I enclose a cheque for
£3—which you can cash at the agent de change (Betts) in the Rue de
Castiglione the next money-changer to the Bodega at the corner of the
Rue de Castiglione & the Rue de Rivoli. The landlord hasn't sent his
bill but it ought to be about 65 francs, as he has had 40 francs on
account. He may want to charge another fortnight if so pay him something on acct. & tell him I will send the rest. Any further expense I will
you may incur I will repay to you when you let me know of it. Will
write again about what to do with the basket. This is a hasty line to
catch post.

affectl yours   ERNEST

P.S. I have sent off the key of basket this morning.

The 40 francs on a/c is marked on enclosed bill.

379. *To William Theodore Peters*

[*c. 20 January 1898*]

1, Guilford Place, Bloomsbury, London, W.C.[1]

My dear Will,

You are a paragon of efficiency, economy & kindness. I am most
awfully obliged to you & fear I have put you to enormous trouble. The
keys have safely arrived & your letter. It is not worth while sending the
balance over. I hope to be over soon. For the moment I am busy at the

1. A lodging-house where Dowson had rooms during most of 1898. It is
described in *The Weird O' It* by M. P. Shiel (1902).

Museum collating the editions of Ben Jonson's "Volpone" for the text which Smithers is to publish with Aubrey Beardsley's illustrations.[2] I have not got my money yet but am promised some hundreds in a week or two. I shall then have to decide upon my plans. It is possible that I may go with Smithers for a short visit to Naples to see Oscar:[3] do not mention this, however. In that case as we shall probably pass through Paris I will get you to dine with us & introduce you to Smithers.

You tell me nothing of your magazine. Is it still preparing? Write to me soon & send me Haskell's[4] address so that I may send him the books he wished. The large paper copies of Pierrot are all sold so that I am unable to get one for you as I had intended. I am dining with Symons tonight. He is very friendly & I think you are wrong in your impression of him; he spoke very well of you.

Present my compliments to the Scherzeffs[5] etc if you see them.

affectly yours   ERNEST

2. Beardsley had begun a series of elaborate illustrations, but died with only a few done. These were published by Smithers late in 1898.
3. Wilde was in Naples until about 10 February, when he moved to Paris. Dowson's plan for a visit fell through and he did not see Wilde again until June 1899.
4. Ernest Haskell, American painter and illustrator (1876–1925), who exhibited in Paris in 1898 and contributed occasionally to *Le Quartier Latin*.
5. Unidentified.

380. *To John Lane*
   [*Early 1898*]

Guilford Place

Dear Mr Lane,

I have just completed a new novel in collaboration with Arthur Moore, with whom I wrote "a Comedy of Masks"—We should be glad to submit it to you, and if you would care to consider it I will bring you round the MSS.[1] I heard from Johnson that you were out of town or I would have called on you.

Yours very truly   ERNEST DOWSON

John Lane Esq

1. Lane did not take *Adrian Rome*, which was published by Methuen in May 1899. The formal tone of this note contrasts sharply with Dowson's earlier letters to Lane. They had probably had no dealings since September 1894, when Dowson transferred *Dilemmas* to Mathews.

381. *To Conal O'Riordan*
[*c. March 1898*]

Guilford Place

My dear Conal,

Forgive my delay in answering you: I was hoping to have raised the money. I am awfully sorry that I must ask you to wait another fortnight. I have had infinite worry & difficulty since June owing to the very complicated legal difficulties in the way of realizing my money. But when I saw my solicitor on the 6th. ult he told me definitely that the matter would be finished in a month's time. I shall then have some hundreds at my disposal & will discharge my debt to you at once. For the moment I have only just enough to carry me through the period of waiting. I am on the very best of terms with Smithers, however, which has cheered me & he has promised me further work. I hope you are well & prospering & that we may meet some day.

Votre bien dévoué   ERNEST DOWSON

Our novel (Moore's & mine) is now with Heinemann. It will be called probably "The Arrangement of Life".

382. *To Leonard Smithers*
[*1898*]

Guilford Place

My dear Smithers,

I am alive although I have had an accident—to my nose—which necessitates confinement to the house. I hope to be presentable by Sat. however, when I will bring you vast amounts of copy.[1] No news from anywhere, I suppose no letter has come to your care for me. Will you not look in sometime and cheer an invalid?

T à vous   E.D.

1. Probably of his translation of *The Memoirs of Cardinal Dubois*.

383. *To Herbert Horne*
    [*Postmark 1 August 1898*]

Guilford Place

My dear Horne,

    I was so very sorry to hear you were ill & have been meaning daily to write and enquire after you. I hope you are on the high road to recovery. I have been very busy lately myself with sundry preparations for departure[1] but I will certainly try & get up to Chelsea before I go, if you are not speedily about again. I don't propose to leave for another week, and may have to postpone my going longer. I will give Smithers your message when he returns from Belgium where he now is.

                  Always yours,   ERNEST DOWSON.

1. Dowson revisited Limerick in the summer of 1898.

384. *Postcard to Herbert Horne*
    Thursday [*Postmark 11 August 1898*]

[*Guilford Place*]

Am so glad you are getting Convalescent—I had an engagement today so could not get out to you but I shall be very glad to come tomorrow (Friday) about 4.0, & am most anxious to see the drawings.[1]

                  yrs   ERNEST DOWSON

1. Horne had a large collection of English eighteenth-century drawings and water-colours.

385. *To Conal O'Riordan*
    [*1898*]

Sophia House, Bloomsbury

My dear Conal,

    Of course I shall be delighted to be translated into the Dutch. I am only sorry that my rudimentary knowledge of the language will prevent me from appreciating the proper values of your friend Van Houten's translation.[1]

I am still in London—still waiting for the completion of my interminable financial transactions, which, however, cannot be spread out beyond another week or two, & then I hope to fly away to some peaceful place in France or Italy & be at rest for a little.

You must come & dine with me if you will before my departure—my really very last departure & we will talk of Ypres.

T à toi   ERNEST DOWSON

You will excuse the flippancy of my note-paper[2] & my language, if you can guess the sadness of my heart.

1. We have not succeeded in tracing this translation.
2. This letter is written on the back of Smithers's prospectus of *Les Liaisons Dangereuses*.

386. *Postcard to Leonard Smithers*
   [*Postmark* [?] *1 March 1899*]

Hôtel Saint Malo, Rue d'Odéssa, Paris

I am intrigued by your card. Is it from a serious Belgian consulate or a jest from Dublin? In either case, perhaps, I had better risk the 2/3. If it is the former, I can only imagine that Leopold has discovered my merit and decided on decorating me.[1]

I am well on with a fat cahier for you.

Toulouse-Lautrec you will be sorry to hear was taken to a lunatic asylum yesterday.[2]

Yrs.   ED

1. The Belgian Government has no record of any decoration being offered to Dowson.
2. Henri de Toulouse-Lautrec (1864–1901), the great French painter and poster artist, was confined in a private asylum at Neuilly late in February 1899.

387. *To Leonard Smithers*
    [? *9 March 1899*]

         Hôtel de la Maison-Rouge, La Roche-Guyon, Eure

My dear Smithers,

    People kept me pottering about at St Germain in an uncomfortable hotel with the promise of an excellent little apartment at 30 francs a month & then broke it to me yesterday that after all it would not be vacant until the end of the month so I came off here & shall stay here for the present. It is cheap & comfortable & as the place is utterly deserted they give me the largest room in the house where I can work splendidly without extra charge. I am sorry the poem[1] slipped my memory. I did not get your letter till yesterday. I have done it to-day & hope it is not too late.

    I have also started work on the Goncourts[2] again & will send you some copy in a day or two. Except for a violent cold I am feeling rather fit & have quite recovered from the results of our excesses of diet when we were in Paris. I hope you are also "going strong" & will drop me a line soon. I will write again in a day or so. It is only about an hour from Paris ~~but~~ & the postal arrangements are singular but I hope this will reach you tomorrow (Friday)

        Ever yours   ERNEST DOWSON

I have duly concerned myself with Smith's[3] beard.

1. Possibly *De Amore*, printed in *Decorations*.
2. *The Confidantes of a King* by Edmond and Jules de Goncourt. Dowson finished his translation in the summer of 1899, but it was not published until 1907.
3. Smith spent 1899 in Paris reading for the degree of Licencié-es-Lettres.

388. *To Leonard Smithers*
    [*April 1899*]

                        Hôtel Saint Malo

My dear Smithers,

    Thanks for returning me the documents. I suppose you are right that I had better accept the arrangement & I am doing so. It is undoubtedly the best thing for me, quâ mortgagee to the amount of £800, through my mother, but what I was uncertain about & wanted to ask you, if I had had more opportunity, was whether it might not be detrimental to me as co-inheritor with my brother of the unfortunate estate on which all these mortgages are charged. I suppose, however, assuming that no better offer then the one Nairne puts before us is obtainable my other interest is not worth considering.

I was awfully disappointed at not getting any money from you to-day. I thought you would send me the £2 . . I lent to Eileen[1] at once. I will forward you £4—worth of work this week (part of it by next post). I am anxious to get back to London, partly in order to see Mr Nairne & get further particulars from him & I will guarantee you the complete translation by the end of this month. If you can let me have an advance, I will and do not think the work sent in entitles me to any further sum as yet, you might surely lend it me as a friend on the understanding that any further sum I obtain from Nairne is placed in your hands at once. I will sign an agreement to that effect if you like. I was very much distressed at what you said to me about Black.[1] I am sure, considering the situation, you would have thought me unspeakably mean if I had not looked after him. The sum I mentioned was simply for his share of dinners etc when we were alone, money advanced, for cigarettes etc. The expense of the night I took him to Barratt's,[2] I paid myself & sundry cabs I took on my own shoulders. If you will send me the £2— however & advance me enough to get back I shall be awfully grateful. I told Methuen to send you a copy of "Adrian Rome". I have not seen it yet but expect a copy to-morrow. Please write by return. Quite apart from any business relations we may have, (and you know how important they are to me) you are the last man in the world I would willingly offend in any way & when I imagine, as I did this last time in Paris, that I had done so it completely unnerves me.

Yrs ever   ERNEST DOWSON

1. Unidentified.
2. Chez Barratte, a café in the Quartier Latin.

389. *To Leonard Smithers*
Monday [? *1 May 1899*]

Hôtel Saint Malo

My dear Smithers,

I have just posted you a budget (2,000 words) & sent you an instalment on Friday. This makes 4 packets of which I have not had an acknowledgement from you. I hope they have not gone astray. I am in much alarm & grief at your silence. I was hoping for money from

you on Saturday & should have been in a fearful state by now had I
not succeeded in borrowing something—on the understanding it should
be repaid at once. If you have not already done so *please* send me a
cheque at once & if you could make it £3—instead of £2—I should be
easier in my mind. I wish you could manage to lend me some time before
the 4th or 5th about £8—. I will make any arrangement you like about
the repayment. I have not the slightest wish to be extravagant but
when my bill is paid, tips etc, I don't know I can get back on any less.
Once in England I may be able to raise money on my interest in the
mortgages. I will send you further copy without fail tomorrow. Smith
tells me you may be over again soon; but in any case I am extremely
anxious to get back. Please don't fail me and let me have a line about
the safe arrival of the copy.

Yours,   ERNEST DOWSON.

390. *Postcard to Leonard Smithers*
  [*Postmark 17 May 1899*]

Hôtel Saint Malo

Thanks for your note. Herewith + 2,500 words. I shall have a further
instalment for next post. This makes nearly 11,000 words during the last
fortnight. J'ai dû acheter une paire de bottines, aussi payer une note à
la crémerie où je dine habituellement, ~~aussi,~~ quoique je vive avec une
économie incroyable je serai bien aise si vous pourrez m'envoyer
quelque ~~chose~~ galette avant *Dimanche* (Dimanche les bureaux de
change sont fermés).

 Je viens de trouver une espèce de brasserie (vraie brasserie) fré-
quentée par des gens de Munich où l'on vend de très bonne bière, à
15 centimes le bock et 25 centimes le demi. Pierre Louys va se marier
avec la fille de Heredia.[1] À demain.

Tout votre   ED.

1. Louÿs announced his engagement to Louise de Heredia in a letter to
Debussy of *c*. 15 May 1899.

391. *To Leonard Smithers*
　　　Sunday [*21 May 1899*]

Hôtel Saint Malo

My dear Smithers,

Thank you for the cheque received last night at a moment when I was about at the end of my tether, having (of necessity) spent no more during the day than 75 centimes & dined on credit. I sent off some 3,700 words this morning & (either on Tuesday or Wednesday) 2,500. Let me know of the safe arrival of these packets. The weather has been very filthy here—constant showers. I have seen no one but Peters & Smith. The latter told me of the amiable Vandyke's[1] indiscretions. I am not surprised in the least. I have seldom met anyone who inspired me with a more profound distrust.

You ~~may~~ will have heard of the sudden & amazing strike of postmen here.[2] You may imagine my feelings, being desirous of seeing your handwriting. It was humorous, however, to see the soldiers, each under the protection of an *agent*. clumsily distributing about 10 of the clock at night the letters which should have been delivered at nine in the morning. The increase in the annual budget necessary to have satisfied the postmen's claim was a vote of 2 millions (francs). The loss incurred sustained by the day & a half's total disorganization of the post, chiefly by people of the banking & *Bourse* genre is estimated at 5 millions.

But I am not a Paris correspondent, unfortunately. I was much delighted with Regie Turner's review.[3] It was not only a very charming review *quâ* review, but an eminently quotable one. If any review could, I should say it would sell the book.

I will send you further copy tomorrow

Tout votre,　　　　ERNEST DOWSON.

1. Paris bookseller and agent for Smithers.
2. The Paris postmen went on strike for one day on 18 May 1899.
3. Reginald Turner (?1870–1938), a close friend of Wilde and Max Beerbohm, at this time on the staff of the *Daily Telegraph* and later the author of ten novels. His review of *Adrian Rome* appeared in the *Daily Telegraph*, 17 May 1899.

392. *Postcard to Leonard Smithers*
　　　Tuesday [*30 May: Postmark of receipt 31 May 1899*]

[*Hôtel Saint Malo*]

Many thanks for enclosure received to-day. I note what you say about the size of packet & will send a bulkier one tomorrow.

Have you seen "Courrier Français" May 21st?[1] There is an article by Lautrec on Beardsley with three reproductions from your last book,

Yrs.   E.D

1. Review of Beardsley's posthumous *A Second Book of Fifty Drawings* (1899).

393. *To Leonard Smithers*[1]

[*Early June 1899*]

[*Hôtel Saint Malo*]

Many thanks for cheque. . . I ran across Oscar last night,[2] also Strong who shook hands with me but objected (through Oscar) to drink with me on the grounds of my relations with Sherard.[3] Oscar quite agreed with me that this conduct was childish and levanted with me to another café. I need not say that *je m'en fous de M. Strong* as much as of Sherard. If you could let me have another cheque by Saturday morning I should be deeply thankful . . . .

P.S. Eleanore[4] whom I saw yesterday told me that Teixeira had been in Paris.

1. Text from *Two Hundred Books from the Library of Richard Butler Glaenzer* (New York, 1911).
2. On 6 June, Wilde wrote to Smithers: 'I saw Ernest Dowson the other night: he forced me to go to the Panthéon at midnight. It was dreadful, a Café-Pandemonium.'
3. They had quarrelled over Strong's part in the Dreyfus affair (see Letter 306).
4. Unidentified.

394. *To Leonard Smithers*

[*5 June 1899*]

Hôtel Saint Malo

My dear Smithers,

Thanks very much for cheque. I wish it could have been for more— but no matter. If you come over for the grand-prix you will probably see a revolution, judging from what happened yesterday.[1] Paris is getting excited as the weather gets hotter. It boils today. After going up to Betts & I have collapsed on my way back to post you your copy. It shall go with further matter tomorrow. Iced coffee is an excellent drink. I forget whether I mentioned to you Lautrec's Beardsley article *Courrier Français* May 31st.[2]

Yours   ERNEST DOWSON

1. The Grand Prix was run on 11 June. A week earlier Royalists had tried to assassinate the President of the Republic on the race-course at Auteuil. A series of political crises kept Paris at fever-pitch throughout the summer.
2. A slip for May 21st.

395. *Postcard to Leonard Smithers*
     Friday [*Postmark 9 June 1899*]

[*Hôtel Saint Malo*]

Have just posted you 2,000 words odd, & have a cahier almost done to follow by next post containing about 3,600. Is there any hope of seeing you over here for Sunday? I am awfully anxious to get back but—alas! I shall be in a fearful state unless I get a letter ETC from you tomorrow. The weather has been awfully trying & has quite knocked me up—but I gather from the papers it has been equally bad in London. PLEASE write & *send* on receipt of this if you have not already done so.

Yrs.   E D

396. *To Leonard Smithers*
     [*c. 13 June 1899*]

Hôtel Saint Malo

My dear Smithers,
    Thanks for cheque. You will have received before now the promised cahier. I am sorry you could not get over this week—the grand prix went off very tamely after all.[1] I was given the winner & second in the

1. The Grand Prix was won by Perth, with Velasquez second.

order of their arrival the previous night but did not invest in them. I am looking forward with all the ardour in the world to seeing you shortly. I wish you could manage to send me this week, if not enough to get away with, at least 100 francs so that I could settle up my bill & move temporarily into a cheaper place. I could get a room for 20 francs. I very much want to see you. I can't help thinking that if you still feel inclined to go in with me to the business you suggested before to me something might be arranged. I gather Vandyck has proved a scoundrel & at any rate you could rely upon my honesty & discretion. Since I have seen the shops in the Palais Royal any previous diffidences or alarms I felt have vanished. I feel also pretty sure that backed up by you, I could get an advance of £100. from my uncle[2] which I would place in your hands for this affair. You would merely have to tell him, as a friend of mine, that you had found a profitable sort of investment for me, advise him, in my interest to advance it, & guarantee the interest & repayment. I would put myself entirely in your hands for the business details—in a sort of monastic obedience—and if you thought it necessary for the success of my endeavours diet myself à la O'Sullivan. *Please think of this seriously.* I am going back now to try & finish up a cahier of equal bulk to the last in time for tonight's post, at any rate it shall go by tomorrow morning's. I sent you a "Figaro" yesterday with one of the most humorous Caran d'Ache's I have yet seen. Treasure it. The "flics" are a joy for ever. Each one has a different face & each one is inevitably and transparently a policeman in plain clothes.[3] Until I saw this picture, when a girl has pointed out to me a harmless looking bourgeois with a tremor & said "Voilà un flic!" I was in the habit of asking: "how do you know?" But the picture teaches.

Let me know of the safe arrival of the *cahiers* & if you can send me a sufficient sum by return to satisfy my landlord please do so.

Yrs ever   ERNEST DOWSON

I met severally & separately yesterday afternoon Oscar, Strong & Sherard—all inveighing bitterly against one another & two of them discussing divers fashions of self-destruction. Oscar was particularly grieved because of a Swedish baron (whom he had met at Marlotte[4] & of whom he hoped much) who had borrowed 5 frances from him on the Boulevard.

2. Stanley Hoole.
3. *Le Chapeau Bastille* in *Figaro*, 12 June 1899. The President is portrayed at the Grand Prix surrounded by a ferociously armed guard of detectives ineffectually disguised as race-goers.
4. Wilde was at Marlotte in the Forest of Fontainebleau in May 1899.

397. *To Leonard Smithers*
[*June 1899*]

Hôtel Saint Malo

My dear Smithers,

I have sent off (registered) copy of the poems,[1] also in same packet about 2.000 words of Goncourt. I should have sent more of the latter, only the poems what with arranging & *redigeant* have taken up all my time. The prose poems I will send on. But do you think they will go well together? I can if necessary send you further verses in a day or two. I am hourly hoping to hear from you & receive enough money to get over to London, or at any rate remove out of reach of my detestable landlord into a room more suitable to my present means. With regard to the verses, the title I have used is quite discretional.[2] I can think of nothing better. Would you kindly hand on the enclosed letter to Bennett.[3] Things are in such a plight that a 2½d stamp is a matter to be considered gravely.

Yrs.   ERNEST DOWSON.

1. Dowson was now preparing his second volume of poems, *Decorations*, for the press. It included five poems in prose, and was published in December 1899.
2. The title at this stage is not known. Dowson later intended to call the book *Love's Aftermath*, but changed to *Decorations: in Verse and Prose* when it was in proof.
3. J. Hannaford Bennett, a friend and assistant of Smithers's and acting editor of *To-Morrow*.

398. *To Leonard Smithers*
[*June–July 1899*]

c/o Paris-Express News Bureau, 105 Boulevard Magenta[1]

My dear Smithers,

Thanks for your letter and cheque. The delay in acknowledging it is due to the fact that I have been staying up here for purposes of

1. Sherard's rooms, where Dowson stayed for about a fortnight. He had by now little more than six months to live and had become weak from neglect. He was again suffering from hallucinations and slept badly.

economy & others, having the place to myself, & that the wretched little chasseur whom I sent daily for my letters pocketed his omnibus fare & never went near the place as I found yesterday, when I got another messenger & received your letter. I was awfully hard up when it came one day having eaten nothing at all but a piece of bread. I wish you could have sent more as it is physically impossible for me to pay my bill & get to England even 3rd class all the way on 100 francs.

With regard to the poems I am sending you the prose poems *registered* and further verses. Your title "Poems in Prose & Verse"— seems all right. That I suggested was in despair of a good inclusive title. If you can do as much as you can ~~this~~ about money I will try to send you 20, or 30,000 words of Goncourt this week. I am also trying to get money elsewhere in order to get over, & to recover certain debts. I feel sure that when once I get over to London & can talk to you there will be little difficulty in raising a hundred as previously suggested. Will you let me have a line acknowledging copy to above address. I certainly have no intention of drinking any monies. Food has lately been too scarce, even tobacco.

Yrs.   ERNEST DOWSON

P.S. The poem on the Renaissance Cloak is included amongst those I sent you. Will you look through them again? I am certain of this or would send you another copy.

399. *To Leonard Smithers*
    Monday [*c. July 1899*]

Hôtel Saint Malo

My dear Smithers,

I herewith enclose cheque for £2. 10. as arranged. I did not send it yesterday as I found I had not my cheque book on me but I suppose it makes no difference. I hope you had a pleasant journey. I saw nobody after leaving you but drank & dined solitary. I will send you a budget of copy tomorrow & also a statement of what I can manage to get back with. Do your best & I will be for ever grateful. By the way Peters has bothered me into writing a preface for his book.[1] I have told him that I think prefaces of the kind ridiculous & have said much the same in the actual preface. It is for you to decide if you will publish it. I am going this afternoon to the Bibliothèque Sainte Geneviève (which is,

---

1. *White Scarabs*, a volume of poems announced as in preparation in Smithers's catalogue for autumn 1899, but not published.

I believe very rich in 18th Century literature, which requires no formalities to use & which unlike the Bte. Nationale has an excellent catalogue) in the hope of finding something traduisible to suggest you.[2] If, by the way, Sherard, as I believe, is now in London, probably maligning me—you will do me a favour by contradicting him. I have lent him money, borne with his temper, stood him & his wretched little w—— of a mistress innumerable meals & been rewarded with nothing but insolence & abuse.[3]

Yours ever   ERNEST DOWSON

2. Dowson's next commission was *The Memoirs of the Duc de Richelieu*. Smithers announced the translation as 'in active preparation', but it was not published. The MS is in Princeton University Library.
3. Dowson is almost certainly exaggerating. Sherard had been at some pains to care for him, and he was glad to accept Sherard's hospitality again at the end of the year.

Epilogue
1899-1900

WHEN Dowson came back to London in the late summer of 1899 he took lodgings at 152 Euston Road. He had still not given up hope of receiving the money due to him from his mother's estate, but the negotiations dragged on without result, while Smithers, who was on the point of bankruptcy himself, found it impossible to pay Dowson regularly.

There must have been some supplies of money, for Dowson was still able to pay for drinks at the Bun House (see Appendix D, *A London Phantom* by R. Thurston Hopkins), but as autumn became winter and the last year of the old century arrived, Dowson became more and more behind with his rent. The rest of the story is best told in Dowson's few remaining letters and in the words of his friends.

400. *To Leonard Smithers*
    [*8 September 1899*]

152 Euston Rd., N.W.

My dear Smithers,
    I wonder if you are back now? I have been ill most of the time since you ~~are~~ left. I tried to get down to see if you were back this evening but was obliged to give it up & return & lie down. I hope to look in tomorrow. It started with a fearful attack of hemhorrhage.
                                        Yrs   ERNEST DOWSON.[1]

1. Smithers's secretary, Florence Brimmacombe, endorsed this letter, 'Answered that you had not returned and that we did not know when to expect you. I wrote this to spare him from coming out in the rain unnecessarily. 9th. Sep. 99. F.S.B.'

SHERARD'S NARRATIVE[1]

One evening I went into the Bodega in Bedford Street to write some letters in the room downstairs. While I was writing, some-one touched me on the shoulder. I turned round and started, for it was as if a being from the grave were standing by my side. It was poor Ernest. He told me that, though he was very ill, he had been driven by the threats of his landlord, who was an Italian music master, to leave his bed and go to the office of his publisher to appeal for help. Smithers had gone off on one of his holidays to Dieppe—with a glare in his eye and a bag full of sovereigns in his pocket—and had left a sarcastic note for Ernest Dowson. There was no chance of getting any money, and he was trying to brace up his courage to return to the Euston Road and to face his land-lord with empty hands. I asked him if half-a-sovereign would help him, and as I passed it to him I felt his hand. It was in an abominable state. "Dowson," I said, "you are very ill, and I am not going to let you return to that place. You must come with me." I told him that just then I was living in a cottage in Cat-ford, of which the lower part was let out to a bricklayer and his wife; but that I could give him a pleasant room to sit in, and that I would look after him until his affairs might take a turn. He said that he would be glad to come, for he had not the courage to wrangle for further grace at his lodgings. "But," he said, "you must take me down to Catford first-class, for I cannot bear to be with people." I remember that he was so weak that I had to take him in a cab to Charing Cross, and again in a cab from Catford Station to my home. He lived with me there just six weeks, the last days of his short life. My first desire after getting him home was to send for a doctor; but he would not allow me to do so. He warned me that if I brought anyone to see him he would leave the house at once.

A few days after these events Sherard wrote to O'Riordan:

Ernest Dowson is here with me in my little cottage. He is not well enough to write to you himself & of course unable to go to see you. He would much like a chat with you & so I am writing to ask you if you would come over here to-morrow afternoon on your bicycle at any hour that may best suit you. Sandhurst Gardens is up a lane to the right just before you come to the Black Horse pub, which is opposite the Catford Fire Station. At the corner of the lane is a wine & spirit merchant. Our fashion-

---

[1] From *The Real Oscar Wilde*.

able residence is in a row of cottages about 200 yards up the lane. The lane is a mud swamp. You pass a big tree before you reach Sandhurst Gardens, also some cottages in course of construction.[1]

[1] MS in the archives of Cassell & Company Ltd.

401. *To Conal O'Riordan*
Tuesday [*February 1900*]

26 Sandhurst Gardens,[1] Catford

My dear Conal,

Thanks many times for your kind letter and remittance. It is a great comfort to me to feel I can come to you now at any time but I fear I am too weak to do it to-morrow. Sherard will not go to Paris this week & Mrs Sherard is most kind in urging me not to leave until I am a little stronger—so I will not inflict myself upon you just yet. Perhaps if the weather improves you will be able to come over & see us. We shall all be delighted to see you. Forgive this short scrawl but it is the first letter I have tried to write & my hand is "nowhere"

always affectly   ERNEST DOWSON

1. Dowson wrote 'Sandown Rd' in error.

402. *To Conal O'Riordan*
[*c. 20 February 1900*][1]

Catford

My dear Conal,

I was going to write & say how grieved I was at the news in your 1st letter when the second came to relieve my mind. Of course my dear old chap nothing you said hurt me & when I get to you & I can't say how much I want to I shall ask my uncle[2] to come & see me. I am deeply grateful for the sums you send me as medicines are so dear & I accept them with less reluctance as I ~~hear~~ had better news from my solo^r the other day & fancy that my money is now within measurable dist. of coming—at any rate I have consented to an arrangement which avoids the necessity of lunatic proceedings & think the ~~tale is~~ affair is now so settled that one of my uncles will at any rate advance me something.

Come over & see us soon, we all wish it

Yrs   ERNEST DOWSON

1. So dated by O'Riordan.
2. Stanley Hoole.

SHERARD'S NARRATIVE CONTINUED

He often used to send me out to get medicines made up for
him from prescriptions which he found in *Health in the Home* or
similar publications. But the seal had been set upon his destiny.
There were no remedies which could have saved his life. He was
dying, though we did not know it, of galloping consumption.
There was nothing to show how near the end was. He made good
meals; he was cheerful; we used to laugh together, as I read him
passages from my work, on the pass to which the Parnassians had
come. Towards the end we used to sit together all day talking of
literature and *les journées de Paris*. At times he put out his
hand and touched mine and said that he was happy that he had
met me. He read all the books that I had in the house, but
Esmond was his favourite volume. He used to take it to bed with
him, and it was by his side when he breathed his last. On the day
before his death, towards evening, his condition began to cause
me serious alarm. He had wished to dictate a letter to me, which
was intended for his friend, the co-author of his novels. But he
could not form the opening phrase. "I feel too tired," he said.
Still I could not induce him that night to go to bed. He sat up
till five in the morning, and even after he had retired to his room
he kept shouting out to me not to go to sleep, but to talk with
him. I remember that we discussed *Oliver Twist*, and to a remark
I made that I did not think that for anything that Fagin could
have told him Bill Sikes would have murdered Nancy he
answered: "No, he would have gone for Fagin." He would not
let me go to sleep. He wished to be convivial. At six in the
morning he asked me to drink some Gilbey's port which was in
his room. At eight he was coughing badly, and he sent me to the
chemist's to get him some ipecacuanha wine, which he said
relieved him. But after this, as he still continued to cough badly,
I declared that the doctor must be fetched. The doctor arrived
an hour after the poor fellow had died. I had gone downstairs to
fetch something and as I was coming up again I called out: "You
had better get up, Ernest, and sit in the arm-chair. You will
breathe more easily." As I entered the room, a woman who was
in attendance in the house pointed to the bed. I looked and saw
that his forehead was bathed in perspiration. I went and raised
him up, and while I was wiping his brow his head fell back on my
shoulder. He was dead.

Sherard wrote to give the news to O'Riordan the same
day:

You will not be able to be kind to Ernest any more. You will be very glad you were the last friend to be good to him. He died suddenly at 10 to 12 to-day. He steadily refused to see a doctor, putting it off until he got to your house. I am to have a Coroner's officer here.[1]

Plarr, who had had almost no news of Dowson since 1897, heard of Dowson's death from the newspaper. "One grey morning in February 1900," he wrote later,[2] ". . . my wife came into the room, and in a very startled and shocked voice announced our friend's death. It was in the morning paper under a sensational heading. Mr. Sherard had written his remarkable and much-quoted account of the poet's last hours. We found ourselves included in the general condemnation of the friends who had let him die. Ye gods! our doors had stood open for him for years! He had stayed many days with us in the dear old seasons: why had he not died with us?"

Among Herbert Horne's papers at the Museo Horne in Florence is a brief account of Dowson's funeral which he wrote on the back of a note from Jepson:

Tuesday, 27th February. The Mass was said at the Catholic church, at Lewisham, at 11 o'clock, and the body afterwards interred in Ladywell Cemetery in a triangular plot of ground just beyond the two chapels, which had recently been reserved for Catholics. The coffin-plate was inscribed: Ernest Christopher Dowson, Died 23 February 1900, aged 32 years. Besides his Uncle, Mr Hoole, & a few relatives, Moore who collaborated with him, Sherard at whose house at Lewisham he died, & his wife, Jepson, Teixeira de Mattos, Mrs Plarr, Bennett, Swanton, Pawle & another actor friend & myself were present."

It was Wilde who paid Dowson the most fitting tribute. Writing to Smithers from Paris just after hearing the news of his death he said: "Poor wounded wonderful fellow that he was, a tragic reproduction of all tragic poetry, like a symbol, or a scene. I hope bay leaves will be laid on his tomb, and rue, and myrtle too, for he knew what love is."[3]

[1] The archives of Cassell & Company Ltd. Dowson died on 23 February 1900.

[2] *Ernest Dowson*, 1888–1897 (1914).

[3] Quoted from *The Letters of Oscar Wilde*.

ADDENDUM

This letter came to light too late to be included in its correct position in the text.

84A. *To William Blackwood*[1]

   [*February 1890*][2]

                                                        Woodford

Dear Sir,
    Enclosed I send you some original verses[3] for which I venture to ask your consideration.
    Should you be able to use them kindly return them to me in the stamped & directed envelope enclosed.
                        Faithfully yours   ERNEST DOWSON

1. Scottish publisher (1836–1912). Head of William Blackwood and Sons and editor of *Blackwood's Magazine*.
2. The letter is endorsed with a note that the poem was returned on 26 February 1890.
3. Probably *Rondel*, completed on 4 February 1890; first published in *Poetical Works*.

Appendices

Appendix A

EXAMPLES OF DOWSON'S CONTRIBUTIONS TO *THE CRITIC*

A WHITE LIE by Sydney Grundy

royal court theatre—*Saturday Evening, May 25th*, 1889

A representative first-night audience was attracted to the Court Theatre on Saturday last to witness the production of a new play by Mr. Sydney Grundy, which had been originally tried in the provinces, although so many alterations and improvements have since been made in it that the preliminary ordeal of *A White Lie* at Nottingham did not seem to have in any way detracted from the freshness of interest with which its inauguration on the London boards was hailed. On the whole we must congratulate Mr. Grundy on this his last effort. There is no play perfect, no play—at least, I can think of none produced in London of late years—which the cavilling critic cannot successfully assail, and *A White Lie* is certainly no exception to this universal rule. It has many obvious blemishes, some of which I shall have to touch upon later, but, at the same time, it is simple captiousness to ignore that it contains work of a very high order, and work, be it said, by no means in that popular and meretricious vein with which Mr. Grundy's name has been far too long associated. In *A White Lie* Mr. Grundy has made an effort which, whatever may be the verdict that it may ultimately receive, is most emphatically a play dealing with serious interests, and demanding necessarily of the critic serious consideration. The plot is briefly as follows: *George Desmond*, a devoted but jealous husband, whom ten years of married felicity have not succeeded in putting out of conceit with his wife, finds himself obliged to run over to America on business, and the curtain rises on the morning of his departure in the *Desmonds'* drawing-room, just as his sister, a young and foolish bride, *Lady Molyneux*, is paying her first call on the *Desmonds* on her return from her honeymoon. She is married to *Sir John Molyneux*, a languid, bored gentleman, who has nothing to do and hates doing it, with a tendency to fall asleep on the smallest provocation—a tendency which has already succeeded in exciting the entire contempt of his young wife, who is exceedingly unhappy at always being allowed to have exactly her own way. *Sir John* appears soon afterwards, and, although he speedily lapses into slumber, it is not long before we guess that his sleepiness is about as superficial as the apparent 'greenness' of *John Mildmay* in *Still Waters*, of

LED–E[1]

which time-honoured comedy, by the way, there are many reminiscences in Mr. Grundy's latest production. It speedily transpires
that *Lady Molyneux* is more than half in love with an unscrupulous
admirer who has followed her from abroad, a *Captain Tempest*,
and when this gentleman calls to escort her ladyship home—her
husband having retired, characteristically satisfied that this
should be so—one immediately becomes aware, firstly, that the
Captain is the inevitable drawing-room villain, who will be responsible for the *lacrimae* to be; secondly, that he is in this case
an ancient lover of *Kate Desmond* (Mrs. Kendal). Indeed, the
husband's ridiculous jealousy is already rampant, and, although
when he questions her and extorts her admission that she was
once engaged to *Tempest*, his anger is appeased by her playful
profession of wifely love, and they bid their *adieux* amicably and
with emotion perhaps hardly justified in view of the shortness of
the period for which they part, the seed of distrust has been sown
and only wants occasion to blossom into a promising misunderstanding. In the second act some time has elapsed, and *George
Desmond* is shortly expected home. The scene has shifted to *Sir
John Molyneux's*, and *Captain Tempest*, who has taken up his
abode there, is making love to his host's wife with the utmost
vigour. *Mrs. Desmond* is also there—an uninvited guest. She is
convinced of *Tempest's* utter want of principle, and endeavours to
stir the languid husband up to some decisive action. But *Jack
Molyneux* is not to be moved, and although he is quite aware of the
critical state of things, and is determined to take a line at his own
time, he still leaves the rest—*Kate*, *Tempest*, and his wife *Dolly*—
under the impression that he is absolutely indifferent. At last he
wakes up from a sleep on the sofa—an episode lacking in probability—to surprise his wife lending a willing ear to *Tempest's* open
avowal of love. He is perfectly calm, but he promptly shows the
Captain to the door, and carries his coolness so far as to see him
to the station. Unfortunately, while waiting there he observes
Tempest give a note to his groom, and although he does not inter-
cept it, he returns in time to take it from his wife's paralysed hands
in the presence of her sister-in-law. It is couched in ambiguous
terms, but entreats her to fly, appointing a rendezvous after dark
in the garden. Then *Kate Desmond* rises to the occasion and tells
her 'white lie,' a big one and a most foolish one in all conscience.
'Give me the letter,' she says; 'it was written to me.' That *Sir John*,
whose shrewdness one has by this time fully gauged, should not
be taken in by this stupendous fiction is only natural; it is even
conceivable that a vain and silly woman like *Lady Molyneux*, who
has all along ascribed the kindly interference of her sister to

jealousy, should herself be deceived by *Kate's* well-meant, if injudicious, effort to shield her; but it is impossible to understand why *George Desmond*, who puts in an unexpected appearance immediately afterwards and is informed by *Sir John* of the state of affairs and of his (*Sir John's*) suspicions as to *Kate's* motives, should immediately throw the experience of his ten years'married life to the winds and come to the conclusion that his wife has dishonoured him. He obtains the compromising letter which *Kate* has claimed, as well as the ambiguous reply that, in her determination to give colouring to her lie and shield her silly sister-in-law at all costs, she has foolishly written; and so—on evidence which would be insufficient to hang the proverbial dog—he brutally accuses his wife of infidelity, and drives her from him. The second act culminates in a passionate scene between husband and wife, in which ample scope is allowed for Mrs. Kendal's emotional acting, and the curtain falls when the child's voice is heard calling from behind, and *George*, with Spartan severity which would be brutal—even if, as in this instance, it was not totally uncalled for—refuses to allow her mother to see her. In the third and last act there is a pretty scene—perhaps the most charming in the play—between *George Desmond* and his little girl. He hears the child her lessons and listens to her innocent prattle concerning 'mamma' with conflicting sentiments of love and repulsion, which would possibly appeal more strongly to the sympathies of the audience if their reason were not so entirely inadequate. The remainder of the act—in which from this point the interest perceptibly flags—is devoted to a clearing-up of the misunderstanding, which one cannot help feeling in real life would never have arisen. *Tempest* is severely humbled, and tells the truth. An unnecessary scene between *George* and his wife, which is excusable, however, for the splendid opportunity it affords Mrs. Kendal for some intensely emotional acting, is cut short by the entrance of *Sir John* and the repentant *Dolly*, who, after a severe but serviceable lesson to her vanity, is quite ready to fall in love again—this time, however, with her husband. *George* is convinced of his absurd mistake—husband and wife, mother and child, are once more happily united, and this 'Storm in a Teacup'—we suggest the name to Mr. Grundy as preferable to that he has chosen—is brought to an end. The weak points of the play, which is redeemed throughout by a constant flow of dialogue of never-flagging brilliancy and by many moving dramatic situations, are sufficiently obvious. It is possible—though not probable—that a woman of *Mrs. Desmond's* calibre might on the spur of the moment tell such a 'white lie' as is the motive of Mr. Grundy's play; it is almost impossible that a husband of ten years' standing should be taken in by it. Apart from this hard morsel for the critical understanding to swallow, there is little else to detract from the very high praise which one can conscientiously bestow on this last and worthiest effort of a playwright of whom even when he seemed most given up to the production of farcical 'pot-boilers,' one could never quite cease to hope that he would at length reassert himself and rise to 'better things.' And it is needless to say that between *A White Lie* and—say—*Merry Margate* there is a very wide gulf. Mrs. Kendal is a most womanly and sympathetic *Kate Desmond*, better, perhaps—although I am aware this is a great heresy—in the pure comedy portions of the play than in the later acts where, although she can be both pathetic and impressive, she has a tendency to be rather more tragic than the situation warrants. Perhaps for this slight tendency to unduly intensify the emotional scenes, which was apparent in Mrs. Kendal, and painfully evident from the first in Mr. Glendinning's *George Desmond*, the author may be a good deal responsible; in any case, he was admirably assisted in this error by the actors. Mr. Kendal was thoroughly at home in the part of *Sir John Molyneux*, and looked and acted his character to perfection. Mr. Arthur Dacre, as *Tempest*, was all that could be wished, and presented a calm and clever study of a 'stage villain,' who was not in the least 'stagey,' and had nothing transpontine about him. Of Mr. Glendinning's *George Desmond* the less said the better. It was the great blemish in the evening, and, although he has that to be said of him that his part was a difficult one, and one which no dramatic ability could ever make very effective, it was evident that Mr. Glendinning entirely failed to give it its proper value, or to infuse into it that small quantum of sympathy of which it might have been capable. Miss Olga Brandon was obviously nervous, a fault which will, no doubt, diminish at each representation, otherwise her performance was well enough. *Lady Molyneux*, however, is a sufficiently unamiable person, even if her constitutional discontent was not exaggerated by Miss Brandon's incessant sneer. On Saturday, moreover, this lady's 'make up' was a great deal too pale. Dear little Minnie Terry, as *Daisy Desmond*, was entirely her own self-possessed little self. Amongst child actresses she stands alone— always natural, always simple, always charming, she treads the boards, plays with her doll, or objects to saying her lessons, with as utter an absence of self-consciousness or affectation, and as perfect a spontaneity, as if she were in her own nursery at home. Her spontaneity, indeed, always strikes me afresh with new amazement —it is difficult to believe at times she is simply saying something she has learnt by rote—and her share in the dialogue on Saturday was so childlike, and withal so appropriate, that I frequently forgot the credit which Mr. Grundy should have for his share in it in my admiration of the cleverness of this wonderful little lady. It is impossible to exaggerate the dramatic efficiency which the part of *Daisy* lends to the play. When this delightful little girl is on the stage the interest is at its highest, and on at least one occasion—at the beginning of the third act—she saved the play at a critical moment, when the false note that Mr. Glendinning had unfortunately struck threatened to turn the situation into a bathos. Altogether, if *A White Lie* attains that success which I hope, and which I feel sure, with a little exertion, it may be made, it will owe as much to the charming acting of this dainty little player as to the less artless efforts of much bigger if not more talented people. At the close of the performance the author was loudly called, and was greeted when he made his appearance with an enthusiasm which, coming from so keenly critical an audience, augurs well for him. *A White Lie* is preceded by a new comedietta, by Rudolf Dircks, called *In the Corridor*. There is some clever dialogue in this little piece, although its interest is of the slightest. Miss Annie Hughes, however, was well applauded in some rather original love-making, in which there is much talk of the 'social status of the actor,' with Mr. Eric Lewis, who also played with a good deal of humour. There is no actress on the English stage who makes a more admirable *ingénue* than Miss Hughes, but surely she is rather wasted on a 'curtain raiser.'

A DOLL'S HOUSE by HENRIK IBSEN

THE NOVELTY THEATRE—*Friday Evening, June 7th, 1889*

THE poor little house in Great Queen Street, with its tradition of failure, has, for once in its inauspicious existence, been the scene of a conspicuous success, a veritable triumph. Ibsen's altogether exceptional power, the rugged strength of his genius, and the uncompromising directness with which he goes straight to the heart of the social problems which he has set himself to tackle, is well known to every reader of his plays. How far, however, these weighty and careful analyses of some of the most vexing sores of humanity would lend themselves to actual dramatic representation was, perhaps, even with some of the greatest admirers of Ibsen's genius, an open question. But the experience of Friday night was conclusive. From the first rising of the curtain the interest of the extraordinary play forced itself upon one, and as it proceeded the characters—so life-like, so intensely real—seemed to have gripped hold of the audience with an intensity which was continuous to the end. The story of *A Doll's House* is too well known to require detailed description. Like all Ibsen's plays it is a ruthless, but severely logical, onslaught on the conventional ideals—if they can be called ideals—of society. In the eyes of the Scandinavian dramatist society is no longer a respectable quantity—it is a society which in its present state has become impossible. But Ibsen, in spite of the popular idea of him, is by no means a Socialist. On the contrary, there is no more marked feature of his theory than the importance which he gives to the individual. And Ibsen is furthermore a pessimist—he has no vulgar and arbitrary Morrison's pill to apply to the universal *malaise*. On the contrary, his genius is destructive, and although in a famous toast, into which he threw something of the solemnity of a libation, he drank to '*Das Kommende das Werdende*'—the future to which he looks out is a distant one. And so, as has been well said, his plays—and this play is not an exception—end in a note of interrogation. *A Doll's House* deals with the much-vexed marriage question, and deals with it with a breadth of view which must fill the average *bourgeois* soul with horror. *Nora* has been the petted daughter of a rich official, and she is, when the action of the play begins, the petted wife of a rising Norwegian lawyer, an amiable egotist, with more than a dash of the prig in him. She is a charming, irresponsible creature, but she has never been at any time of her life treated as other than a doll, and of the moral facts of life she has remained in severe ignorance. She is simply a child, and the first act is devoted, with a precision of detail which can only seem trivial to persons who fail to realise its dramatic necessity, to the unfolding of her childishness. But this charming creature is destined to suffer a rude awakening. In perfect ignorance of the criminal nature of her act, in order to procure the necessary funds to take her delicate husband to a warmer climate she has forged her dead father's name as security for a loan which she has procured from one of her husband's subordinates. *Nils Krogstad*, who has *Nora* thus in his power, has himself been ostracised for a fault of a similar nature, and when her husband, *Torvald*, dismisses him, for a petty, inadequate motive enough, from his post in the bank he uses this document to insure his reinstatement, and with it his last chance of retrieving his reputation. In spite of her entreaties the man is resolute, and when the letter which is to inform *Torvald* of his wife's indiscretion falls into the letter-box her whole energies are concentrated on a postponement of the discovery. The scene which follows, in which the unhappy woman wrought up to a pitch of hysterical frenzy rehearses a *tarantella* for the fancy dress ball which she must go to that night, is one of indescribable power; and the natural effect of the part is so enhanced by the wonderful acting of Miss Janet Achurch that the audience hails the inevitable discovery, when it comes, with a sigh of almost physical relief. When *Helmer* becomes aware of his wife's childish peccadillo he is incapable of considering motives, and so far from taking her innocent guilt on his own shoulders as she had dreaded, and at the same time half hoped, he upbraids her furiously for having dishonoured him. The storm passes; *Krogstad*, the victim of society, has joined hands with *Mrs. Linden*, one of Ibsen's most characteristic women, who persuades him to return the forged surety, and *Torvald*, in the revulsion caused by this unexpected lightening of his load, turns once more to his wife with the expansive forgiveness of the consummate prig. She is once more his 'lark,' his 'song-bird', and he is prepared to pet her as much as ever, and watch over her more carefully than before. But to *Nora* a change has come: in the terrible strain of the last few hours she has snapped her chains; she is no longer a doll but a woman, and in the *Doll's House* which her husband has made for her she can have henceforth no part or portion. The short dialogue between the husband and wife, in which she announces her intention of leaving him, and meets all his pleadings with a stony resolution, is not only eminently dramatic, but it points and concludes the argument of the play. A great wrong, *Nora* declares, has been done to her, first by her father and then by her husband. They have treated her as a doll; she has not been happy, only merry; her husband has not loved her, it has simply amused him to be in love with her; and the children she has borne to him have been her dolls, and until she has learnt more of life—and he is no fit teacher for her—their instruction must pass out of her hands. After eight years of marriage she has awakened to the fact that her husband is a stranger to her, and in the house of a strange man she cannot continue to live. He reproaches her with ingratitude, with a failure in her duty, but her primary duty she tells him is to herself. 'You are a wife and mother before everything,' he says. 'No, Torvald,' she answers, 'before everything I am an individual, a human being, just as much as you are.' And so, leaving him with bowed head to accept this unanswerable truth, and telling him that in the future they must both be free, she casts off the Neapolitan fisher girl's dress in which she has come from the ball, as if it were the visible sign of her dollhood, and goes out into the dark, blindly, resolutely, to know and see, and find out for herself. And what will be the issue of her scepticism is for the audience, as doubtless for the author, a matter which is yet to seek. The acting of this remarkable play, which goes so sternly and with such relentless disregard of our conventional prejudices to the very heart of things, was almost uniformly excellent. Miss Achurch's impersonation of *Nora* was simply faultless. She seemed to have grasped from the first the true significance of the character, and with a grace and refinement of execution which cannot be too highly praised, she consistently retained her hold of the sympathies of the audience until the end. It was a part which even the most subtle actress might have easily misinterpreted, and a part, be it said, in which, entailing such immense physical exertion as it does, a less fragile-looking actress than Miss Achurch might excusably flag towards the end; and this lady, therefore, deserves all the more credit for a successful creation which must at once reveal her to all lovers of really artistic acting as an actress of a very high order indeed. Mr. Waring as the egotistic, severely conventional husband, played a thankless part with discretion and intelligence, and Mr. Royce Carleton as the corrupt but human *Nils Krogstad* was very effective. The small and grisly part of *Dr. Rank*, a character brought in to illustrate the force of heredity—a ghastly factor in life, which seems to exercise as great a fascination over Ibsen as over Emile Zola—was played with a terrible, subdued power by Mr. Charrington. The visit of the *Doctor*, who is suffering in his own person for the sins of his ancestors, when he comes in after the ball for the last time to announce his own death, is indescribably impressive, it grips hold of one—it is the quality of all Ibsen's work at its finest—with a sense of overpowering reality, and the footlights, for the nonce, go for nothing. And one cannot help hoping that if ever the brave little band of Ibsenites repeat their experiment, and produce the very tragedy of heredity and Ibsen's most characteristic work, *Ghosts*, that the part of *Alving* may be entrusted to that actor of genius whose *Dr. Rank* was a study so lifelike, so unpleasantly vivid, and so full of an almost unnatural gruesomeness, that its final impression will not be easily forgotten by those who have seen it.

THE CULT OF THE CHILD

August 17th, 1889

THE clause in the Protection of Children's Bill relating to the employment of young children in theatres has been exciting a good deal of discussion lately, and doubtless the end of it all has not yet been heard. As to the merits of the clause in question we do not propose to speak, chiefly we must confess because our sympathies are somewhat divided. It would, of course, be obviously shameful that these 'little eyases that cry out on the top of question, and are most tyrannically clapped for it,' should be in any way sacrificed for the sake of the public's amusement. If these children do, by their contact with the stage, suffer any detriment in mind, body, or estate, which they would not sustain equally in their own homes—presumably humble—without a doubt the clause prohibiting their employment should stand. But is this the case? It is a difficult question, and one on which we should like some less disinterested opinions than have yet been evoked. In the meantime, however, doubtless we must be contented with Lord Dunraven's compromise, for whatever may be said about pantomime children, the case of 'star' children is hardly the same. With them the question is one of aesthetics rather than of ethics, and if, like the former one, it is a question upon which theatre-goers are not in unison, it is one upon which we ourselves have a very strong conviction. Artistically we find the child-actress an enormous boon to the modern stage. There are cases within our recollection in which a play, in itself foolish, or, at the best, trivial, has been redeemed and made artistically possible by the marvellous acting of a tiny child. And there is no greater fallacy than the assumption which we have seen quite lately expressly stated in an article by one of our smartest dramatic critics, that a child's acting is necessarily inartistic. In our opinion it is generally the reverse. At the risk of appearing paradoxical, we must even assert that there is every reason why a child's acting should be artistic—more artistic even than that of most 'grown ups.' The men and women who are naturally actors and actresses are, as we know by painful experience, in the exception. But in childhood we are all spontaneously dramatic. Without effort children take up poses the most delightfully naive in the world. Tragedy, comedy, romantic drama, they play it all by turns. A child who is a real child and not a precocious little prig, a child who has entered into its inheritance, lives all its real life in the kingdom of pretence. It is only when we have turned our first decade that we begin to grow out of the 'passion for

making believe.' Anyone who has been a sympathetic observer of
a little girl with her doll must admit the truth of this. What
dramas! what romances! what a wealth of histrionic power is
lavished on the wooden puppet! To the gross adult vision it is
hideous—even repulsive; it has probably—assuming it to be the
best beloved of dolls—a smudged countenance, and a mutilated
body, but it suffices to the glorious imagination of seven for an
infinity of *rôles*. Her name is legion—this staring Dutch atrocity—
and she has a personality in the mind of her diminutive mistress
for each one of her names. And why should not this charming,
childish instinct be trained and cultivated for the pleasure of dis-
criminating folk who can appreciate it. Why should not we have
children on the stage—if it does not hurt them? We may be told
that, after all, it is unfair; it is making them toil for our amusement. Well, if that is so, if it is really a hardship, people are right
to protest. But we doubt if this is the case. Our opinion is that it is
a pleasure to them; we believe that they delight in it. And if they
work hard at it, it must be remembered that they work very hard
at play. As Montaigne says, 'the play of children is not performed
in play, but to be judged as their most serious action.' And to let
children go on the stage is, after all, to do nothing worse than to
cultivate their playful instinct. And the children whom we applaud
the most, who touch us most, are precisely those who are most
themselves, who play with the fewest limitations, who, in a word,
are the greatest children. Of course, there are persons who are
incapable of delighting in the childish character. But with these
we need hardly concern ourselves. It is enough that there are an
ever increasing number of people who receive from the beauty of
childhood, in art as in life, an exquisite pleasure. There is no more
distinctive feature of the age than the enormous importance
which children have assumed. We have only to look at a bookstall
—to catalogue the countless children's books, assuredly not
chiefly read in the nursery—to go to the Academy, to take up a
newspaper to realise this. '*Que l'enfant veut doit être à lui, s'il le
préfère.*' It is in this adage of Victor Hugo which has taken the
place of the repressive maxims of our grandsires. And, on the
whole, we agree with Victor Hugo, and, indeed, make it our business to 'spoil' all our childish acquaintance as much as we are
allowed. Indeed, it is not surprising that an age which is, after all,
chiefly pessimist, an age which is so deeply disillusioned, should
turn with an immense delight to the constant charm of childhood.
Sentimental unrealities *à la* Buchanan no longer appeal to us; our
realism has made us difficult, and, profoundly disgusted with the
result of our scepticism, we naturally hail the more eagerly the

one unimpeachable consolation which our scepticism cannot touch. And not less in the drama than in the rest of art the cult of the child should have a place, so that just as we seek relief from the sombre and relentless psychology of M. Paul Bourget in the realism of the nursery, the charming pages of Mrs. Ewing, we may find it now and again across the footlights, and acknowledge, as we must all have done a year ago, when we applauded the exertions of the charming little player who performed the *title-rôle* in Mrs. Winter's play of *Bootle's Baby*, that art can still offer us the counterfeit presentment of one exquisite relation.

THE NOBILITY OF ART IN DEATH

The Obsequies of Emile Augier—Dramatist

November 2nd, 1889

All literary and dramatic Paris was called together on Monday last to pay the final honours, at the church of the Trinity, to the illustrious dramatist which France and that universal world embraced by Art have just lost.

The porch of the church was temporarily turned into a mortuary, and was an impressive spectacle, with its black drapery fringed with silver, and relieved with the initials of the dead artist.

On the bier the academical sword and hat of the dramatist were placed. The Academy was represented in force; the Duc d'Aumale, Sully Prudhomme, Dumas, Claretie, and Sardou taking prominent places in the obsequies. MM. Tirard and Spuller were present, representing the Government. The service was sadly impressive, the orchestra of the Opéra Comique playing the introductory funeral march of Méhul under the direction of M. Viardot, and assisting the organist, M. Bonichère, in the mass which followed.

The orations—so inseparable a part of the French funeral— were given by M. Claretie and M. Larroumet. If they, perhaps, erred a little on the side of panegyric, the fault in this instance was a generous one. Excellent as their speeches were, I will refrain from giving them in their entirety. Here, however, are the passages with which I was most struck. M. Larroumet said:—

'Gentlemen, Emile Augier was in every sense of the word a national writer, and no one more than he merited that noble title. He unites in himself many of the essential qualities of the French character, with a vigour and frankness of expression which have made of him not only the glory of half a century, but one of those men in whom the soil of a great country asserts itself. Numbers of writers represent above all—themselves; that is one particular turn of character and sentiment; such writers pass away without taking with them aught else than their individuality. There are some, on the contrary, who combine with personal originality so large a quantum of the national character, that the people regret in them an expressive and faithful type in which they delight to recognise themselves. Emile Augier was one of those; each one of his successes was hailed by us with a pride which associates us with the glory of authorship by all that is best in every citizen—I should say the community of spirit which unites the sons of one mother and constitutes the soul of a nation.

'It would only need to enumerate his works to enumerate each one of his qualities, which since the day that France grew conscious of herself have developed through the centuries, and have finished by constituting the French character, that is to say a *mélange* as unique as it is charming, of sense, experience and idealism, of frankness and subtlety, of wit and of logic, of common sense and of poetry.'

With many other such rhetorical utterances was the body of Emile Augier consigned to the tomb, the mortal man and the immortal work of the same fleshly hand gaining in one second of Eternal Time that immeasurable nobility which is only conferred by the greatest and most blessed of donors—Death!

Appendix B

HERBERT HORNE'S DRAFT FOR THE CONTRACT OF *DILEMMAS*[1]

E.M. undertakes to print at least 600 copies of five stories by E.D. which have appeared in Temple Bar, Macmillans, & Hobby Horse, to be sold at 3/6 a copy net, out of which E.M. will pay E.D. 6d a copy royalty exclusive of review & presentation copies. In the event of an American edition being published the royalty paid to be 3d a copy. E.M. will pay E.D. royalty of 6d per copy for the first three hundred copies, on the day of publication. E.D. undertakes not to reprint the above stories until the whole of the above edition shall have been disposed of by E.M. provided that in any event the copyright shall revert to E.D. at the end of 4 years from the date of publication.

[2] I promise to provide you with six gratuitous copies and as many further copies as you may require at the ordinary trade terms.
[2] I should like to publish towards the end of November.
[2] I agree to the above terms.

[3] c-o Teixeira de Mattos,
    3 Plowden Buildings,
        in the Temple.

[1] Manuscript in Princeton University Library.
[2] Notes in pencil by Elkin Mathews.
[3] Added on back by E.C.D.

Appendix C
PROCES VERBAL

Extrait

des minutes du Greffe de la Justice
de Paix du canton de Pont-Aven

Audience de simple police du 21 juillet 1896. Entre: M. René Canéret adjoint au maire de la commune de Pont-Aven y demeurant.

(Jugement simple police Dowson Ernest et Denos Raymond.)

1° Dowson Ernest, âgé de 28 ans, homme de lettres, demeurant à Pont-Aven hôtel Gloanec, né à Londres le 2 août 1867.

2° Denos Raymond, âgé de 25 ans, sans profession, demeurant à Quimperlé où il est né rue du Bourgneuf, domicilié à Lorient.

La cause appelée, le greffier a donné lecture d'un procès verbal dressé le 11 juillet 1896 par MM. Richard et Moreau gendarmes à Pont-Aven affirmé et enregistré, duquel il résulte que le dit jour, sur plainte du sieur Limbour Louis boulanger à Pont-Aven, les dits sieurs Dowson et Denos vers une heure du matin et à deux reprises différentes—étant sous l'influence de la boisson—ont secoué fortement la porte de la boulangerie du plaignant et après ouverture faite par celui-ci ils sont entrés précipitamment chez lui, l'ont saisi au collet, déchiré et enlevé sa chemise et cassé deux carreaux de la croisée.

Les contrevenants ont reconnu le fait constaté à leur charge et ont exprimé le vif regret de s'être ainsi oubliés et d'avoir commis la faute qui leur est reprochée et ont demandé l'indulgence du tribunal.

Ouï les contrevenants en leurs aveux et explications.

Attendu que de ce procès verbal il résulte que les sieurs Dowson et Denos, vers une heure du matin, étant sous l'influence de la boisson ont secoué fortement la porte de la boulangerie du sieur Limbour plaignant—que celui-ci, croyant que c'étaient des marins qui venaient lui demander du pain, s'est levé—qu'à l'ouverture de son domicile les prévenus se sont précipités sur lui, l'ont pris au collet et déchiré sa chemise—qu'un instant après avoir été mis à la porte les dits prévenus sont revenus à la charge et n'ayant pu rentrer de force ils ont brisé deux carreaux sur la fenêtre:

Attendu que les contrevenants ont reconnu le fait constaté à leur charge:

Attendu que si le sieur Limbour a retiré sa plainte les faits dont se sont rendus coupables Dowson et Denos n'en doivent pas moins être punis:

Par ces motifs le Tribunal:

Déclare les contrevenants convaincus de la contravention qui leur est reprochée et les condamne à l'amende d' un franc chacun pour ivresse et à quatre francs chacun également pour tapage nocturne: les condamne en outre solidairement au dépens de l'instance liquidée à la somme de quatre francs huit centimes compris le coût du présent jugement:

Fixe quant à l'amende et au paiement des frais envers l'Etat la durée de la contrainte par corps à deux jours chacun.

Ainsi jugé et prononcé par Nous Guigner Francisque Le Galher Juge de Paix du canton de Pont-Aven présidant l'audience de simple police assisté de Mᵉ Pierre Le Mastric greffier en audience publique tenue à deux heures de soir au prétoire de la Justice de Paix.

Appendix D

A LONDON PHANTOM

by

R. Thurston Hopkins

Towards the end of the eighteen-nineties I was a student at University College in Gower Street, London. That seems to be all that is necessary to say about a fact that is not of the faintest interest to anyone but the writer of this narrative. But what may be of interest to the reader is that it was during this time that there walked into my life (via the Bun House, a haunt of bohemianism in the Strand) that amazing and erratic poet Ernest Dowson. Thin, small-boned, light brown wavy hair which was always curiously upstanding, blue eyes, a tired voice and nerveless, indeterminate hands, with thin fingers, such as are in the habit of letting things fall and slip from them. That is Dowson as I resurrect him from the mists of the dear dead London of the eighteen-nineties. He wore a disreputable out-of-elbows coat that seemed to be distressingly short above his rump. His collar was, I distinctly remember, tied together with a piece of wide black moire ribbon which acted as a poet's bow and a fastening for his shirt at the same time.

Dowson seldom smiled. His face was lined and grave, and yet it was the round face of a schoolboy and sometimes one might catch a gleam of youth in his blue eyes. At such moments a ghost of a smile would flit over his sombre features and wipe out the fretful expression which generally lurked there.

At that time he carried a small silver-plated revolver in his hip pocket and he seemed ridiculously proud of it. He would produce it, and hand it round for inspection in bars and cafés, without comment, and for no apparent reason at all. I never discovered what risky tortuous paths impinged on Dowson's life, that he should think it necessary to carry a gun; but perhaps he was toying with the idea of suicide. God knows, he must have found life a very distressing affair, for his thirty years' existence on earth had been one long catalogue of disillusionments, financial worries and heartbreaks.

I spent many evenings with Dowson in the Bun House. Though the name of this rendezvous has a doughy sound, it never at any time offered buns to its customers. It is just a London tavern, but it was part of the literary and newspaper life of the eighteen-nineties. It was there that I saw Lionel Johnson, the poet, John Evelyn Barlas, poet and anarchist who tried to 'shoot up' the

House of Commons, Edgar Wallace, just out of a private soldier's uniform, Arthur Machen in a caped 'Inverness' coat which he told me had been his regular friend for twenty years. 'I hope to wear out four of these magnificent cloaks during my lifetime—anyway I can make four last out a hundred years!'

At that time absinthe was a popular spirituous drink amongst the young poets and literary vagabonds, and I can still see Dowson sitting on a high stool, lecturing on the merits of this opalescent anaesthetic. 'Whisky and beer for fools; absinthe for poets'; 'absinthe has the power of the magicians; it can wipe out or renew the past, and annul or foretell the future' were phrases which recurred in his discourse. 'Tomorrow one dies' was a saying which was often on his lips, and he would sometimes add, 'and nobody will care—it will not stop the traffic passing over London Bridge'.

After I had met Dowson a few times at the Bun House we would sometimes rove forlornly about the foggy London streets, initiated bohemians, tasting each other's enthusiasms. Sharing money and confessions, Dowson wielding a cheap Austrian cigar artfully and blowing smoke rings through his nostrils. As we wandered about London at night we often played a sort of game which we called Blind Chivvy. The idea was to find short cuts or round-about-routes from one busy part of London to another by way of slinking alleys and byways which then were not well known to the average London man.

One evening we were blind chivvying in a puzzle of by-ways, yards, courts and alleys when we became aware of a dark form following us—a figure wrapped up, intent and carrying a gladstone bag. We turned and twisted and he turned and twisted. We could not be mistaken—he was following us. Soon our unwanted 'companion' was so close on our heels that we could hear him heavily breathing. At this a foolish feeling of alarm gripped me, but I struggled to save myself from getting panicky.

Nevertheless as soon as we turned into a busy main street I pulled Dowson across to the friendly gas lamps and said to him: 'Run like the Devil!!'

When we had shaken this unwelcome wayfarer off I asked Dowson if he had caught sight of the man's face. No he had not; nor had I. But we both had an idea of a dark wrapped-up scare-crow following us through the empty courts with a debauched-looking gladstone bag in his hand.

A few nights later Dowson and I were in a bar parlour having a couple of frugal 'beers' when I noticed Dowson patting his pockets to locate his cigarette case. Dowson—who wrote that poem *Cynara* that has since been popularized all over the world by

LED–F[1]

its use as a title and a motif in one of Ronald Colman's famous films—was an absent-minded dreamer who never could return his cigarette case to the same pocket twice running. At that moment somebody slipped through the swing door of the bar. He was tall and thin; carried a horrible old gladstone bag; a mummified figure in an overcoat with a crazy old mackintosh over it. His face was almost hidden by a dirty silk scarf which was bound round his jaw as though he had toothache.

Yes! it was the same man who had followed us through the back streets only recently. It is a funny thing to say, but I felt that this figure (or 'personage' shall we say?) was not bound by the limits of youth or of age—there was some strange quality about him that was other-worldly. I found it difficult to think of him as a *live* human being.

Meanwhile Dowson fumbled for his cigarette case with ineffective fingers, without result.

Then a low voice came from the mummy-like figure: 'Try your hip pocket.'

Dowson dived into the hip pocket and found the elusive cigarette case. We looked up and met the eyes of the visitor. Afterwards we tried to recall why we felt that this man—this personage—was so horrible: why he filled us with the essence of terror and repulsion. I do not remember that we could find any sound reason for thinking that he was so ghastly and abnormal. But certainly we did both agree about one thing. That was that our visitor had a *cold* kind of face which as Dowson remarked 'reminded him of a wizened bladder of lard'. It may be guessed that we did not linger over our beer. The idea of speaking to this personage was intolerable to us and so we emptied our glasses and vamoosed.

Yet once again we were to run into this sinister personage. One evening we had walked towards the house in which Dowson lodged (I think it was 111 Euston Road) and when we were about a hundred yards from the iron railings which stood before the basement we saw once again the man with the dissipated gladstone bag. We watched (with frightful perplexity) as the man walked up the front steps of Dowson's lodgings. That was enough for us. Somehow the idea of sleeping in the same house with this personage was intolerable to Dowson—for we had guessed that our visitor was looking for a bedroom—and so Dowson arranged to sleep at my home at Crouch End for a night or so.

Before we went to sleep that night we spoke, together and to ourselves, asking each other: Why a derelict hawker with a gladstone bag could appear to us so evil and dangerous?

Dowson could not be persuaded to return to the Euston Road

caravansary until several days had passed. But when he did enter the house he could not help but observe that his landlady was very agitated about something. She told him that a man who had called and engaged a bedroom for a week had been found dead in his bed the following morning. She said that he had not a penny in his pockets and his gladstone bag, when opened by the police, contained nothing but garden mould or fine soft earth. No one ever came forward to say who the dead man was, so he was buried in a pauper's grave. He had told Dowson's landlady that his name was Lazarus. As far as I remember, the police could not trace any of his kinsmen or friends.

I asked Dowson what he made of the affair some time afterwards; and the poet shrugged his shoulders and said in his low and hesitating voice: 'Let me tell you something, Hopkins. That mould in his bag was graveyard mould . . . And was it not Lazarus *"that had been dead that did come forth from his grave bound in a winding sheet and his face bound about with a napkin"*?'

Even after all these years I can still see Dowson's rather pallid face, and the sombre light in his eyes as he said these words.

There are times when I believe that Dowson and I were inclined to exaggerate the strangeness of a not very unusual set of co-incidences, but that I must confess is not my final decision about the case. I am more than convinced that this wretched errant soul was dying on his feet—possibly starving and looking for someone who would take pity on him. But his appearance was so forbidding that no one would heed him. Also I believe that, in truth, he may have possessed some abnormal gift of hanging on to his body some days after death had really claimed it.

SELECT BIBLIOGRAPHY

A. Books by Ernest Dowson:

1893 *A Comedy of Masks* (in collaboration with Arthur Moore)
1895 *Dilemmas: Stories and Studies in Sentiment*
1896 *Verses*
1897 *The Pierrot of the Minute*
1899 *Adrian Rome* (in collaboration with Arthur Moore)
1899 *Decorations: in Verse and Prose*
1934 *Poetical Works*, edited by Desmond Flower
1947 *The Stories of Ernest Dowson*, edited by Mark Longaker

B. Translations:

1894 *La Terre* by Emile Zola
1894 *Majesty* by L. M. A. Couperus (in collaboration with Teixeira de
        Mattos)
1895–6 *History of Modern Painting* by Richard Muther (in collabora-
        tion with G. A. Greene and A. C. Hillier)
1896 *La Fille aux Yeux d'Or* by Honoré de Balzac
1898 *Les Liaisons Dangereuses* by Choderlos de Laclos
1899 *La Pucelle* by Arouet de Voltaire (the translation edited by
        Dowson)
1899 *The Memoirs of Cardinal Dubois*
1907 *The Confidantes of a King* by Edmond and Jules de Goncourt
1907 *The Story of Beauty and the Beast* (this translation, though pub-
        lished under Dowson's name, is almost certainly the work of
        Edward Strangman)

Unpublished Translation:

   The Memoirs of the Duc de Richelieu (Dowson's MS is in Princeton
        University Library)

C. Principal Contributions to Books and Periodicals:

1886 'Sonnet of a Little Girl' in *London Society*
1888 'Souvenirs of an Egoist' in *Temple Bar*
1889 Numerous unsigned contributions to *The Critic*
1890 'The Diary of a Successful Man' in *Macmillan's Magazine*
1891 'The Story of a Violin' in *Macmillan's Magazine*
        'A Case of Conscience' in *The Century Guild Hobby Horse*
        Four poems in *The Century Guild Hobby Horse*
1892 Six poems in *The Book of the Rhymers' Club*
1893 'The Statute of Limitations' in *The Hobby Horse*
1894 Six poems in *The Second Book of the Rhymers' Club*
        'Apple Blossom in Brittany' in *The Yellow Book*
        Three poems in *The Hobby Horse*

1896 'The Eyes of Pride' in *The Savoy*
      'Countess Marie of the Angels' in *The Savoy*
      'The Dying of Francis Donne' in *The Savoy*
      Seven poems in *The Savoy*
1897 'In a Breton Cemetery' in *The Pageant*
1898 *Volpone* by Ben Jonson (the text edited by Dowson).

D. PRINCIPAL BIOGRAPHICAL REFERENCES:

BEARDSLEY, Aubrey: *Letters to Smithers*, edited by R. A. Walker, 1937
FLOWER, Desmond: Introduction to Dowson's *Poetical Works*, 1934
GAWSWORTH, John: *The Dowson Legend*, 1939
JEPSON, Edgar: *Memories of a Victorian*, 1933
LONGAKER, Mark: *Ernest Dowson*, 1944
O'RIORDAN, Conal: *Bloomsbury and Beyond in the Eighteen Nineties*, 1948
O'SULLIVAN, Vincent: *Aspects of Wilde*, 1936
PLARR, Marion: *Cynara: The Story of Ernest Dowson and Adelaide*, 1933
PLARR, Victor: *Ernest Dowson, 1888–1897*, 1914
ROTHENSTEIN, William: *Men and Memories*, Volume I, 1931
SHERARD, Robert Harborough: *Twenty Years in Paris*, 1905
      The Real Oscar Wilde, N.D.
SYMONS, Arthur: Introduction to *The Poems of Ernest Dowson*, 1902
THOMAS, W. R.: 'Ernest Dowson at Oxford' in *The Nineteenth Century*, April 1928. (Thomas's typescript contains many details omitted from the published text.)
WILDE, Oscar: *Letters*, edited by Rupert Hart-Davis, 1962
YEATS, W. B.: *The Trembling of the Veil*, 1922

MANUSCRIPT LOCATIONS AND SOURCES

Every effort has been made to give up-to-date locations and sources for the letters. Certain privately owned collections have, however, been dispersed and their whereabouts are not known.

1–26. Pierpont Morgan Library, New York

27. William Andrews Clark Memorial Library, University of California

28–40. Pierpont Morgan Library, New York

41. Princeton University Library

42–44. Pierpont Morgan Library, New York

45. Michael Holland Collection

46–49. Pierpont Morgan Library, New York

50. A. J. A. Symons Collection

51–114. Pierpont Morgan Library, New York

115. McPherson Library, University of Victoria, British Columbia

116–122. Pierpont Morgan Library, New York

123. Arthur Moore Collection

124. A. J. A. Symons Collection

125. Pierpont Morgan Library, New York

126. Museo Horne, Florence

127. Pierpont Morgan Library, New York

128. McPherson Library, University of Victoria, British Columbia

129–131. Pierpont Morgan Library, New York

132. British Museum

133. Pierpont Morgan Library, New York

134. Arthur Moore Collection

135. Princeton University Library

136. Pierpont Morgan Library, New York

137–138. Princeton University Library

139. Pierpont Morgan Library, New York

140. Text from J. Gawsworth, *The Dowson Legend* (1939)

141–151. Pierpont Morgan Library, New York

152. Michael Holland Collection

153–155. Pierpont Morgan Library, New York

156. Desmond Flower Collection

157–158. Pierpont Morgan Library, New York

159. A. J. A. Symons Collection

160–162. Pierpont Morgan Library, New York

163. Manchester University Library

164. Museo Horne, Florence

165. Arthur Moore Collection

166–167. Museo Horne, Florence

168–169. Pierpont Morgan Library, New York

170. Sold by Messrs. Dulau, 27/11/1931

171. Pierpont Morgan Library, New York

172. George Greene Estate

173. Pierpont Morgan Library, New York

174. Michael Holland Collection

175. Mrs. M. Barwell Collection

176. Manchester University Library

177–178. Mrs. M. Barwell Collection

179. Sold by Mr. Anthony d'Offay, 1961

180. Pierpont Morgan Library, New York

181. Patricio Gannon Collection

182. Princeton University Library

183. Text from Gawsworth, op. cit.

184. A. J. A. Symons Collection

185. Text from Gawsworth, op. cit.

186. British Museum

187. Museo Horne, Florence

188. Michael Holland Collection

189. Text from Plarr, op. cit.

190. Henry W. and Albert A. Berg Collection, New York Public Library

191–192. Sold by Messrs. Dulau, 27/11/1931

193. Museo Horne, Florence

194. Henry W. and Albert A. Berg Collection, New York Public Library

195. A. J. A. Symons Collection

196. Henry W. and Albert A. Berg Collection, New York Public Library

197. Museo Horne, Florence

198. Text from Plarr, op. cit.

199. Henry W. and Albert A. Berg Collection, New York Public Library

200. Pierpont Morgan Library, New York

201–202. Henry W. and Albert A. Berg Collection, New York Public Library

203. Pierpont Morgan Library, New York

204. Henry W. and Albert A. Berg Collection, New York Public Library

205. Princeton University Library

206–208. Henry W. and Albert A. Berg Collection, New York Public Library

209. George Greene Estate

210. Harvard College Library

211–216. Henry W. and Albert A. Berg Collection, New York Public Library

217. Pierpont Morgan Library, New York

218. Museo Horne, Florence

219. Pierpont Morgan Library, New York

220. Museo Horne, Florence

221. Henry W. and Albert A. Berg Collection, New York Public Library

222. Museo Horne, Florence

223–229. Henry W. and Albert A. Berg Collection, New York Public Library

230. Princeton University Library

231. Henry W. and Albert A. Berg Collection, New York Public Library

232. Museo Horne, Florence

233. A. J. A. Symons Collection

234. Sold by Messrs. Dulau, 27/11/1931

235. Text from Plarr, op. cit.

236. Michael Holland Collection

237. Manchester University Library

238–239. Henry W. and Albert A. Berg Collection, New York Public Library

240. Sold by Messrs. Dulau, 2/12/1931

241. Henry W. and Albert A. Berg Collection, New York Public Library

242. Mrs. M. Barwell Collection

243. Sold by Messrs. Davis and Orioli

244. Henry W. and Albert A. Berg Collection, New York Public Library

245. Text from Plarr, op. cit.

246. Mrs. M. Barwell Collection

247. Text from Gawsworth, op. cit.

248–249. Henry W. and Albert A. Berg Collection, New York Public Library

250. Text from Plarr, op. cit.

251–254. Henry W. and Albert A. Berg Collection, New York Public Library

255–256. Pierpont Morgan Library, New York

257. Princeton University Library

258. George Greene Estate

259. Text from Plarr, op. cit.

260–261. Pierpont Morgan Library, New York

262. Text from Plarr, op. cit.

263. Pierpont Morgan Library, New York

264. Henry W. and Albert A. Berg Collection, New York Public Library

265. Princeton University Library

266. Text from Plarr, op. cit.

267–269. Henry W. and Albert A. Berg Collection, New York Public Library

270. Princeton University Library

271. George Greene Estate

272. Text from Plarr, op. cit.

84A. Royal Library of Scotland, Edinburgh

273. Henry W. and Albert A. Berg Collection, New York Public Library
274. George Greene Estate
275. Michael Holland Collection
276–277. Sold by Messrs. Dulau, 27/11/1931
278. A. J. A. Symons Collection
279–280. Text from Plarr, op. cit.
281. Text from Gawsworth, op. cit.
282. George Greene Estate
283. Pierpont Morgan Library, New York
284. George Greene Estate
285. Text from Jepson, *Memories of a Victorian* (1933)
286. McPherson Library, University of Victoria, British Columbia
287. Allen Lane Collection
288. Text from Longaker, *Ernest Dowson* (1944)
289. Reading University Library (the property of Miss N. C. Elkin Mathews)
290. Princeton University Library
291. Sold by Messrs. Davis and Orioli
292. Text from Plarr, op. cit.
293. Formerly property of Mr. Ben Abramson
294. Text from *Two Hundred Books from the Library of Richard Butler Glaenzer* (New York, 1911)
295. Michael Holland Collection
296. Pierpont Morgan Library, New York
297. Sold by Messrs. Dulau, 27/11/1931
298. Patricio Gannon Collection
299. Text from Gawsworth, op. cit.
300–302. Cassell & Co.
303. Manchester University Library
304. Cassell & Co.
305. Pierpont Morgan Library, New York
306. Cassell & Co.
307. Pierpont Morgan Library, New York
308–309. Cassell & Co.

310. Pierpont Morgan Library, New York
311. Manchester University Library
312. Cassell & Co.
313. Pierpont Morgan Library, New York
314. Cassell & Co.
315. McPherson Library, University of Victoria, British Columbia
316. Pierpont Morgan Library, New York
317. Princeton University Library
318. Manchester University Library
319. Sold by Messrs. Elkin Mathews (Catalogue No. 80)
320. Museo Horne, Florence
321. Princeton University Library
322. Pierpont Morgan Library, New York
323. Manchester University Library
324. British Museum
325. Sold by Messrs. C. A. Stonehill, 7/3/1934
326. Mark Longaker Collection
327. McPherson Library, University of Victoria, British Columbia
328. Pierpont Morgan Library, New York
329. Princeton University Library
330. H. Bradley Martin Collection
331. Text from Gawsworth, op. cit.
332. Manchester University Library
333. Pierpont Morgan Library, New York
334. Text from Gawsworth, op. cit.
335. Text from Plarr, op. cit.
336. Text from *Books from the Library of John Lane* (Dulau, 1928)
337. Princeton University Library
338. Late A. J. A. Symons Collection
339. Sold by Messrs. Elkin Mathews (Catalogue 93)
340. Princeton University Library
341. Text from Gawsworth, op. cit.

342. British Museum
343. Pierpont Morgan Library, New York
344–345. Princeton University Library
346. Sold by Messrs. Dulau, 27/11/1931
347–348. Cassell & Co.
349. William Andrews Clark Memorial Library, University of California
350. Text from *Books from the Library of John Lane* (Dulau, 1928)
351. Text from Gawsworth, op. cit.
352. Cassell & Co.
353. Princeton University Library
354. Cassell & Co.
355. University of Texas Library
356. A. J. A. Symons Collection
357. Cassell & Co.
358–360. A. J. A. Symons Collection
361. Cassell & Co.
362. Princeton University Library
363. H. Bradley Martin Collection
364. Desmond Flower Collection
365–366. A. J. A. Symons Collection
367. Henry W. and Albert A. Berg Collection, New York Public Library
368. Baker Library, Dartmouth College, New Hampshire
369. Henry W. and Albert A. Berg Collection, New York Public Library
370. H. Bradley Martin Collection
371. A. J. A. Symons Collection
372. Baker Library, Dartmouth College, New Hampshire

373. H. Bradley Martin Collection
374. William Andrews Clark Memorial Library, University of California
375. Henry W. and Albert A. Berg Collection, New York Public Library
376. Sold by Messrs. C. A. Stonehill, 7/3/1934
377. H. Bradley Martin Collection
378–379. Henry W. and Albert A. Berg Collection, New York Public Library
380. Allen Lane Collection
381. Cassell & Co.
382. Property of Mr. Russell Goldfarb
383–384. Museo Horne, Florence
385. Cassell & Co.
386. Baker Library, Dartmouth College, New Hampshire
387. Yale University Library
388–389. Pierpont Morgan Library, New York
390–392. Baker Library, Dartmouth College, New Hampshire
393. Text from *Two Hundred Books from the Library of Richard Butler Glaenzer* (New York, 1911)
394–395. Baker Library, Dartmouth College, New Hampshire
396. University of Texas Library
397. Princeton University Library
398–400. Baker Library, Dartmouth College, New Hampshire
401–402. Cassell & Co.

General Index

Index of Recipients